THE
BOOK

Nissan Micra
Service and Repair Manual

Colin Brown

Models covered

(931-240-5Y7)

Nissan Micra (K10 series) Hatchbacks, including special/limited edition models
988 cc & 1235 cc 8-valve engines

Does not cover new (K11 series) Nissan Micra range with 16-valve engines introduced January 1993

Printed in the USA

ABCDE
FGHIJ
KLMNO
PQ
3

Haynes Publishing
Sparkford, Nr Yeovil, Somerset BA22 7JJ, England

Haynes North America, Inc
861 Lawrence Drive, Newbury Park, California 91320, USA

Editions Haynes S.A.
Tour Aurore - La Défense 2, 18 Place des Reflets,
92975 PARIS LA DEFENSE Cedex, France

Haynes Publishing Nordiska AB
Box 1504, 751 45 UPPSALA, Sweden

© Haynes Publishing 1996

A book in the **Haynes Service and Repair Manual Series**

ISBN 1 85960 270 3

British Library Cataloguing in Publication Data
A catalogue record for this book is available from the British Library.

Contents

LIVING WITH YOUR NISSAN MICRA

Roadside Repairs

Routine Maintenance

Recommended Lubricants and Fluids

Contents

Introduction to the Nissan Micra

The Nissan Micra was introduced to the UK in June 1983, and quickly established itself in the small economy car class.

The range of models was revised in June 1985, when the SGL was added; mechanically similar to the preceding L, DX and GL models, but with higher trim level. Other cosmetic changes were also made at this time, to update the appearance of the model.

In February 1986, Nissan introduced the Colette, with a high level of trim, but using a low compression engine and 4-speed manual gearbox for economy motoring.

In 1987, the range of models was again revised, and 5-door models became available. The development continued when, in 1988, the higher specification 'S' series was introduced.

All versions use the 988cc MA10 or 1235cc MA12 S overhead camshaft engines, mounted transversely and driving the front wheels. Power-assisted steering, although covered in this manual, is not optionally available in the UK market. This also applies to the air conditioner. The vehicle is quite conventional in design and the DIY home mechanic should find most maintenance tasks quite straightforward .

Nissan Micra GL

Acknowledgements

Thanks are due to Champion Spark Plug who supplied the illustrations showing spark plug conditions. Certain other illustrations are the copyright of the Nissan Motor Company Limited, and are used with their permission. Thanks are also due to Sykes-Pickavant who supplied some of the workshop tools, and to all those people at Sparkford who assisted in the production of this manual.

We take great pride in the accuracy of information given in this manual, but vehicle manufacturers make alterations and design changes during the production run of a particular vehicle of which they do not inform us. No liability can be accepted by the authors or publishers for loss, damage or injury caused by errors in, or omissions from, the information given.

Nissan Micra Colette (3-door)

Working on your car can be dangerous. This page shows just some of the potential risks and hazards, with the aim of creating a safety-conscious attitude.

General hazards

Scalding

• Don't remove the radiator or expansion tank cap while the engine is hot.
• Engine oil, automatic transmission fluid or power steering fluid may also be dangerously hot if the engine has recently been running.

Burning

• Beware of burns from the exhaust system and from any part of the engine. Brake discs and drums can also be extremely hot immediately after use.

Crushing

• When working under or near a raised vehicle, always supplement the jack with axle stands, or use drive-on ramps. *Never venture under a car which is only supported by a jack.*

• Take care if loosening or tightening high-torque nuts when the vehicle is on stands. Initial loosening and final tightening should be done with the wheels on the ground.

Fire

• Fuel is highly flammable; fuel vapour is explosive.
• Don't let fuel spill onto a hot engine.
• Do not smoke or allow naked lights (including pilot lights) anywhere near a vehicle being worked on. Also beware of creating sparks (electrically or by use of tools).
• Fuel vapour is heavier than air, so don't work on the fuel system with the vehicle over an inspection pit.
• Another cause of fire is an electrical overload or short-circuit. Take care when repairing or modifying the vehicle wiring.
• Keep a fire extinguisher handy, of a type suitable for use on fuel and electrical fires.

Electric shock

• Ignition HT voltage can be dangerous, especially to people with heart problems or a pacemaker. Don't work on or near the ignition system with the engine running or the ignition switched on.

• Mains voltage is also dangerous. Make sure that any mains-operated equipment is correctly earthed. Mains power points should be protected by a residual current device (RCD) circuit breaker.

Fume or gas intoxication

• Exhaust fumes are poisonous; they often contain carbon monoxide, which is rapidly fatal if inhaled. Never run the engine in a confined space such as a garage with the doors shut.
• Fuel vapour is also poisonous, as are the vapours from some cleaning solvents and paint thinners.

Poisonous or irritant substances

• Avoid skin contact with battery acid and with any fuel, fluid or lubricant, especially antifreeze, brake hydraulic fluid and Diesel fuel. Don't syphon them by mouth. If such a substance is swallowed or gets into the eyes, seek medical advice.
• Prolonged contact with used engine oil can cause skin cancer. Wear gloves or use a barrier cream if necessary. Change out of oil-soaked clothes and do not keep oily rags in your pocket.
• Air conditioning refrigerant forms a poisonous gas if exposed to a naked flame (including a cigarette). It can also cause skin burns on contact.

Asbestos

• Asbestos dust can cause cancer if inhaled or swallowed. Asbestos may be found in gaskets and in brake and clutch linings. When dealing with such components it is safest to assume that they contain asbestos.

Special hazards

Hydrofluoric acid

• This extremely corrosive acid is formed when certain types of synthetic rubber, found in some O-rings, oil seals, fuel hoses etc, are exposed to temperatures above 400ºC. The rubber changes into a charred or sticky substance containing the acid. *Once formed, the acid remains dangerous for years. If it gets onto the skin, it may be necessary to amputate the limb concerned.*
• When dealing with a vehicle which has suffered a fire, or with components salvaged from such a vehicle, wear protective gloves and discard them after use.

The battery

• Batteries contain sulphuric acid, which attacks clothing, eyes and skin. Take care when topping-up or carrying the battery.
• The hydrogen gas given off by the battery is highly explosive. Never cause a spark or allow a naked light nearby. Be careful when connecting and disconnecting battery chargers or jump leads.

Air bags

• Air bags can cause injury if they go off accidentally. Take care when removing the steering wheel and/or facia. Special storage instructions may apply.

Diesel injection equipment

• Diesel injection pumps supply fuel at very high pressure. Take care when working on the fuel injectors and fuel pipes.

⚠ *Warning: Never expose the hands, face or any other part of the body to injector spray; the fuel can penetrate the skin with potentially fatal results.*

Remember...

DO

• Do use eye protection when using power tools, and when working under the vehicle.

• Do wear gloves or use barrier cream to protect your hands when necessary.

• Do get someone to check periodically that all is well when working alone on the vehicle.

• Do keep loose clothing and long hair well out of the way of moving mechanical parts.

• Do remove rings, wristwatch etc, before working on the vehicle – especially the electrical system.

• Do ensure that any lifting or jacking equipment has a safe working load rating adequate for the job.

DON'T

• Don't attempt to lift a heavy component which may be beyond your capability – get assistance.

• Don't rush to finish a job, or take unverified short cuts.

• Don't use ill-fitting tools which may slip and cause injury.

• Don't leave tools or parts lying around where someone can trip over them. Mop up oil and fuel spills at once.

• Don't allow children or pets to play in or near a vehicle being worked on.

For information applicable to later models, see Supplement at end of manual

Dimensions mm (in)

Overall length 3645 (143.5)
Overall width 1560 (61.4)
Overall height 1395 (54.9)
Ground clearance 165 (6.5)
Wheelbase 2300 (90.6)
Turning circle . . . . 9.8 metre (32.2 ft)

Kerb weights kg (lb)

Manual transmission 645 (1420)
Automatic transmission 675 (1490)

Capacities

Fuel tank . . . . 8.8 Imp gal (40 litre)
Cooling system - total capacity, including heater and expansion tank:
   1.0 models . . . . 8.3 Imp pt (4.7 litre)
   1.2 models . . . . 9.7 Imp pt (5.5 litre)
Engine oil - including filter . . . . 4.9 Imp pt (2.8 litre)
Transmission - including final drive:
   Four-speed manual . . . . 4.4 Imp pt (2.5 litre)
   Five-speed manual . . . . 4.6 Imp pt (2.6 litre)
   Automatic transmission . . . . 10.6 Imp pt (6.0 litre)
Power steering system . . . . 1.7 Imp pt (1.0 litre)
Water reservoirs:
   Windscreen wash . . . . 2.6 Imp pt (1.5 litre)
   Windscreen and rear screen wash . . . . 5.2 Imp pt (3.0 litre)

Jump starting

Jump starting will get you out of trouble, but you must correct whatever made the battery go flat in the first place. There are three possibilities:

1 *The battery has been drained by repeated attempts to start, or by leaving the lights on.*

2 *The charging system is not working properly (alternator drivebelt slack or broken, alternator wiring fault or alternator itself faulty).*

3 *The battery itself is at fault (electrolyte low, or battery worn out).*

When jump-starting a car using a booster battery, observe the following precautions:

✔ Before connecting the booster battery, make sure that the ignition is switched off.

✔ Ensure that all electrical equipment (lights, heater, wipers, etc) is switched off.

✔ Make sure that the booster battery is the same voltage as the discharged one in the vehicle.

✔ If the battery is being jump-started from the battery in another vehicle, the two vehcles MUST NOT TOUCH each other.

✔ Make sure that the transmission is in neutral (or PARK, in the case of automatic transmission).

1 Connect one end of the red jump lead to the positive (+) terminal of the flat battery

2 Connect the other end of the red lead to the positive (+) terminal of the booster battery.

3 Connect one end of the black jump lead to the negative (-) terminal of the booster battery

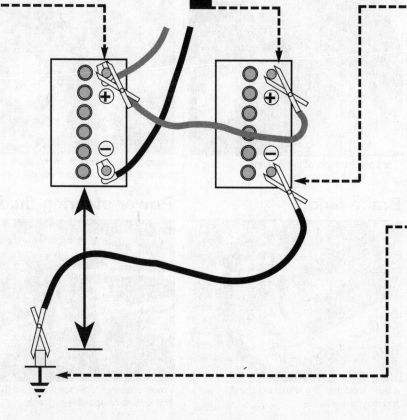

4 Connect the other end of the black jump lead to a bolt or bracket on the engine block, well away from the battery, on the vehicle to be started.

5 Make sure that the jump leads will not come into contact with the fan, drive-belts or other moving parts of the engine.

6 Start the engine using the booster battery, then with the engine running at idle speed, disconnect the jump leads in the reverse order of connection.

Identifying leaks

Puddles on the garage floor or drive, or obvious wetness under the bonnet or underneath the car, suggest a leak that needs investigating. It can sometimes be difficult to decide where the leak is coming from, especially if the engine bay is very dirty already. Leaking oil or fluid can also be blown rearwards by the passage of air under the car, giving a false impression of where the problem lies.

⚠ **Warning: Most automotive oils and fluids are poisonous. Wash them off skin, and change out of contaminated clothing, without delay.**

 HAYNES HiNT *The smell of a fluid leaking from the car may provide a clue to what's leaking. Some fluids are distinctively coloured. It may help to clean the car carefully and to park it over some clean paper overnight as an aid to locating the source of the leak.*
Remember that some leaks may only occur while the engine is running.

Sump oil

Engine oil may leak from the drain plug...

Oil from filter

...or from the base of the oil filter.

Gearbox oil

Gearbox oil can leak from the seals at the inboard ends of the driveshafts.

Antifreeze

Leaking antifreeze often leaves a crystalline deposit like this.

Brake fluid

A leak occurring at a wheel is almost certainly brake fluid.

Power steering fluid

Power steering fluid may leak from the pipe connectors on the steering rack.

Jacking, wheel changing and towing

Jacking

The jack supplied with the vehicle should only be used for emergency roadside wheel changing (photo).

The roadwheels on the opposite side to those being worked on should be chocked. Put manual transmission vehicles in reverse gear and automatic transmission vehicles to P. Apply the handbrake in all cases. **Caution:** *ensure the vehicle is standing on firm, level ground before jacking.*

Place the jack under the cut-out in the base of the sill (front or rear, as required), and slowly raise the vehicle by turning the cranked jack handle clockwise. When the vehicle is raised, supplement the jack with axle stands.

Wheel changing

Prepare the vehicle as described in the preceding paragraphs, but do not raise the vehicle at this stage.

Remove the centre cap of the wheel or wheel trim and loosen the wheel nuts one or two turns by turning them anti-clockwise with the wheel nut wrench. Do not remove the wheel nuts completely until the vehicle is off the ground.

Jack stowage in luggage compartment

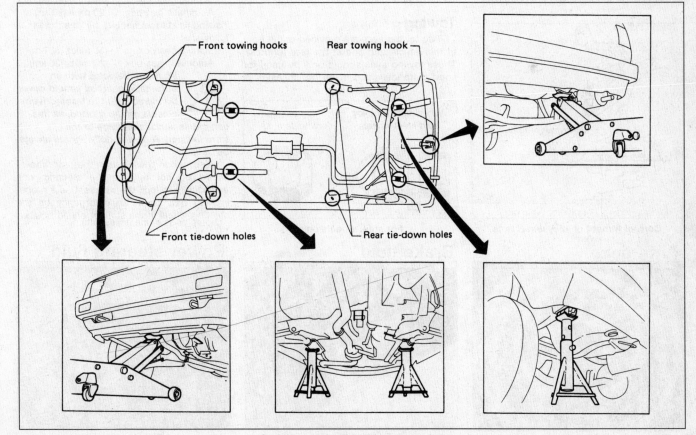

Jacking, axle stand and towing points

Raise the vehicle slowly until the wheel is clear of the ground. Remove the wheel nuts and the wheel. Position the spare wheel onto the studs and refit the wheel nuts, bevelled ends facing inward.

Tighten the wheel nuts evenly and in an alternate pattern.

Where aluminium wheels are fitted. use only the nuts designed for these wheels. When refitting the nuts, slightly pull back the wheel to align the nuts with the bolt holes in the wheel, and again tighten the nuts evenly and alternately.

Lower the vehicle to the ground by turning the jack handle anti-clockwise.

Remove the jack from the jacking point.

Tighten the wheel nuts to the specified torque. Where this operation is done at the roadside, torque tightening should be carried out at the earliest opportunity, and with aluminium wheels, should be rechecked after 1000 km (600 miles).

Towing

Two towing eyes are provided at the front of the vehicle and one at the rear (photos). These towing eyes should only be used for short distances, and if the transmission is faulty, then a proper towing dolly should be used, which raises the front wheels (the driven wheels) off the ground.

Before towing commences, put the gearbox in neutral and release the handbrake. The ignition key should remain in the OFF position to prevent the steering lock from locking.

Towing speeds should be restricted as follows:

Manual gearbox   50 mph (80 km/h)
Automatic gearbox   20 mph (30 km/h)

Towing distance should be restricted as follows:

Manual gearbox   50 miles (80 km)
Automatic gearbox   20 miles (30 km)

⚠️ **Warning: Vehicles with an automatic gearbox should never be towed with the front (driven) wheels on the ground, as this can cause serious damage to the transmission. A towing dolly should always be used.**

Also, when towing with the rear wheels raised do not rely on the steering lock mechanism to lock the wheels. Use a proper locking bar. Or in an emergency tie the steering wheel in the straight-ahead position with rope.

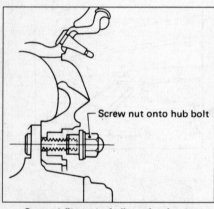

— Screw nut onto hub bolt

Correct fitment of alloy wheel nuts

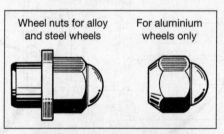

Wheel nuts for alloy and steel wheels

For aluminium wheels only

For steel wheels only

Spare wheel stowage under luggage compartment floor

Front towing eye

Rear towing eye

Tyre condition and pressure

It is very important that tyres are in good condition, and at the correct pressure - having a tyre failure at any speed is highly dangerous. Tyre wear is influenced by driving style - harsh braking and acceleration, or fast cornering, will all produce more rapid tyre wear. As a general rule, the front tyres wear out faster than the rears. Interchanging the tyres from front to rear ("rotating" the tyres) may result in more even wear. However, if this is completely effective, you may have the expense of replacing all four tyres at once! Remove any nails or stones embedded in the tread before they penetrate the tyre to cause deflation. If removal of a nail does reveal that the tyre has been punctured, refit the nail so that its point of penetration is marked. Then immediately change the wheel, and have the tyre repaired by a tyre dealer.

Regularly check the tyres for damage in the form of cuts or bulges, especially in the sidewalls. Periodically remove the wheels, and clean any dirt or mud from the inside and outside surfaces. Examine the wheel rims for signs of rusting, corrosion or other damage. Light alloy wheels are easily damaged by "kerbing" whilst parking; steel wheels may also become dented or buckled. A new wheel is very often the only way to overcome severe damage.

New tyres should be balanced when they are fitted, but it may become necessary to re-balance them as they wear, or if the balance weights fitted to the wheel rim should fall off. Unbalanced tyres will wear more quickly, as will the steering and suspension components. Wheel imbalance is normally signified by vibration, particularly at a certain speed (typically around 50 mph). If this vibration is felt only through the steering, then it is likely that just the front wheels need balancing. If, however, the vibration is felt through the whole car, the rear wheels could be out of balance. Wheel balancing should be carried out by a tyre dealer or garage.

1 Tread Depth - visual check

The original tyres have tread wear safety bands (B), which will appear when the tread depth reaches approximately 1.6 mm. The band positions are indicated by a triangular mark on the tyre sidewall (A).

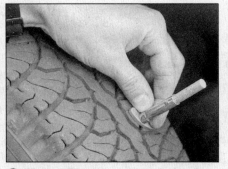

2 Tread Depth - manual check

Alternatively, tread wear can be monitored with a simple, inexpensive device known as a tread depth indicator gauge.

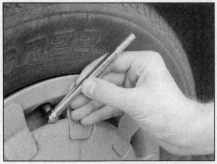

3 Tyre Pressure Check

Check the tyre pressures regularly with the tyres cold. Do not adjust the tyre pressures immediately after the vehicle has been used, or an inaccurate setting will result.

Tyre tread wear patterns

Shoulder Wear

Underinflation (wear on both sides)
Under-inflation will cause overheating of the tyre, because the tyre will flex too much, and the tread will not sit correctly on the road surface. This will cause a loss of grip and excessive wear, not to mention the danger of sudden tyre failure due to heat build-up.
Check and adjust pressures
Incorrect wheel camber (wear on one side)
Repair or renew suspension parts
Hard cornering
Reduce speed!

Centre Wear

Overinflation
Over-inflation will cause rapid wear of the centre part of the tyre tread, coupled with reduced grip, harsher ride, and the danger of shock damage occurring in the tyre casing.
Check and adjust pressures

If you sometimes have to inflate your car's tyres to the higher pressures specified for maximum load or sustained high speed, don't forget to reduce the pressures to normal afterwards.

Uneven Wear

Front tyres may wear unevenly as a result of wheel misalignment. Most tyre dealers and garages can check and adjust the wheel alignment (or "tracking") for a modest charge.
Incorrect camber or castor
Repair or renew suspension parts
Malfunctioning suspension
Repair or renew suspension parts
Unbalanced wheel
Balance tyres
Incorrect toe setting
Adjust front wheel alignment
Note: *The feathered edge of the tread which typifies toe wear is best checked by feel.*

The routine maintenance instructions given here are basically those recommended by the manufacturer. They are sometimes supplemented by additional tasks, which have proved to be necessary. Since no two vehicles operate under identical circumstances or conditions, the DIY mechanic, who does not have repair costs to take in to consideration, may wish to shorten the specified intervals. Experience will show if this is necessary.

Maintenance schedule for models up to mid-1987

Weekly or before a long journey
- [ ] Check engine oil level (Chapter 1, Section 2)
- [ ] Check engine coolant level (Chapter 2, Section 3)
- [ ] Check automatic transmission fluid level (Chapter 7, Section 3)
- [ ] Check brake fluid level (Chapter 9, Section 2)
- [ ] Check all tyres for condition and pressure (including spare) (Chapter 10, Section 22)
- [ ] Check operation of all lights, horn, wipers and washers (Chapter 12)
- [ ] Check washer fluid level, adding a screen wash (Chapter 12, Section 23)

Every 6000 miles (10 000 km) or 6 months - whichever comes first
- [ ] Renew engine oil and filter (Chapter 1, Sections 2 and 10)
- [ ] Check engine idle speed (Chapter 3, Section 10)
- [ ] Check distributor contact breaker points (Chapter 4, Section 3)
- [ ] Check ignition timing (Chapter 4, Section 8)
- [ ] Check spark plugs (Chapter 4, Section 10)
- [ ] Check manual transmission oil level (Chapter 6, Section 2)
- [ ] Check disc brake pads (Chapter 9, Section 2)
- [ ] Check power steering fluid level (Chapter 10, Section 2)
- [ ] Check brake, fuel and exhaust systems for leaks, cracks, chafing, deterioration and security
- [ ] Lubricate locks, hinges and latches
- [ ] Check operation of brakes (including handbrake) and clutch (Chapters 5 and 9)

Every 12 000 miles (20 000 km) or 12 months - whichever comes first
- [ ] Check valve clearances (Chapter 1, Section 5)
- [ ] Check positive crankcase ventilation system (Chapter 1, Section 24 and Chapter 13, Section 4)
- [ ] Check cooling system hoses and connections (Chapter 2, Section 2)
- [ ] Check all drivebelts for cracks, fraying, wear and tension (Chapter 2, Section 9)
- [ ] Renew distributor contact breaker points (Chapter 4, Section 3)
- [ ] Renew spark plugs (Chapter 4, Section 10)
- [ ] Check steering gear and linkage, suspension and driveshafts for damage, security and lubrication (Chapters 8 and 10)
- [ ] Check brake shoes and drums (Chapter 9, Section 4)
- [ ] Check wheels for alignment and balance (Chapter 10, Section 21)
- [ ] Check seat belts, buckles, retractors, anchor points and adjusters for wear and security (Chapter 11, Section 25)

Every 24 000 miles (40 000 km) or 24 months - whichever comes first
- [ ] Renew positive crankcase ventilation system filter (Chapter 13, Section 4)
- [ ] Renew engine coolant (Chapter 2, Sections 3 and 4)
- [ ] Renew air filter element (Chapter 3, Section 3)
- [ ] Renew fuel filter and check all fuel lines and connections (Chapter 3, Section 8)
- [ ] Check ignition wiring (Chapter 4, Section 2)
- [ ] Renew brake fluid (Chapter 9, Section 13)
- [ ] Check brake servo vacuum hoses, connections and non-return valve (Chapter 9, Section 14)
- [ ] Check front wheel bearing grease (Chapter 10, Section 5)

Every 60 000 miles (100 000 km)
- [ ] Renew the timing belt (Chapter 1, Section 6)

Tyre pressure plate

Maintenance schedule for models from mid-1987 to mid-1989

Weekly or before a long journey

- [ ] Check engine oil level (Chapter 1, Section 2)
- [ ] Check engine coolant level (Chapter 2, Section 3)
- [ ] Check automatic transmission fluid level (Chapter 7, Section 3)
- [ ] Check brake fluid level (Chapter 9, Section 2)
- [ ] Check all tyres for condition and pressure (including spare) (Chapter 10, Section 22)
- [ ] Check operation of all lights, horn, wipers and washers (Chapter 12)
- [ ] Check washer fluid level, adding a screen wash (Chapter 12, Section 23)

Every 4500 miles (7500 km) or 6 months - whichever comes first

Note: *Frequent oil and filter changes are good for the engine. We recommend changing the oil at the mileage specified here, or at least twice a year if the mileage covered is less.*

- [ ] Renew engine oil and filter (Chapter 1, Sections 2 and 10)

Every 9000 miles (15 000 km) or 6 months - whichever comes first

- [ ] Check engine idle speed (Chapter 3, Section 10)
- [ ] Where fitted, renew distributor contact breaker points (Chapter 4, Section 3)
- [ ] Check ignition timing (Chapter 4, Section 8)
- [ ] Renew spark plugs (Chapter 4, Section 10)
- [ ] Check manual transmission oil level (Chapter 6, Section 2)
- [ ] Check disc brake pads (Chapter 9, Section 2)
- [ ] Check power steering fluid level (Chapter 10, Section 2)
- [ ] Check brake, fuel and exhaust systems for leaks, cracks, chafing, deterioration and security
- [ ] Lubricate locks, hinges and latches
- [ ] Check operation of brakes (including handbrake) and clutch (Chapters 5 and 9)

Topping-up the engine oil level

Every 18 000 miles (30 000 km) or 12 months - whichever comes first

- [ ] Check valve clearances (Chapter 1, Section 5)
- [ ] Check positive crankcase ventilation system (Chapter 1, Section 24 and Chapter 13, Section 4)
- [ ] Check cooling system hoses and connections (Chapter 2, Section 2)
- [ ] Check all drivebelts for cracks, fraying, wear and tension (Chapter 2, Section 9)
- [ ] Renew fuel filter (Chapter 3, Section 8)
- [ ] Check condition of vacuum hoses and connections (Chapters 3 and 4)
- [ ] Renew distributor contact breaker points (Chapter 4, Section 3)
- [ ] Renew spark plugs (Chapter 4, Section 10)
- [ ] Check steering gear and linkage, suspension and driveshafts for damage, security and lubrication (Chapters 8 and 10)
- [ ] Check brake shoes and drums (Chapter 9, Section 4)
- [ ] Renew brake fluid (Chapter 9, Section 13)
- [ ] Check front wheel bearings for wear and grease leakage (Chapter 10, Section 5)
- [ ] Check wheels for alignment and balance (Chapter 10, Section 21)
- [ ] Check bodywork (Chapter 11, Sections 2 and 4)
- [ ] Check seat belts, buckles, retractors, anchor points and adjusters for wear and security (Chapter 11, Section 25)

Every 36 000 miles (60 000 km) or 24 months - whichever comes first

- [ ] Renew positive crankcase ventilation system filter (Chapter 13, Section 4)
- [ ] Renew engine coolant (Chapter 2, Sections 3 and 4)
- [ ] Renew air filter element (Chapter 3, Section 3)
- [ ] Check all fuel lines and connections (Chapter 3, Section 8)
- [ ] Check ignition wiring (Chapter 4, Section 2)
- [ ] Check brake servo vacuum hoses, connections and non-return valve (Chapter 9, Section 14)

Every 60 000 miles (100 000 km)

- [ ] Renew the timing belt (Chapter 1, Section 6)

Maintenance schedule for models without catalytic converters from mid-1989

Weekly or before a long journey

- ☐ Check engine oil level (Chapter 1, Section 2)
- ☐ Check engine coolant level (Chapter 2, Section 3)
- ☐ Check automatic transmission fluid level (Chapter 7, Section 3)
- ☐ Check brake fluid level (Chapter 9, Section 2)
- ☐ Check all tyres for condition and pressure (including spare) (Chapter 10, Section 22)
- ☐ Check operation of all lights, horn, wipers and washers (Chapter 12)
- ☐ Check washer fluid level, adding a screen wash (Chapter 12, Section 23)

Every 6000 miles (10 000 km) or 6 months - whichever comes first

- ☐ Renew engine oil and filter (Chapter 1, Sections 2 and 10)

Every 12 000 miles (20 000 km) or 12 months - whichever comes first

- ☐ Check valve clearances (Chapter 1, Section 5)
- ☐ Check Positive Crankcase Ventilation (PCV) system (Chapter 13, Section 4 and Chapter 1, Section 24)
- ☐ Check condition of cooling system hoses and connections (Chapter 2, Section 2)
- ☐ Check idling speed and mixture, and adjust if required (Chapter 3, Section 10)
- ☐ Check condition of vacuum hoses and connections (Chapters 3 and 4)
- ☐ Renew spark plugs (Chapter 4, Section 10)
- ☐ Check operation of the clutch; check clutch cable for security and condition (Chapter 5)
- ☐ Check manual transmission oil level (Chapter 6, Section 2)
- ☐ Where appropriate, check level and condition of automatic transmission fluid (Chapter 7, Section 3)
- ☐ Check operation of brakes, including handbrake; check brake fluid level; check system and system lines for leaks or damage (Chapter 9, Sections 12, 13 and 16)
- ☐ Check front brake pads for wear; check condition of brake calipers, discs and hydraulic hoses (Chapter 9, Sections 2, 3, 5, 6 and 12)
- ☐ Check roadwheel balance and alignment (Chapter 10, Sections 21 and 22)
- ☐ Check bodywork (Chapter 11, Sections 2 and 4)

Every 24 000 miles (40 000 km) or 2 years - whichever comes first

- ☐ Renew Positive Crankcase Ventilation (PCV) system filter (Chapter13, Section 4)
- ☐ Check all drivebelts for cracks, fraying, wear and tension (Chapter 2, Section 9)
- ☐ Renew engine coolant (Chapter 2, Sections 3 and 4)
- ☐ Check condition and security of fuel and exhaust system hoses, pipes and connections (Chapter 3, Section 2)
- ☐ Renew air filter element (Chapter 3, Section 3)
- ☐ Renew fuel filter (Chapter 3, Section 8)
- ☐ Check condition of spark plug HT leads (Chapter 4, Section 10)
- ☐ Renew brake fluid (Chapter 9, Section 13)
- ☐ Check condition and security of braking system vacuum servo unit hose, connections and non-return valve (Chapter 9, Sections 2 and 14)
- ☐ Check rear brake shoes for wear; check condition of brake drums, wheel cylinders and hydraulic hoses/pipes (Chapter 9, Sections 2, 4, 7, 8 and 12)
- ☐ Check condition and security of steering gear and linkage, driveshafts and suspension components (Chapters 8 and 10)
- ☐ Check condition and security of seat belts, buckles, retractors, anchorage points and adjuster (Chapter 11, Section 25)

Every 60 000 miles (100 000 km)

- ☐ Renew the timing belt (Chapter 1, Section 6)

Topping-up the brake fluid level

Maintenance schedule for all models with a catalytic converter

Weekly or before a long journey
- [ ] Check engine oil level (Chapter 1, Section 2)
- [ ] Check engine coolant level (Chapter 2, Section 3)
- [ ] Check automatic transmission fluid level (Chapter 7, Section 3)
- [ ] Check brake fluid level (Chapter 9, Section 2)
- [ ] Check all tyres for condition and pressure (including spare) (Chapter 10, Section 22)
- [ ] Check operation of all lights, horn, wipers and washers (Chapter 12)
- [ ] Check washer fluid level, adding a screen wash (Chapter 12, Section 23)

Every 4500 miles (7500 km) or 6 months - whichever comes first
Note: *Frequent oil and filter changes are good for the engine. We recommend changing the oil at the mileage specified here, or at least twice a year if the mileage covered is less.*
- [ ] Renew engine oil and filter (Chapter 1, Sections 2 and 10)

Every 18 000 miles (30 000 km) or 12 months - whichever comes first
- [ ] Check valve clearances (Chapter 1, Section 5)
- [ ] Check Positive Crankcase Ventilation (PCV) system (Chapter 13, Section 4, and Chapter 1, Section 24)
- [ ] Check condition of cooling system hoses and connections (Chapter 2, Section 2)
- [ ] Check all drivebelts for cracks, fraying, wear and tension (Chapter 2, Section 9)
- [ ] Check operation of air filter automatic air temperature control system (Chapter 13, Section 7)
- [ ] Renew fuel filter (Chapter 3, Section 8)
- [ ] Check operation of exhaust gas sensor (Chapter 13, Section 7)
- [ ] Check condition of Evaporative Emission Control system vacuum hoses and connections (Chapter 13, Section 7)
- [ ] Renew spark plugs (Chapter 4, Section 10)
- [ ] Check operation of the clutch, check clutch cable for security and condition (Chapter 5)
- [ ] Check manual transmission oil level (Chapter 6, Section 2)
- [ ] Where appropriate, check level and condition of automatic transmission fluid (Chapter 7, Section 3)
- [ ] Check operation of brakes, including handbrake; check brake fluid level; check system and system lines for leaks or damage (Chapter 9, Sections 2, 12,13 and 16)

- [ ] Check front brake pads for wear; check condition of brake calipers, discs and hydraulic hoses (Chapter 9, Sections 2, 3, 5, 6 and 12)
- [ ] Check roadwheel balance and alignment (Chapter 10, Sections 21 and 22)
- [ ] Check bodywork (Chapter 11, Sections 2 and 4)

Every 36 000 miles (60 000 km) or 2 years - whichever comes first
- [ ] Renew Positive Crankcase Ventilation (PCV) system filter (Chapter 13, Section 4)
- [ ] Renew engine coolant (Chapter 2, Sections 3 and 4)
- [ ] Check condition and security of fuel and exhaust system hoses, pipes and connections (Chapter 3, Section 2)
- [ ] Renew air filter element (Chapter 3, Section 3)
- [ ] Check condition of spark plug HT leads (Chapter 4, Section 10)
- [ ] Renew brake fluid (Chapter 9, Section 13)
- [ ] Check condition and security of braking system vacuum servo unit hose, connections and non-return valve (Chapter 9, Sections 2 and 14)
- [ ] Check rear brake shoes for wear; check condition of brake drums, wheel cylinders and hydraulic hoses/pipes (Chapter 9, Sections 2, 4, 7, 8 and 1 2)
- [ ] Check condition and security of steering gear and linkage, driveshafts and suspension components (Chapters 8 and 10)
- [ ] Check condition and security of seat belts, buckles, retractors, anchorage points and adjuster (Chapter 11, Section 25)

Every 60 000 miles (100 000 km)
- [ ] Renew the timing belt (Chapter 1, Section 6)

Greasing the bonnet lock

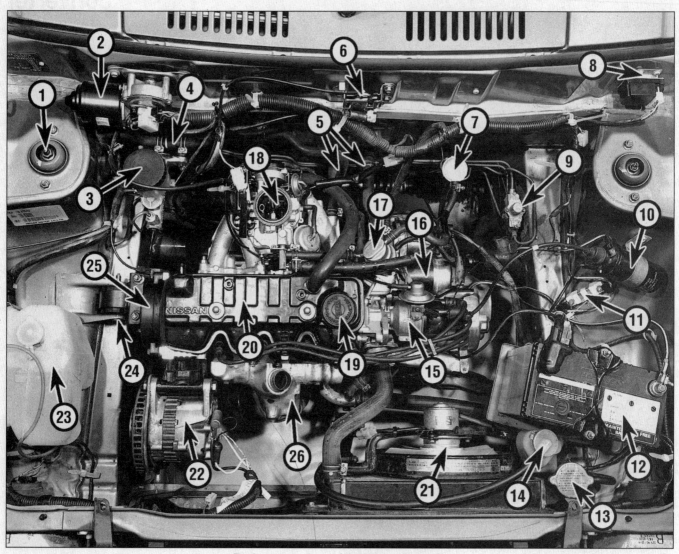

Engine compartment (air cleaner removed)

1 Shock absorber top mounting
2 Windscreen wiper motor assembly
3 Brake master cylinder fluid reservoir cap
4 Brake vacuum servo hose to inlet manifold
5 Heater hoses (inlet and outlet)
6 Bonnet release catch mechanism
7 Fuel filter
8 Intermittent wipe relay amplifier
9 Brake system dual proportioner valve
10 Ignition coil
11 Ignition system ballast resistor
12 Battery
13 Radiator filler cap
14 Radiator expansion bottle
15 Distributor
16 Starter motor
17 Fuel pump
18 Carburettor
19 Engine oil filler cap
20 Rocker cover
21 Radiator cooling fan
22 Alternator
23 Windscreen wash reservoir
24 Engine mounting
25 Timing cover
26 Exhaust manifold and collector plate

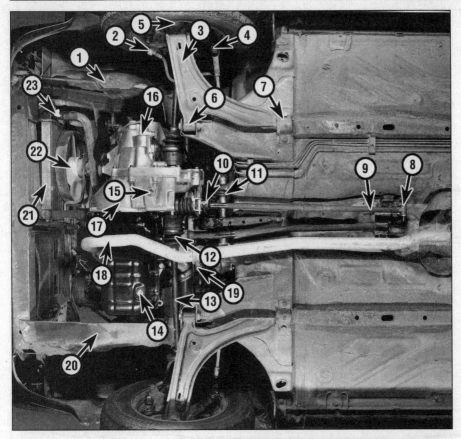

View of front underside of car

1 Engine shield
2 Brake caliper and hose
3 Suspension transverse link
4 Steering rod balljoint
5 Transverse link balljoint
6 Transverse link front mounting
7 Transverse link rear mounting
8 Gear change lever connection
9 Gear change control rod
10 Gear change control rod to transmission
    unit input shaft connection
11 Steering rack assembly
12 Inboard driveshaft joint
13 Driveshaft
14 Engine oil drain plug
15 Transmission unit drain plug
16 Transmission unit
17 Clutch bellhousing
18 Exhaust downpipe
19 Exhaust pipe front mounting
20 Engine shield
21 Radiator
22 Radiator cooling fan
23 Radiator drain plug

View of rear underside of car

1 Fuel and hydraulic brake pipes
2 Rear suspension location link rods
3 Fuel tank filler pipe
4 Fuel tank drain plug
5 Handbrake cable
6 Link rod attachment brackets
7 Rear shock absorber lower mounting
8 Rear axle tube
9 Exhaust silencer and mounting
10 Handbrake cable adjustment point
11 Handbrake cable pivot arm
12 Intermediate exhaust mounting
13 Heat shield
14 Intermediate silencer

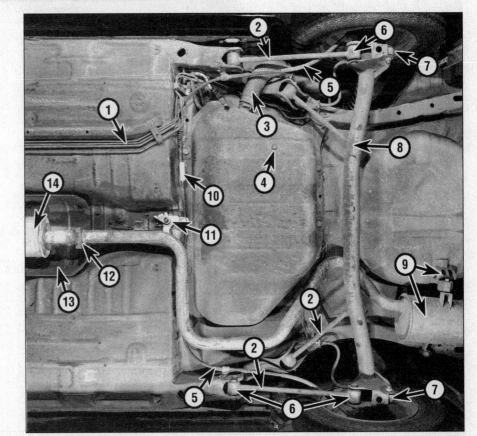

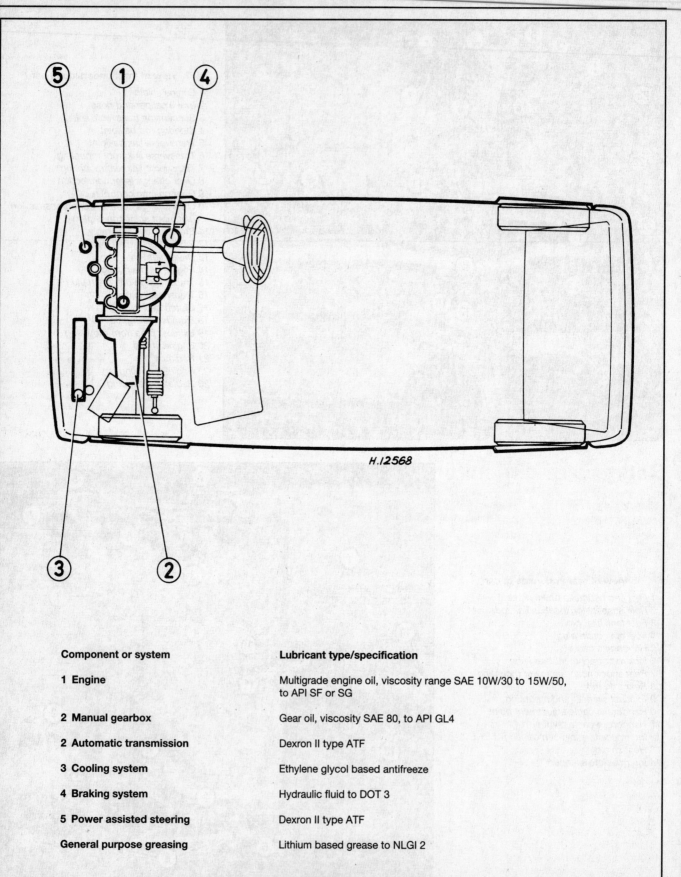

H.12568

Component or system	Lubricant type/specification
1 Engine	Multigrade engine oil, viscosity range SAE 10W/30 to 15W/50, to API SF or SG
2 Manual gearbox	Gear oil, viscosity SAE 80, to API GL4
2 Automatic transmission	Dexron II type ATF
3 Cooling system	Ethylene glycol based antifreeze
4 Braking system	Hydraulic fluid to DOT 3
5 Power assisted steering	Dexron II type ATF
General purpose greasing	Lithium based grease to NLGI 2

Chapter 1 Engine

For modifications, and information applicable to later models, see Supplement at end of manual

Contents

Degrees of difficulty

Easy, suitable for novice with little experience	**Fairly easy,** suitable for beginner with some experience	**Fairly difficult,** suitable for competent DIY mechanic	**Difficult,** suitable for experienced DIY mechanic	**Very difficult,** suitable for expert DIY or professional

Specifications

General

Type	Transverse, four cylinder, in-line overhead camshaft
Designation	MA10
Bore	68.0 mm (2.68 in)
Stroke	68.0 mm (2.68 in)
Capacity	988 cc (60.29 cu in)
Compression ratio	9.5:1 (4-speed) or 10.3:1
Compression pressure (at 350 rev/min):	
Standard	192 lbf/in² (13.5 kgf/cm²)
Minimum	164 lbf/in² (11.5 kgf/cm²)
Maximum difference between cylinders	14 lbf/in² (1 kgf/cm²)
Firing order	1 - 3 - 4 - 2

Cylinder block

Material	Aluminium alloy
Cylinder bore:	
Standard	68.00 to 68.03 mm (2.6772 to 2.6783 in)
Wear limit	0.1 mm (0.0039 in)
Maximum out-of-round	0.02 mm (0.0008 in)
Maximum taper	0.02 mm (0.0008 in)
Normal difference between bores	0.05 mm (0.002 in)
Maximum difference between bores	0.2 mm (0.0079 in)

Crankshaft

Number of main bearings 5
Main journal diameter .... 44.95 to 44.97 mm (1.7697 to 1.7705 in)
Crankpin diameter .... 39.96 to 39.97 mm (1.5732 to 1.5736 in)
Maximum journal and crankpin out-of-round .... Less than 0.01 mm (0.0004 in)
Endfloat (standard) .... 0.06 to 0.22 mm (0.0024 to 0.0087 in)
Endfloat (maximum) .... 0.5 mm (0.0197 in)
Main bearing running clearance:
    Standard .... 0.03 to 0.05 mm (0.0012 to 0.0020 in)
    Maximum .... 0.075 mm (0.0030 in)
Connecting rod bearing clearance:
    Standard .... 0.02 to 0.06 mm (0.0008 to 0.0024 in)
    Maximum .... 0.12 mm (0.0047 in)
    Main bearing undersize .... 0.25 mm (0.0098 in)

Flywheel run-out .... 0.15 mm (0.0059 in) maximum

Connecting rods

Big-end side play .... 0.10 to 0.37 mm (0.0039 to 0.0146 in)
Wear limit .... 0.5 mm (0.020 in)

Gudgeon pin

Pin to piston clearance .... 0.008 to 0.012 mm (0.0003 to 0.0005 in)
Interference fit in small-end .... 0.017 to 0.038 mm (0.0007 to 0.0015 in)

Pistons

Piston skirt diameter (standard) .... 67.967 to 67.997 mm (2.6759 to 2.6770 in)
Oversize .... 0.5 mm (0.030 in)
Clearance in block .... 0.023 to 0.043 mm (0.0009 to 0.0017 in)

Piston rings

Type .... Two compression, one oil control
Clearance in groove (standard):
    Top .... 0.04 to 0.08 mm (0.0016 to 0.0031 in)
    2nd .... 0.03 to 0.06 mm (0.0012 to 0.0024 in)
    Oil control .... 0.0 to 0.175 mm (0.0 to 0.0069 in)
Wear limit .... 0.2 mm (0.008 in)
Ring end gap:
    Top No 1 grade .... 0.21 to 0.30 mm (0.0083 to 0.0118 in)
    Top No 2 and No 3 grade .... 0.18 to 0.30 mm (0.0071 to 0.0118 in)
    2nd .... 0.15 to 0.39 mm (0.0059 to 0.0154 in)
    Oil control .... 0.20 to 0.79 mm (0.0079 to 0.0311 in)

Camshaft

Outer diameter of journal .... 39.95 to 39.97 mm (1.5728 to 1.5736 in)
Camshaft bearing inner diameter .... 40.00 to 40.03 mm (1.5748 to 1.5760 in)
Journal-to-bearing clearance:
    Standard .... 0.03 to 0.07 mm (0.0012 to 0.0028 in)
    Wear limit .... 0.15 mm (0.0059 in)
Endfloat .... 0.03 -to 0.31 mm (0.0012 to 0.0122 in)
Cam lobe height:
    Inlet .... 33.77 to 34.02 mm (1.3295 to 1.3394 in)
    Exhaust .... 33.73 to 33.98 mm (1.3280 to 1.3378 in)

Valves

Clearances (cold):
    Inlet .... 0.22 mm (0.009 in)
    Exhaust .... 0.22 mm (0.009 in)
Clearances (hot):
    Inlet .... 0.25 mm (0.0098 in)
    Exhaust .... 0.30 mm (0.0118 in)
Valve seat angle (inlet and exhaust) .... 45°15' to 45°45'
Valve spring free length .... 46.70 mm (1.8386 in)
Valve guides:
    Outer diameter .... 11.023 to 11.034 mm (0.4340 to 0.4344 in)
    Inner diameter .... 7.005 to 7.020 mm (0.2758 to 0.2164 in)
Cylinder head valve guide hole diameter .... 10.960 to 10.978 mm (0.4315 to 0.4322 in)
Interference fit of valve guides .... 0.045 to 0.074 mm (0.0018 to 0.0029 in)
Stem to guide clearance:
    Inlet .... 0.015 to 0.045 mm (0.0006 to 0.0018 in)
    Exhaust .... 0.045 to 0.075 mm (0.0018 to 0.0030 in)

Timing belt deflection (measured) midway on longest run .... 2.0 mm (0.08 in) with applied force of 1.06 to 1.28 lbf (0.48 to 0.58 kgf)

Cylinder head
Material .... Aluminium alloy
Surface out-of-true (limit) .... 0.1 mm (0.004 in)

Lubrication
Oil pressure at 1200 rev/min .... 28 lbf/in² (2.0 kgf/cm²)
Oil pressure at 2000 rev/min .... 43 lbf/in² (3.0 kgf/cm²)
Oil pump:
   Rotor tip clearance .... 0.2 mm (0.008 in)
   Outer rotor to body clearance .... 0.2 mm (0.008 in)
   Rotor endfloat .... 0.2 mm (0.008 in)
Engine oil capacity (including oil filter) .... 2.8 litre (4.9 pt)
Oil type/specification .... Multigrade engine oil, viscosity range SAE 10W/30 to 15W/50, to API SF or SG
Oil filter .... Champion C131

Torque wrench settings

	lbf ft	kgf m
Alternator bracket bolt	6.7 to 8.7	0.93 to 1.2
Alternator adjuster link bolt	6.7 to 8.7	0.93 to 1.2
Alternator to bracket	16 to 22	2.2 to 3.0
Clutch pressure plate bolts	12 to 15	1.6 to 2.1
Engine mounting to cylinder head	29 to 36	4.0 to 5.0
Engine mounting to cylinder block	29 to 36	4.0 to 5.0
Fuel pump mounting nuts	6.5 to 8.7	0.9 to 1.2
Inlet and exhaust manifold nuts	12 to 15	1.6 to 2.1
Oil pump idler gear bolts	4.3 to 5.1	0.6 to 0.7
Oil pump securing bolt	13 to 16	1.8 to 2.2
Power-steering pump bracket	12 to 15	1.6 to 2.1
Power steering pump mounting bolt	23 to 31	3.2 to 4.3
Spark plugs	18 to 22	2.5 to 3.0
Water pump bolts	2.9 to 3.6	0.4 to 0.5
Air conditioner compressor bracket	22 to 30	3.1 to 4.1
Crankshaft pulley bolt	61 to 69	8.5 to 9.5
Thermostat housing bolts	2.0 to 3.6	0.4 to 0.5
Oil pressure switch	9 to 12.7	1.25 to 1.75
Camshaft pulley bolt	6.5 to 8.7	0.9 to 1.2
Connecting rod nut	22 to 25	3.0 to 3.5
Cylinder head bolts:		
1st stage	25 to 29	3.5 to 4.0
2nd stage	43 to 47	6.0 to 6.5
Flywheel bolts	43 to 51	6.0 to 7.0
Driveplate bolts	51 to 58	7.0 to 8.0
Main bearing cap bolts	34 to 38	4.7 to 5.3
Oil sump bolts	2.9 to 3.6	0.4 to 0.5
Oil sump drain plug	26 to 35	3.6 to 4.8
Oil strainer bolts	4.3 to 5.8	0.6 to 0.8
Rocker shaft bolts	13 to 15	1.8 to 2.1
Tensioner lock nut	11 to 12	1.5 to 1.7
Rocker cover nut	2.2 to 3.6	0.3 to 0.5
Valve clearance adjuster screw locknut	8 to 11	1.1 to 1.5

1 General description

The new MA10 engine, designed specifically for the Micra is a lightweight, compact, all alloy engine. It is conventional, being of four-cylinder, in-line overhead cam design.

The cylinder head has a crossflow design, with hemispherical combustion chambers, the valves being driven from the camshaft, which in turn is driven by toothed belt from the crankshaft.

The crankshaft is supported in five main bearings mounted within a one-piece bearing cap. Main bearings and big-end bearings are of the white metal lined shell type, and are readily renewed, but the gudgeon pins require specialist equipment for removal and refitting. The camshaft runs in bearings machined directly into the cylinder head.

2 Routine maintenance

1 At weekly intervals, check the engine oil level. Do this by withdrawing the dipstick, wiping it clean, reinserting it and withdrawing it for the second time.
2 The oil level should be between the L and H marks. Top up if necessary.
3 Change the engine oil and oil filter at the

2.4 Oil sump drain plug

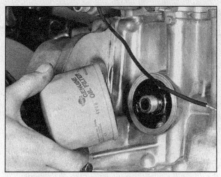

2.5 Removing the oil filter cartridge

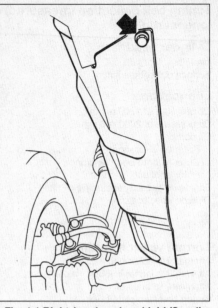

Fig. 1.1 Right-hand engine shield (Sec 4)

intervals indicated in the Routine maintenance schedule.

4 The oil should be drained when hot by removing the oil filler cap and the sump drain plug (photo). Use a large bowl to catch the oil.

5 Using a suitable filter removal tool, unscrew the cartridge type oil filter which is located on the cylinder block just to the rear of the alternator (photo). Be prepared for some spillage of oil.

6 Wipe the filter mating face on the cylinder block clean and smear the rubber sealing ring of the new filter with a little oil. Screw on the filter hand-tight only.

7 Refit the sump drain plug.

8 Refill with the correct quantity and type of engine oil. Refit the oil filler cap.

9 At the intervals indicated in the Routine

maintenance schedule, check the crankcase ventilation system hoses for condition and security.

3 Major operations possible without removing the engine

The following operations may be carried out with the engine in position in the vehicle.
Removal and refitting of the cylinder head
Adjustment of the valve clearances
Removal and refitting of the timing belt
Removal and refitting of the oil pump
Removal and refitting of the sump
Removal of piston rings and big-end bearings

4 Cylinder head - removal and refitting

Note: *the procedure given here describes the removal operation with the engine in situ. Later texts describe the overhaul procedure with the engine removed from the vehicle.*

1 Disconnect the battery.

2 Disconnect the HT and LT leads to the distributor and remove it and the spark plugs (Chapter 4).

3 Remove the air cleaner, then disconnect all fuel lines, control cables, hoses and electrical leads to the carburettor (Chapter 3).

4 Drain the cooling system and remove the radiator (Chapter 2).

5 Remove the collector plate from around the exhaust manifold, and disconnect the exhaust downpipe (Chapter 3).

6 Remove the exhaust manifold and inlet manifold, complete with carburettor.

7 Raise the car and support the front end of the vehicle on axle stands.

8 Remove the right-hand engine shield.

9 Remove the right-hand road wheel.

10 Support the engine under the oil sump and remove the right-hand engine mounting (photo). (This gives access to the timing belt covers).

11 Remove the alternator drivebelt, and if fitted the power and air conditioner pump drivebelts (Chapter 2).

12 By means of a socket on the crankshaft pulley bolt, set the engine timing marks to TDC on the compression stroke (photo).

13 Remove the crankshaft pulley.

14 Remove the timing cover (photo). Note the earth lead attached to the cover securing bolt (photo).

4.10 Right-hand engine mounting

4.12 Aligning the crankshaft pulley mark with the 0° (TDC) mark

4.14A Timing belt upper cover retaining bolts (arrowed)

4.14B Remember the earth lead when refitting

4.15 Timing belt tensioner pulley

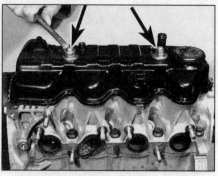

4.16 Remove the rocker cover (retaining nuts arrowed)

4.17 Oil pump idler gear. The bulb in the plate faces downwards (arrowed)

15 Release the timing belt tensioner (photo) and return spring and remove the timing belt. Do not rotate either the camshaft or crankshaft once the timing belt has been removed as damage may result from a valve hitting a piston.

16 Remove the rocker cover (photo).

17 Undo and remove the two bolts retaining the oil pump idler gear and remove the idler gear and driveshaft (photo).

18 Loosen the cylinder head bolts progressively in the reverse order to the tightening sequence (photo). Remove the bolts.

19 Remove the cylinder head carefully. If further dismantling is to be carried out, refer to the relevant Sections of this Chapter. If difficulty is experienced removing the head,

tap it gently around the sides using a soft-faced mallet.

20 Before refitting the cylinder head, make sure all traces of old gasket are removed from the mating surfaces of the cylinder head and block. **Note:** *the alloy used in the construction of the engine is easily damaged by scrapers and screwdrivers so be careful when cleaning off old gasket. Paint stripper will help to remove stubborn pieces of gasket and carbon.*

21 Clean out oil from the cylinder block bolt holes, clean the cylinder head bolts and oil them lightly with clean engine oil.

22 Fit a new cylinder gasket to the cylinder block (photo).

23 Before lowering the cylinder head into position turn the camshaft by means of the drive sprocket to line up the zero mark with

the notch on the cylinder head. This will prevent damage to the pistons and valves by ensuring their correct relative position.

24 Lower the cylinder head carefully onto the block (photo) and ensure it seats correctly.

25 Fit the cylinder head bolts, with their washers. Tighten the bolts progressively in the correct sequence (Fig. 1.2) to the 1st stage torque figures given in the Specification, then loosen each bolt. again in reverse sequence, and finally re-torque to the 2nd stage specified setting, again on the sequence shown in Fig. 1.2.

Note: *Do not rotate the crankshaft or camshaft without the drivebelt being fitted or the valves will hit the pistons.*

26 Refit the oil pump driveshaft (photo).

27 Refit the oil pump idler gear (photo).

1

4.18 Loosening the cylinder head bolts

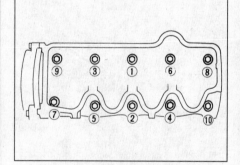

Fig. 1.2 Cylinder head bolt tightening sequence (Sec 4)

4.22 Cylinder head gasket in position

4.24 Placing the cylinder head on the cylinder block

4.26 Fitting the oil pump driveshaft . . .

4.27 . . . and the idler gear

4.29A Camshaft sprocket alignment marks

4.29B Crankshaft sprocket alignment marks

4.29C Checking alignment

28 Bolt on the oil pump retainer plate, ensuring the dish faces downwards.
29 Check the alignment marks on the crankshaft sprocket and camshaft sprocket are lined up (photos).
30 If they were removed, refit the tensioner spring and pulley (photos) .
31 Slide the tensioner pulley to the left in its slot and temporarily tighten the bolt.
32 Check that both the tensioner pulley and coolant pump sprocket turn freely.
33 Ensure the timing belt is clean and free from oil and water, before fitting it in position, make sure its directional arrow faces the correct way (it rotates clockwise as you look at it).
34 Loosen the tensioner pulley locknut.
35 Using a peg spanner on the camshaft sprocket, rotate the whole assembly two turns anti-clockwise.
36 Tighten the tensioner locknut and re-check the alignment marks on the camshaft and crankshaft sprockets.
37 Check the deflection at the camshaft belt (see Fig. 1.3) (see Specifications) .
38 Fit the lower camshaft drivebelt cover (photo).
39 Fit the upper camshaft drivebelt cover (photo).
40 Refit the crankshaft pulley.
41 Refit the alternator drivebelt and the power steering and air conditioning pump bolts if these are fitted.
42 Refit the right-hand engine mounting, remove the support from under the oil sump,
refit the roadwheel and lower the vehicle to the ground
43 Refit the right-hand engine shield.
44 Refit the exhaust manifold (photo) and connect up the downpipe. Fit the collector plate.
45 Refit the inlet manifold, and reconnect the carburettor fuel lines, electrical leads, control cables and hoses (refer to Chapter 3).
46 Refit the distributor HT and LT leads and spark plugs (Chapter 4).
47 Refill the cooling system (Chapter 2).
48 Adjust valve clearances (see Section 5).
49 Refit the rocker cover as described in Section 5 (photos).
50 Check engine oil level.
51 Reconnect the battery.

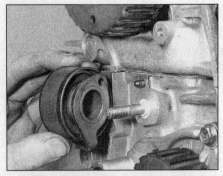

4.30A Refitting the tensioner pulley . . .

4.30B . . . and spring

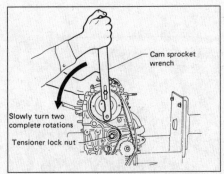

Fig. 1.3 Check belt deflection after tightening the locknut (Sec 4)

Cam sprocket wrench

Slowly turn two complete rotations

Tensioner lock nut

4.38 Timing belt lower cover

4.39 Fitting the timing belt upper cover

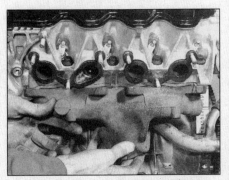

4.44 Fitting the exhaust manifold

4.49A Ensure rubber gasket is located correctly . . .

4.49B . . . when fitting the rocker cover

5 Valve clearances - adjustment

1 If the valve clearances are being checked as part of 'Routine maintenance' the engine must be fully warmed up to normal operating temperature. If the clearances are being checked after engine overhaul work, they must be set provisionally with the engine cold, then rechecked and set accurately once it has been restarted and has warmed up. Ensure that the specified clearances are used that are appropriate to the engine's temperature.

2 Remove the air cleaner (Chapter 3) and the spark plugs (Chapter 4). Disconnect the remaining crankcase breather hose from the rocker cover, unscrew the rocker cover retaining nuts (collecting the cupped washers), then withdraw the cover. Check the

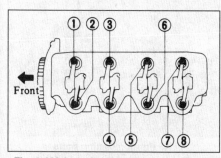

Fig. 1.4 Valve adjusting sequence (Sec 5)

rocker cover rubber gasket and seals, which can be re-used several times, but must be renewed if distorted, split or otherwise unserviceable. If improved access is required to the crankshaft pulley, jack up the front of the car and support it securely on axle stands, then remove the right-hand engine shield.

3 Using a spanner applied to the crankshaft pulley bolt, rotate the crankshaft clockwise until No 1 cylinder's inlet valve (valve 1, Fig. 1.4) has opened and closed again, then rotate the crankshaft slightly further until the crankshaft pulley notch aligns with the O mark on the timing belt lower cover scale. No 1 cylinder is now at TDC on the compression stroke.

4 Using feeler gauges inserted between the valve stem tip and the adjuster screw, measure the clearances of valves Nos 1, 2, 3 and 6 (Fig. 1.4). Note that, with reference to Fig. 1.4, the odd-numbered valves are the inlets, and the even numbers are the exhausts. The clearance of any valve is correct when a feeler gauge of the specified thickness is a firm sliding fit; as noted above, ensure that the specifications used are appropriate to the engine's temperature.

5 If adjustment is required, slacken the adjuster screw locknut, turn the screw until the clearance is correct, then retighten the locknut without altering the screw's setting (photo).

6 When the clearances are correct on the first four valves, rotate the crankshaft through one full turn clockwise until No 4 cylinder is at TDC on the compression stroke, then check the clearances on valves Nos 4, 5, 7 and 8 (Fig. 1.4).

7 On completion, refit the rocker cover. Ensure that its seals and gasket are correctly located on clean mating surfaces, do not forget the cupped washers, and do not overtighten the cap nuts; note the specified torque wrench setting. Reconnect the breather hose, then refit the spark plugs, air cleaner and any other components removed for access.

6 Timing belt - removal and refitting

1 The timing belt must be renewed as a precautionary measure every 60 000 miles (100 000 km), irrespective of its apparent condition.

2 Removal is as described in Section 4, paragraphs 7 to 15, refitting from paragraph 30 onwards.

7 Sump pan - removal and refitting

1 Drain the engine oil.

2 Unbolt the reinforcement struts from the rear corner of the sump and transmission.

3 Disconnect the exhaust downpipe from the manifold and release the exhaust pipe front mounting.

4 Unscrew and remove the sump pan bolts and nuts. The nut nearest the transmission is very inaccessible and will require the use of a universally-jointed drive extension and socket to remove it.

5 Remove the sump pan by pulling the exhaust pipe downwards.

6 Remove and discard the old gaskets.

7 Before fitting the sump pan, stick new side gaskets and end sealing strips in position with gasket cement. Make sure that the ends of the sealing strips overlap the side gaskets. Cover the seam with a generous blob of cement (photo).

8 Screw in the sump bolts and fit the nuts, tightening them evenly (photo) .

9 Reconnect the exhaust pipe.

10 Fill the engine with oil.

5.5 Adjusting the valve clearances

7.7 Fitting new gaskets, using sealing compound

7.8 Sump pan bolts – note the four nuts are located at the sump corners (two arrowed)

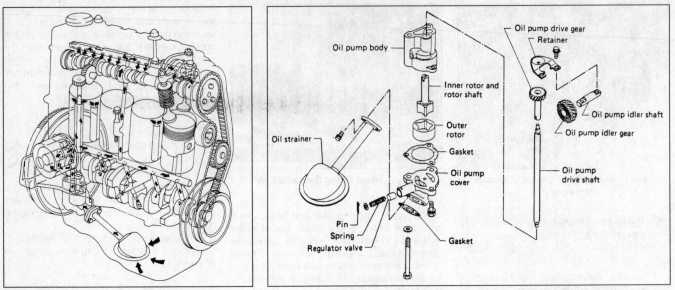

Fig. 1.5 Oil system flow diagram (Sec 8)

Fig. 1.6 Exploded view of oil pump (early models) (Sec 9)

8 Oil pump - general

1 The oil pump, which is trochoidal, is bolted to the cylinder block within the sump.
2 It is driven by skew gear and shafts from the camshaft.
3 A spring plate, which is held in place by the bolts which retain the idler gear, keeps the vertical shaft in position.
4 The oil pump may be removed with the engine in situ, but note that our photographs in the following text were taken with the engine removed for clarity.

9 Oil pump - removal, inspection and refitting

1 Remove the sump pan as described in Section 7.

2 Undo the two retaining nuts and remove the oil pick up arm and strainer (photo).
3 Remove the bolts holding the pump to the cylinder block (photo) and remove the pump. (Be ready to catch the vertical driveshaft if this is being done in situ.)
4 Remove the remaining bolt and take off the end cap (photo).

5 Extract the split pin from the relief valve housing and remove the spring and plunger (photos).
6 The inner rotor and shaft and outer rotor may now be removed (photo).
7 Measure the rotor tip clearance, outer rotor clearance and endfloat (photos) and compare them with the tolerances in the Specifications.

9.2 Removing the oil strainer

9.3 Pump retaining bolts

9.4 Remove the remaining bolt and remove end cap

9.5A Split pin retaining the relief valve plunger

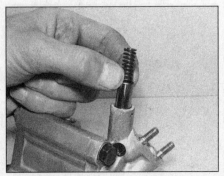

9.5B Removing the relief valve

9.6 Component parts of the oil pump

9.7A Measuring rotor tip clearance . . .

9.7B . . . outer rotor clearance . . .

If any parts are worn beyond the specified limits renew the whole assembly.

8 Refitting is a reversal of removal, but use new gaskets. If the job is being done in situ then remove the rocker cover and the oil pump idler gear as described in Section 4 and refit the driveshaft and idler gear after the pump is bolted in place (photo). This will ensure the driveshaft slots and tongues are meshed correctly. Wash the oil strainer in petrol and dry it before refitting. Oil all parts liberally during reassembly.

9 On later models a spring stopper has been added to the idler gear assembly and to improve performance, the direction of the oil pump drivegear teeth has been changed. This changes the rotational direction of the pump from clockwise to anti-clockwise.

9.7C . . . and endfloat

9.8 Strainer bolted in position

10 This means that the new pumps can only be fitted with the new camshaft. Ensure all new parts are compatible.

10 Oil filter - removal and refitting

1 The oil filter screws into its housing on the rear face of the engine block, below the inlet manifold.
2 If an old filter is difficult to remove, use a strap wrench, or alternatively, drive a screwdriver right through the body of the filter and use it to unscrew the filter. Be prepared for some oil spillage during removal.
3 The oil filter housing incorporates a bypass valve, which is a spring loaded ball bearing. This will open to allow oil passage should the

filter become blocked during service (photo).
4 When fitting a new filter, oil the seal lightly to prevent sticking, and only do the filter canister up hand tight.
5 Fill the engine with oil, then run the engine and check for leaks. It is usual for the oil pressure warning light to remain on for a few seconds whilst the new filter is filling with oil.

11 Piston rings and big-end bearing shells - renewal

1 The choice of renewal of piston rings or substitution with special proprietary rings may be made as a means of reducing heavy oil consumption. The opportunity should also be taken to examine and renew if necessary the big-end bearings.
2 Remove the cylinder head and sump, as described in earlier Sections.
3 Note that the connecting rod big-end caps are numbered with matching numbers on

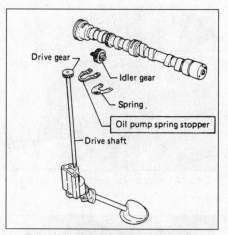

Fig. 1.7 Later models have a sprung stopper (Sec 9)

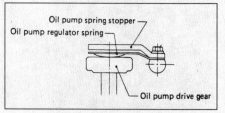

Fig. 1.8 Correct assembly of regulator spring (Sec 9)

10.3 Oil filter housing (bypass valve arrowed)

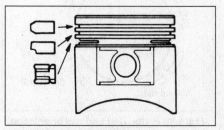

Fig. 1.9 Piston ring arrangement (Sec 11)

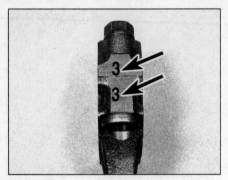

11.3 Matching numbers are stamped on the faces

11.4A Big-end cap bolts

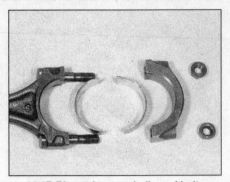

11.4B Big-end caps, shells and bolts

adjacent machined surfaces on the connecting rod (photo). Note to which side of the crankcase the numbers face.

4 Undo the big-end cap bolts and remove the caps (photo).

5 If the bearing shells are to be used again, keep them in their correct order with the connecting rods. Do not mix them.

6 Push the pistons and connecting rods up and out of the cylinder bores. If the cylinder bores are severely worn and a ridge can be felt around the top of the bores, this may have to be reduced by careful reaming before the pistons will pass through.

7 Remove the piston rings by sliding pieces of old feeler gauge blades under them at three equidistant places and then sliding the rings off the piston.

8 Clean the piston ring grooves, removing all

traces of gum and carbon. (A piece of old piston ring is ideal for this purpose.)

9 Check that the new rings have the correct groove clearance (photo) and end gap (photo).

10 Fit the rings to the pistons by reversing the removal operation.

11 The rings are marked on their upper surfaces.

12 If using new rings then the bores should be honed to remove the hard glaze. Use a rotary abrasive flap wheel.

13 The piston ring gaps should be staggered at equidistant points around the piston circumference, oil the rings and pistons liberally and use a ring compressor when fitting the pistons to bores.

14 Oil the cylinder bores and insert the first piston/con rod assembly, con rod first, into No 1 cylinder. Push it in until the piston ring compressor rests on the block (photo).

15 Now push the piston into the bore, which will release the ring compressor. Repeat on the remaining pistons.

16 Make sure the mark on the piston faces the timing belt end of the block (photo).

17 Draw each con rod/piston assembly down to the crankshaft. Oil each crankpin liberally and check that the big-end bearing shells are returned to their original positions.

18 Unless the shells are in excellent condition, with no signs of the copper underlay showing through, they should be renewed. The size is stamped on the back of the shell. Standard shells are unmarked or stamped 0-00.

19 Fit the big-end bearing caps with their shells, ensuring the numbers match, and tighten the nuts to the specified torque (photo).

11.9A Measuring piston ring groove clearance . . .

11.9B . . . and end gap

11.14 Using a ring compressor on the piston

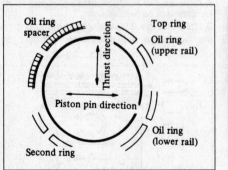

Fig. 1.10 Piston ring end gap orientation (Sec 11)

11.16 Piston alignment mark should face the timing belt end when inserting the piston

11.19 Fitting a big-end bearing cap

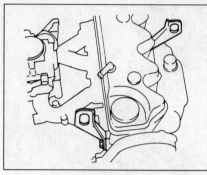

Fig. 1.11 Engine lifting brackets (Sec 13)

20 Refit the cylinder head and oil sump as described in earlier Sections.
21 Refill the engine with oil and coolant.

12 Engine removal - method

The engine should be removed from the vehicle as a unit complete with transmission. The help of an assistant will definitely be required.

For vehicles with air conditioning

If components of the air conditioning system obstruct the overhaul of the engine and cannot be moved sufficiently within the limits of their flexible hoses to avoid such obstruction, the system should be discharged by your dealer or competent refrigeration engineer.

As the system must be completely evacuated before recharging, the necessary vacuum equipment to do this is only likely to be held by your dealer.

The refrigerant fluid is Freon 12 and, although harmless under normal conditions, contact with eyes or skin must be avoided. If Freon comes into contact with a naked flame a poisonous gas is created which is injurious to health.

13 Engine/manual transmission - removal and separation

Note: *Refer to Chapter 6 where necessary*
1 With the help of an assistant, unbolt and remove the bonnet (see Chapter 11).
2 Disconnect the battery and remove it together with its support bracket.
3 Remove the air cleaner.
4 Drain the cooling system, retaining the coolant if it is suitable for further use.
5 Remove the radiator complete with electric cooling fan (see Chapter 2).

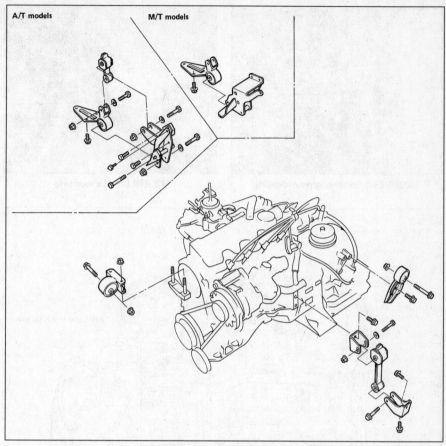

Fig. 1.12 Engine mounting brackets (Sec 13)

6 If power steering is fitted, unbolt the pump and move it to one side of the engine compartment.
7 If air conditioning is fitted, unbolt the compressor and belt tensioner pulley and move them aside. *Do not disconnect the refrigerant circuit pipelines* (see Chapter 11).
8 Disconnect the exhaust downpipe from the manifold and the mounting bracket.
9 Unbolt and disconnect the gearchange control rod and its stabiliser rod from the transmission.
10 Support the vehicle under its side-member and then disconnect the front suspension lower balljoints. Do this by unscrewing the three nuts which hold the balljoint to the suspension arm. It is recommended that new nuts are used at reassembly.
11 Remove the front roadwheels.
12 Drain the engine and transmission oils.
13 Unbolt the disc calipers and tie them up out of the way.
14 Unscrew, but do not remove, the nuts at the front suspension strut top mountings. This is to allow movement of the struts when the driveshafts are withdrawn from the transmission.
15 To disconnect a driveshaft, insert a large screwdriver or suitable lever behind the inboard joint flange and prise to overcome the

resistance of the joint circlip. Take care not to damage the transmission oil seal and do not pull on the outer end of the driveshaft or the joints may come apart. Insert a rod into the side gears in the transmission casing to prevent them moving from the differential case.
16 Disconnect the clutch operating cable from the release lever.
17 Disconnect the speedometer drive cable from the transmission.
18 Disconnect the throttle and choke cables as applicable.
19 Disconnect the fuel hoses from the fuel pump and plug them. Also disconnect all vacuum and air hoses from the engine.
20 Disconnect all electrical leads, including those from the coolant temperature switch, oil pressure switch, reverse lamp switch and alternator, also the HT and LT leads from the ignition coil.
21 On models with an automatic choke, disconnect the electrical lead from the choke terminal. Withdraw the complete wiring harness from under the intake manifold after releasing the clips.
22 Lifting eyes should be bolted to the engine. Attach suitable lifting gear and take the weight of the engine.
23 Disconnect the four engine/transmission flexible mountings by unscrewing either the

13.23A Left-hand engine mounting

13.23B Front mounting

13.23C Right-hand mounting

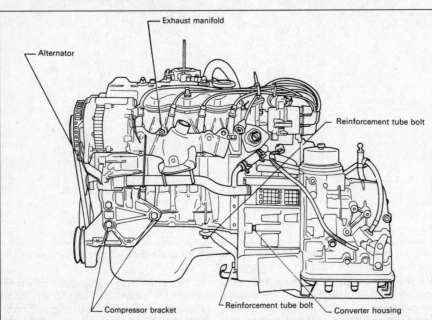

Alternator

Exhaust manifold

Reinforcement tube bolt

Compressor bracket

Reinforcement tube bolt

Converter housing

Fig. 1.13 Engine external components viewed from front (automatic version shown) (Sec 13)

13.23D Rear mounting

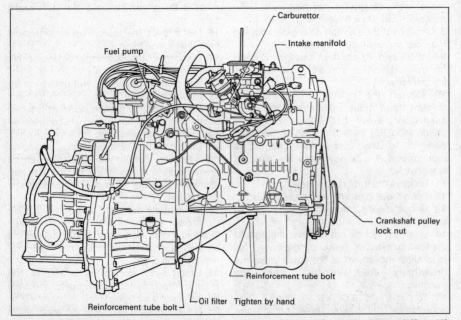

Fuel pump

Carburettor

Intake manifold

Crankshaft pulley lock nut

Reinforcement tube bolt

Reinforcement tube bolt

Oil filter Tighten by hand

Fig. 1.14 Engine external components viewed from rear (automatic version shown) (Sec 13)

13.24 Lifting the engine out

bush pivot or the nut according to location (photos).

24 Lift the engine/transmission up and out of the engine compartment (photo). Take care not to damage adjacent components or the wing surface.

25 With the unit removed, clean away external dirt using a water soluble solvent or paraffin and a stiff brush.

26 To separate the engine from the transmission unbolt and remove the starter motor and then withdraw the bolts which connect the clutch bellhousing to the engine. Note that some of these bolts retain the upper coolant tube, the sump pan-to-bellhousing reinforcement tube and the transmission mounting brackets. Mark their positions for ease of refitting.

27 Support the weight of the transmission and then withdraw it in a straight line from the engine.

14 Engine/automatic transmission - removal and separation

1 The operations for removal are very similar to those described for vehicles with manual transmission in the preceding Section but observe the following differences. Refer also to Chapter 7.

2 Ignore any reference to the clutch cable.

3 Remove the front wing protective shield where fitted.

4 Disconnect the speed selector cable from the transmission, also the inhibitor switch leads.

5 Disconnect and plug the oil cooler hoses.

6 To separate the engine from the automatic transmission first unbolt and remove the starter motor. Also disconnect the kick-down cable.

7 Mark the relationship of the torque converter to the driveplate using a dab of quick-drying paint.

8 Unscrew the torque converter-to-driveplate connecting bolts. The crankshaft will have to be turned to bring each bolt into view in the cut-out in the torque converter housing before a spanner or socket wrench can be used. Remove the engine-to-transmission connecting bolts.

9 Withdraw the automatic transmission, at the same time have an assistant hold the torque converter in full engagement with the oil pump driveshaft to avoid loss of transmission fluid.

15 Engine dismantling - general

1 Before commencing a major engine overhaul, make sure that you have gathered together clean rags, brushes, freeing fluid and a good selection of tools - including a torque wrench.

2 A number of clean tins or other containers is useful to keep the various nuts and bolts safely. Mark the tins as a guide to where the fixings belong.

16.12 Removing the camshaft drive sprocket

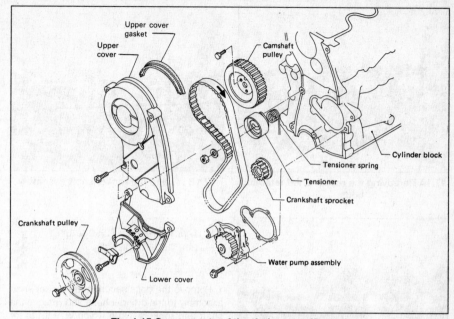

Fig. 1.15 Components of the timing gear (Sec 16)

Upper cover gasket — Upper cover — Camshaft pulley — Cylinder block — Tensioner spring — Tensioner — Crankshaft sprocket — Water pump assembly — Crankshaft pulley — Lower cover

3 Have a pencil and paper handy to record sequences of assembly of small items, or to sketch an item which may present difficulty at reassembly or refitting.

4 Obtain all the necessary gaskets and oil seals in advance.

5 If it is known that only one component of the engine is worn or damaged the dismantling operations should only be pursued as far as is necessary to rectify the problem, the engine need not be completely dismantled.

16 Engine - complete dismantling

1 Place the engine upright, preferably on a bench.

2 Remove the ancillary components such as the alternator, distributor, fuel pump, carburettor, inlet and exhaust manifolds, and remove the transmission unit and clutch assembly. (Refer to the relevant Chapter).

16.14 Water pump retaining bolts

3 Remove the oil filter.

4 Remove the thermostat and housing.

5 Remove the alternator mounting bracket. If fitted also remove those for power steering and air conditioner pumps.

6 Remove the coolant tube which runs along the side of the engine.

7 Remove the timing belt covers.

8 Remove the rocker cover.

9 Turn the engine on its side and remove the oil sump.

10 Prevent the crankshaft from rotating and remove the flywheel bolts. As these bolts are not offset, mark the flywheel and crankshaft relationship before removing the flywheel, and the engine rear plate.

11 Remove the timing belt and belt tensioner pulley.

12 Remove the camshaft sprocket by inserting a dowel through one of the holes so that it contacts an engine web to prevent it turning while undoing the three bolts (photo).

13 Remove the crankshaft sprocket, which is keyed to the crankshaft. Use a puller if it is tight.

14 Undo the five bolts and remove the water pump (photo).

15 Remove the oil pump and the oil pump idler gear, and lift out the driveshaft.

16 Remove the cylinder head bolts and lift off the cylinder head and gasket.

17 Remove the piston and con rod assemblies as described in Section 11.

18 Unscrew the main bearing cap bolts progressively and in sequence. Remove the main bearing cap.

19 Lift out the crankshaft, keeping the bearings in their correct order, and note the thrust washers either side of the No 4 bearing.

20 The engine is now ready for inspection as described in the following Sections.

1

17.1A Removing the rocker shaft retaining bolts . . .

17.1B . . . and the rocker shaft assembly

17.2 Removing the thermostat housing

17.3 Withdrawing the camshaft

17 Cylinder head - dismantling and decarbonizing

1 Remove the bolts securing the rocker shaft assembly to the cylinder head and remove the shaft and rockers. Note which way it fits for correct reassembly (photos). Note where the spring locking clips are fitted over the bolts.

2 Remove the bolts from the thermostat housing on the end of the cylinder head and remove the housing (photo).

3 Carefully withdraw the camshaft, taking care not to damage the bearings as the lobes pass through (photo).

4 The valves and their associated components should now be removed. Owing to the depth of the cylinder head a valve spring compressor having a long reach will be required. If this is not available, temporarily refit the rocker shaft and then make up a lever with a fork at one end to compress the valve spring by using the underside of the rocker shaft as a fulcrum.

5 Compress the first valve spring, extract the split collets. If the valve spring refuses to compress, do not apply excessive force but

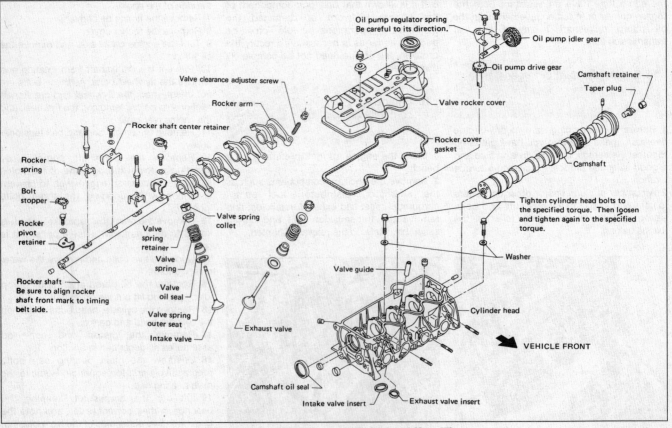

Fig. 1.16 Exploded view of cylinder head (Sec 17)

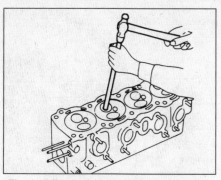

Fig. 1.17 Removing a valve guide (Sec 17)

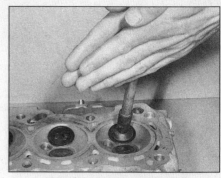

Fig. 1.18 Valve guide projection (Sec 17)

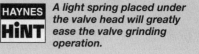
17.11 Grinding in a valve seat

remove the compressor and place a piece of tubing on the spring cap and strike it a sharp blow to release the collets from the valve stem. Refit the compressor and resume operations.

6 Gently release the compressor, take off the spring retaining cap, the valve spring and the spring seat. Remove the valve. Keep the valve with its associated components together and in numbered sequence so that it can be refitted in its original position. A small box with divisions is useful for this purpose.

7 Remove the other valves in a similar way.

8 Bearing in mind that the cylinder head is of light alloy construction and is easily damaged use a blunt scraper or rotary wire brush to clean all traces of carbon deposits from the combustion spaces and the ports. The valve heads, stems and valve guides should also be freed from any carbon deposits. Wash the combustion spaces and ports down with a suitable solvent and scrape the cylinder head surface free of any foreign matter with the side of a steel rule, or a similar article.

9 If the engine is installed in the car, clean the pistons and the top of the cylinder bores. If the pistons are still in the block, then it is essential that great care is taken to ensure that no carbon gets into the cylinder bores as this could scratch the cylinder walls or cause damage to the piston and rings. To ensure this does not happen, first turn the crankshaft so that two of the pistons are at the top of their bores. Stuff rag into the other two bores or seal them off with paper and masking tape. The waterways should also be covered with small pieces of masking tape to prevent particles of carbon entering the cooling

system and damaging the coolant pump.

10 Press a little grease into the gap between the cylinder walls and the two pistons which are to be worked on. With a blunt scraper carefully scrape away the carbon from the piston crown, taking great care not to scratch the aluminium. Also scrape away the carbon from the surrounding lip of the cylinder wall. When all carbon has been removed, scrape away the grease which will now be contaminated with carbon particles, taking care not to press any into the bores. To assist prevention of carbon build-up the piston crown can be polished with a metal polish. Remove the rags or masking tape from the other two cylinders and turn the crankshaft so that the two pistons which were at the bottom are now at the top. Place rag in the cylinders which have been decarbonized, and proceed as just described.

11 Examine the head of the valves for pitting and burning, especially, the heads of the exhaust valves. The valve seatings should be examined at the same time. If the pitting on the valve and seat is very slight, the marks can be removed by grinding the seats and valves together with coarse, and then fine valve grinding paste (photo).

12 Where bad pitting has occurred to the valve seats it will be necessary to recut them and fit new valves. This latter job should be entrusted to the local agent or engineering works. In practice it is very seldom that the seats are so badly worn. Normally it is the valve that is too badly worn for refitting, and the owner can easily purchase a new set of valves and match them to the seats by valve grinding.

13 Valve grinding is carried out as follows. Smear a trace of coarse carborundum paste on the seat face and apply a suction grinding tool to the valve head. With a semi-rotary motion, grind the valve head to its seat, lifting the valve occasionally to redistribute the grinding paste. When a dull matt even surface is produced on both the valve seat and the valve, wipe off the paste and repeat the process with fine carborundum paste, lifting and turning the valve to redistribute the paste as before.

HAYNES HiNT *A light spring placed under the valve head will greatly ease the valve grinding operation.*

When a smooth unbroken ring of light grey matt finish is produced on both valve and valve seat faces, the grinding operation is complete. Carefully clean away every trace of grinding compound, take great care to leave none in the ports or in the valve guides. Clean the valves and valve seats with a solvent-soaked rag, then with a clean rag, and finally, if an air line is available. blow the valves, valve guides and valve ports clean.

14 Check that all valve springs are intact. If any one is broken, all should be renewed. Check the free height of the springs against new ones. If some springs are not within specifications, replace them all. Springs suffer from fatigue and it is a good idea to renew them even if they look serviceable.

15 Check that the oil supply holes in the rocker arms are clear.

16 The cylinder head can be checked for warping either by placing it on a piece of plate glass or using a straight-edge and feeler blades. If there is any doubt or if its block face is corroded, have it re-faced by your dealer or motor engineering works.

17 Test the valves in their guides for side-to-side rock. If this is any more than almost imperceptible, new guides must be fitted. This, as with valve seat renewal, is really a job for your dealer as the cylinder head must be warmed and the old guide driven out. New guides should be pressed in to protrude 12.7 mm (0.50 in) above the cylinder head and then reamed using a 7.005 to 7.020 mm (0.2758 to 0.2764 in) reamer.

18 Renew the valve stem oil seals (photos).

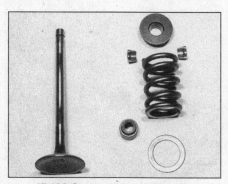
17.18A Components of the valve

17.18B Fitting valve stem oil seal

17.19 Pushing in a valve

17.20A Fitting the spring seat . . .

17.20B . . . spring . . .

17.20C . . . and cap

17.21 Using a valve spring compressor

19 Commence reassembly by oiling the stem of the first valve and pushing it into its guide (photo).

20 Fit the spring seat (photo), the valve spring (photo) and the spring cap (photo). The closer coils of the valve spring must be towards the cylinder head.

21 Compress the valve spring and locate the split collets in the valve stem cut-outs (photo).

22 Gently release the compressor, checking to see that the collets are not displaced (photo).

23 Fit the remaining valves in the same way (photo).

24 Tap the end of each valve stem with a plastic or copper-faced hammer to settle the components.

25 Fit a new camshaft oil seal to the cylinder head, spring faces inwards (photo). Oil all bearing surfaces and the camshaft, and insert the camshaft into the cylinder head.

26 For correct valve timing, the spigot should be centralised at the top. Fit the camshaft retainer at the other end of the camshaft.

27 Fit a new gasket to the thermostat housing, apply sealant to the mating surfaces, and bolt the housing in position on the cylinder head.

28 Fit the camshaft sprocket (photo).

29 Before refitting the rocker shaft and arms, check the shaft for wear and the rocker arms for pitting of the case hardened contact points with the valve stems. Keep all parts in order, and replace in their original positions (photo).

17.22 Check the collets are in position before releasing the compressor

17.23 Valve stems and springs assembled

17.25 Camshaft oil seal in position

17.28 Camshaft sprocket correctly located

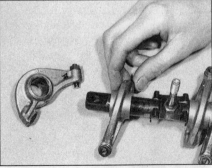

17.29 Put all parts back in their original positions

17.30A Pivot retainer legs face inwards

17.30B Refitting the rocker arm assembly

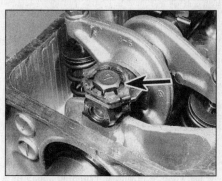

17.30C Don't forget the spring locking washers

30 Refit the rocker shaft, making sure the legs of the pivot retainers face inwards, and use new sprung locking washers on the bolt heads. These push on after the bolts have been tightened (photos).

18 Examination and renovation

Cylinder block and crankcase

1 Examine the casting carefully for cracks, especially around the bolt holes and between cylinders.
2 The cylinder bores must be checked for taper, ovality, scoring and scratching. Start by examining the top of the cylinder bores. If they are worn, a ridge will be felt on the thrust side. This ridge marks the top of piston travel. The owner will have a good indication of bore wear prior to dismantling by the quantity of oil consumed and the emission of blue smoke from the exhaust, especially when the engine is cold.
3 An internal micrometer or bore gauge should be used to check bore wear and taper.
4 Slight wear and scoring may be taken out by honing, and the appropriate size piston selected from the five grades shown in the Specifications in the Supplement (Chapter 13).
5 If the degree of wear is such that it cannot be rectified by honing, the cylinders can be rebored. Refer to the Supplement (Chapter 13) for details.
6 Excessive oil consumption may also be eliminated by fitting proprietary oil control rings, as described in Section 11.

Crankshaft and bearings

7 Examine the surfaces of the crankpins and journals for signs of scoring or scratching, and check for ovality or taper. If a crankpin or journals are not within the dimensional tolerances given in the Specifications Section at the beginning of this Chapter the crankshaft will have to be reground.
8 Wear in a crankshaft can be detected while the engine is running. Big-end bearing and

crankpin wear is indicated by distinct metallic, knocking, particularly noticeable when the engine is pulling from low engine speeds. Low oil pressure will also occur.
9 Main bearing and journal wear is indicated by engine rumble increasing in severity as the engine speed increases. Low oil pressure will again be an associated condition.

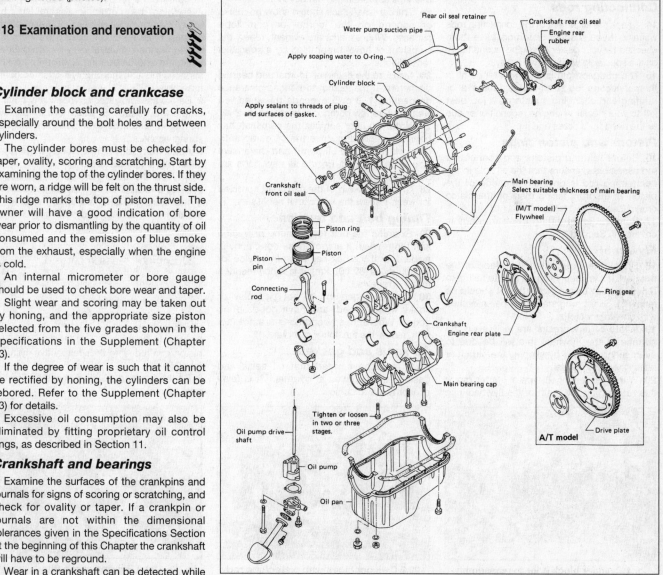

Fig. 1.19 Exploded view of cylinder block (Sec 18)

10 Crankshaft grinding should be carried out by specialist engine reconditioners who will supply the matching undersize bearing shells to give the required running clearance.

11 Inspect the connecting rod big-end and main bearing shells for signs of general wear, scoring, pitting and scratching. The bearings should be matt grey in colour. If a copper colour is evident, then the bearings are badly worn and the surface material has worn away to expose the underlay. Renew the bearings as a complete set.

12 At the time of major overhaul it is worthwhile renewing the bearing shells as a matter of routine even if they appear to be in reasonably good condition.

13 Bearing shells can be identified by the marking on the back of the shell. Standard sized shells are usually marked STD or 0.00. Undersized shells are marked with the undersize, such 0.25 mm.

Connecting rods

14 Check the alignment of the connecting rods visually. If you suspect distortion, have them checked by your dealer or engine reconditioner on the special jig which he will have.

15 The gudgeon pin is an interference fit in the connecting rod small-end and removal or refitting and changing a piston is a job best left to your dealer or engine reconditioner due to the need for a press and jig.

Pistons and piston rings

16 Before refitting pistons and connecting rod assemblies, ensure that the oil hole in the connecting rod is on the same side of the piston as the front facing mark on the piston crown (see photo 11.16).

17 Removal and refitting of piston rings is covered in Section 11.

Flywheel

18 Check the clutch mating surface of the flywheel. If it is deeply scored (due to failure to renew a worn driven plate) then it should be renewed. Slight roughness may be smoothed with fine emery cloth.

19 If lots of tiny cracks are visible on the surface of the flywheel this will be due to overheating caused by slipping the clutch or riding the clutch pedal.

20 With a pre-engaged type of starter motor it is rare to find the teeth of the flywheel ring gear damaged or worn, but if they are the ring gear will have to be renewed.

21 To remove the ring gear, drill a hole between the roots of two teeth, taking care not to damage the flywheel, and then split the ring with a sharp cold chisel.

22 The new ring gear must be heated to between 180 and 220°C (356 and 428°F) which is very hot, so if you do not have facilities for obtaining these temperatures, leave the job to your dealer or engine reconditioner.

Driveplate (automatic transmission)

23 Should the starter ring gear on the driveplate require renewal, the driveplate should be renewed complete.

Camshaft

24 Examine the camshaft bearings for scoring or pitting. If evident then the complete cylinder head will have to be renewed as the bearings are machined directly in it.

25 The camshaft itself should show no marks or scoring on the journal or cam lobe surfaces. Where marks are evident, renew the camshaft or have it reprofiled by a specialist reconditioner.

26 Measure the camshaft journal and bearing diameters. If the journal-to-bearing clearance on bearing 1, 3 or 5 exceeds the specified wear limit, renew components as necessary.

27 **Note:** On later engines the camshaft has been redesigned to drive the oil pump anti-clockwise, and the oil pump and drive have also been changed. Ensure all new parts are compatible.

28 Check the teeth of the camshaft sprocket for wear. Renew the sprocket if necessary.

Timing belt and tensioner

29 Examine the belt for cracking or fraying and tooth wear. If any of these conditions is evident, or if the belt has been in service for 50 000 miles (80 000 km), it is recommended that it is renewed.

30 The tensioner should not be noisy or shaky when turned, and have good spring action. Where these conditions are not met with, renew the tensioner complete.

Oil seals and gaskets

31 It is recommended that oil seals and gaskets are renewed at overhaul. It is false economy not to do so.

TOOL TiP *Sockets are useful for removing and fitting seals.*

An arrow may be stamped on the end to indicate the rotational direction of the component which it seals. Fit seals the correct way round, complying with the arrow. This is usually with the spring facing into the housing into which the seal is being fitted .

Cylinder head

32 It is dealt with in Section 17, during dismantling and decarbonizing.

19 Engine reassembly - general

1 To ensure maximum life with minimum trouble from a rebuilt engine, not only must everything be correctly assembled, but everything must be spotlessly clean, all the oilways must be clear, locking washers and spring washers must always be fitted where indicated and all bearing and other working surfaces must be thoroughly lubricated during assembly.

2 Before assembly begins renew any bolts or studs, the threads of which are in any way damaged, and wherever possible use new spring washers.

3 Apart from your normal tools, a supply of clean rag, an oil can filled with engine oil (an empty plastic detergent bottle thoroughly cleaned and washed out, will do just as well), a new supply of assorted spring washers, a set of new gaskets, and a torque wrench, should be collected together.

20 Engine - reassembly

1 Place the cleaned cylinder block onto the bench (photo).

2 Refer to Section 11 and fit the assembled piston/con rods into their respective cylinders (photo).

3 Fit the big-end bearing shells to the con rods (photo).

20.1 Cylinder block prior to reassembly

20.2 Cylinder block with piston/con rod assemblies fitted in the bores

20.3 Big-end shells fitted

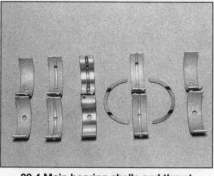

20.4 Main bearing shells and thrust washers

20.5 Main bearing shell and thrust washer fitted to No 4 main bearing

20.6 Lowering the crankshaft into position

4 Place the main bearing shells on the bench in order, together with the thrust washers. Note that Nos 2 and 4 lower shells are grooved (which fit into the bearing cap) and Nos 2, 3 and 4 upper shells are grooved (which fit into the cylinder block). Also note that the thrust washers fit either side of number 4 bearing (photo).

5 Lightly oil the upper shells and fit them into the cylinder block together with the thrust washers (photo).

6 Carefully lower the crankshaft into position (photo).

7 Draw the piston/con rod assemblies up each cylinder and fit them to the crankshaft as described in Section 11 (photo).

8 Fit the main bearing lower shell halves to the main bearing cap, oil all parts liberally, then fit the main bearing cap (photo).

9 Before tightening the bolts to their correct torque (see Specifications) and in the sequence shown in Fig. 1.20, bed the crankshaft in by shifting it back and forward axially a few times (photo).

10 Crankshaft endfloat should now be checked, using a dial gauge as shown in Fig. 1.21.

11 If the endfloat does not comply with the tolerances given in the Specification, then the thrust washers either side of No 4 main bearing should be changed to bring endfloat within limits.

12 Fit a new oil seal to the crankshaft front end and push it fully home (photos).

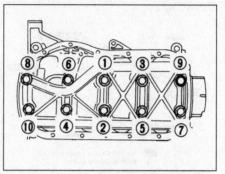

Fig. 1.20 Main bearing cap bolt tightening sequence (Sec 20)

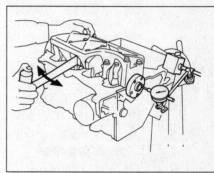

Fig. 1.21 Using a dial gauge to check crankshaft endfloat (Sec 20)

20.7 Tightening the big-end bearing caps

20.8 Fitting the main bearing cap

20.9 Tightening the main bearing cap bolts

20.12A Fit a new oil seal to crankshaft front end . . .

20.12B . . . and push it fully home

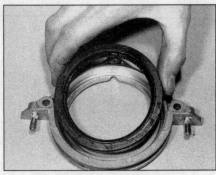

20.13A Fitting an oil seal to the crankshaft rear oil seal housing

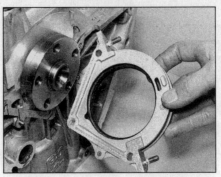

20.13B Fitting the oil seal housing to the block

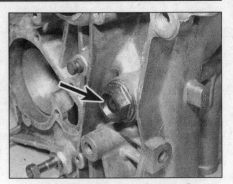

20.14 Oil gallery plug (arrowed)

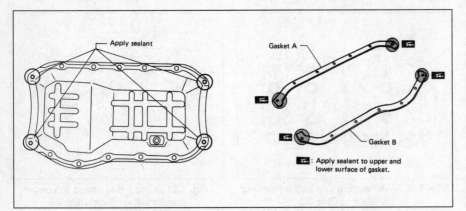

Apply sealant

Gasket A

Gasket B

⊞ : Apply sealant to upper and lower surface of gasket.

Fig. 1.22 Areas to apply sealant to oil sump gasket (Sec 20)

13 Fit a new oil seal to the rear crankshaft oil seal housing, fit a new gasket and apply sealing compound to its mating surfaces before bolting on the oil seal and housing (photo).
14 Ensure the oil gallery plug is fitted at the timing belt end of the block (photo).
15 Refit the oil pump as described in Section 9.
16 Apply sealant to the areas indicated in Fig. 1.22 and using a new gasket, fit the oil sump. Make sure the drain plug is fitted to the sump.
17 Apply sealant to the threads of the coolant pump retaining bolts, and to the gasket and mating surfaces of the pump housing, and fit the pump to the cylinder block (photo).
18 Using a new cylinder head gasket, fit the cylinder head as described in Section 4.
19 Also refering to Section 4, fit the oil pump driveshaft, idler gear and retainer. Also fit the camshaft and crankshaft drive sprockets, tensioner assembly and camshaft belt.
20 Set the valve clearances initially and fit the rocker cover using a new gasket. There is a wire filter mesh over the breather hole. Make sure it is not clogged (photo).
21 Offer up the engine rear shield, fit it over the locating dowels (photo) and keep it in place with one bolt fitted loosely.
22 Offer up the flywheel, fit the bolts, and ensure that the alignment marks, made previously, match up. Tighten the bolts to the specified torque (photos).

20.17 Fit a new gasket to the water pump housing

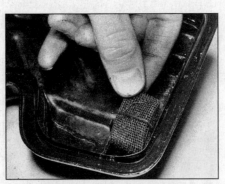

20.20 Wire mesh filter over breather hole

20.21 Fit the rear engine shield

20.22A Offer up the flywheel . . .

20.22B . . . fit and tighten the bolts

20.23 Bolting on the clutch

20.25A Use a new O-ring seal . . .

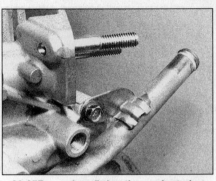

20.25B . . . when fitting the coolant pipe

1

23 Fit the clutch, as described in Chapter 5 (photo).

24 Using a new gasket, and with sealant applied to the mating surfaces, fit the thermostat, distributor and fuel pump housing.

25 Using a new O-ring seal fit the coolant pipe to the coolant pump outlet. Lubricate the seal and push it home (photo) and bolt the securing bracket in place below the fuel pump housing (photo).

26 Fit the oil pressure switch (photo) and the water temperature sender unit (photo).

27 Fit new gaskets to the inlet manifold, then bolt on the manifold. Repeat this procedure with the exhaust manifold and fit the heat collector shield.

28 Bolt on the alternator mounting bracket (photo). Fit the timing belt covers if this was not done earlier, then fit the crankshaft pulley.

29 Fit the oil filter, smearing the rubber seal with fresh oil to ensure an oil tight seal.

30 The ancillaries, such as carburettor and alternator may be fitted now or left until the engine is back in the vehicle.

31 Check round the engine to ensure there are no obvious omissions.

32 Clean out the inside of the clutch bellhousing then bolt the transmission unit to the engine (refer to Chapter 6 or 7) (photo).

20.26A Oil pressure switch . . .

20.26B . . . and water temperature transmitter

20.27A Use new gaskets . . .

20.27B . . . when fitting the inlet manifold . . .

20.27C . . . and exhaust manifold and shield

20.28 The alternator mounting bracket

20.32 Transmission unit ready to be bolted to the engine

20.33 Bolt on the starter motor

20.34A Fit the engine mountings . . .

20.34B . . . in their appropriate positions

33 Fit the starter motor (photo) and tighten its retaining bolts.
34 Fit the engine mountings, ensuring any other component brackets are in position (photos). Make sure the engine stays (reinforcement tubes) between the oil sump and transmission unit are fitted.
35 After a final check the engine transmission unit is ready for installation.

21 Engine/transmission unit - refitting

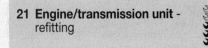

1 Connect the hoist to the lifting lugs, raise the engine and lower it slowly into the engine compartment.
2 Manoeuvre the engine around gently while fitting the bolts to the engine mountings. Once all the mountings are fitted and bolts tightened, remove the lifting gear.
3 From underneath the vehicle, connect the gear change control rod (Chapter 6).
4 Refer to Chapter 8 and refit the driveshafts. Do not forget to tighten the top suspension strut bolts if they were undone.
5 Refit the brake calipers and roadwheels.
6 Bolt up the exhaust downpipe and the exhaust pipe intermediate bracket if this has been undone for access (photos).

7 Refit the speedometer drive cable after filling the transmission with oil.
8 Reconnect the clutch operating cable to the operating arm, and check the clutch adjustment (Chapter 5) (photo).
9 Reconnect the fuel lines to the pump and carburettor (photos).
10 Connect the throttle and choke control cable as appropriate. On models with an automatic choke reconnect the electrical lead.
11 Reconnect the reversing lamp lead, oil pressure switch lead and water temperature transmitter leads (photo).
12 Refer to the relevant Chapters and refit the distributor and alternator if these were not fitted previously. Fit the alternator belt and

21.6A Connect the exhaust downpipe

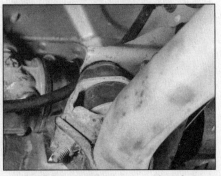

21.6B Intermediate support bracket

21.8 Clutch control cable end fitting

21.9A Fuel pump supply hose (arrowed)

21.9B Connections at the carburettor

21.10 Throttle control cable

21.11 Water temperature electrical lead

21.13A Top radiator hose

21.13B Bottom radiator hose . . .

tension it. Fit the drivebelts to the power steering and air conditioner if fitted.

13 Refit the radiator, connect the coolant hoses and heater hoses, reconnect the electric fan cable and refill the system (Chapter 2) (photos) .

14 Refill the engine with oil, refit the dipstick.

15 Refit the air cleaner to the carburettor, ensuring all vent hoses from the rocker cover are connected, and connect also the vacuum hoses.

16 Reconnect the battery.

17 Refit the bonnet and radiator grille.

22 Engine/automatic transmission - reconnection and refitting

Reconnection

Refer also to Chapter 7

1 The operations are very similar to those described in the preceding Section, but the following special points should be noted.

2 Before connecting the driveplate to the torque converter, check to see that the converter is pushed fully home by referring to Chapter 7.

3 Align the marks on the driveplate and torque converter (made before dismantling). Apply thread locking fluid to the clean threads of the connecting bolts and tighten them to the specified torque. Bolt on the starter motor, and reconnect the kick-down cable.

Refitting

4 Reconnect the speed selector control cable and adjust it, if necessary.

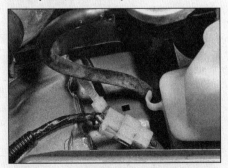

21.13C . . . and the cooling fan electrical connection

5 Reconnect the inhibitor switch leads.

6 Reconnect the oil cooler hoses.

7 Refit the front wing protective shield where fitted.

8 Top up the automatic transmission fluid.

23 Initial start-up after major overhaul

1 Set the idle speed screw to a higher setting than normal to offset the drag caused by new engine components.

2 Start the engine. This may take rather longer than usual as the fuel pump has to fill the carburettor with fuel.

3 Once the engine starts, allow it to warm without racing and then check for oil leaks.

4 There will be some odd smells caused by oil and grease burning off metal surfaces.

5 Treat the engine as a new unit for the first few hundred miles by restricting speed and load.

6 Once the engine is run-in after 1000 km (600 miles), check the idle speed, the valve

clearances and the tightening torque of all engine nuts and bolts. Change the engine oil and filter at the same time.

24 Crankcase ventilation system (PCV)

1 This is of positive, dual-line type which returns blow-by gas (which has passed the piston rings) from the crankcase to either the air filter or the intake manifold, according to manifold vacuum. According to engine load conditions a valve regulates the routing of the gas.

2 Check the system connecting hoses regularly and clean them out.

3 To test the operation of the valve, have the engine idling and disconnect the hoses from the side of the valve which is furthest from the intake manifold. Vacuum hiss should be heard coming from the open end of the valve and a strong suction felt if a finger is placed over it. If this is not so, renew the valve.

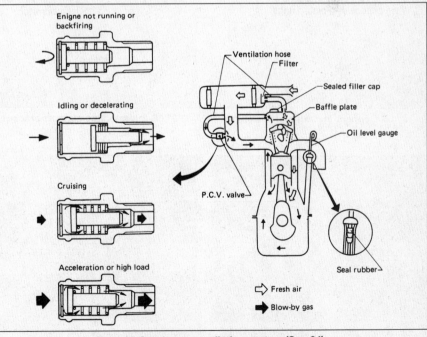

Fig. 1.23 Crankcase ventilation system (Sec 24)

Fault finding - engine

Engine fails to turn when starter control operated

No current at starter motor

- ☐ Flat or defective battery
- ☑ Loose battery leads
- ☐ Defective starter solenoid or switch or broken wiring
- ☐ Engine earth strap disconnected

Current at starter motor

- ☐ Jammed starter motor drive pinion
- ☐ Defective starter motor

Engine turns but will not start

No spark at spark plug

- ☐ Ignition leads or distributor cap damp or wet
- ☐ Ignition leads to spark plugs loose
- ☐ Shorted or disconnected low tension leads
- ☐ Dirty, incorrectly set, or pitted contact breaker points
- ☐ Faulty condenser
- ☐ Defective ignition switch
- ☐ Ignition leads connected wrong way round
- ☐ Faulty coil
- ☐ Contact breaker point spring earthed or broken

No fuel at engine

- ☐ No petrol in petrol tank
- ☐ Vapour lock in fuel line (in hot conditions or at high altitude)
- ☐ Blocked float chamber needle valve
- ☐ Fuel pump filter blocked
- ☐ Choked or blocked carburettor jets (where applicable)
- ☐ Faulty fuel pump

Lack of power and poor compression

Mechanical wear

- ☐ Burnt out valves
- ☐ Sticking or leaking valves
- ☐ Worn or broken valve springs
- ☐ Worn valve guides or stems
- ☐ Worn pistons and piston rings

Engine stalls and will not restart

Excess of petrol in cylinder or carburettor flooding

- ☐ Too much choke allowing too rich a mixture or wet plugs
- ☐ Float damaged or leaking or needle not seating
- ☐ Float lever incorrectly adjusted

No spark at spark plug

- ☐ Ignition failure - sudden
- ☐ Ignition failure - misfiring precedes total stoppage
- ☐ Ignition failure - in severe rain or after traversing water splash

No fuel at jet

- ☐ No petrol in petrol tank
- ☐ Petrol tank breather choked
- ☐ Sudden obstruction in carburettor
- ☐ Water in fuel system

Engine misfires or idles unevenly

Intermittent spark at spark plug

- ☐ Ignition leads loose
- ☐ Battery leads loose on terminals
- ☐ Battery earth strap loose on body attachment point
- ☐ Engine earth lead loose
- ☐ Low tension leads on coil loose
- ☐ Low tension lead on distributor loose
- ☐ Dirty or incorrectly gapped plugs
- ☐ Dirty, incorrectly set, or pitted contact breaker points
- ☐ Tracking across inside of distributor cover
- ☐ Ignition too retarded
- ☐ Faulty coil
- ☐ Slack timing belt

Fuel shortage at engine

- ☐ Mixture too weak
- ☐ Air leak in carburettor
- ☐ Air leak at inlet manifold to cylinder head, or inlet manifold to
- ☐ carburettor

Chapter 2 Cooling system

For modifications, and information applicable to later models, see Supplement at end of manual

Contents

Degrees of difficulty

Easy, suitable for novice with little experience	Fairly easy, suitable for beginner with some experience	Fairly difficult, suitable for competent DIY mechanic	Difficult, suitable for experienced DIY mechanic	Very difficult, suitable for expert DIY or professional

Specifications

System type .... Pressurised, circulation pump driven from camshaft drivebelt, radiator, thermostat and electric cooling fan

Radiator cap relief pressure .... 13 lbf/in² (0.9 kgf/cm²)

Thermostat
Opening temperature .... 88°C (190°F)
Maximum valve lift .... 8 mm at 100°C (0.31 in at 212°F)

Coolant temperature switch
Switches on at .... 90°C (194°F)

Drivebelt tensions
The deflection is to be measured midway between pulleys on the belt's longest run. The tension of a new belt should be checked after the vehicle's first operating period, when the belts should be set to the 'used belt' values.

Standard or air conditioner equipped models:	Deflection (used belt)	Deflection (new belt)
Alternator	18 to 22 mm (0.71 to 0.87 in)	15 to 19 mm (0.59 to 0.75 in)
Air conditioner compressor	7.5 to 11.5 mm (0.295 to 0.453 in)	7 to 9 mm (0.28 to 0.35 in)
Power steering equipped models:	Deflection (used belt)	Deflection (new belt)
Alternator	13.5 to 16 mm (0.531 to 0.630 in)	12.5 to 14 mm (0.492 to 0.551 in)
Power steering oil pump	6.5 to 8.5 mm (0.256 to 0.335 in)	6 to 7.5 mm (0.236 to 0.295 in)
Air conditioning and power steering equipped models:	Deflection (used belt)	Deflection (new belt)
Alternator	10 to 12 mm (0.39 to 0.47 in)	9.5 to 10.5 mm (0.374 to 0.413 in)
Air conditioner compressor	6.5 to 7.5 mm (0.256 to 0.295 in)	5.5 to 6.5 mm (0.217 to 0.256 in)
Power steering oil pump	6.5 to 8.5 mm (0.256 to 0.335 in)	6 to 7.5 mm (0.236 to 0.295 in)

Coolant
Capacity - total, including heater and expansion tank .... 8.3 Imp pt (4.7 litre)
Coolant type .... Ethylene glycol based antifreeze

Torque wrench settings	**lbf ft**	**kgf m**
Water pump bolts	2.9 to 3.6	0.4 to 0.5
Thermostat housing bolts	3.6 to 5.8	0.5 to 0.8
Temperature switch in radiator	2.2 to 3.6	0.3 to 0.5
Radiator mounting bolts	2.3 to 3.2	0.32 to 0.44
Radiator fan shroud nuts	2.3 to 3.2	0.32 to 0.44

2

1 General description

The cooling system consists of a front mounted radiator, a pump driven by the camshaft belt, and an electric fan mounted behind the radiator. An expansion tank, mounted on the side of the radiator, eliminates the need for frequent topping up of the system.

Coolant is circulated around the cylinder block water jacket, where it extracts heat from the cylinders and is passed back to the inlet side of the pump. When the coolant is heated to the operating temperature of the thermostat, this will open and allow coolant to flow through the radiator, where it now loses heat to atmosphere, thus being cooled. Should the temperature of the coolant rise sufficiently, the temperature switch in the radiator will operate the electric fan thus providing even more cooling action by drawing more air through the radiator. This is especially effective in slow moving traffic or when the vehicle is stationary, when little or no air is being drawn through the radiator by the vehicle's forward motion.

2 Routine maintenance

1 At the intervals indicated in the Routine maintenance schedule, check all drivebelts for cracks, fraying, wear and tension, renewing them as necessary. Check all hoses and connections for leaks.
2 At the intervals indicated in the Routine maintenance schedule, drain the cooling system and refill with fresh antifreeze solution (photo).

3 Cooling system - draining, flushing and refilling

Warning: To avoid danger of scalding do not attempt to drain the system when the engine is hot.

1 Set the heater control lever inside the vehicle to the HOT position.
2 Open the drain cock at the bottom of the radiator (photo) and remove the radiator filler cap. Allow the coolant to drain.
3 If the coolant being drained is in a clean condition, then the drain cock can be replaced and the system refilled with fresh antifreeze solution.
4 If however, the coolant is badly contaminated with sludge and rust, the system should be flushed through with clean water by inserting a hosepipe into the radiator filler cap. In severe cases it may be necessary to use a descaling agent. In this case follow the manufacturer's instructions.
5 An alternative method of flushing the system is to refill with clean water, refit the radiator cap and run the engine for five or ten minutes before draining, repeating this process until the system is clean.
6 Refill the radiator with coolant to the specified level. On vehicles without a reservoir tank this should be 0.79 to 1.57 in (20 to 40 mm) below the bottom edge of the filler neck, and for those with a reservoir tank, to the MAX mark on the side of the tank.
7 Run the engine for a few minutes and check for leaks, then stop the engine and recheck coolant level, topping up as necessary.

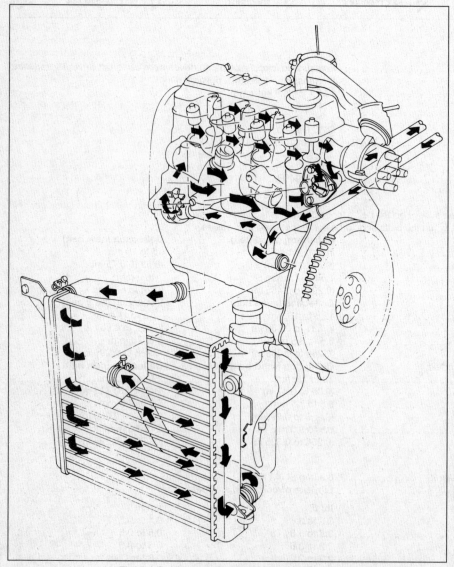

Fig. 2.1 Cooling system flow diagram (Sec 1)

2.2 Topping-up with antifreeze

3.2 Radiator drain plug

5.2 Removing the thermostat housing

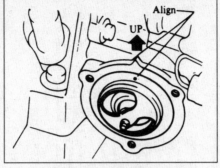

Fig. 2.2 Correct alignment of the thermostat (Sec 5)

5.3 Remove the thermostat (note the arrow indicating fitment)

4 Coolant mixture - general

1 It is desirable to keep the cooling system filled with an antifreeze mixture all year round. Apart from the obvious frost protection in winter, antifreeze liquids also contain corrosion inhibitors and should be left in the system all year round.

2 Antifreeze should be mixed according to the manufacturer's instructions, and mixed with clean water in proportion to the frost protection desired. Generally a 50/50 mixture will give maximum protection.

3 Make sure the antifreeze chosen is suitable for aluminium engines.

4 The coolant mixture should be renewed every two years as the inhibitors used deteriorate with time, and will be of little value after this time. Also, buy a top quality antifreeze with an ethylene glycol base, as cheaper products usually contain chemicals which evaporate and quickly lose their protection value.

5 When topping up during service, use the same mixture proportion as before, to avoid dilution.

6 If the vehicle is being used in tropical climates, then do remember to use a corrosion inhibitor.

5 Thermostat - removal, testing and refitting

1 The coolant should be drained sufficiently to bring its level below the thermostat housing, which is situated at the top left-hand side of the engine, by the distributor.

2 Disconnect the hose from the thermostat housing, and then remove the three bolts securing the housing cover and remove the cover (photo) .

3 Remove the thermostat. If it is stuck, do not try to lever it out with a screwdriver or similar, but cut around its rim using a sharp knife, being careful not to damage the soft aluminium housing (photo).

4 Check the operation of the thermostat by suspending it in water and bringing the water to the boil, observing that the thermostat opens fully, and that it closes when allowed to cool.

5 If the thermostat is defective a replacement should be fitted. It is not wise to run an engine without a thermostat.

6 Clean the thermostat housing and fit the thermostat with its bleed hole or jiggle pin at the top. Use a new gasket and refit the cover, tightening the bolts to the specified torque. Do not overtighten (photo).

7 Refit the hose, tightening the clip, then refill the system and finally run the engine and check for leaks.

6 Radiator - removal, repair and refitting

1 Drain the system as described in Section 3. **Note:** *If the coolant is in good condition and is not due for periodical change, it may be drained into clean containers and re-used.*

2 Where fitted, unbolt the power steering pump and support it on one side, without disconnecting the fluid supply and return lines.

3 Disconnect the top and bottom radiator hoses.

4 Disconnect the electrical leads to the cooling fan and the temperature transmitter.

5 Remove the radiator securing bolts (this varies depending on the type of radiator fitted, but is generally three or four bolts), and lift it out from the engine compartment (photos).

6 The cooling fan and shroud may now be removed, and the radiator leak and pressure tested.

7 It is best to take the radiator to a specialist repairer, or your Nissan dealer, who has the necessary equipment for testing and repairing radiators, or to exchange it for a replacement.

8 Refitting is a reversal of removing, refilling the system as described in Section 3.

2

5.6 Use a new gasket on refitting

6.5A The radiator and cooling fan assembly removed

6.5B Radiator bottom mounting rubbers

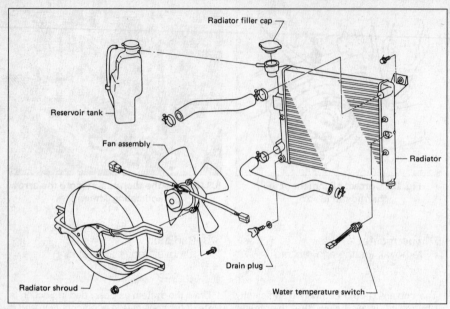

7.10 Radiator cooling fan switch

Fig. 2.3 Components of the radiator (Sec 6)

7 Radiator cooling fan and temperature transmitter switch - removal and refitting

Fan

1 Disconnect the battery negative lead.
2 Disconnect the electrical supply leads at the connector.
3 Remove the bolts securing the fan and shroud to the radiator and lift it clear.
4 The three bolts which secure the fan to the shroud can now be removed and the two separated.
5 On some models, it may be necessary to remove the fan blade assembly from the fan before they can be dismantled. This is held on by a nut.
6 Refitting is a reversal of removal.

Switch

7 Disconnect the battery negative lead.
8 Drain the cooling system as described in Section 3.

9 Disconnect the electrical supply lead to the switch at the multi-block connector.
10 Unscrew the switch, remove and discard the sealing washer (photo).
11 The switch can be tested by connecting a battery and bulb in line between the two terminals, lowering the switch into water and raising the temperature of the water to the specified switching on temperature.
12 Refitting is a reversal of removal, but use a new sealing washer under the switch and refill the system as described in Section 3.

8 Water pump - removal and refitting

Removal

1 The water pump is driven by the camshaft/timing drivebelt, and reference should be made to Chapter 1 for removal of the alternator drivebelt, right-hand engine mounting bracket and the timing belt covers.

Before removing the engine mounting, the engine should be supported from underneath the oil pan. If fitted, then the power steering and air conditioning unit drivebelts will also have to be removed. It is also important that the engine is set at TDC, No 1 cylinder on its compression stroke, so as not to lose engine timing. Refer to Chapter 1 for details.
Caution: with the timing belt removed do not turn the crankshaft or camshaft sprockets, or the valves may hit the pistons causing damage.
2 Once the timing belt covers are removed and access to the drivebelt gained, slacken the bolt at the centre of the tensioner unit and remove the timing belt.
3 Remove the five bolts which secure the water pump to the cylinder block, and remove it. The water pump is a sealed unit and cannot be repaired. If it is defective, replace it with a new unit (photo).

Refitting

4 Clean both mating surfaces thoroughly, ensuring all traces of old gasket are removed.
5 Smear a little grease or petroleum jelly on the mating surface of the water pump, then position a new paper gasket in place on it.
6 Fit the pump in place on the cylinder block and fit and tighten the five securing bolts to the specified torque (photo). These bolts must be fitted using sealing compound on their threads or water leaks will be apparent after assembly.
7 Refit the timing belt covers, crankshaft pulley, alternator and drivebelt, and the power steering and air conditioning drive belts as necessary.
8 Tension the drivebelts as described in Section 9.
9 Fill the cooling system on completion, run the engine and check for leaks.

9 Drivebelts - removal, fitting and adjustment

1 An alternator is fitted to all models, driven by belt from the crankshaft pulley. Some models may also have power steering and air conditioning units fitted, and these too are driven by belt from the crankshaft pulley.

8.3 Water pump assembly removed

8.6 Use a new gasket when refitting the pump

9.4 Checking alternator drivebelt tension

2 Belts should be checked for cracking, fraying, general wear and oil contamination and renewed as necessary. Drivebelts should not touch the bottom of the groove of the pulley in which they run.

Alternator drivebelt

3 Slacken the alternator mounting and adjuster link bolts and push the alternator in sufficiently to allow the belt to be slipped off its pulleys.
4 Fit a new belt and tension it to the values given in the Specification (photo). The figures given measure the required deflection of the belt, along its longest run, under moderate thumb pressure.

Power steering drivebelt

5 Slacken the power steering pump mounting bolts and the bolt on the adjuster link and push the pump in sufficiently to allow the belt to be slipped off its pulleys. Fit a new belt and tension it, as described in paragraph 4.

Air conditioning belt

6 Where an air conditioning unit is fitted, then the drivebelt arrangement is different from those without it.
7 The arrangement is as shown in Fig. 2.4 and the belt is removed by slackening off the idler pulley adjusting bolt until the belt can be removed.
8 The belt is tensioned by tightening the idler pulley adjusting bolt, as described in paragraph 4.

Fig. 2.4 Drivebelt tensioning and adjustment (Sec 9)

1 *Alternator belt*
2 *With air conditioner*
3 *With power steering*
4 *With air conditioner and power steering*

10 Coolant temperature switch

1 Drain the system sufficiently to allow the temperature transmitter switch to be removed without loss of coolant.
2 Testing requires special electrical meters, and should be left to your dealer or auto-electrician.
3 Before removing a switch which is suspected of malfunction, check the switch-to-gauge lead is not being earthed by faulty insulation.
4 A maximum temperature reading on the gauge as soon as the ignition is switched on indicates a fault in either the switch or the gauge.
5 To remove the switch which is situated in the cylinder head, by the thermostat housing (photo), disconnect its electrical lead and unscrew it from its housing. On refitting, use a new sealing washer.

10.5 Water temperature transmitter switch

Fault finding - cooling system

Overheating

- ☐ Loss of coolant
- ☐ Faulty fan or switch
- ☐ Faulty thermostat
- ☐ Radiator matrix clogged

Underheating

- ☐ Faulty thermostat
- ☐ Faulty fan or switch

Loss of coolant

- ☐ External leakage
- ☐ Internal leakage (cylinder head gasket blown)
- ☐ Overheating (causing evaporation)

Poor performance from heater

- ☐ Air lock in heater matrix or pipes (loosen outlet hose clip from heater, with engine running, and allow trapped air to escape

Notes

Chapter 3
Fuel, exhaust and emission control systems

For modifications, and information applicable to later models, see Supplement at end of manual

Contents

Degrees of difficulty

| Easy, suitable for novice with little experience 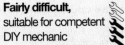 | Fairly easy, suitable for beginner with some experience | Fairly difficult, suitable for competent DIY mechanic | Difficult, suitable for experienced DIY mechanic | Very difficult, suitable for expert DIY or professional |

Specifications

General

System type .... Mechanical fuel pump, twin barrel downdraught carburettor, with manual or automatic choke
Fuel tank capacity .... 8.8 gal (40 litre)
Fuel pump pressure .... 2.8 to 3.8 lbf/in² (0.20 to 0.27 kgf/cm²)
Recommended fuel - minimum octane rating:
  Models with four-speed manual transmission .... 88 RON, unleaded or leaded
  All other models .... 97 RON, unleaded or leaded
Note: *Refer to Chapter 13 for further details*

Fuel filter .... Champion L102

Air filter element .... Champion W123

Carburettor

Type:
  Manual transmission .... Hitachi DCZ 306-81
  Automatic transmission .... Hitachi DCZ 306-82
Idling speed:
  Manual transmission .... 750 to 850 rev/min
  Automatic transmission .... 850 to 950 rev/min
Fast idling speed:
  Manual transmission .... 1700 to 2100 rev/min
  Automatic transmission .... 1800 to 2200 rev/min
CO content at idle .... 1.5 ± 0.5%

Jet sizes:

	Primary	Secondary
Main jet	94	130
Main air bleed	80	80
Slow jet	43	75
Slow air bleed	160	80
Power jet	45	-
Fuel inlet needle valve	20	-

3

Carburettor settings

Vacuum break clearance R	1.26 ± 0.15 mm (0.0496 ± 0.0059 in)
Choke unloader clearance C	2.01 mm (0.079 in)
Primary and secondary valve plate interlock clearance G	5.49 ± 0.3 mm (0.216 ± 0.012 in)
Dashpot/stop lever contact engine speed	1800 to 2200 rev/min
Primary throttle valve-to-inner wall clearance A (automatic choke)	
Manual transmission	0.44 ± 0.07 mm (0.0173 ± 0.0028 in)
Automatic transmission	0.62 ± 0.07 mm (0.0244 ± 0.0028 in)
Primary throttle valve-to-inner wall clearance A (manual choke)	1.33 ± 0.07 mm (0.0524 ± 0.0028 in)
Float heights:	
Fuel inlet needle valve closed ('H', Fig. 3.17)	14.0 mm (0.55 in)
Fuel inlet needle valve fully open ('h', Fig. 3.18)	46.0 mm (1.81 in)
Throttle cable adjustment a	1.0 to 3.0 mm (0.04 to 0.12 in)
Choke cable adjustment s	21 to 25 mm (0.83 to 0.98 in)

Note: *See text for explanation of dimensional letters*

Torque wrench settings

	lbf ft	kgf m
Anti-dieseling valve	13 to 16	1.8 to 2.2
Idle speed control valve	13 to 16	1.8 to 2.2
Fuel tank mounting bolts	19.7 to 26.6	2.72 to 3.68
Fuel tank drain plug	12 to 15	1.6 to 2.1
Exhaust downpipe to manifold	22 to 26	3.0 to 3.6
Exhaust mounting bolts	5.8 to 8.7	0.8 to 1.2
Intermediate exhaust clip	12 to 15	1.6 to 2.1

1 General description

The fuel system consists of a rear mounted tank, the fuel pump being mechanical and mounted on the engine, where it draws fuel via a filter mounted on the engine bulkhead, pumping it to the carburettor.

The carburettor, a Hitachi DCZ 306, is of twin barrel, downdraught type, with either manual or automatic choke, depending on model.

All models have emission control systems.

3.2 Air filter central retaining nut

2 Routine maintenance

1 At the intervals indicated in the Routine maintenance schedule, check and adjust the engine idle speed. Also check the condition and security of the fuel lines and exhaust system.

2 Renew the air cleaner at the intervals indicated in the Routine maintenance schedule. Also renew the fuel filter.

3 Air filter element - removal and refitting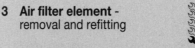

1 The air filter paper element should be renewed at the intervals indicated in the Routine Maintenance schedule. The element requires no special cleaning in between these intervals.

2 To renew the element, undo the central retaining nut (photo), remove the cover and lift out the element.

3 Refitting is a reversal of this procedure.

4 Air filter housing - removal and refitting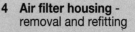

1 Remove the element as described in Section 3, then undo the two bolts attaching the air filter housing to the rocker cover (photo).

2 Remove the air hose connecting the filter housing to the hot air collector plate on the exhaust manifold (photo).

3 Disconnect the air tube to the idle compensator device.

4 Disconnect all breather hoses as necessary to clear the filter housing, and remove it from the carburettor.

5 Refitting is a reversal of removal.

5 Winter/Summer changeover valve - general

1 This changeover valve is situated in the air filter housing air intake (photo).

2 It is a simple flap valve, drawing air either directly from atmosphere (summer), or warmed air from around the exhaust manifold (winter).

3 It is operated manually by a lever on the side of the intake.

4.1 Two bolts secure the housing to the rocker cover (arrowed)

4.2 Air hose from exhaust manifold to air filter housing

5.1 Winter/summer changeover valve

6 Idle compensator device - description and inspection

1 The idle compensator device is situated in the air filter housing (photo) .

2 It is a simple contact switch of bi-metallic material, and its purpose is to allow an air bleed to the carburettor to stabilise engine idle speed under high temperature conditions.

3 Under cold conditions of idle the valve will be closed. Under hot conditions, the bi-metal strip will open the air bleed hole to allow air to be drawn in to the inlet manifold, where it is mixed with the normal fuel/air mixture. This weakens the fuel/air ratio, and prevents rich mixtures under these conditions.

4 The idle compensator is in good condition if a hissing noise can be heard coming from it with the engine running and the temperature above that at which the idle compensator should operate (see Fig. 3.1).

5 It can be tested for correct operation by using a hair dryer to blow hot air on it and checking to see if it operates.

7 Fuel pump - removal and refitting

Caution: Before working on any part of the fuel system involving fuel lines, disconnect the battery.

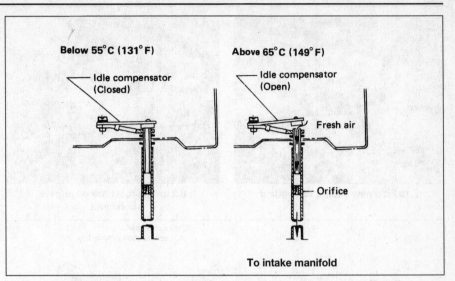

Below 55°C (131°F)

Idle compensator (Closed)

Above 65°C (149°F)

Idle compensator (Open)

Fresh air

Orifice

To intake manifold

Fig. 3.1 Diagrammatic views of idle compensator valve operation (Sec 6)

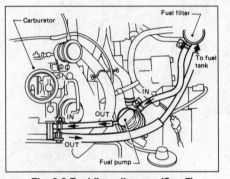

Carburetor

Fuel filter

To fuel tank

IN

IN

OUT

OUT

Fuel pump

Fig. 3.2 Fuel flow diagram (Sec 7)

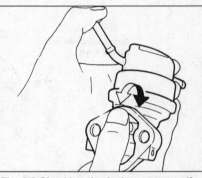

Fig. 3.3 Checking the fuel pump operation (Sec 7)

1 The fuel pump is situated to the rear of the cylinder block, by the distributor and water thermostat.

2 To remove the pump disconnect the fuel lines and plug the line from the fuel tank.

3 Undo the two nuts securing it to the housing (photo).

4 Clean the pump and then test it as follows.

5 Drain all fuel from the pump, then block off the inlet port with your finger. You should not now be able to operate the cam lever.

6 Remove your finger from the inlet port and listen for a suction sound. This will indicate that sufficient suction was produced.

7 Next, block off the outlet port with your finger and operate the cam lever. After air pressure had been built up, check that pressure remains for two or three seconds.

8 If the pump appears not to be working, change the complete unit, as it cannot be dismantled for repair.

9 Remove the lever operating rod from the fuel pump housing and check it for wear. Lubricate the rod and refit it (photo).

6.1 The bi-metal idle compensator in air filter housing

7.3 Fuel pump securing nuts

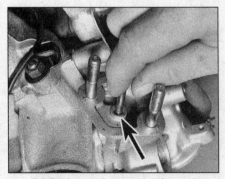

7.9 Fuel pump lever operating rod

3

7.10 Fit a new gasket on refitting

8.2 In-line fuel filter on engine bulkhead

10 Use a new gasket (photo) before bolting the pump back into position and connecting up the fuel lines.

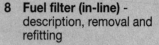

8 Fuel filter (in-line) - description, removal and refitting

1 An in-line fuel filter is used between the tank and the pump.
2 It is mounted on the engine bulkhead (photo).
3 The filter is a sealed unit and if it becomes blocked, or leaks, it should be renewed.

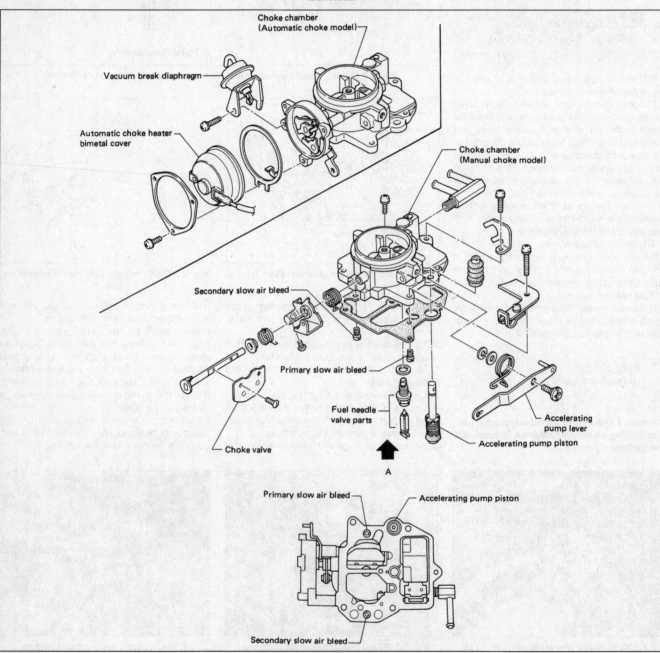

Fig. 3.4 Exploded view of choke chamber (Sec 9)

4 Undo the fuel line clips, pull the filter from the bulkhead clip, and pull off the fuel hoses.
5 Refit a new unit in the reverse order.

9 Carburettor - general description

1 The carburettor is a Hitachi DCZ 306-81 for manual transmission and a DCZ 306-82 for automatic transmission versions.
2 It is a twin barrel, downdraught type, fitted with either manual or automatic choke, anti-dieseling device, a temperature sensitive idle compensation system (see Section 6). A secondary throttle vacuum diaphragm is also fitted, which links the primary and secondary throttles. A choke unloader weakens the fuel/air mixture during warm up and a vacuum break diaphragm acts on the choke plate, again to give increased control under starting conditions.
3 The DCZ 306-82 for automatic versions has a dashpot device to prevent the engine stalling under certain conditions.
4 These items will be dealt with individually in the following Sections.
5 The fuel system also has a total system inspection facility, which requires specialist equipment.

10 Carburettor - idle speed and mixture adjustment

1 The mixture is preset during production and should not normally require altering. However, adjustment may be necessary if the carburettor has been overhauled or after a high mileage when the engine characteristics may have changed slightly due to the build-up of carbon or wear in the engine components.
2 On some models, the idle mixture screw is fitted with a limiter cap (photo). The screw can be turned if a screwdriver blade is ground to a shape similar to that shown in Fig. 3.6.
3 Have the engine at normal operating temperature with the ignition timing and valve clearances correctly set.
4 Connect a tachometer to the engine in accordance with the manufacturer's instructions.
5 If an air conditioner is fitted, make sure that it is switched off.
6 With the engine idling, turn the throttle speed screw (photo 10.2) as necessary to bring the speed within the range given in Specifications.
7 For accuracy, the idle mixture should be adjusted using a CO meter (exhaust gas analyser). Rev up the engine two or three times to clear it and then let it idle. Turn the idle mixture screw until the meter indicates a CO content within the specified tolerance. This adjustment should be carried out quickly. If it extends over more than two minutes, rev

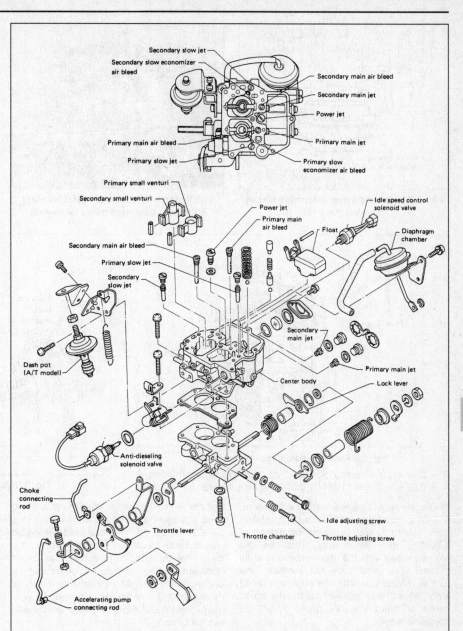

Fig. 3.5 Exploded view of carburettor (Sec 9)

Note: *Component location may vary according to model*

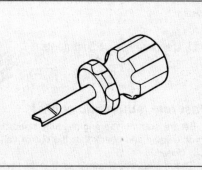

Fig. 3.6 Special screwdriver to turn idle mixture screw (Sec 10)

10.2 Idle mixture screw A and throttle speed screw B

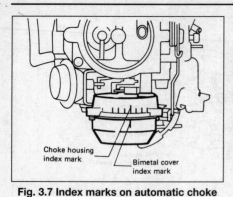

Fig. 3.7 Index marks on automatic choke housing (Sec 11)

11.2 Automatic choke bi-metal housing showing securing screws (arrowed)

11.4 Fast idle cam steps

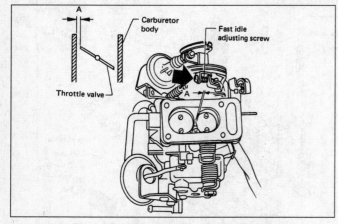

Fig. 3.8 Fast idle adjusting screw (Sec 11)

A = 0.44 ± 0.07 mm (0.0173 ± 0.0028 in) for manual transmission
A = 0.62 ± 0.07 mm (0.0244 ± 0.0028 in) for automatic transmission

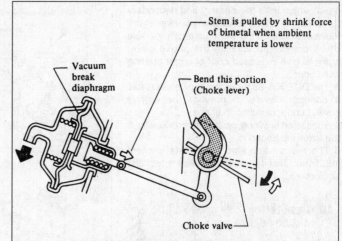

Fig. 3.9 Vacuum break diaphragm (Sec 11)

the engine again before resuming adjustment.
8 If an exhaust gas analyser is not available, carry out the following alternative method of adjusting the idle mixture. Turn the idle mixture screw until the engine speed is at its highest level and does not increase any further. Make sure that the engine is idling smoothly and then readjust the throttle speed screw to bring the idle speed within the specified range.

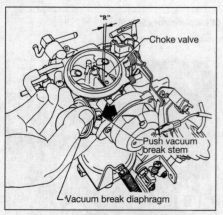

Fig. 3.10 Checking vacuum break adjustment (Sec 11)

R = 1.26 ± 0.15 mm (0.0496 ± 0.0059 in)

9 If the territory in which the vehicle is being used is subject to strict emission regulations the idle mixture CO content should **always** be checked with an exhaust gas analyser.
10 If the idle mixture screw has been removed during carburettor overhaul, a starting point for mixture adjustment can be established if the screw is turned in very gently until it just seats and then unscrewed two full turns.
11 Note that on power steering models the front wheels should be in the straight ahead position to ensure the pump does not affect the idle speed. Refer to Chapter 12, Section 26 for details of the idle speed control system.

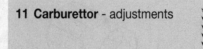

11 Carburettor - adjustments

Fast idle (automatic choke)

1 Before starting the engine, fully open the throttle valve and check that the choke valve fully closes.
2 Check the index marks on the bi-metal cover of the choke housing are lined up in the mid position (Fig. 3.7) (photo).

3 Start the engine and when fully warmed up, check that the choke valve has fully opened.
4 Stop the engine, remove the choke housing cover and set the fast idle lever on the second step of the fast idle cam (photo).
5 Start the engine and check that the idle speed is as specified. If not adjust on the fast idle adjusting screw (Fig. 3.8).

Vacuum break

6 With the engine cold, remove the air cleaner and close the choke valve plate.
7 Depress the diaphragm rod fully and then check the clearance R is as specified (Fig. 3.10). The clearance is measured between the edge of the valve plate and the wall of the carburettor. To adjust bend the choke lever.

Choke unloader (automatic choke)

8 With the engine cold remove the air cleaner and automatic choke housing cover, and close the choke valve plate.
9 Turn the throttle lever until the primary throttle valve is fully open. If the clearance C is not as specified, bend the tongue of the unloader (Fig. 3.11).

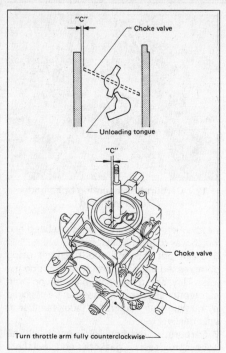

Fig. 3.11 Checking choke unloader setting (Sec 11)

C = 2.01 mm (0.0791 in)

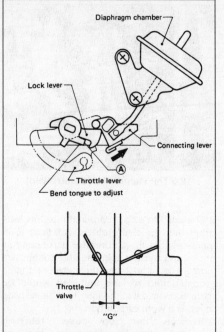
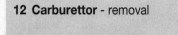

Fig. 3.12 Valve plate interlock setting diagram (Sec 11)

G = 5.49 ± 0.3 mm (0.2161 ± 0.012 in)

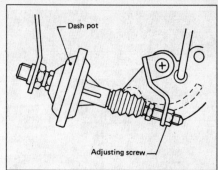

Fig. 3.13 Dashpot adjustment (Sec 11)

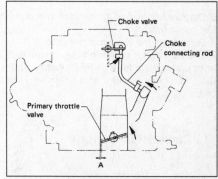

Fig. 3.14 Fast idle adjustment – manual choke (Sec 11)

A = 1.33 ± 0.07 mm (0.0524 ± 0.0028 in)

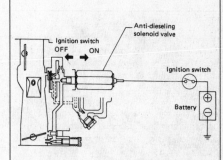

Fig. 3.15 Diagram of anti-dieseling valve (Sec 11)

Primary and secondary valve plate interlock

10 Turn the throttle lever until the throttle arm contacts the lever at point A (Fig. 3.12).
11 Check that the clearance G is as specified. If it is not, bend the tongue on the throttle arm as necessary.

Dashpot (automatic transmission)

12 The engine should be idling at normal operating temperature.
13 Turn the throttle lever on the carburettor by hand and have an assistant record the engine speed shown on the tachometer at the point where the dashpot just makes contact with the stop lever. If the speed is not as specified, release the locknut and turn the dashpot rod (Fig. 3.13).
14 Tighten the locknut and make sure that engine speed drops from 2000 to 1000 rpm in approximately 3 seconds.

Fast idle - manual choke

15 Remove the carburettor and close the choke valve completely.
16 Measure clearance A between primary throttle valve and inner wall (see Fig. 3.14).
17 Adjust by bending the choke connecting rod if the clearance is outside that specified.

Anti-dieseling valve

18 If the engine continues running when the anti-dieseling valve electrical connector is disconnected, the valve has stuck.

19 To check, connect the valve electrical connections direct to the battery, and listen for a clicking sound. If there is none, renew the valve (see photo 12.4).

12 Carburettor - removal

1 Disconnect the battery, and remove the air filter assembly.
2 Disconnect the accelerator control cable from the carburettor.
3 Disconnect the idle speed control solenoid valve wiring (photo).
4 Disconnect, as applicable, the (manual) choke cable or the (automatic) choke/anti-dieseling valve wiring (photo).

12.3 Idle speed control solenoid valve (arrowed)

12.4 Automatic choke/anti-dieseling valve wiring (arrowed)

12.5 Inlet and outlet fuel hoses

12.6 The vacuum hoses (arrowed)

12.7 Carburettor mounting bolts under inlet manifold

5 Disconnect and plug the inlet and outlet fuel hoses (photo).
6 Disconnect the vacuum pipes (photo).
7 The carburettor retaining bolts are reached from under the inlet manifold (photo). Undo the retaining bolts and remove the carburettor.

13 Carburettor - overhaul

1 Clean the exterior of the carburettor thoroughly using petrol or proprietary engine cleaner. Dirt entry into the carburettor can be disastrous.

2 The need to strip a carburettor to this level other than to clean jets or set float level indicates that the carburettor parts such as choke and throttle spindles and bushes are worn. It is almost certain therefore that a reconditioned replacement unit would be more economical in the long term than trying to repair a worn carburettor.
3 Remove the top cover retaining screws, there are five of them, and gently lift off the top cover. Note the inlet and outlet union locking plate under one of them (photo).
4 The float and fuel inlet needle valve can be removed from the top cover by pushing out the float pivot arm.
5 Clean out the float chamber, being careful not to lose any springs, pistons or steel balls.

Keep a note of where the parts are fitted and which way round they fit (photo).
6 Clean out the jets and bearings using compressed air, never use wire to probe the jets. Tiny scratches can play havoc with carburettor settings. Jet sizes can be checked by quoting your carburettor index number to your dealer.
7 Carburettor overhaul kits contain all the necessary seals, gaskets and washers required. Renew items as needed, and check the following adjustments on reassembly. A twist drill is very useful for measuring throttle and choke plate clearances.

Float level

8 The level of fuel in the float chamber, which is controlled by the action of the float lever arm on the inlet valve, can be checked externally.
9 Stand the vehicle on level ground, with the engine idling, and check that the fuel level is as shown in Fig. 3.16 through the sight glass on the side of the carburettor (photo).
10 If it is not as shown carry out the following adjustments.
11 Remove the carburettor top cover as described earlier in this Section .
12 The float can be removed by extracting the pivot pin. Shake the float to hear if it is punctured and contains fuel (photo).
13 Remove the inlet needle valve and clean it (photo 13.12).
14 Refit both the needle valve and float.

13.3 Top cover retaining screws and inlet/outlet union locking plate

13.5 Beware of losing springs, pistons and steel balls

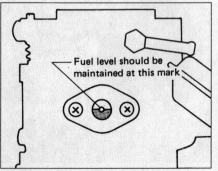

Fig. 3.16 Fuel level in float chamber (Sec 13)

Fuel level should be maintained at this mark

13.9 Fuel level sight glass

13.12 Float pivot pin A and below it the inlet needle valve B

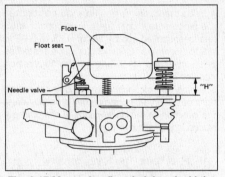

Fig. 3.17 Measuring float height – fuel inlet needle valve closed (Sec 13)

H = 14.0 mm (0.55 in)

13.15 Measuring float height – fuel inlet needle valve closed

Fig. 3.18 Measuring float height – fuel inlet needle valve fully open (Sec 13)

h = 46.0 mm (1.81 in)

15 With reference to Fig. 3.17, hold the top cover inverted and horizontal, then measure the distance (dimension 'H') from the top of the float to the cover's mating surface (photo). If adjustment is required, gently bend the float seat.

16 With reference to Fig. 3.18, hold the top cover upright and horizontal, then measure the distance (dimension 'h') from the bottom of the float to the cover's mating surface (photo). If adjustment is required, gently bend the float stopper arm.

17 Refit the cover as described later in this Section and recheck the fuel level as previously described.

Accelerator pump

18 With the engine stopped and the carburettor float bowl full, operate the accelerator pump by opening the throttle lever.

19 Observe that the pump injects fuel into the primary venturi, smoothly and without delay.

20 If this is not the case, check the pump and linkage for wear or damage.

Assembly

21 Use a new gasket when refitting the top cover, and ensure all springs, pistons and steel balls are in their correct location.

14 Carburettor - refitting

1 Refitting the carburettor is largely a matter of reversing the removal operations in Section 12.

2 Use a new gasket on the inlet manifold (photo).

3 Make sure the inlet and outlet hoses are connected to the correct union (photo).

4 Reconnect all breather hoses, vacuum pipes and electrical leads as applicable.

5 Refit the air filter assembly.

6 Check accelerator and choke cable for correct adjustment.

15 Emission control system - general

The emission control system consists of the crankcase ventilation system, described in Chapter 1, and the idle compensator device described in Section 6 of this Chapter.

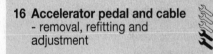

13.16 Measuring float height – fuel inlet needle valve fully open

16 Accelerator pedal and cable - removal, refitting and adjustment

Pedal

1 Release the cable from the top of the pedal arm.

2 Extract the E-clip from the pedal pivot shaft, disengage the return spring and remove the pedal.

3 Refitting is a reversal of removal, but apply grease to the moving parts.

13.21 Top cover gasket in position before fitting top cover

14.2 Use a new gasket when refitting

14.3 Inlet and outlet fuel union

3

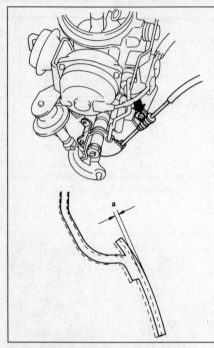

Fig. 3.19 Throttle cable adjustment (Sec 16)

a = 1 to 3 mm (0.04 to 0.12 in)

Cable

4 Disconnect the cable from the top of the pedal arm.

5 Release the plastic grommet at the engine compartment rear bulkhead.

6 Disconnect the cable at the throttle and then withdraw it into the engine compartment.

7 Refitting is the reverse of the removal procedure; adjust the cable as described below.

8 To adjust the accelerator cable on early models (cable secured by a single clamp screw), position the cable outer as necessary in the clamp to give the specified free play at the pedal pad, then tighten the clamp screw (see Fig. 3.19). On later models (cable secured by a locknut on each side of the adjuster bracket), slacken both locknuts and pull the cable outer up as far as possible through the bracket while holding the carburettor throttle lever in the closed (idle) position. Screw down the upper nut until it just touches the bracket,

Fig. 3.20 Choke cable adjustment (Sec 17)

S = 21 to 25 mm (0.83 to 0.98 in)

then unscrew it 1.5 to 2.0 turns and tighten the lower nut securely against the bracket.

9 When adjustment is completed, check that the throttle valve is fully open when the accelerator pedal is fully depressed, and fully closed when the pedal is released, with the specified free play at the pedal pad.

10 On vehicles equipped with automatic transmission, check that the pedal can be pressed fully into the kickdown position. If necessary, check/adjust the kickdown cable as described in Section 7 of Chapter 7.

17 Choke control cable - removal and refitting

1 Remove the air filter assembly from the carburettor, release the cable pinch screw on the trunnion at the carburettor and the cable clamp screw.

2 Working inside the vehicle at the facia panel, unscrew the choke control knob bezel nut and withdraw the cable into the vehicle interior. If a choke warning lamp switch is fitted, disconnect the electrical leads.

3 Refitting is a reversal of removal. Make sure that the bulkhead cable grommet makes a good seal.

4 With the cable in position, do not tighten the pinch screw until the choke control knob has been pulled out by about 0.83 to 0.98 in (21 to 25 mm) and the choke valve plate has been checked as being in the fully open position (Fig. 3.20).

5 Finally check that with the control pulled right out, the valve plate is fully closed. Adjust the position of the outer cable in the clamp if necessary to achieve this.

18 Fuel tank - removal, repair and refitting

1 Jack up the rear of the car and support on axle stands, then drain the fuel by unscrewing the drain plug from the base of the tank.

2 Working within the luggage compartment, remove the cover plate from the tank transmitter unit and then disconnect the wiring harness plug (photos).

3 Disconnect the battery.

4 Working under the rear wing, disconnect the fuel filler and ventilation hoses (photo). Stuff a piece of rag into the openings to prevent the entry of dirt. If required, the filler pipe can be removed by removing the upper and lower mounting plates.

5 Working at the front of the fuel tank, disconnect the fuel flow and return hoses.

6 Support the tank and then unscrew and remove the six mounting bolts from the tank flange (photo). Lower and remove the tank from the vehicle.

18.2A Removing the fuel tank transmitter cover

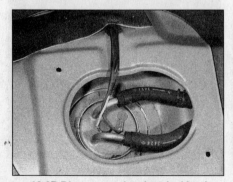

18.2B Disconnect the electrical lead

18.4 Fuel filter and vent hose connections

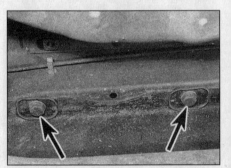

18.6 Fuel tank mounting bolts (there are six altogether)

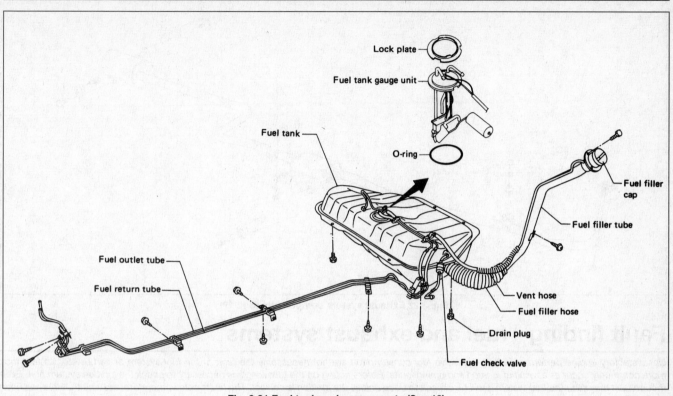

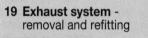

Fig. 3.21 Fuel tank and components (Sec 18)

Lock plate

Fuel tank gauge unit

Fuel tank

O-ring

Fuel filler cap

Fuel filler tube

Fuel outlet tube

Fuel return tube

Vent hose

Fuel filler hose

Drain plug

Fuel check valve

7 A leak in a fuel tank can be sealed using one of the several products available at motor accessory stores. For a permanent repair the tank will have to be soldered or brazed, but *on no account attempt to do this work yourself* owing to the risk of explosion unless the tank has been steamed out thoroughly. Radiator repairers can usually undertake fuel tank repair work.

8 Removal of sediment, water or sludge can be carried out after first having removed the tank transmitter unit. Pour in some paraffin, or petrol, and shake the tank vigorously. Empty the tank and repeat the operations as many times as is necessary to clean it and then give a final rinse with clean fuel.

9 Refitting is a reversal of removal.

19 Exhaust system - removal and refitting

1 The exhaust system can be broken down into three parts, the exhaust manifold (described in Chapter 1) the downpipe and intermediate silencer, and the rear silencer.

2 Should any part become corroded and holed, the whole system should be replaced.

3 The time and effort required to replace an exhaust system is hardly worthwhile, with so many quick fit specialists around.

4 Should you decide to do the job yourself, then proceed as follows.

5 Soak all clamp and mounting bolts in

releasing fluid. Do not waste time in removing these. If they are so corroded they will not budge, then cut them off with a hacksaw.

6 Undo the exhaust downpipe connection at the manifold.

7 Undo the intermediate pipe clamp (photo).

8 Undo the intermediate silencer mounting (photo).

9 Undo the rear silencer mounting (photo).

10 Refit the new exhaust, starting at the exhaust manifold and working rearwards.

11 Use a proprietary sealing compound, for exhaust joints, and fit everything loosely, until the parts can be properly lined up and are not under stress.

12 Tighten all mounting bolts and clamps, then run the engine and check for leaks.

3

19.7 Intermediate exhaust pipe clamp

19.8 Intermediate silencer mounting

19.9 Rear silencer mounting

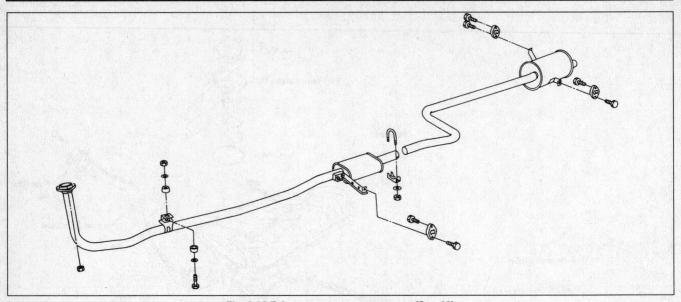

Fig. 3.22 Exhaust system components (Sec 19)

Fault finding - fuel and exhaust systems

Unsatisfactory engine performance and excessive fuel consumption are not necessarily the fault of the fuel system or carburettor. In fact they more commonly occur as a result of ignition and timing faults. Before acting on the following it is necessary to check the ignition system first. Even though fault may lie in the fuel system it will be difficult to trace unless the ignition is correct. The faults below, therefore, assume that this has been attended to first (where appropriate).

Smell of fuel when engine is stopped

☐ Leaking fuel lines or unions
☐ Leaking fuel tank

Smell of fuel when engine is idling

☐ Leaking fuel line unions between pump and carburettor injectors
☐ Overflow of fuel from float chamber due to wrong level setting,
☐ ineffective needle valve or punctured float

Excessive fuel consumption for reasons not covered by leaks or float chamber faults

☐ Worn jets
☐ Over-rich setting
☐ Sticking mechanism
☐ Dirty air cleaner element
☐ Sticking air cleaner thermostatic mechanism

Difficult starting when cold

☐ Choke control or automatic choke maladjusted
☐ Automatic choke not cocked before starting

Difficult starting when hot

☐ Automatic choke malfunction
☐ Accelerator pedal pumped before starting
☐ Vapour lock (especially in hot weather or at high altitude)

Difficult starting, uneven running, lack of power, cutting out

☐ One or more jets blocked or restricted
☐ Float chamber fuel level too low or needle valve sticking
☐ Fuel pump not delivering sufficient fuel
☐ Faulty solenoid fuel shut-off valve (if fitted)
☐ Induction leak

Engine does not respond properly to throttle

☐ Faulty accelerator pump
☐ Blocked jet(s)
☐ Slack in accelerator cable

Engine idle speed drops when hot

☐ Defective temperature compensator
☐ Overheated fuel pump

Fault finding - emission control system

Excessive HC or CO in exhaust gas

☐ Air cleaner clogged
☐ Float level too high
☐ Faulty spark control system
☐ Faulty throttle opener control system
☐ Leaking intake manifold gasket

HC Hydrocarbons
CO Carbon monoxide
NOx Nitrogen oxide

Excessive HC, CO and NOx in exhaust gas

☐ Worn piston rings
☐ Incorrect valve clearances
☐ Fault thermostat
☐ Blown cylinder head gasket
☐ Clogged PCV valve
☐ Incorrect idle mixture
☐ Clogged fuel filter
☐ Faulty idle compensator
☐ Choke not fully off
☐ Incorrect ignition settings
☐ Malfunction of emission control system component

Chapter 4 Ignition system

For modifications, and information applicable to later models, see Supplement at end of manual

Contents

Degrees of difficulty

Easy, suitable for novice with little experience	**Fairly easy,** suitable for beginner with some experience	**Fairly difficult,** suitable for competent DIY mechanic	**Difficult,** suitable for experienced DIY mechanic	**Very difficult,** suitable for expert DIY or professional

Specifications

System type . . . . Conventional with coil and contact breaker points

Distributor

Firing order . . . . 1 - 3 - 4 - 2 (No 1 at timing belt end)
Rotation of rotor . . . . Anti-clockwise
Minimum protrusion of carbon brush . . . . 3 mm (0.12 in)
Contact breaker point gap . . . . 0.45 to 0.55 mm (0.018 to 0.022 in)
Dwell angle . . . . 49° to 55°

Coil

Primary resistance . . . . 1.3 to 1.5 ohm
Secondary resistance . . . . 8.7 to 11.7 k ohm

Ignition timing

Four-speed manual transmission . . . . 2° ± 1° ATDC at idle speed with distributor vacuum hose disconnected
All other models . . . . 5° ± 1° BTDC at idle speed with distributor vacuum hose disconnected·

HT leads . . . . Champion S 05 boxed set

Spark plugs

Type . . . . Champion RN9YCC or RN9YC
Gap . . . . 0.8 to 0.9 mm (0.032 to 0.036 in)

Torque wrench setting	lbf ft	kgf m
Spark plug	18 to 22	2.5 to 3.0

1 General description

The ignition system is conventional in design consisting of coil, the distributor, which incorporates the contact points, and the spark plugs, one in each cylinder.

The ignition system is based on feeding low tension voltage from the battery to the coil where it is converted to high tension voltage. The high tension voltage is powerful enough to jump the spark plug gap in the cylinders many times a second under high compression pressures, providing that the system is in good condition and that all adjustments are correct.

The ignition advance is controlled both mechanically and by vacuum, to ensure that the spark occurs at just the right instant for the particular engine load and speed. The mechanical governor comprises two lead weights, which move out from the distributor shaft as the engine speed rises, due to centrifugal force.

The vacuum control consists of a diaphragm, one side of which is connected via a small bore tube to the carburettor, and the other side to the contact breaker plate. Depression in the inlet manifold and carburettor, which varies with engine speed and throttle opening, causes the diaphragm to move, so moving the contact breaker plate, and advancing or retarding the spark.

2 Routine maintenance

1 At the intervals indicated in the Routine maintenance schedule, check and adjust as necessary the ignition timing. Also check the distributor contact points.
2 At the intervals indicated in the Routine maintenance schedule, renew the contact breaker points and spark plugs.
3 At the intervals indicated in the Routine maintenance schedule, check the condition of all ignition wiring and associated components, and renew as necessary.

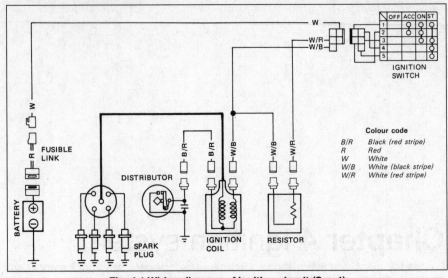

Fig. 4.1 Wiring diagram of ignition circuit (Sec 1)

3 Contact breaker points - servicing and adjustment

1 The contact breaker points should be serviced and adjusted as specified in the routine maintenance Section.
2 Remove the distributor cap and move it to one side; there is no need to disconnect the HT leads (photo). On early models, the cap is secured by two clips, while on later models it is secured by two screws, a gasket being fitted between the cap and distributor body.
3 This will give access to the rotor arm, which should be pulled off the driveshaft. This will give access to the contact breaker points.
4 The point may be gently prised apart and the two contacts examined, one on the fixed plate, the other on the moving spring arm. If they are badly pitted, burnt, or eroded, they should be renewed. If the wear is minimal, the contacts may be dressed clean using fine abrasive paper or by rubbing squarely on an oilstone.
5 To change the contact points, disconnect the LT lead from the terminal on the distributor body.

6 Loosen, but do not remove completely the two screws securing the contact breaker to the base plate (photo).
7 Slide the contact breaker out from under the screw head, and remove it from the distributor.
8 To remove the spring contact arm, extract the circlip from its slot on the post and slide the arm off.
9 New contacts should have their faces cleaned with a solvent, to remove any traces of protective grease before being fitted.
10 Apply a few drops of oil to the pivot post, then fit the spring arm contact and the circlip.
11 Fit the contact breaker assembly back under the two retaining screws, and tighten the screws finger tight only.
12 Re-connect the LT lead.
13 By turning the engine using a spanner on the crankshaft pulley nut, position the heel of the moving spring arm contact on to one of the lobes of the cam on the distributor driveshaft.
14 Now adjust the gap between the two contacts by sliding the fixed contact plate in or out under its two retaining screws, until a feeler gauge set of the correct gap size is a sliding fit between them (photo). **Note:** *a cut-out is provided in the contact plate to enable a screwdriver to be used to rotate the plate.*

3.2 Removing the distributor cap

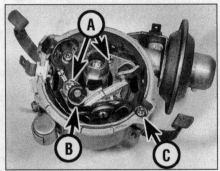

3.6 Removing the contact breaker points

A Baseplate securing screws   B E-Clip
C LT terminal

3.14 Adjusting the contact breaker points

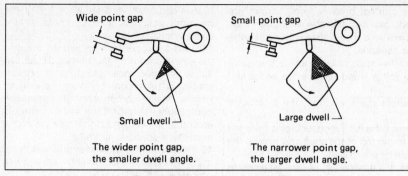

Fig. 4.2 Setting of dwell angle (Sec 4)

6.3 Removing the distributor securing nut

15 Once the gap is correct, tighten the two screws, and re-check the gap.
16 Apply a smear of high melting point grease to the lobes of the distributor driveshaft, and oil the felt pad in the recess at the top of the driveshaft with one or two drops of engine oil.
17 Fit the rotor arm, ensuring it seats properly in the location slot, then refit the distributor cap.
18 Check the HT leads are seating correctly on their location housings.
Note: *This is a basic setting procedure, and should be undertaken in conjunction with more precise methods of setting the ignition timing, described in the following Sections.*

4 Dwell angle - checking and adjusting

1 The setting of contact breaker points gap using feeler gauges has nowadays become a basic setting only, and more emphasis is placed on the dwell angle.
2 The dwell angle may be expressed as the number of degrees through which the distributor driveshaft turns with the contact points closed. The wider the gap, the smaller the dwell angle. Checking the dwell angle gives a more accurate setting of the contact breaker points and tends to even out the effects of wear in the distributor and differences in height between the cam lobes.

3 To check the dwell angle requires the use of a dwell meter, connected according to the manufacturer's instructions. Refer to the Specifications for the correct dwell angle.
4 With the dwell angle meter connected and the engine running, check the dwell angle. If it is too large, increase the points gap and vice versa. The dwell angle should always be checked before checking and adjusting the ignition timing.

5 Condenser - testing, removal and refitting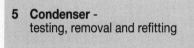

1 The purpose of the condenser is to minimise arcing across the contact breaker points, which would otherwise cause premature wear of the contacts and reduced spark strength.
2 The condenser is mounted on the outside of the distributor body, but its lead is terminated inside.
3 To remove the condenser, remove the distributor cap and rotor arm and remove the terminal nut from the condenser lead. Remove the screw securing the condenser to the distributor body and remove the condenser.
4 Refitting is a reversal of removal.
5 Condensers should be changed along with contact points and spark plugs to ensure optimum performance of the ignition system generally. Poor starting and uneven running can often be traced to a faulty condenser.

6 Without special equipment proper fault diagnosis of the condenser is impossible, but an indication that the condenser is in poor condition can be obtained by opening the points while the ignition is switched on. If this results in a strong blue flash, then suspect the condenser of reduced performance.

6 Distributor - removal and refitting

1 The distributor is mounted on the cylinder head at the left-hand side of the engine.
2 Remove the spark plugs and turn the engine so that the 0° mark on the crankshaft pulley is lined up with the pointer on the crankcase.
3 Remove the distributor cap and rotor arm, mark the relationship of the distributor clamp plate to the cylinder head, then release the nut securing the distributor to the engine housing (photo).
4 Pull off the hose to the vacuum unit, disconnect the wires, noting their connections, then remove the distributor (photo).
5 Refitting is a reversal of this operation. but note that the distributor drive tongue and the slot in the distributor driveshaft are off-set, to prevent the distributor being replaced with the timing 180° out (photos).
6 Check ignition timing.

6.4 Removing the distributor

6.5A Distributor drive tongue in engine housing

6.5B Slot in distributor driveshaft

7 Distributor - overhaul

1 With the distributor removed from the engine (Section 6), clean away external dirt.
2 Prise off the spring clips and take off the cap. On later models, the cap is attached by two screws, and a gasket is fitted between the cap and distributor body.
3 Pull off the rotor.
4 Extract the fixing screws and remove the vacuum advance capsule. It will need tilting in order to release the link rod from the pivot on the baseplate once the E-clip has been prised off the pivot.
5 Extract the two screws and remove the baseplate.
6 Remove the contact breaker from the baseplate.

7 If the contact breaker fixing screws are removed, take care that the anti-friction balls are not lost as the baseplate upper and lower sections separate.
8 Mount the shaft collar in a vice then drive out the roll pin and remove the collar and washer.
9 Withdraw the shaft from the distributor body.
10 Extract the felt lubrication pad from the recess in the top of the shaft and remove the screw which is exposed.
11 Mark the relationship of cam assembly to shaft and separate them.
12 If the cam counter weights and springs must be dismantled, make quite sure that the springs are marked with a dab of quick-drying paint so that they can be reconnected in their original positions.
13 With the distributor dismantled, clean and examine all components for wear. If the shaft

bushes and other items are worn, it may well be more economical to purchase a new distributor complete.
14 Take the opportunity to carefully examine the cap and rotor for tiny cracks. These can cause conductance paths and prevent starting or be responsible for erratic running. Renew these components if necessary, particularly the rotor if the metal contact is eroded or the carbon brush inside the cap is worn to the specified minimum.
15 Reassembly is a reversal of dismantling, apply light grease to all components as work proceeds and make quite sure that they are aligned with each other in their original positions.

8 Ignition timing - adjustment

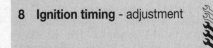

1 For the engine to run efficiently the spark produced at the spark plugs must occur at precisely the right moment during the engine's combustion cycle. To set ignition timing proceed as follows.
2 Run the engine until it reaches normal operating temperature.
3 Disconnect and blank off the idle compensator vacuum hoses, on the inlet manifold side. Disconnect the electrical connection to the cooling fan switch. (This is

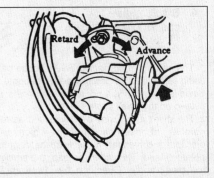

Fig. 4.4 Adjusting ignition timing by turning the distributor in its housing (Sec 8)

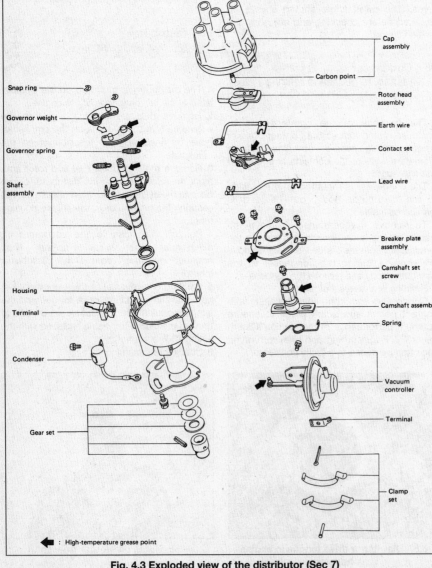

Fig. 4.3 Exploded view of the distributor (Sec 7)

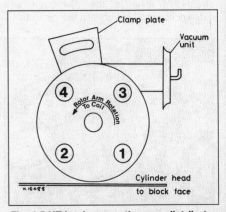

Fig. 4.5 HT lead connections on distributor to spark plugs (Sec 8)

to prevent the fan switching on during the adjustment, which would cause a drop in engine speed.)

4 Run the engine at between 2000 and 3000 rev/min for a few moments, under 'no-load' conditions then allow it to idle.

5 Using a tachometer, check idle speed is 900 rev/min or just below. If it is not, then adjust the carburettor throttle adjusting screw. (See Chapter 3.)

6 With the engine idling in this condition check ignition timing using a strobe light. (See Section 9.)

7 If the ignition timing is not as specified, adjust by loosening the clamp nut on the distributor and turning the distributor in its housing. Once the timing is correct, tighten the clamp nut.

8 Remove the blanks from the vacuum hoses and re-connect the hoses, then run the engine at between 2000 and 3000 rev/min for a few moments, then allow it to idle.

9 Adjust the idle speed to that specified by turning the carburettor throttle adjusting screw in or out.

10 Now re-check ignition timing with the strobe light.

9 Timing procedures - static and dynamic

1 There are two generally used methods to set ignition timing. The first being set with the engine stationary (static timing) and the second with the engine running (dynamic timing). Static timing should be regarded as a basic setting only. Dynamic timing is far more accurate, but requires the use of a tachometer and a strobe light. These are a worthwhile investment for the home mechanic, and will recoup their cost in fuel savings.

Static timing procedure

2 Remove the spark plugs, enabling the engine to be turned easily by hand (use a socket wrench on the crankshaft pulley nut) and turn the engine so that No 1 cylinder is just approaching its compression stroke. This can be verified by placing your thumb over the spark plug hole of No 1 cylinder and feeling for the build up of pressure as the engine is turned. Both valves on No 1 cylinder should be closed and the rotor arm in the distributor will be pointing to the HT terminal lead which feeds No 1 spark plug.

3 Continue to turn the engine until the notch in the crankshaft pulley wheel is in line with the specified timing mark on the fixed plate on the lower camshaft drivebelt cover.

4 Connect a 12 volt test lamp between the contact breaker terminal and a good earth.

5 Switch on the ignition, slacken off the clamp nut on the distributor, and turn the distributor anti-clockwise until the lamp goes out. Now slowly turn the distributor back until the lamp just lights.

6 Tighten the clamp nut and turn the engine through two complete revolutions before re-checking that the timing is set correctly.

7 Remove the test lamp, refit the distributor cap, spark plugs and HT leads.

Dynamic timing procedure

8 Connect up a tachometer and strobe light according to the manufacturer's instructions, having first ensured that the distributor dwell angle is correct (Section 4).

9 Start the engine, then point the strobe light at the timing mark on the crankshaft pulley.

10 As the strobe light flashes on and off, the timing marks will appear to be stationary and can be easily read.

11 Adjust the timing by turning the distributor body in its housing, as previously described, until the desired timing value is obtained. Remember to blank off vacuum hoses as described and check engine speed is correct for the operation undertaken.

12 Remove the strobe light and tachometer, check the clamp nut on the distributor has been fully tightened, and reconnect any vacuum hoses disconnected.

10 Spark plugs, HT leads and distributor cap - general

1 The correct functioning of the spark plugs is vital for the correct running and efficiency of the engine. It is essential that the plugs fitted are appropriate for the engine, and the suitable type is specified at the beginning of this chapter. If this type is used and the engine is in good condition, the spark plugs should not need attention between scheduled replacement intervals. Spark plug cleaning is rarely necessary and should not be attempted unless specialised equipment is available as damage can easily be caused to the firing ends.

2 To remove the plugs, remove the air cleaner, pull off the HT leads from the spark plugs. (Do this only by gripping the rubber cover, not the lead itself, or damage to the lead may result.)

3 Clean the area around the spark plug recesses with a brush to remove dirt which may fall into the cylinder when the plugs are removed.

4 Remove each spark plug using a double depth socket or box spanner.

5 Examination of the spark plugs can provide a good indication of engine condition.

6 If the nose of the plugs is clean and white, with little or no deposits, it indicates the fuel/air mixture is too weak.

7 If the nose of the plug is covered with a hard black deposit, then it shows the mixture is too rich.

8 If the deposit is black, wet and oily, it may indicate that internal wear of the engine has occurred to the degree where oil is passing the pistons and being burned in the combustion chambers. Do not confuse this condition with that of an engine 'flooded' with petrol, where excessive use of throttle and choke has resulted in the plugs being soaked in petrol, with a resultant failure to start.

9 The ideal condition for the plugs to be in is that of an even light brown to greyish brown deposit, indicating the mixture is correct.

10 The size of the spark plug gap is vitally important to engine efficiency, and must be set correctly. To do this, measure the gap with feeler gauges, then bend the outer electrode either in or out until the gap is correct. Never try to bend the centre electrode or damage to the insulation will occur. Special tools for gap setting are available commercially at little expense, and are worth having.

11 Lightly grease the plug threads using graphite or high melting point grease, then screw each plug by hand, ensuring the plugs are not cross threaded.

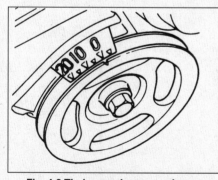

Fig. 4.6 Timing marks on crankcase (Sec 9)

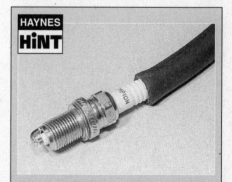

HAYNES
HINT

It's often difficult to insert spark plugs into their holes without cross-threading them. To avoid this possibility, fit a short piece of rubber hose over the end of the spark plug. The flexible hose acts as a universal joint, to help align the plug with the plug hole. Should the plug begin to cross-thread, the hose will slip on the spark plug, preventing thread damage.

4

12 Tighten to the correct torque, using a torque wrench, to avoid danger of stripping the threads in the aluminium cylinder head.

13 Refit the HT leads, in their correct firing order 1 - 3 - 4 - 2, No 1 cylinder being at the timing belt end of the engine.

14 HT leads require little or no attention except to check their general condition and that they are making good electrical contact with the plugs and where they connect to the distributor cap.

15 Whenever the distributor cap is removed, take the opportunity of wiping the inside clean, and checking the inner terminals are not fouled up. A hard shellac type deposit often forms on them, and may be removed using a file or sharp instrument.

16 Check also the spring-loaded carbon conductor in the centre of the cap for minimum protrusion.

17 Thin lines running between electrodes in the cap are an indication of 'electrical tracking' and the cap should be removed and a new one fitted in its place.

11 Coil - description and testing

1 The coil is located to the left-hand side of the engine compartment (photo).

2 To ensure correct HT polarity at the spark plugs, the LT coil leads must always be connected correctly. These are usually marked positive and negative (+ or -) and reference should be made to the wiring diagrams at the end of this manual for correct colour coding.

3 The coil may be tested using an ohmmeter, connected across the two LT terminals on the coil to check the primary winding resistance, and across the negative LT terminal and central HT terminal to check the secondary winding resistance. If the

11.1 Electrical connections to the coil

resistance figures obtained fall outside that given in the Specifications, the coil should be renewed.

4 A ballast resistor is mounted next to the coil, and its purpose is to supply battery voltage to the coil during starting. Under normal running conditions the coil operates on a reduced voltage.

Fault finding - ignition system

1 If the engine suddenly fails to start after a period of normal operation, first check that there is fuel in the tank. If the engine turns over normally on the starter motor and the battery is evidently well charged, check the HT circuit.

2 Wet or damp components is a common cause of non starting. If dampness is suspected then wipe all components dry, especially the inside of the distributor cap, and then refit it.

3 If the engine still fails to start, disconnect an HT lead from one of the spark plugs and holding the lead with well insulated pliers so that it is almost touching the cylinder block, have someone operate the starter. A regular blue spark should occur. If it does then the spark plugs themselves should be suspected of malfunction.

4 If no spark occurs, disconnect the main feed HT lead from the distributor cap and again check for a spark, as in paragraph 3. If there is a spark check the distributor cap rotor arm and HT leads.

5 To test the ignition switch supply, connect a voltmeter or test lamp between the LT wire on the battery side of the coil and earth, and with ignition switched on and the points open. No reading indicates a break in supply from the ignition switch.

6 Test between the LT terminal on the distributor side of the coil and earth. If there is no reading, this indicates a faulty coil or condenser.

Chapter 5 Clutch

For modifications, and information applicable to later models, see Supplement at end of manual

Contents

Degrees of difficulty

Easy, suitable for novice with little experience	**Fairly easy,** suitable for beginner with some experience	**Fairly difficult,** suitable for competent DIY mechanic	**Difficult,** suitable for experienced DIY mechanic	**Very difficult,** suitable for expert DIY or professional

5

Specifications

Type .... Cable operated, single dry plate with diaphragm spring and pressure plate

Driven plate
Diameter .... 160 mm (6.30 in)
Maximum wear limit (lining surface to rivet) .... 0.3 mm (0.012 in)
Maximum run-out .... 0.5 mm (0.020 in)
Hub spline play .... 0.6 mm (0.024 in)

Clutch cover
Diaphragm spring finger maximum variation .... 0.5 mm (0.020 in)

Clutch pedal
Pedal height (dimension H) .... 203 to 213 mm (7.99 to 8.39 in)
Free play (dimension A) .... 18 to 28 mm (0.71 to 1.10 in)
Release lever free play .... 2 to 4 mm (0.08 to 0.16 in)
Note: *See text for explanation of dimensions*

Torque wrench settings	lbf ft	kgf m
Pedal stop bolt locknut	9 to 11	1.2 to 1.5
Cable adjustment locknut	2.2 to 2.9	0.3 to 0.4
Pressure plate bolts	12 to 15	1.6 to 2.1
Clutch cable securing bracket bolt	6.7 to 8.7	0.93 to 1.2

1 General description

The clutch is of single dry plate type operated by cable from a pendant pedal. When the pedal is depressed, the cable pulls the release lever which forces the ball bearing type release bearing against the diaphragm spring fingers of the cover assembly. This releases the pressure plate from the linings of the driven plate, so disengaging the drive between the engine and transmission.

When the pedal is released, the pressure plate is forced against the driven plate which in turn is forced against the flywheel. Drive is then restored from the engine, through the driven plate and into the transmission via the input shaft.

2 Routine maintenance

At the intervals indicated in the Routine maintenance schedule, check the clutch pedal height and cable free play, adjusting if necessary. Check the pedal for smooth operation and lightly oil the pivot bushes with clean engine oil.

3 Clutch - adjustment

1 Remove the carpeting from the area immediately below the clutch pedal, and

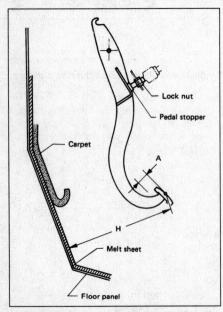

Fig. 5.2 Clutch pedal adjustment (Sec 3)
A = 0.71 to 1.10 in (18 to 28 mm)
H = 7.99 to 8.39 in (203 to 213 mm)

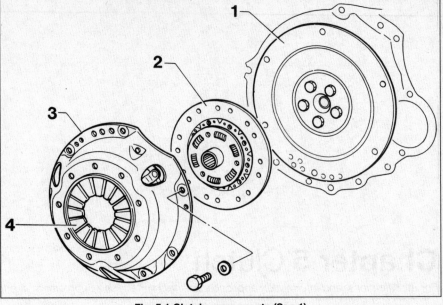

Fig. 5.1 Clutch components (Sec 1)

| 1 Flywheel | 3 Pressure plate | 4 Diaphragm and spring |
| 2 Driven plate | | fingers |

using a ruler measure the distance from the top surface of the clutch pedal to the floor, as shown in Fig. 5.2.
2 If the figure obtained is not as laid down in the Specifications then make adjustment on the pedal stop bolt until it is within limits.
3 Now check the free play at the clutch release lever arm in the engine compartment, adjusting as necessary using the knurled adjusting nut.
4 Fully depress the clutch pedal several times and recheck the dimensions.
5 Finally check the clutch pedal free play, then check all locknuts are fully tightened.
Note: *Sometimes cables may stretch with age, and the tolerances laid down in the Specifications will not be met because the cable is too long. A new cable is the only answer.*

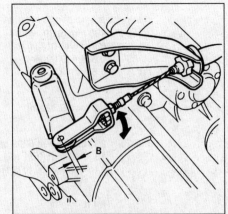

Fig. 5.3 Release lever free play adjustment (Sec 3)
B = 0.08 to 0.16 in (2 to 4 mm)

4 Clutch cable - renewal

1 Loosen the locknut on the knurled adjuster on the clutch release lever arm in the engine compartment and loosen the adjuster sufficiently for the cable end assembly to be disconnected from the release arm lever and the clutch cable bracket (photo).
2 From inside the vehicle, unhook the cable end assembly from the top of the clutch pedal.
3 Unscrew the two bolts holding the grommet panel where the cable passes through the bulkhead, and feeding the cable through the bulkhead, remove it from the vehicle.
4 The fitting of a new cable is a reversal of the removal operations, and then adjusting the cable as described in Section 3.

4.1 Clutch pedal adjusting bolt A

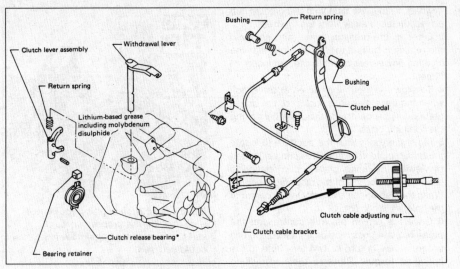

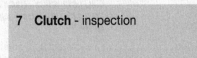

Fig. 5.4 Clutch cable components (Sec 4)

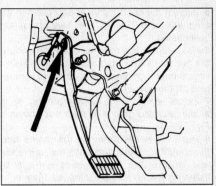

Fig. 5.5 Clutch pedal E-clip location (Sec 5)

5 Clutch pedal - removal and refitting

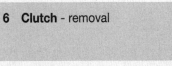

1 Disconnect the cable end from the top end of the pedal.
2 Extract the E-clip from the end of the pedal pivot shaft.
3 Unhook the pedal return spring and slide the pedal off the pivot shaft.
4 Inspect the pivot bushes for wear and renew if necessary.
5 Refitting is a reversal of removing, but apply grease to all pivot points and bushes. Finally adjust the pedal and clutch cable as described in Section 3.

6 Clutch - removal

1 To gain access to the clutch, the transmission must be removed as described in Chapter 6.
2 Unscrew the clutch pressure plate bolts progressively a turn at a time until the pressure being exerted by the diaphragm spring is relieved. (This prevents danger of

warping to the diaphragm and cover.) It may be necessary to jam the flywheel to prevent it turning while unscrewing the bolts.
3 Remove the pressure plate, catching the driven plate as it is released from the flywheel.
4 The bolts are offset, so it can only be replaced in one position.

7 Clutch - inspection

1 Examine the driven plate. If the linings are worn down to the limit given in the Specifications, or is close to it, then renew the plate.
2 Examine the linings also for burnt or discoloured patches, and contamination from oil or grease, which will all impair the efficiency of the clutch.
3 Check the amount of backlash between the driven plate and splines of the input shaft. Also check the driven plate for run-out. Inspect the torsion springs for damage, wear and cracks.
4 Check the pressure plate assembly for general wear, cracks or severe corrosion. and the fingers of the diaphragm for wear, especially where they come into contact with the release bearing. Renew as necessary. (A

complete new assembly will have to be obtained, as the diaphragm cannot be dismantled further.)
5 Inspect the friction surfaces of both the pressure plate and the flywheel, for grooves, cracking or pitting. The flywheel may be smoothed with fine emery cloth if it is slightly rough, but anything more serious requires renewal. The pressure plate will have to be renewed if it shows any signs of wear.
6 If contamination by oil is evident on clutch removal, then inspect the crankshaft rear oil seal for leaking, and renew it before replacing the clutch (refer to Chapter 1).

8 Release bearing, operating fork arm and cross-shaft - removal and refitting

1 Whenever the transmission is dismantled for clutch renewal, the release bearing should also be renewed, and the fork arm and cross-shaft inspected.
2 Remove the release bearing from the fork arm by releasing the spring clips which hold it, and slide it off its mounting sleeve on the bellhousing (photo).
3 Inspect the fork arm for cracks and wear, and the return spring for tension.
4 The fork arm may be removed from the cross-shaft by punching out the two roll pins which hold it in place on the cross-shaft. To do this the roll pins must be in line with the cavity in the bellhousing as they are punched out (photo).

8.2 Clutch release bearing

8.4 Release fork arm retaining roll pins

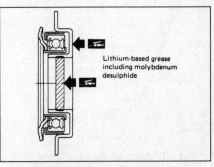

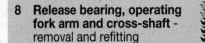

Fig. 5.6 Area to apply grease on clutch release bearing (Sec 8)

5 Inspect the shaft for wear especially in the area where it sits in the bearing of the bellhousing.

6 Reassembly is a reversal of this procedure, but grease all moving, mating surfaces with a lithium based grease, and always use new roll pins on the fork arm.

7 Before replacing the release bearing, apply a lithium based grease in the areas shown in Fig. 5.6.

8 Push the release bearing fully home over the mounting shaft and onto the fork ends, and ensure the spring clips engage by listening for an audible click as they snap home.

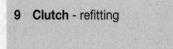

9 Clutch - refitting

1 Ensure the flywheel and pressure plate are free from protective coatings, and clean off any oil or grease.

2 Position the driven plate against the flywheel so that the side with the greater hub projection faces away from the flywheel.

3 Offer up the pressure plate, and screw in the retaining bolts finger tight. Note that the locating dowels are offset to prevent incorrect fitment.

4 To allow the input shaft to enter the clutch when the transmission is replaced, the driven plate must be centralised before tightening the retaining bolts.

5 Move the tool within the aperture to locate the driven plate centrally. This can be judged by viewing the driven plate hub in relation to the hole in the centre of the diaphragm spring. When the hub appears exactly in the centre of the hole, all is correct.

6 Once the driven piate is centralised the pressure plate bolts may be tightened. Do this progressively, a turn or two at a time to the specified torque. Remove the centralising tool.

Note: *Difficulty in refitting the transmission will indicate the driven plate has not been properly centralised, and this procedure will need to be repeated until the input shaft slides home without trouble.*

7 Refit the transmission with reference to Chapter 6.

> **TOOL TiP**
>
> *If a special clutch aligning tool is not available, then a broom handle, suitable size socket or similar item could be used*

Fault finding - clutch

Judder when taking up drive

☐ Loose engine or gearbox mountings
☐ Badly worn friction linings or contaminated with oil
☐ Worn splines on gearbox input shaft or driven plate hub

Clutch drag (or failure to disengage) so that gears cannot be meshed

☐ Incorrect adjustment
☐ Rust on splines (may occur after vehicle standing idle for long periods)
☐ Damaged or misaligned pressure plate assembly
☐ Cable stretched or broken

Clutch slip (increase in engine speed does not result in increase in car speed - especially on hills)

☐ Incorrect adjustment
☐ Friction linings worn out or oil contaminated

Noise from clutch

☐ Worn release bearing
☐ Worn or loose components of pressure plate or driven plate

Chapter 6 Manual transmission

For information applicable to later models, see Supplement at end of manual

Contents

Degrees of difficulty

Easy, suitable for novice with little experience	**Fairly easy,** suitable for beginner with some experience	**Fairly difficult,** suitable for competent DIY mechanic	**Difficult,** suitable for experienced DIY mechanic	**Very difficult,** suitable for expert DIY or professional

Specifications

Type . . . . Transverse, four- or five-speed with reverse. Synchromesh on all forward gears, floor mounted gearchange

Designation
Four-speed RN4F40A
Five-speed RSSF41A

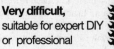

Ratios
1st . . . . 3.412 : 1
2nd . . . . 1.958 : 1
3rd . . . . 1.258 : 1
4th . . . . 0.921 : 1
5th (if fitted) . . . . 0.721 : 1
Reverse . . . . 3.385 : 1
Final drive ratio . . . . 3.810 : 1 (4-speed) or 3.591 : 1

Lubrication
Oil capacity:
  Four-speed . . . . 4.4 pints (2.5 litres)
  Five-speed . . . . 4.6 pints (2.6 litres)
Oil type/specification . . . . Gear oil, viscosity SAE 80 to API GL4

Gearbox setting tolerances
Gear endfloat:
  1st gear . . . . 0.22 to 0.44 mm (0.0087 to 0.0173 in)
  2nd gear . . . . 0.22 to 0.54 mm (0.0087 to 0.0213 in)
  3rd . . . . 0.22 to 0.49 mm (00087 to 0.0193 in)
  4th gear . . . . 0.22 to 0.39 mm (0.0087 to 0.0154 in)
  5th gear . . . . 0.22 to 0.29 mm (0.0087 to 0.0114 in)
Side gear-to-pinion mate gear clearance . . . . 0 to 0.3 mm (0 to 0.012 in)
Available side gear thrust washers . . . . 0.77 mm (0.0303 in)
  0.82 mm (0.0323 in)
  0.87 mm (0.0343 in)

Gearbox setting tolerances (continued)

Baulk ring-to-1st gear clearance:
 Standard .... 1.0 to 1.35 mm (00394 to 0.0531 in)
 Wear limit .... 0.7 mm (0.028 in)
Mainshaft groove clearance (after fitment of snap-ring) .... 0 to 0.15 mm (0 to 0.0059 in)
Available mainshaft snap-rings .... 2.0 mm (0.079 in)
 2.1 mm (0.083 in)

Input shaft groove clearance (after fitment of snap-ring) .... 0 to 0.13 mm (0 to 0.0051 in)
Available input shaft snap-rings .... 1.65 mm (0.650 in)
 1.75 mm (0.0689 in)
 1.85 mm (0.0728 in)

Reverse check plunger lengths:

Distance X (see text):	Plunger length Y
Less than 17.78 mm (0.7000 in)	17.17 mm (0.6760 in)
17.78 to 18.18 mm (0.7000 to 0.7157 in)	17.57 mm (0.6917 in)
18.18 to 18.58 mm (0.7157 to 0.7315 in)	17.97 mm (0.7075 in)
More than 18.58 mm (0.7315 in)	18.58 mm (0.7315 in)

Turning torque (new bearings):
 Final drive only .... 8.7 to 26.0 lbf in (10 to 30 kgf cm)
 Total assembly .... 22.0 to 52.0 lbf in (25 to 60 kgf cm)

Torque wrench Settings

	lbf ft	kgf m
Clutch housing to transmission case	12 to 15	1.6 to 2.1
5th and reverse gear check plug	14 to 22	2.0 to 3.0
5th and reverse check ball plug	12 to 15	1.6 to 2.1
Shift check ball plug	6.5 to 8.7	0.9 to 1.2
Shift rod plate to clutch housing	4.3 to 5.8	0.6 to 0.8
Guide plate to clutch housing	4.3 to 5.8	0.6 to 0.8
Reverse bracket assembly to clutch housing	4.3 to 5.8	0.6 to 0.8
Reverse light switch to transmission case	1.6 to 2.9	0.25 to 0.4
Bearing retainer to clutch housing	12 to 15	1.6 to 2.1
Drain plug	7 to 14	1.0 to 2.0
Final gear to differential case	54 to 65	7.5 to 9.0
Support rod to gearbox	21 to 27	2.9 to 3.7
Control rod to gearbox	4.3 to 5.8	0.6 to 0.8
Selector stopper bolt	2.9 to 3.6	0.4 to 0.5
Rubber holder to body	2.2 to 2.9	0.3 to 0.4
Rubber holder nut	2.2 to 2.9	0.3 to 0.4
Speedometer pinion gear	2.2 to 2.9	0.3 to 0.4

1 General description

Both the four-speed and five-speed gearboxes are a new lightweight unit designed exclusively for use with a transverse engine. They are identical to each other, the five-speed simply having the extra gear added.

Synchromesh is provided on all forward gears, and the gear lever is of the conventional, floor mounted type.

The transmission unit, which includes the differential unit, is mounted transversely, in line with the engine. Power is transmitted from the clutch via an input shaft and mainshaft to the final drive/differential unit, and on to the front roadwheels via the driveshaft.

The overhaul procedure given here describes a five-speed gearbox, those owners working on a four-speed box should ignore references to the 5th gear.

2 Routine maintenance

1 At the intervals indicated in the Routine maintenance schedule, check the oil level in the gearbox and top up as necessary.

2.1A Removing the speedometer drive securing bolt

Remove the bolt holding the speedometer drive cable in place (photo) and remove the speedometer drivegear (photo). This acts as a dipstick, as shown in Fig. 6.1 and filler hole. Replace the speedometer drive and securing bolt on completion.

2 When operating under severe or dusty conditions renew the transmission oil every

2.1B Withdrawing the speedometer drive unit

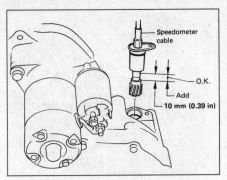

Fig. 6.1 Checking the gearbox oil level (Sec 2)

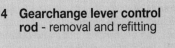

2.2 Gearbox oil drain plug

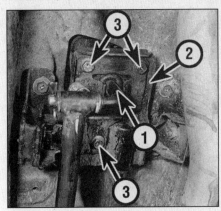

3.3 Adjustment point between gear lever and stopper plate

1 Adjustment point   3 Securing bolts
2 Stopper plate

24 000 miles (40 000 km) or 2 years, whichever comes first. The drain plug is situated on the underside of the transmission casing (photo).

3 Gearchange lever - adjustment

1 Twist off the gearchange lever knob. It may be necessary to protect the knob with rags and use a wrench.
2 Remove the rubber boot then refer to Chapter 12 for removal of the clock and its plastic housing.
3 Select first gear and check that there is a 0.039 in (1.0 mm) clearance between the lever and the stopper plate. If the clearance is incorrect loosen the three securing bolts and move the plate to obtain the correct clearance

(photo). Tighten the bolts and check the selection of all gears.
4 Refit the clock and its housing and the rubber boot, before refitting the gear lever knob.

4 Gearchange lever control rod - removal and refitting

1 Remove the gear lever knob, clock and housing as described in the previous Section.
2 Undo and remove the three screws holding the dust cover and remove it from the gear lever (photos).
3 Remove the bolt from the front end of the support rod (photo).
4 Then remove the locking spring pin from the control rod end, and slide the control rod

4.2A Gearlever dust cover and securing screws

4.2B Removing the dust cover

4.3 Support rod securing bolt

1 Support rod   2 Securing bolt

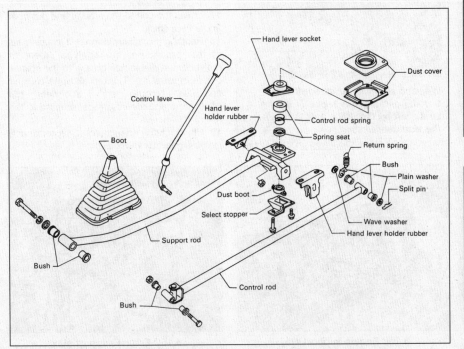

Fig. 6.2 Exploded view of gear lever, control rod and support tube (Sec 3)

6

4.4 Control rod-to-gear lever connection

4.5 Removing control lever-to-selector shaft bolt

5.15A Engine mounting bracket

off the gear lever, noting the order of all washers and bushes (photo).

5 Remove the bolt securing the control lever to the gearbox selector shaft (photo).

6 Now remove the bolts holding the support rod rear plate position.

7 The whole assembly may now be manoeuvred from the vehicle and the gear lever seating further dismantled as required.

8 Reassembly is a reverse of the above procedure greasing all moving parts and finally adjusting the gear lever stop plate as described in Section 3.

5 Transmission - removal and refitting

1 The transmission unit is removed complete with the clutch bellhousing. The driveshafts are disconnected at their inboard ends, where they enter the differential unit.

2 It will be helpful to refer to Chapter 8 regarding the driveshafts at this point, remembering that the intention is to disconnect the driveshafts from the transmission and not remove them completely.

3 Jack the vehicle at the front end jacking points and support it on suitable stands. The engine should also be supported under the oil sump with suitable blocks. Drain the transmission oil.

4 Remove the front roadwheels.

5 Undo and remove the steering rod balljoints (refer to Chapter 10).

6 Undo and remove the two bolts securing the wheel hub knuckle to the lower end of the suspension strut.

7 Lower each hub sufficiently to allow the inboard ends of each driveshaft to be levered from the transmission housing.

8 Support the driveshafts, hubs and steering rods with wire or string so that they are out of the way and will not be damaged.

9 Once the driveshafts are removed, the side gears need to be retained in place to prevent them falling into the differential housing.

TOOL TiP

We used short, tapered lengths of broom handle gently tapped into the space left by the driveshaft to retain the side gears.

10 Disconnect the front ends of the gear lever control and support rods (see Section 4).

11 Disconnect the clutch operating cable from the release lever (Chapter 5).

12 Disconnect the speedometer cable drive unit from the transmission casing (Section 2).

13 Disconnect the electrical leads from the reversing light switch.

14 Remove the starter motor.

15 Ensure the engine is suitably supported under the oil sump with blocks before removing the rear engine mounting bracket, and the front right-hand mounting. Also remove the two support tubes between the oil sump and transmission casing (photos).

16 Supporting the transmission unit, remove the five bolts securing it to the engine, noting their lengths and any brackets or clips which may fit under their heads, so that all will be in place on reinstallation.

17 Lower the unit to the ground and out from under the vehicle.

18 Refitting the transmission unit is a reversal of this procedure, but apply a smear of molybdenum disulphide grease to the splines of the input shaft. Tighten all bolts to their specified torque, and reconnect the driveshafts and steering rods, refering to the relevant Chapters.

19 Check clutch adjustment (Chapter 5) and refill the gearbox with oil.

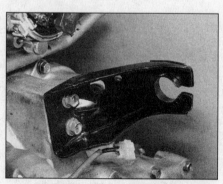

5.15B Engine mounting bracket

5.15C Engine support stay

5.15D Engine support stay

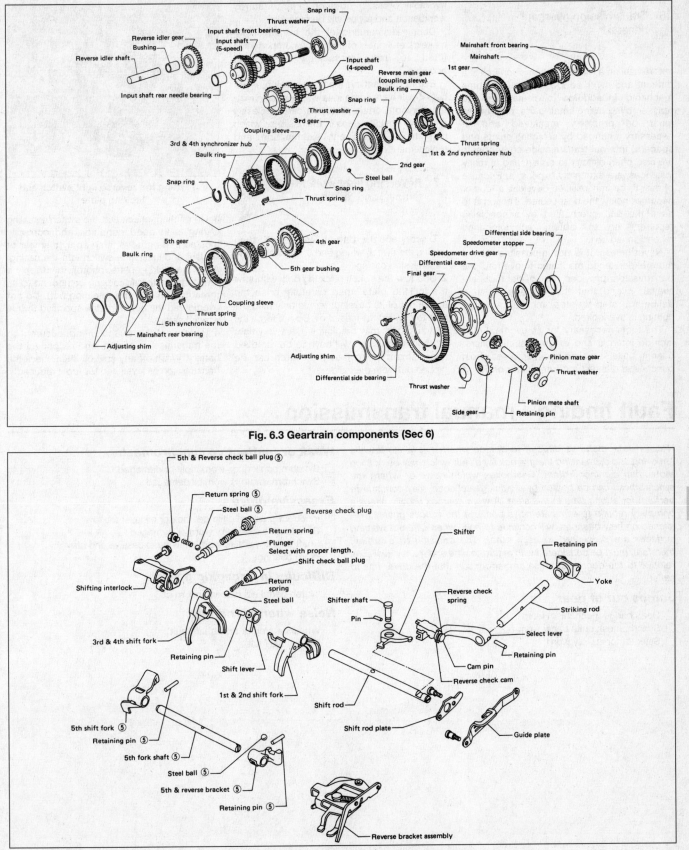

Fig. 6.3 Geartrain components (Sec 6)

Fig. 6.4 Gear change shift components (Sec 6)

6 Transmission overhaul - general

Overhauling a manual transmission unit is a difficult and involved job for the DIY home mechanic. In addition to dismantling and reassembling many small parts, clearances must be precisely measured and, if necessary, changed by selecting shims and spacers. Internal transmission components are also often difficult to obtain, and in many instances, are extremely expensive. Because of this, if the transmission develops a fault or becomes noisy, the best course of action is to have the unit overhauled by a specialist repairer, or to obtain an exchange reconditioned unit.

Nevertheless, it is not impossible for the more experienced mechanic to overhaul the transmission, provided the special tools are available, and that the job is done in a deliberate step-by-step manner so that nothing is overlooked.

The tools necessary for an overhaul may include internal and external circlip pliers, bearing pullers, a slide hammer, a set of pin punches, a dial test indicator, and possibly a hydraulic press. In addition, a large, sturdy workbench and a vice will be required.

During dismantling of the transmission, make careful notes of how each component is fitted, to make reassembly easier and accurate.

Before dismantling the transmission, it will help if you have some idea which area is malfunctioning. Certain problems can be closely related to specific areas in the gearbox, which can make component examination and replacement easier.

7 Reversing light switch - removal and refitting

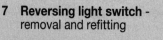

1 Disconnect the battery earth lead, then unplug the switch wiring and unclip it from the transmission casing.
2 Unscrew the switch retaining bolt, withdraw the locking plate, then carefully prise the switch out of its housing; temporarily plug the hole to prevent the loss of oil. Do not force the switch, or you may break it; if it is a very tight fit, the transmission will have to be removed and dismantled so that the switch can be tapped out from the inside.

7.3 Fitting the reverse light switch and locking plate

3 On refitting, check that the switch's sealing O-ring is in good condition and correctly located in its groove, then apply a smear of sealant and insert the switch into the casing. Align the locking plate (photo), then apply a few drops of thread-locking compound to its threads, and refit the retaining bolt. Do not overtighten the bolt; note the specified torque wrench setting.
4 Reconnect the switch wiring, secure it to the transmission casing, and reconnect the battery. Wash off any spilt oil, then check the transmission oil level, and top-up if required.

Fault finding - manual transmission

Note: *It is sometimes difficult to decide whether it is worthwhile removing and dismantling the gearbox for a fault which may be nothing more than a minor irritant. Gearboxes which howl, or where the synchromesh can be beaten by a quick gearchange, may continue to perform for a long time in this state. A worn gearbox usually needs a complete rebuild to eliminate noise because the various gears, if re-aligned on new bearings, will continue to howl when different wearing surfaces are presented to each other. The decision to overhaul, therefore, must be considered with regard to time and money available, relative to the degree of noise or malfunction that the driver has to suffer.*

Jumps out of gear

☐ Gearchange mechanism worn
☐ Synchromesh units badly worn
☐ Selector fork badly worn

Weak or ineffective synchromesh

☐ Synchro baulk rings worn, split or damaged
☐ Synchromesh units worn or damaged

Excessive noise

☐ Incorrect grade of oil in gearbox or oil level too low
☐ Gear teeth excessively worn or damaged
☐ Shaft thrust washers worn allowing excessive end play
☐ Worn bearings

Difficulty in engaging gears

☐ Clutch pedal adjustment incorrect

Noise when cornering

☐ Wheel bearing or driveshaft fault
☐ Differential fault

Chapter 7 Automatic transmission

For modifications, and information applicable to later models, see Supplement at end of manual

Contents

Degrees of difficulty

Easy, suitable for novice with little experience	**Fairly easy,** suitable for beginner with some experience	**Fairly difficult,** suitable for competent DIY mechanic	**Difficult,** suitable for experienced DIY mechanic	**Very difficult,** suitable for expert DIY or professional

Specifications

Type	RL3FO1B fully automatic, air-cooled, lock up design, providing three forward and one reverse gear

Ratios

1st	2.826:1
2nd	1.543:1
3rd	1.000:1
Reverse	2.364:1
Final drive:	
MA10/MA10 S	3.737 1
MA12 S	3.600:1

Lubrication

Fluid capacity	10.6 Imp pts (6.0 litres)
Fluid type	Dexron II type ATF

Torque wrench settings	**lbf ft**	**kgf m**
Driveplate to torque converter	29 to 36	4 to 5
Torque converter housing to engine	12 to 16	1.6 to 2.2
Sump pan bolts	3.6 to 5.1	0.5 to 0.7
Control valve body to transmission casing	5.1 to 6.5	0.7 to 0.9
Governor valve body to shaft	3.6 to 5.1	0.5 to 0.7

1 General description

The automatic transmission incorporates a torque converter with planetary geartrains and the final drive differential unit.

Six speed selector control lever positions are used as follows:

P *Park - to lock the transmission*
R *Reverse gear*
N *Neutral*
D *Forward speed, changes automatically up and down between 1st, 2nd and 3rd gear*
2 *Second gear hold, will change only between 1st and 2nd gears*
1 *First gear, will hold the transmission in 1st gear*

An automatic kickdown device is incorporated which allows for rapid acceleration during overtaking, or for hill climbing, actuated by fully depressing the accelerator.

The torque converter is air cooled.

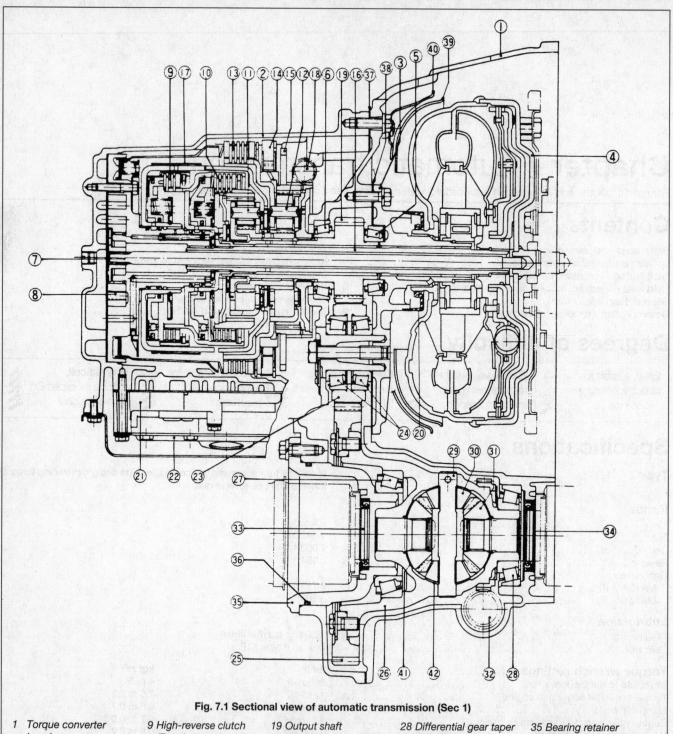

Fig. 7.1 Sectional view of automatic transmission (Sec 1)

1 Torque converter housing	9 High-reverse clutch (Front)	19 Output shaft	28 Differential gear taper roller bearing	35 Bearing retainer
2 Transmission case	10 Forward clutch (Rear)	20 Front cover oil seal	29 Pinion mate shaft	36 O-ring
3 Front cover	11 Front planetary gear	21 Control valve	30 Pinion mate gear	37 Gasket
4 Torque converter	12 Rear planetary gear	22 Oil strainer	31 Side gear	38 Gasket
5 Output shaft taper roller bearing	13 Low and reverse brake	23 Idler gear	32 Speedometer pinion gear	39 Converter shroud
6 Output shaft taper roller bearing	14 One-way clutch	24 Idler gear taper roller bearing	33 Differential gear side oil seal	40 Shroud separator
7 Oil pump shaft	15 Parking gear	25 Final gear	34 Differential gear side oil seal	41 Side gear thrust washer
8 Oil pump	16 Input shaft	26 Differential gear case		42 Pinion mate gear thrust washer
	17 Brake band	27 Differential gear taper roller bearing		
	18 Governor valve shaft			

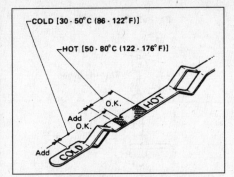

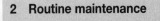

Fig. 7.2 Checking automatic transmission fluid level (Sec 3)

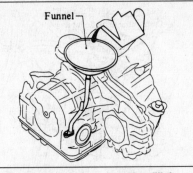

Fig. 7.3 Use a clean funnel to fill the automatic transmission (Sec 3)

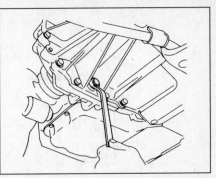

Fig. 7.4 The transmission drain plug (Sec 3)

2 Routine maintenance

1 At the intervals indicated in the Routine maintenance schedule, check the transmission fluid level. Visually inspect the fluid on the dipstick for discoloration due to contamination, which may indicate internal wear.

2 If the car is operating under severe conditions, renew the transmission fluid every 24000 miles, (40000 km) or two years, whichever comes first.

3 Fluid level - checking, topping up and changing

1 Check the fluid level at the intervals given in Section 2.

2 The precise level of the fluid will depend on the ambient temperature (see Fig. 7.2). First park the car on a level surface and apply the handbrake.

3 Run the engine for ten minutes and allow it to idle.

4 Move the selector lever slowly through each position ending in Park (P).

5 With the engine idling, withdraw the transmission dipstick, wipe it clean, re-insert it and then withdraw it again and read off the fluid level.

6 If it is not as indicated in the illustrations, top up.

7 On no account overfill the automatic transmission or run it with too low a fluid level.

 HAYNES HiNT *Renewal of the automatic transmission fluid is only specified by the manufacturers if the vehicle is operated under arduous conditions such as trailer towing. However, it would seem to make sense to change the fluid on all vehicles after a reasonably high mileage in order to remove any impurities from the system. The additives in the fluid will almost certainly have lost some of their characteristics by this time as well.*

8 Before draining the fluid, have it at normal operating temperature by running on the road for a distance of at least five miles (eight kilometres).

9 Unscrew and remove the transmission drain plug and catch the fluid in a container.

10 The condition of the fluid is an indication of the serviceability of the transmission. If it is very dark or nearly black and smells of burning, suspect worn friction components within the transmission. If there is no odour then the discoloration may be due to a small leak of coolant coming from the fluid cooler within the radiator.

11 If the fluid is an opaque pink in colour this will be due to a coolant leak or flood water contamination.

12 If the fluid is dark brown in colour and sticky, this will probably be due to overheating by under or over filling.

13 Refit the drain plug, withdraw the dipstick and pour the fresh fluid into the transmission through the dipstick guide tube.

14 Check the fluid level, as previously described.

4 Overhaul and adjustment - general

1 Owing to the need for special tools and equipment, operations to the automatic transmission should be limited to the in-vehicle work described in the following Sections.

2 Where more extensive overhaul is required,

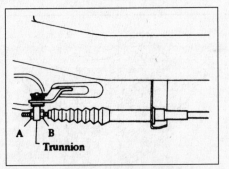

Fig. 7.5 Selector cable adjustment at transmission end (Sec 5)

A Locknut   B Locknut

Trunnion

it is best to leave this to your dealer, or, where necessary, remove the transmission for professional repair or renewal, as described in Section 11.

5 Speed selector cable - adjustment

1 When the hand control lever is moved to all positions on the index, the individual detents should be positively felt. If this is not so, adjust in the following way.

2 Set the control lever to P.

3 Working at the selector lever on the transmission casing, disconnect the cable.

4 With the fingers, move the selector lever positively into its P detent.

5 Using the cable end fitting locknuts, adjust the cable until it applies no tension in either direction to the selector lever on the transmission. Tighten the locknuts.

6 Check that the selector positions are positively obtained.

6 Inhibitor switch - adjustment

1 The inhibitor switch controls the reversing lamps when R is selected, and also prevents operation of the starter when the hand control lever is in any position but P or N.

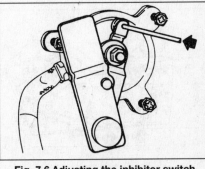

Fig. 7.6 Adjusting the inhibitor switch (Sec 6)

Arrow indicates alignment pin

7

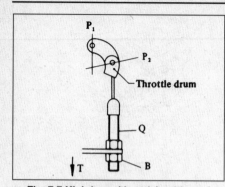

Fig. 7.7 Kickdown (throttle) cable end fitting at carburettor (Sec 7)

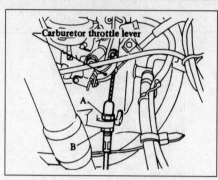

Fig. 7.8 Kickdown (throttle) cable locknuts A and B at carburettor end (Sec 7)

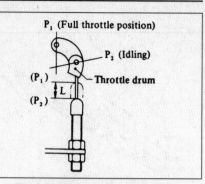

Fig. 7.9 Kickdown (throttle) cable movement diagram (Sec 7)

B Locknut
P1 Full throttle position
P2 Idle position
Q Cable end fitting
T Adjustment movement direction

2 If the inhibitor switch does not operate correctly, adjust in the following way.
3 Loosen, but do not remove, the switch screws.
4 Set the hand control lever to N.
5 Push a 2.5 mm (0.098 in) diameter pin through the switch lever and switch body holes to align them. Hold the pin and tighten the switch screws. Remove the pin.

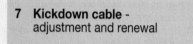

7 Kickdown cable - adjustment and renewal

1 Release the cable locknuts at the carburettor (see Fig. 7.8).
2 With the carburettor throttle lever held in the full throttle position, move the cable end fitting in the direction T (see Fig. 7.7). Tighten nut B to eliminate any free movement.
3 Unscrew nut B between one and one and a half turns and secure it in this position by tightening nut A (see Fig. 7.8).
4 Check that the throttle cable end fitting movement L is within the specified tolerances (see Fig. 7.9).
5 To renew the cable, first remove the fluid sump pan and control valve assembly, as described in the next Section.

6 Disconnect the kickdown cable from the carburettor.
7 Disconnect the other end of the cable from the lever and then release the cable conduit from the casing by flattening the lockplate tab and unscrew the nut.
8 Fit the new cable by reversing the removal operations. Bend up the locktab around the nut.
9 Adjust as previously described, and finally check that the rubber bellows (if fitted) on the inner cable at the carburettor end is not twisted.

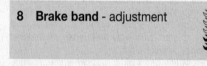

8 Brake band - adjustment

1 This will normally only be required if a fault develops, indicated by one of the following symptoms.
No change from 1st to 2nd
Speed changes direct from 1st to 3rd
Severe jerk on 1st to 2nd upshift
Poor acceleration
Maximum speed not obtained
No 3rd to 2nd downshift
No kickdown when in 3rd gear
Slip in 3rd to 2nd downshift
No manual 3rd to 2nd downshift
Transmission overheats
2 Drain the transmission fluid.
3 Remove the sump pan shield, the sump

L 1.079 to 1.236 in (27.4 to 31.4 mm)
P1 Full throttle position
P2 Idle position

pan and the gasket from the transmission.
4 Unscrew the bolts evenly and progressively and withdraw the control valve assembly.
5 Release the brake band anchor pin locknut and then, using a torque wrench, tighten the pin to between 4.0 and 6.0 Nm (3 and 4 lbf ft).
6 Now unscrew the anchor pin through 2 1/2 complete turns. Hold the anchor pin stationary and tighten the locknut to between 16.0 and 22.0 Nm (12 and 16 lbf ft).
7 Refit the control valve assembly and tighten the bolts. Make sure that the manual and detent valves are correctly engaged - the manual valve should be set at neutral, and the groove on the detent valve should face forward.
8 Refit the sump pan together with a new gasket, followed by the shield. Fill the transmission with the specified fluid then check the level as described in Section 3.

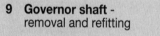

9 Governor shaft - removal and refitting

1 On pre 1984 models disconnect the battery, remove the cooling system expansion tank, and remove the battery and its support bracket.
2 On 1984 on models remove the distributor cap.

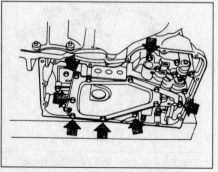

Fig. 7.10 Control valve assembly bolt locations (Sec 8)

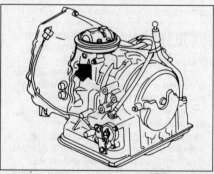

Fig. 7.11 Adjusting the brake band anchor pin (Sec 8)

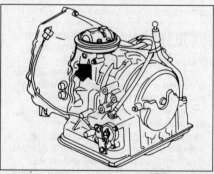

Fig. 7.12 Governer shaft lockbolt location (Sec 9)

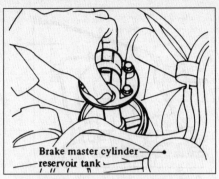

Fig. 7.13 Removing the governor shaft (Sec 9)

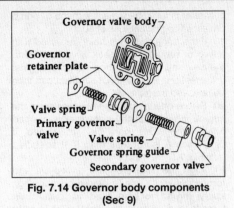

Fig. 7.14 Governor body components (Sec 9)

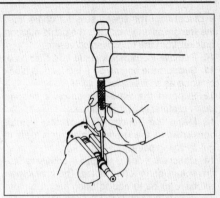

Fig. 7.15 Driving out the governor shaft worm pin (Sec 9)

3 Release the governor cap snap retainer, the cap with breather hose, and the sealing ring.
4 Unscrew the governor shaft lockbolt.
5 Withdraw the governor shaft.
6 The governor body may be unbolted from the shaft, and scratched or worn components renewed. The worm may be removed from the governor shaft after driving out the securing pin.
7 Refitting is a reversal of removal, but make sure that the cap is located on the case protrusion correctly.

gears are worn excessively, and renewal of the transmission should be considered.
4 If the side gear wear is not excessive remove the driveshafts as described in Chapter 8 and extract the oil seals using a two-legged puller.
5 Apply transmission fluid to the lips of the new oil seals before fitting them. A piece of tubing applied to the outer rim of the oil seal can then be used to drive them into their seats.
6 Refit the driveshafts with reference to Chapter 8.

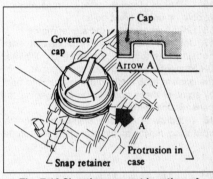

Fig. 7.16 Showing correct location of governor cap (Sec 9)

10 Differential bearing oil seals - renewal

1 In the event of oil leakage from the differential bearing oil seals, it is necessary to ascertain whether the cause is simply worn oil seals or additionally, excessive wear of the side gears resulting in lateral movement in the oil seal. If the latter is the case, new oil seals will not necessarily cure the problem and the transmission should be renewed.
2 Jack up the front of the car and support on axle stands. Apply the handbrake.
3 Using a dial gauge at right angles to the driveshaft bellows clip (Fig. 7.17), push the driveshaft joint fully towards the transmission then lightly move the joint up and down. If the play is more than 1.0 mm (0.039 in) the side

11 Transmission - removal and refitting

1 Place the vehicle over an inspection pit or raise the front end and support it securely on axle stands positioned under the side-members.
2 Disconnect the battery.
3 Remove the left-hand roadwheel.
4 Drain the transmission fluid.
5 Remove the left-hand plastic wing shield.
6 Disconnect both driveshafts, as described in Chapter 6, Section 5, paragraphs 3 to 8.
7 Disconnect the speedometer cable from the transmission.
8 Disconnect the throttle cable from the carburettor and the leads from the inhibitor switch.

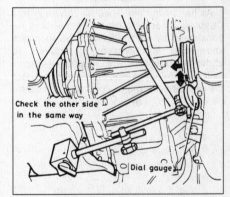

Fig. 7.17 Using a dial gauge to check the differential side gear wear (Sec 10)

7

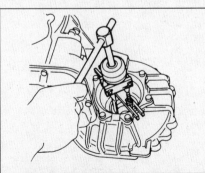

Fig. 7.18 Using a puller to remove a differential bearing oil seal (Sec 10)

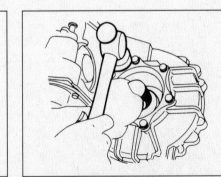

Fig. 7.19 Driving in a new differential bearing oil seal (Sec 10)

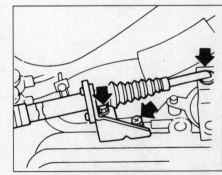

Fig. 7.20 Speed selector cable fixings at transmission end (Sec 11)

9 Disconnect the speed selector cable from the transmission lever, and the cable support bracket from the transmission casing.

10 Remove the dipstick guide/fluid filler tube.

11 Support the engine on a jack with a block of wood as an insulator.

12 Support the transmission on a second jack - preferably of trolley type.

13 Mark the relationship of the torque converter to the driveplate using a dab of quick-drying paint.

14 Unscrew the torque converter-to-driveplate connecting bolts. The crankshaft will have to be turned to bring each bolt into view within the cut-out of the torque converter housing before a spanner or socket wrench can be used.

15 Withdraw the automatic transmission flexible mounting pivot bolts.

16 Unbolt and remove the starter motor.

17 Unscrew and remove the torque converter housing-to-engine connecting bolts. Disconnect, plug and record the location of the coolant tube and mounting brackets held by some of these bolts. Unbolt the engine-to-transmission reinforcement strut.

18 Withdraw the transmission from under the front wing, having an assistant hold the torque converter in full engagement with the oil pump driveshaft to prevent loss of fluid.

19 If the transmission is being replaced with a new or rebuilt unit, check what is fitted to the new unit before parting with the original transmission. The parts not supplied can then be removed from the old unit.

20 Before offering up the transmission to the engine, check that the converter is pushed fully home. This can be determined if dimension A is not less than that specified (see Fig. 7.21).

21 Align the marks on the driveplate and torque converter (made before dismantling), apply thread locking fluid to clean bolt threads, and screw in and tighten the bolts to the specified torque.

22 Bolt on the starter motor.

23 Fit the engine-to-transmission connecting bolts, making sure to locate the coolant tube and mounting brackets under their correct bolts. Refit the mounting pivot bolts. Refit the reinforcement strut.

24 Reconnect the speed selector control cable, and adjust if necessary.

25 Reconnect the inhibitor switch leads.

26 Reconnect the fluid cooler hoses.

27 Refit the wing protective shield.

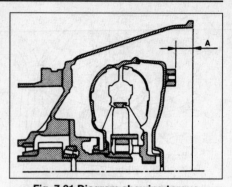

Fig. 7.21 Diagram showing torque convertor dimension when fully installed (Sec 11)

A = Not less than 21.1 mm (0.831 in)

28 Refit the dipstick guide/fluid filler tube.

29 Reconnect the throttle cable.

30 Reconnect the speedometer drive cable.

31 Reconnect the driveshafts, as described in Chapter 8.

32 Refit the left-hand roadwheel.

33 Reconnect the battery.

34 Fill the transmission with the specified fluid then check the level as described in Section 3.

Fault finding - automatic transmission

1 As has been mentioned elsewhere in this Chapter, no service repair work should be considered by anyone without the specialist knowledge and equipment required to undertake this work. This is also relevant to fault diagnosis. If a fault is evident, carry out the various adjustments previously described, and if the fault still exists consult the local garage or specialist.

2 Before removing the automatic transmission for repair, make sure that the repairer does not require to perform diagnostic tests with the transmission installed.

3 Most minor faults will be due to incorrect fluid level, incorrectly adjusted selector control or throttle cables and the internal brake band being out of adjustment (refer to Sections 3, 5, 7 and 8).

Chapter 8
Driveshafts

For modifications, and information applicable to later models, see Supplement at end of manual

Contents

Degrees of difficulty

Easy, suitable for novice with little experience	**Fairly easy,** suitable for beginner with some experience	**Fairly difficult,** suitable for competent DIY mechanic	**Difficult,** suitable for experienced DIY mechanic	**Very difficult,** suitable for expert DIY or professional

Specifications

Type .... Open shafts with ball and cage joints at each end

Lubrication
Quantity of grease required for each driveshaft .... 90 g (3.17 oz)
Grease type .... Lithium based molybdenum disulphide grease

Torque wrench settings	lbf ft	kgf m
Lower ball joint to arm	36 to 43	5.0 to 6.0
Suspension strut to knuckle	58 to 72	8.0 to 10.0
Driveshaft nut	58 to 116	8.0 to 16.0

1 General description

The driveshafts are of the open type, transmitting power from the differential unit in the final drive assembly to the front roadwheels. Ball and cage joint are employed at both ends, but only the transmission side joint can be dismantled for repair, the roadwheel side being changed as a complete unit.

2 Routine maintenance

At the intervals indicated in the Routine maintenance schedule, check the driveshaft rubber bellows for damage, cracks, leakage and security (photos). Where the car is operating under extreme conditions, reduce the service interval by half.

3 Driveshaft - checking, removal and refitting

1 Jack up the front of the car and support on axle stands. Apply the handbrake.
2 Grip the driveshaft and attempt to turn it in alternate directions against the rotation of the roadwheel. If possible, have an assistant depress the brake pedal during the check. If any play is evident, the joint must be renewed

8

2.1A Driveshaft outer rubber bellows

2.1B Driveshaft inner bellows (right-hand shaft)

2.1C Driveshaft inner bellows (left-hand shaft)

3.4 Remove the split pin and nut retainer, and loosen the nut

3.9 Prising free the driveshaft inboard joint

3.12A Removing the driveshaft nut . . .

(Section 4 or 5) or the complete driveshaft replaced.

3 To remove the driveshaft-first remove the roadwheel.

4 Extract the split pin, take off the nut retainer (photo), and loosen the driveshaft-to-hub retaining nut in order to hold the hub against rotation, either refit the roadwheel and lower the vehicle to the ground, have an assistant apply the brakes, or use a length of steel rod or bar placed between two roadwheel studs as a lever. Take steps to prevent damage to the stud threads by screwing on the nuts.

5 Unbolt the brake caliper and tie it up out of the way. There is no need to disconnect the hydraulic line. Remove the disc pads and pull the disc from the hub.

6 Extract the split pin, unscrew the nut, and detach the steering tie-rod from the steering knuckle using a separator tool.

7 Disconnect the front suspension lower balljoint. Do this by unscrewing the nuts which hold the balljoint to the suspension arm. It is recommended that new nuts are used at reassembly.

8 Place a suitable container beneath the transmission to catch any spilled oil.

9 Insert a large screwdriver or other lever between the transmission casing and the inboard joint flange of the driveshaft. On the right-hand side of the casing an aperture is provided for inserting the lever. Prise the joint to overcome resistance of the retaining clip (photo). Take care not to damage the transmission oil seal, and do not pull on the outer end of the driveshaft as the joints may come apart.

10 Unscrew and remove the bolts holding the knuckle to the strut, then withdraw the driveshaft from the transmission together with the hub and knuckle.

11 Once the inboard end of the shaft has been disconnected, insert a short bar into the differential side gear as it is possible for the side gear to rotate and to fall into the differential case.

12 Working at the outboard end of the shaft, remove the driveshaft nut and washer and push the driveshaft out of the hub (photos). If it is tight, use a two or three-legged puller to push it out.

13 It is recommended that a new oil seal is fitted to the transmission whenever the driveshaft is removed. Refer to Chapter 6 or 7 for the procedure.

14 Refitting is a reversal of removal, but use a new circlip when fitting the inboard end of the driveshaft (photo). Push the shaft fully home in the side gear, after having first removed the temporary gear retaining bar and having applied grease to the oil seal lips. Pull the joint

3.12B . . . and washer

3.12C Withdrawing the outboard joint from the knuckle

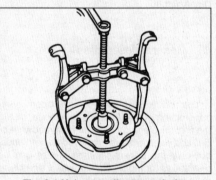

Fig. 8.1 Using a puller to push the driveshaft from the hub (Sec 3)

3.14A Circlip at driveshaft inboard end

3.14B Tightening the driveshaft nut

3.14C Insert a new split pin . . .

3.14D . . . and bend up the legs

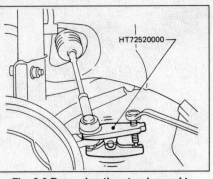

Fig. 8.2 Removing the steering rod to steering knuckle balljoint (Sec 3)

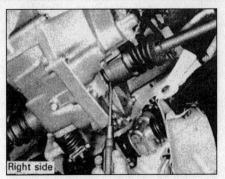

Fig. 8.3 Prising out the driveshaft from the transmission housing (Sec 3)

4.3 Removing the driveshaft outboard joint

4.6A Slide on the small clip . . .

4.6B . . . then the rubber bellows

cover to check that the circlip is positively engaged. The flange of the joint casing may be tapped with a plastic-faced hammer if necessary to drive shaft fully home. Tighten all nuts and bolts to the specified torque and fit a new split pin to the hub nut (photos). Top up the transmission oil level as necessary, and finally depress the footbrake pedal several times to set the disc pads in their normal position.

4 Driveshaft outboard joint - removal and refitting

1 With the driveshaft removed, as described in the preceding Section, remove and discard the bellows securing bands.

2 Using quick-drying paint, put alignment marks on the shaft and joint.
3 Using a plastic or copper-faced hammer tap the outboard joint assembly off the shaft against the resistance of the retaining circlip (photo). Quite heavy blows will be required to release it.
4 Withdraw the flexible bellows from the shaft.

5 If the joint is worn it can only be renewed as an assembly.
6 Commence refitting by sliding the bellows onto the shaft and fitting a new securing band to the narrower diameter (photos).
7 If the original joint is being fitted, use a new retaining circlip and, having wiped away as much lubricant as possible, tap the joint onto the shaft until the circlip snaps home (photo).

4.7 Fitting the joint to the shaft

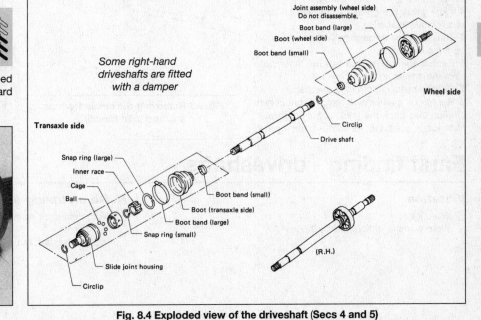

Fig. 8.4 Exploded view of the driveshaft (Secs 4 and 5)

Some right-hand driveshafts are fitted with a damper

Joint assembly (wheel side)
Do not disassemble
Boot band (large)
Boot (wheel side)
Boot band (small)
Wheel side
Circlip
Drive shaft
Transaxle side
Snap ring (large)
Inner race
Cage
Ball
Boot band (small)
Boot (transaxle side)
Boot band (large)
Snap ring (small)
Slide joint housing
Circlip
(R.H.)

8

4.8 Pack with grease

4.9A Fit the large clip . . .

4.9B . . . and bend over the tabs

The marks made before removal should be in alignment.

8 Peel back the bellows and apply the specified quantity of the special grease which is supplied with each new joint. If the original joint is being refitted use a suitable molybdenum disulphide based grease (photo). See Specifications for quantity of grease required.

9 Set the bellows length (Fig. 8.5) then fit the large securing band. Tighten both bands using pliers and a screwdriver, bend over the tabs then bend back the remaining end and cut off the excess (photos).

5 Driveshaft inboard joint - removal and refitting

1 With the driveshaft gripped in the jaws of a vice fitted with jaw protectors, remove the bellows retaining bands and discard them.

2 Pull back the bellows and prise out the large circlip now exposed.

3 Pull off the slide joint housing.

4 Wipe away the grease from the ball cage and remove the balls.

5 Turn the cage through half a turn and pull it from the inner race.

6 Extract the circlip and tap the inner race from the driveshaft.

7 Pull the bellows from the driveshaft.

8 Refitting is a reversal of removal, but fit new circlips and pack the joint with new grease. New joints are supplied with a grease pack,

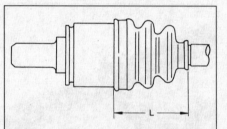

Fig. 8.6 Setting bellows length. inboard joint (Sec 5)

Length L = 3.23 in (82 mm)

but if the original joint is being refitted use a suitable molybdenum disulphide grease. See Specifications for quantity of grease required.

9 Set the bellows length (Fig. 8.6) then fit the large securing band. Tighten both bands using pliers and a screwdriver, bend over the tabs, then bend back the remaining end and cut off the excess.

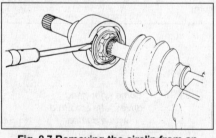

Fig. 8.7 Removing the circlip from an inboard joint (Sec 5)

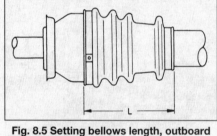

Fig. 8.5 Setting bellows length, outboard joint (Sec 4)

Length L = 3.35 in (85 mm)

6 Driveshaft bellows - renewal

Renewal of either driveshaft bellows is only possible after removal of the relevant joint as described in Section 4 or 5.

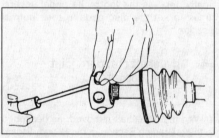

Fig. 8.8 Removing the balls from the joint (Sec 5)

Fault finding - driveshafts

Vibration
☐ Worn joints
☐ Worn wheel or differential bearings

Noise on taking up drive
☐ Worn driveshaft splines
☐ Worn joints
☐ Loose driveshaft nut

Chapter 9 Braking system

For modifications, and information applicable to later models, see Supplement at end of manual

Contents

Degrees of difficulty

Easy, suitable for novice with little experience	**Fairly easy,** suitable for beginner with some experience	**Fairly difficult,** suitable for competent DIY mechanic	**Difficult,** suitable for experienced DIY mechanic	**Very difficult,** suitable for expert DIY or professional

Specifications

System type .... Front disc, rear drum, servo-assisted. Diagonally split hydraulic circuit, with proportioning valve. Automatic adjustment. Cable operated handbrake, acting on rear wheels

Brake fluid type/specification .... Hydraulic fluid to DOT 3

Front brake discs
Diameter .... 214.0 mm (8.43 m)
Maximum run-out .... 0.07 mm (0.0028 in)
Minimum thickness of disc .... 11.0 mm (0.433 in)

Pad friction material minimum thickness .... 2.0 mm (0.079 in)

Rear brakes
Drum inner diameter .... 180.0 mm (7.09 in)
Drum maximum inner diameter .... 181.0 mm (7.13 in)
Drum maximum run-out .... 0.05 mm (0.002 in)

Shoe friction material minimum thickness .... 1.5 mm (0.059 in)

Brake pedal
Free height:
   Manual transmission .... 203.0 to 213.0 mm (7.99 to 8.39 in)
   Automatic transmission .... 205.0 to 215.0 mm (8.07 to 8.46 in)
Stop lamp switch clearance .... 0 to 1.0 mm (0 to 0.04 in)
Depressed height (engine running, force of 110 lb/50 kg) .... At least 105 mm (4.13 in)

Torque wrench settings	**lbf ft**	**kgf m**
Pedal bracket to body	5.8 to 8.0	0.8 to 1.1
Servo unit to pedal bracket	5.8 to 8.0	0.8 to 1.1
Master cylinder to servo unit	5.8 to 8.0	0.8 to 1.1
Servo unit input rod locknut	12 to 16	1.6 to 2.2
Stop lamp switch locknut	9 to 11	1.2 to 1.5
Pressure regulating valve mounting bolt	2.9 to 3.6	0.4 to 0.5
Air bleed valves	5.1 to 6.5	0.7 to 0.9
Brake tube flare nut	11 to 13	1.5 to 1.8
Brake caliper lockpin bolts	29 to 36	4.0 to 5.0
Drum brake back plate bolts	25 to 33	3.4 to 4.6
Wheel cylinder to back plate	4.3 to 5.8	0.6 to 0.8

9

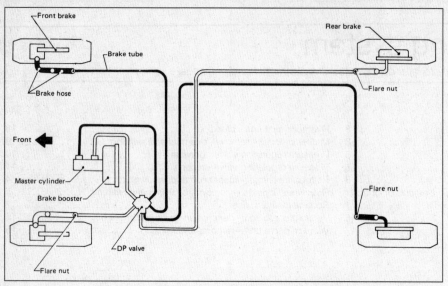

Fig. 9.1 Circuit diagram of the braking system (Sec 1)

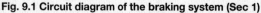

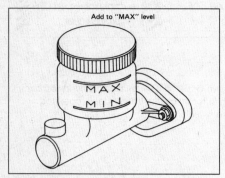

Fig. 9.2 Hydraulic fluid reservoir (Sec 2)

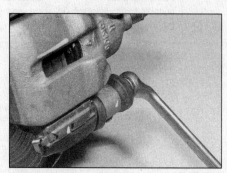

3.4 Unscrewing the caliper lower lockpin bolt

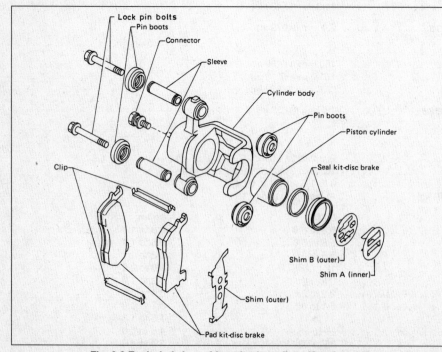

Fig. 9.3 Exploded view of front brake caliper (Sec 3 and 5)

1 General description

The braking system is of dual-line four wheel hydraulic type with servo assistance. The hydraulic circuit is split diagonally.

A pressure regulating valve is incorporated in the hydraulic circuit to prevent the rear wheels locking up during heavy applications of the brake pedal.

The handbrake operates mechanically on the rear wheels and incorporates an 'on' warning-lamp switch.

2 Routine maintenance

1 At the intervals indicated in the Routine maintenance schedule, check the front brake disc pads for wear and check the condition and security of the discs, calipers and all hydraulic hoses and lines. Check the footbrake pedal and handbrake for wear and correct adjustment. Check that the brake fluid level in the reservoir is at or near the maximum mark, and top up if necessary. Slight variations of level will occur according to the wear of the brake linings, however if the level drops considerably the complete hydraulic system should be checked for leaks.
2 At the intervals indicated in the Routine maintenance schedule, check the rear brake shoes and drums for wear.
3 At the intervals indicated in the Routine maintenance schedule, renew the brake fluid. Check the servo vacuum hoses, connections and non-return valve for operation, condition and security.

3 Disc pads -
inspection and renewal

1 Raise the front of the vehicle, support it securely, and remove the roadwheels.
2 Check the thickness of the friction material. This must not be less than that specified.
3 If the thickness is less than that figure the pads must be renewed as an axle set (four pads).
4 Unscrew and remove the caliper lockpin bolts (photo).
5 Remove the caliper and tie it up out of the way (photo).
6 Note that, on some models, the caliper will pivot around the upper lockpin bolt, so it need not be removed.
7 Take out the pads (photo).
8 The retaining springs can be prised out, if required (photo), also the piston shim (photo).
9 Brush away dirt and dust. *Avoid inhaling it*

3.5 Removing the caliper to gain access to the disc pads

3.7 Removing the disc pads

3.8A Removing the pad retaining spring . . .

as it is injurious to health. Do not depress the brake pedal while the pads are out of the caliper.

10 Smear a trace of high melting-point grease onto the pad backplates and then locate the pads (friction surface to disc) and the anti-squeal shim.

11 The piston must now be fully depressed into the cylinder in order to accommodate the increased thickness of the new pads. Depressing the piston will cause the fluid level to rise in the master cylinder reservoir, so anticipate this by syphoning out some fluid using a clean battery hydrometer or meat baster.

12 Refit the caliper, or swivel it down, and secure with the lockpin bolt(s). Tighten both lockpin bolts to the specified torque.

13 Renew the pads on the opposite side, refit the roadwheels and lower the vehicle.

14 Apply the brakes hard to position the pads against the disc.

15 Check the fluid level, and top up the reservoir if necessary.

3.8B . . . and piston shims

4.7A Removing a shoe steady spring cap . . .

purchased complete with linings. Attempting to reline old shoes yourself seldom proves satisfactory.

6 If the old shoes appear oil stained, this will be due to a leaking wheel cylinder (defective seal) or to a faulty bearing oil seal.

7 Remove the shoe steady springs. To do this, grip the edges of the spring cup with a pair of pliers (photo), depress it against pressure of the coil spring and turn it through 90°. Release the spring cup and take off the spring (photo).

---

4 Rear brake linings -
inspection and renewal

1 Chock the front wheels. Raise the rear of the vehicle, support it securely and remove the roadwheels. Release the handbrake.

2 Prise off the hub grease cap, extract the cotter pin, take off the nut retainer and unscrew and remove the nut.

3 Pull off the brake drum, catching the outboard bearing which will be displaced. It is possible for the brake drum to be held on the axle due to the brake shoes being locked in grooves which have been worn in the drum. Should this occur, prise the plug from the brake backplate and, using a screwdriver. Lift the toggle lever from the automatic adjuster star wheel and turn the star wheel to contract the shoes.

4 Inspect the shoe linings. If their thickness is less than that specified the shoes must be renewed as an axle set (four shoes).

5 It is recommended that new shoes are

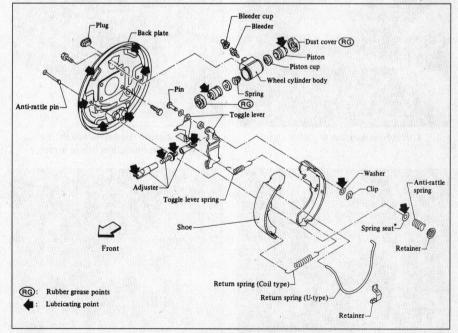

Fig. 9.4 Exploded view of rear brake (Sec 4)
Deleted after 1985

9

4.7B . . . and spring

4.9A Prise off the spring clip . . .

4.9B . . . followed by the shoe return spring

8 Note the location of the shoes on the backplate with respect to the leading and trailing ends, as the lining material does not cover both ends of the shoes equally. Also note the spring location points on the shoes.
9 Prise off the shoe return spring clip (photo), and then release the shoe return spring. This is a U-shaped spring and one arm should be gripped and levered towards the other arm to release it from the hole in the shoe (photos). It is recommended that a rag is placed over the spring to prevent it flying out accidently.
10 Pull the upper ends of the shoes apart and remove the adjuster strut (photo).
11 Unhook and remove the lower return spring and at the same time remove the shoes (photo). As they come away, disconnect the handbrake cable. Do not depress the brake pedal while the shoes are removed.

12 The handbrake and automatic adjuster toggle levers (photo) must be removed from the old shoe and fitted to the new one using the pin, washer, spring and U-shaped clip.
13 Apply a smear of grease to the shoe contact high spots on the brake backplate and to the ends of the wheel cylinder pistons.
14 Fit the new shoes by reversing the removal operations, but before fitting the automatic adjuster strut turn the star wheel to contact the strut fully.
15 Refit the brake drum and adjust the bearing preload, as described in Chapter 10.
16 Repeat the operations on the opposite brake.
17 Apply the handbrake several times to actuate the automatic adjuster and to position the shoe linings as close as possible to the drum.

18 Refit the roadwheels and lower the vehicle.

5 Caliper - removal, overhaul and refitting

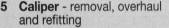

1 Raise the front of the vehicle and support it securely. Remove the roadwheel. Fit a suitable clamp to the flexible hydraulic hose or alternatively tighten the fluid reservoir filler cap onto a sheet of polythene to prevent the loss of brake fluid, then disconnect the hydraulic hose from the caliper by unscrewing the hollow bolt from the banjo union. Note the copper washers, one each side of the union.
2 Unscrew the caliper lockpin bolts and remove the caliper from the carrier bracket (photos).

4.10 Removing the adjuster strut

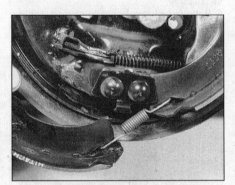

4.11 Releasing the lower return spring when removing the brake shoes

4.12 Showing the handbrake and automatic adjuster toggle lever and spring

5.2A Front brake caliper viewed from inside

5.2B Removing the lock pin bolts

5.2C The cylinder body comes away . . .

5.2D . . . leaving the pads in the caliper bracket

3 Clean away external dirt, *avoiding inhaling any dust*.

4 Remove the lockpin/sleeve boots and the sleeves.

5 Apply air pressure (such as is generated by a foot-operated pump) to the fluid entry hole in the caliper and eject the piston and the dust excluding seal.

6 Inspect the surfaces of the piston and cylinder bore. If pitted or corroded, renew it complete.

7 If the piston and cylinder are in good condition, use a sharp instrument to pick the piston seal out of its groove and discard it.

8 Wash all components in methylated spirit or clean hydraulic fluid and obtain a repair kit which will contain all the necessary new seals and other renewable items.

9 Commence reassembly by manipulating the new piston seal into its groove using the fingers only.

10 Push the piston part way into its bore, having first lubricated it with hydraulic fluid.

11 Fit the dust excluder to the piston. Push the piston fully into its bore.

12 Smear the sleeves with a little rubber grease and locate them in the caliper, along with their boots.

13 Connect the cylinder body to the caliper bracket then insert and tighten the lockpin bolts.

14 Connect the hydraulic hose to the caliper.

15 Bleed the hydraulic system as described in Section 13 then apply the brakes several times to position the pads on the disc.

6 Disc - inspection and renovation

1 Whenever the disc pads are inspected for wear, take the opportunity to examine the disc for deep scoring, grooving or cracks. Light scoring is normal.

2 The disc should not run out-of-true by more than the specified tolerance (see Specifications). This may be checked using a dial gauge or feeler blades between the disc and a fixed point as the disc is rotated.

3 Provided the thickness of the brake disc will not be reduced below the specified minimum,

a scored disc may be reground for further use.

4 To remove the disc, first unbolt the brake caliper from the caliper bracket and support it out of the way. Remove the disc pads. Pull the disc from the hub.

5 Clean the disc-to-hub mating faces before refitting the disc.

6 Push the disc into place and refit the brake pads and caliper.

7 Rear wheel cylinder - removal, overhaul and refitting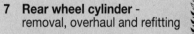

1 Remove the brake shoes, as described in Section 4.

2 Disconnect the hydraulic line from the cylinder.

3 Unbolt the wheel cylinder from the brake backplate (photo).

4 Clean away external dirt and pull off the dust covers.

5 Eject the internal components by tapping the cylinder on a block of wood or by applying air pressure from a foot-operated tyre pump to the fluid entry hole. Note which direction the seal lips face.

6 Examine the surface of the pistons and cylinder bore. If scored or corroded, renew the wheel cylinder complete.

7 If these components are in good condition, clean everything in either methylated spirits or hydraulic fluid, nothing else.

8 Discard the old seals and fit the new ones. These are contained in a repair kit, together with other renewable items.

9 Assemble the cylinder, applying hydraulic fluid as a lubricant as work progresses.

10 Refit the cylinder to the backplate, connect the fluid line and fit the brake shoes.

11 Bleed the brake circuit, as described in Section 13.

8 Brake drum - inspection and renovation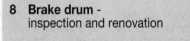

1 Whenever the brake drum is removed to inspect the wear of the shoe linings, take the

7.3 Rear wheel cylinder mounting bolt location

opportunity to examine the interior friction surface of the drum.

2 If it is badly scored or grooved it is possible to have it machined, provided the internal diameter will not exceed the maximum specified dimension (see Specifications).

9 Master cylinder - removal, overhaul and refitting

1 Disconnect the fluid lines from the master cylinder and allow the fluid to drain into a suitable container.

2 Unbolt the master cylinder from the front face of the vacuum servo unit. Disconnect the low fluid switch wiring where applicable.

3 Withdraw the master cylinder, taking care not to spill hydraulic fluid on the paintwork.

4 Clean away external dirt.

5 Prise off the end cap and be prepared for the primary piston to be ejected.

6 Where applicable slightly depress the secondary piston and unscrew and remove the stop screw.

7 Shake out the secondary piston. Note the direction in which all seal lips face.

8 Inspect the surfaces of the pistons and the cylinder bore. If they are scored or corroded, renew the master cylinder complete.

9 If these components are in good condition, clean them in either methylated spirit or hydraulic fluid, nothing else. Discard the seals, and obtain a repair kit which will contain all the necessary new seals and other renewable components. It should be noted that a primary piston of Nabco make is supplied as an assembly.

10 Manipulate the new seals into position with the fingers only.

11 Renew the reservoir seals. Where applicable, the fast-fill valve assembly can be removed after extracting the circlip. Renew the valve O-ring.

12 As reassembly progresses, lubricate the components with clean hydraulic fluid.

13 Insert the secondary piston spring and then the assembled secondary piston into the cylinder.

14 Where applicable, depress the secondary piston slightly with a rod and screw in the stop screw.

15 Fit the primary piston spring and the primary piston assembly and stake a new end cap into position.

16 Fit the master cylinder to the front face of the vacuum servo unit.

17 Reconnect the fluid pipelines and wiring as applicable.

18 Bleed the complete system, as described in Section 13, however if the fluid reservoir aperture in the master cylinder incorporates a fast-fill valve it is only necessary to bleed the master cylinder using the following procedure.

19 Top up the reservoir and keep it full during the procedure.

9

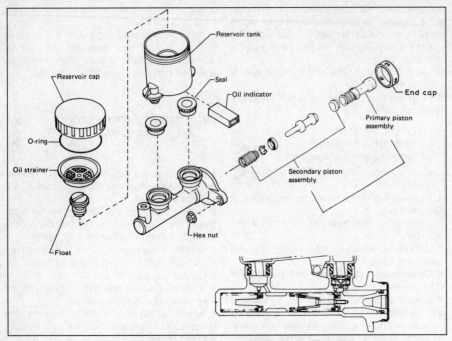

Fig. 9.5 Exploded view of master cylinder (Sec 9)

20 Disconnect the primary line (nearest the servo), place a container beneath the master cylinder, then fully depress the brake pedal.
21 Release the pedal and wait five seconds.
22 Repeat until clear fluid emerges from the master cylinder, then refit and tighten the primary line.
23 While an assistant depresses the brake pedal loosen the primary line union to bleed the remaining air then tighten the union. If air is still present release the pedal, wait five seconds, and bleed out the remaining air.
24 Bleed the secondary line in a similar manner but instead of waiting five seconds after releasing the pedal, wait twenty seconds.
25 After bleeding the master cylinder, depress the brake pedal and check that it feels firm. If it feels 'spongy', air must be present in another section of the hydraulic circuit and the complete system should then be bled.

10 Pressure regulating valve - general

1 This valve (also referred to as a dual proportioning valve) is located on the engine compartment rear bulkhead.
2 Any fault can only be rectified by renewal of the valve, no repair being possible.
3 Removal is simply a matter of disconnecting the fluid lines and the central anchor bolt. Note the reconnection points for the individual pipelines to facilitate refitting.
4 Bleed the system on completion (Section 13).

11 Pressure regulating valve - testing

1 Undo the unions to the valve and remove it.
2 Apply air pressure to the brake servo side of the valve by blowing into it.
3 If the valve does not open then it needs replacing.

12 Hydraulic pipes and hoses - general

1 Periodically inspect the condition of the flexible brake hoses. If they appear swollen, chafed or when bent double with the fingers tiny cracks are visible they must be renewed.
2 Always uncouple the rigid pipe from the flexible hose first, then release the end of the flexible hose from the support bracket (photo).

12.2 Flexible hose to rigid pipeline connection

To do this, pull out the lockplate using a pair of pliers.
3 Now unscrew the flexible hose from the caliper or connector. On calipers, a banjo type hose connector is used. When installing the hose, always use a new sealing washer.
4 When installation is complete, check that the flexible hose does not rub against the tyre or other adjacent components. Its attitude may be altered to overcome this by pulling out the clip at the support bracket and twisting the hose in the required direction by not more than one quarter turn.
5 Bleed the hydraulic system (Section 13).
6 At regular intervals wipe the steel brake pipes clean and examine them for signs of rust or denting caused by flying stones.
7 Examine the fit of the pipes in their insulated securing clips and bend the tongues of the clips if necessary to ensure a positive fit.
8 Check that the pipes are not touching any adjacent components or rubbing against any part of the vehicle. Where this is observed, bend the pipe gently away to clear.
9 Any section of pipe which is rusty or chafed should be renewed. Brake pipes are available to the correct length and fitted with end unions from most dealers and they can also be made to pattern by many accessory suppliers. When installing the new pipes use the old pipes as a guide to bending and do not make any bends sharper than is necessary.
10 The system will of course have to be bled when the circuit has been reconnected.

13 Hydraulic system - bleeding

1 The two independent hydraulic circuits are as follows:
(a) Front right-hand caliper and left rear wheel cylinder
(b) Front left-hand caliper and right rear wheel cylinder

On RHD models (a) is the primary circuit and (b) is the secondary circuit, however on LHD models the circuits are reversed. The *secondary* circuit should be bled first (rear wheel then front wheel), followed by the *primary* circuit (rear wheel then front wheel).
2 If the master cylinder or the pressure regulating valve has been disconnected and reconnected then the complete system (both circuits) must be bled.
3 If the component of only one circuit has been disturbed then only the particular circuit need be bled.
4 Owing to the design of the hydraulic system and pipeline layout, it will be found easier to bleed the system using a pressure bleeding kit. Unless the pressure bleeding method is being used, do not forget to keep the fluid level in the master cylinder reservoir topped-up to prevent air from being drawn into the

13.10 Bleed tube connected to front caliper bleed screw

system which would make any work done worthless.

5 Before commencing operations, check that all system hoses and pipes are in good condition with all unions tight and free from leaks.

6 Take great care not to allow hydraulic fluid to come into contact with the vehicle paintwork as it is an effective paint-stripper.

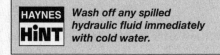

HAYNES HiNT *Wash off any spilled hydraulic fluid immediately with cold water.*

7 As the system incorporates a vacuum servo, destroy the vacuum by giving several applications of the brake pedal in quick succession.

Bleeding - two-man method

8 Gather together a clean glass jar and a length of rubber or plastic tubing which will be a tight fit on the brake bleed screws.

9 Engage the help of an assistant.

10 Push one end of the bleed tube onto the first bleed screw and immerse the other end in the glass jar which should contain enough hydraulic fluid to cover the end of the tube (photo).

11 Open the bleed screw one half turn and have your assistant depress the brake pedal fully then slowly release it. Tighten the bleed screw at the end of each pedal downstroke to obviate any chance of air or fluid being drawn back into the system.

12 Wait between 10 and 20 seconds then repeat the operations as many times as is necessary until clean hydraulic fluid, free from air bubbles can be seen coming through into the jar.

13 Tighten the bleed screw at the end of a pedal downstroke and remove the bleed tube. Bleed from the remaining screws in a similar way.

Bleeding - using one-way valve kit

14 There are a number of one-man, one-way brake bleeding kits available from motor accessory shops. It is recommended that one of these kits is used wherever possible, rather than just a tube, as it will greatly simplify the bleeding operation and reduce the risk of air

or fluid being drawn back into the system, quite apart from being able to do the work without the help of an assistant.

15 To use the kit, connect the tube to the bleed screw and open the screw one half turn.

16 Depress the brake pedal fully and slowly release it. The one-way valve in the kit will prevent expelled air from returning at the end of each pedal downstroke. Repeat this operation several times to be sure of ejecting all air from the system. Some kits include a translucent container which can be positioned so that the air bubbles can actually be seen being ejected from the system.

17 Tighten the bleed screw, remove the tube and repeat the operations in the remaining brakes.

18 On completion, depress the brake pedal. If it still feels spongy repeat the bleeding operations as air must still be trapped in the system.

Bleeding - using a pressure bleeding kit

19 These kits are available from motor accessory shops and are usually operated by air pressure from the spare tyre.

20 By connecting a pressurised container to the master cylinder fluid reservoir, bleeding is then carried out by simply opening each bleed screw in turn and allowing the fluid to run out, rather like turning on a tap, until no air is visible in the expelled fluid.

21 By using this method, the large reserve of hydraulic fluid provides a safeguard against air being drawn into the system during bleeding which often occurs if the fluid level in the reservoir is not maintained.

22 Pressure bleeding is particularly effective when bleeding 'difficult' systems or when bleeding the complete system at a time of routine fluid renewal.

All methods

23 When bleeding is completed, check and top up the fluid level in the master cylinder reservoir.

24 Check the feel of the brake pedal. If it feels at all spongy, air must still be present in the system and further bleeding is indicated. Failure to bleed satisfactorily after a reasonable repetition of the bleeding operations may be due to worn master cylinder seals.

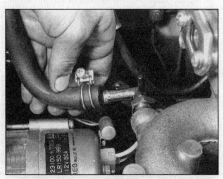

14.6 Vacuum servo hose at the intake manifold

25 Discard brake fluid which has been expelled. It is almost certain to be contaminated with moisture, air and dirt, making it unsuitable for further use. Clean fluid should always be stored in an airtight container as it absorbs moisture readily (hygroscopic) which lowers its boiling point and could affect braking performance under severe conditions.

14 Vacuum servo unit - description and maintenance

1 The vacuum servo unit is fitted into the brake hydraulic circuit in series with the master cylinder to provide assistance to the driver when the brake pedal is depressed. This reduces the effort required by the driver to operate the brakes under all braking conditions.

2 The unit operates by vacuum obtained from the induction manifold and comprises, basically, a booster diaphragm and non-return valve. The servo unit and hydraulic master cylinder are connected together so that the servo piston rod acts on the master cylinder pushrod: The driver's effort is transmitted through another pushrod to the servo unit piston and its built-in control system. The servo unit piston does not fit tightly into the cylinder, but has a strong diaphragm to keep its edges in constant contact with the cylinder wall, so assuring an airtight seal between two parts. The forward chamber is held under vacuum conditions created in the inlet manifold of the engine and, during periods when the brake pedal is not used, the controls open a passage to the rear chamber so placing it under vacuum conditions as well. When the brake pedal is depressed, the vacuum passage to the rear chamber is cut off and the chamber opened to atmospheric pressure. The consequent rush of air pushes the servo piston forward in the vacuum chamber and operates the main pushrod to the master cylinder.

3 The controls are designed so that assistance is given under all conditions and when the brakes are not required, vacuum in the rear chamber is established when the brake pedal is released. All air from the atmosphere entering the rear chamber is passed through a small air filter.

4 If the vacuum servo unit is thought to be faulty, have the operation of the brakes checked by an experienced Nissan mechanic; if the unit is faulty, it must be renewed, as no component parts are available with which it can be reconditioned.

5 It is emphasised that the servo unit assists in reducing the braking effort required at the foot pedal and, in the event of its failure, the hydraulic braking system is in no way affected except that the need for higher pedal pressure will be noticed.

6 Periodically inspect the condition of the vacuum hose in which is incorporated a non-return valve (photo). Renew the hose if it is split or has hardened.

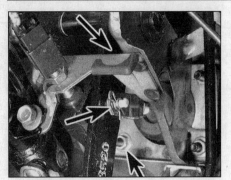

15.4 Showing brake pedal pushrod and vacuum servo unit mounting nuts (arrowed)

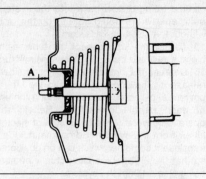

Fig. 9.6 Vacuum servo unit-to-master cylinder pushrod dimension (Sec 15)

A = 0.406 to 0.413 in (10.3 to 10.3 mm)

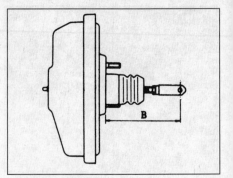

Fig. 9.7 Brake pedal-to-vacuum servo unit pushrod setting dimension (Sec 15)

B = 5.20 in (132.0 mm)

7 The non-return valve in the vacuum hose can be checked by disconnecting the hose (at either end) then sucking and blowing through it; air must be able to pass freely through the valve **out of** the servo, but **not into** the servo. If the valve is faulty (air either cannot flow out of the servo, or can leak back into the servo), it must be renewed.

8 If the valve is removed, note which way round it is fitted before slackening the retaining clamps, then ensure it is refitted as noted on removal (with its tapered end towards the manifold). Tighten the clamps securely, and check the valve's operation before fastening the hose.

15 Vacuum servo unit - removal and refitting

1 Remove the master cylinder, as described in Section 9.

2 Disconnect the vacuum hose from the servo unit.

3 Working inside the vehicle, disconnect the pushrod from the brake pedal.

4 Unbolt the brake servo unit from the bulkhead and remove it (photo).

5 Refitting is a reversal of removal, but carry out the following checks before actually installing it.

6 Check the projection (A) of the pushrod which enters the master cylinder (see Fig. 9.6). The projection is set in production and the threads locked, so if it does not conform to specifications renew the complete unit.

7 Now check the length (B) of the pushrod which connects with the brake pedal (see Fig. 9.7). Adjust if necessary by turning the clevis fork after having released the locknut.

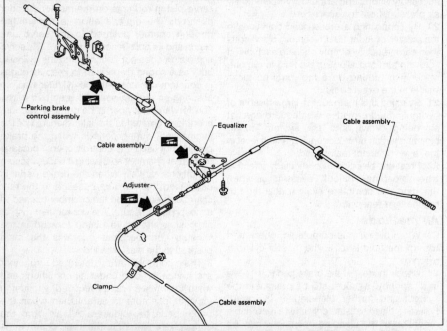

Fig 9.8 Diagrammatic view of handbrake cable assembly (Sec 16 and 17)

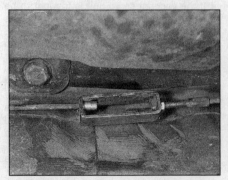

16.3A Handbrake cable adjustment point

16.3B Handbrake cable equaliser

16 Handbrake - adjustment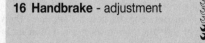

1 The handbrake is adjusted by the action of the rear shoe automatic adjuster and will require no further attention unless the cable stretches, normally only after a high mileage has been covered.

2 The handbrake should be fully applied with the rear wheels locked if the handbrake control lever is pulled up 6 to 7 notches (clicks) of the ratchet.

3 If the lever moves over an excessive number of notches, release the handbrake and adjust the cable by moving the locknuts at the cable stirrup which is adjacent to the equaliser under the vehicle (photos).

4 Keep the groove in the equaliser well greased at all times.

5 Working inside the vehicle, remove the centre console (see Chapter 11) and bend the handbrake warning switchplate down so that, with the ignition on, the warning lamp comes on when the lever is pulled up one notch.

17 Handbrake cables - renewal

Primary cable

1 Disconnect the secondary cable from the connecting stirrup which is adjacent to the equaliser under the vehicle (see photo 16.3B). Do this by unscrewing the locknuts and then passing the cable end fitting through the groove in the equaliser.

2 Working inside the vehicle, remove the centre console, as described in Chapter 11.

3 Disconnect the lead from the handbrake warning switch (photo).

4 Remove the seat belt stalks.

5 Remove the hand control lever fixing screws and the cable bush fixing screws (photo).

6 Withdraw the hand control lever with the primary cable attached into the vehicle interior.

7 To separate the primary cable from the control lever, drill out the connecting pin.

8 Refitting is a reversal of removal, a clevis pin and split pin are supplied for connecting the new cable to the hand control lever.

17.3 Handbrake warning switch lead

9 Adjust, as described in the preceding Section.

Secondary cable

10 Disconnect the cable at the stirrup which is adjacent to the equaliser under the vehicle.

11 Draw the longer cable through the groove in the equaliser.

12 Bend back the cable clips on the rear suspension arms and release the cables.

13 Raise the rear of the vehicle, support it securely and chock the front wheels. Remove both roadwheels and brake drums.

14 Unhook the handbrake cable and fittings from the handbrake lever on the brake shoes.

15 Remove both cables through the brake backplates.

16 Fit the new cables by reversing the removal operations. Apply grease to the cable friction surfaces.

17 Refit the brake drums and adjust the bearings, as described in Chapter 10.

17.5 Handbrake lever fixing bolts

18 Refit the roadwheels.

19 Adjust the cables, as described in the preceding Section.

18 Brake pedal - removal, refitting and adjustment

1 Working within the vehicle, under the facia panel, disconnect the pushrod from the brake pedal arm. Where necessary the lower facia panel and heater duct must be removed.

2 Prise the clip from the end of the pivot shaft, then unhook the return spring and withdraw the clutch pedal.

3 Slide the pivot shaft from the bracket and lower the brake pedal.

4 The pivot bushes may be renewed.

5 Refitting is a reversal of removal, but apply grease to the pivot shaft and bushes and check the pedal height as follows.

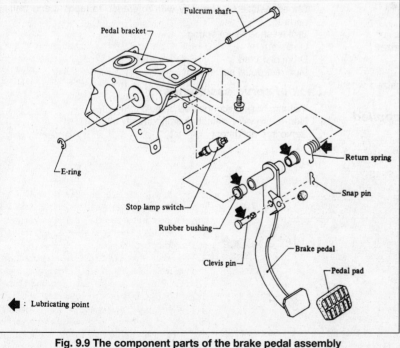

Fig. 9.9 The component parts of the brake pedal assembly (Sec 18)

Fulcrum shaft
Pedal bracket
E-ring
Stop lamp switch
Rubber bushing
Clevis pin
Return spring
Snap pin
Brake pedal
Pedal pad

◀ : Lubricating point

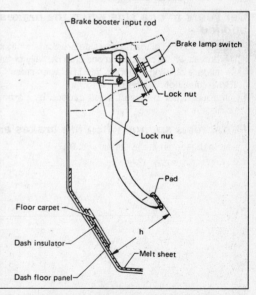

Fig. 9.10 Brake pedal height adjustment (Sec 18)

Brake booster input rod
Brake lamp switch
Lock nut
Lock nut
Pad
Floor carpet
Dash insulator
Dash floor panel
Melt sheet

h = 7.99 to 8.39 in (203.0 to 213.0 mm) *manual transmission*
h = 8.07 to 8.46 in (205.0 to 215.0 mm) *automatic transmission*
c = 0 to 0.04 in (0 to 1.0 mm)

9

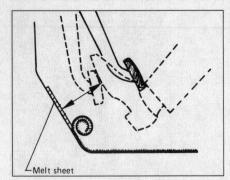

Fig. 9.11 Brake pedal depressed height (Sec 18)

Depressed height = 4.13in (105.0 mm) (under a force of 110 lbf (50 kgf). engine running)

18.7 Stop lamp switch locknut

6 Measure the distance from the upper surface of the brake pedal pad to the floor pan or steering hole cover as shown in Fig. 9.10. If the dimension is not as specified, loosen the locknut and turn the pedal pushrod as required making sure that the end of the rod protrudes into the clevis. Tighten the locknut after adjusting the rod.

7 With the pedal fully released check that the specified clearance exists between the pedal and stop-lamp switch. If not, loosen the locknut and adjust the stop-lamp as necessary, then tighten the locknut (photo).

8 Finally run the engine and check that the depressed height of the pedal is as specified (Fig. 9.11). If below the minimum amount check the hydraulic system for leaks or accumulation of air.

Fault finding - braking system

Pedal travels a long way before the brakes operate

☐ Incorrect pedal adjustment
☐ Brake shoes set too far from the drums (seized adjuster)

Stopping ability poor, even though pedal pressure is firm

☐ Linings, discs or drums badly worn or scored
☐ One or more wheel hydraulic cylinders seized, resulting in some brake
☐ shoes not pressing against the drums (or pads against disc)
☐ Brake linings contaminated with oil
☐ Wrong type of linings fitted (too hard)
☐ Brake shoes wrongly assembled
☐ Servo unit not functioning

Car veers to one side when the brakes are applied

☐ Brake pads or linings on one side are contaminated with oil
☐ Hydraulic wheel cylinder on one side partially or fully seized
☐ A mixture of lining materials fitted between sides
☐ Brake disc not matched
☐ Unequal wear between sides caused by partially seized wheel cylinders

Pedal feels spongy when the brakes are applied

☐ Air is present in the hydraulic system

Pedal feels springy when the brakes are applied

☐ Brake linings not bedded in (after fitting new ones)
☐ Master cylinder or brake backplate mounting bolts loose
☐ Severe wear in brake drums causing distortion when brakes are applied
☐ Discs out of true

Pedal travels right down with little or no resistance and brakes are virtually non-operative

☐ Leak in hydraulic system resulting in lack of pressure for operating wheel cylinders
☐ If no signs of leakage are apparent the master cylinder internal seals are failing to sustain pressure

Binding, juddering, overheating

☐ One or a combination of reasons given above
☐ Shoes installed incorrectly with reference to leading and trailing ends
☐ Broken shoe return spring
☐ Disc worn
☐ Drum distorted
☐ Incorrect pedal adjustment

Lack of servo assistance

☐ Vacuum hose disconnected or leaking
☐ Non-return valve defective or incorrectly fitted
☐ Servo internal defect

Chapter 10 Suspension and steering

For modifications, and information applicable to later models, see Supplement at end of manual

Contents

Degrees of difficulty

Easy, suitable for novice with little experience	**Fairly easy,** suitable for beginner with some experience	**Fairly difficult,** suitable for competent DIY mechanic	**Difficult,** suitable for experienced DIY mechanic	**Very difficult,** suitable for expert DIY or professional

Specifications

Front suspension

Type .... MacPherson type strut and transverse links
Hub bearing turning effort .... 3.5 to 12.3 lbf (1.6 to 5.6 kgf)

Rear suspension

Type .... Dead axle with four link location, coil spring and telescopic dampers

Steering

Type .... Rack and pinion with universally jointed column. Optional power assistance

Steering angles:
  Camber (non-adjustable) .... -0°25' to + 1°05'
  Castor(non-adjustable) .... + 1°30' to + 3°00'
  Kingpin inclination(non-adjustable) .... + 12°25' to + 13°55'
  Toe-in .... 2.0 to 4.0 mm (0.08 to 0.16 in)
Steering ratio:
  Manual steering .... 18.9 : 1
  Power-assisted steering .... 16.2 : 1
Number of turns lock-to-lock:
  Manual steering 3.5
  Power-assisted steering 3.0
System fluid capacity:
  Power-assisted steering .... 1.76 pt (1.0 litre)
Power-assisted steering fluid type .... Dexron II type ATF

Roadwheels

Type .... Pressed steel or light alloy
Size:
  Pressed steel .... 4J-12 or 4.50B-12
  Light alloy 4 1/2J-12

10

Tyres

Size .... 145 SR 12 or 155 SR 12
Pressures .... Refer to tyre pressure plate on vehicle

Torque wrench settings

	lbf ft	kgf m
Front suspension		
Strut piston rod self-locking nut	23 to 31	3.2 to 4.3
Strut upper mounting bolts	19 to 22	2.6 to 3.1
Strut-to-knuckle	58 to 72	8 to 10
Lower balljoint to transverse link	36 to 43	5 to 6
Transverse link front bush	65 to 80	9 to 11
Transverse link rear bush	27 to 35	3.7 to 4.8
Steering tie-rod:		
Lock nut	27 to 34	3.7 to 4.7
Stud nut	22 to 29	3.0 to 4.0
Rear suspension		
Shock absorber upper mounting	14 to 19	1.9 to 2.6
Shock absorber lower mounting bolt	35 to 44	4.9 to 6.1
Brake back plate attachment bolts	25 to 33	3.4 to 4.6
Roadwheel nuts	58 to 72	8.0 to 10.0
Wheel hub nut (preliminary setting - see text)	29 to 33	4.0 to 4.5
Steering		
Steering wheel nut	29 to 40	4.0 to 5.5
Steering shaft lower pinch-bolt:		
M10 size	23 to 31	3.2 to 4.3
M8 size	17 to 22	2.4 to 3.0
Lower bracket to pedal bracket	6.5 to 10.1	0.9 to 1.4
Steering column clamp to body	6.5 to 10.1	0.9 to 1.4
Steering gear rack mounting brackets	43 to 58	6.0 to 8.0
Fluid pump to engine mounting	23 to 31	3.2 to 4.3
Belt tensioning bolt locknut	6.5 to 8.7	0.9 to 1.2
Pulley locknut	23 to 31	3.2 to 4.3
High pressure pipe connections	22 to 36	3.0 to 5.0
Low pressure pipe connections	0.7 to 1.4	0.1 to 0.2

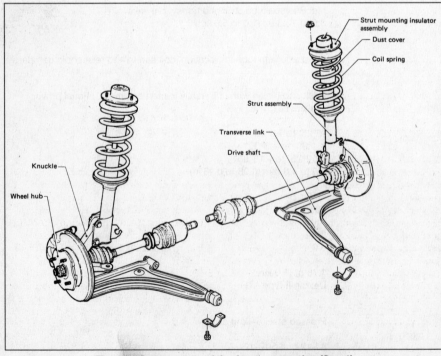

Fig. 10.1 Components of the front suspension (Sec 1)

Strut mounting insulator assembly
Dust cover
Coil spring
Strut assembly
Transverse link
Drive shaft
Knuckle
Wheel hub

1 General description

Front suspension is by MacPherson type strut and transverse link.

Rear suspension is by dead axle with four link location, coil springs and double-acting telescopic dampers.

Steering is by rack and pinion, with a universally jointed steering column.

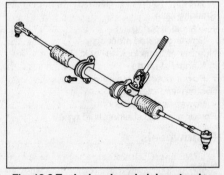

Fig. 10.2 Typical rack and pinion steering assembly (Sec 1)

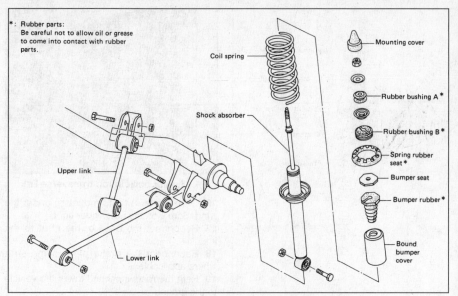

*: Rubber parts:
Be careful not to allow oil or grease to come into contact with rubber parts.

Coil spring

Shock absorber

Upper link

Lower link

Mounting cover

Rubber bushing A *

Rubber bushing B *

Spring rubber seat *

Bumper seat

Bumper rubber *

Bound bumper cover

Fig. 10.3 Components of the rear suspension (Sec 1)

3.5 Remove the two pinch-bolts

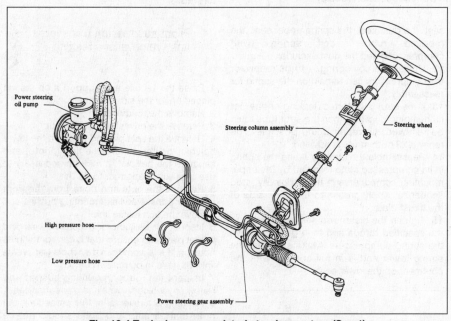

Power steering oil pump

Steering column assembly

Steering wheel

High pressure hose

Low pressure hose

Power steering gear assembly

Fig. 10.4 Typical power-assisted steering system (Sec 1)

3.6 Showing top of shock absorber mounting in engine compartment

3.7 Looking under the wing at the strut assembly

Front and rear wheels run on taper roller bearings, but only the rear bearings are adjustable in service, the front bearings having preload applied to them by means of spacers of different thicknesses.

2 Routine maintenance

1 At the intervals indicated in the Routine maintenance schedule, check the power steering fluid level in the reservoir and top up as necessary. Also check the power steering hoses for conditions and security.

2 At the intervals indicated in the Routine maintenance schedule, check the power steering pump drivebelt for condition and tension .

3 At the intervals indicated in the Routine maintenance schedule, check the steering and suspension components including all balljoints for excessive wear, adjust the rear wheel bearings and check the front wheel bearings for wear and leakage of grease. Check, and if necessary, adjust the front wheel alignment. Change the roadwheel positions and have them balanced.

4 If the car is operated under extreme conditions the maintenance intervals should be more frequent, and the mileages reduced accordingly.

3 Front suspension strut - removal, overhaul and refitting

10

1 Raise the front of the vehicle and support it securely on axle stands placed under the side-members.

2 Remove the roadwheel.

3 Disconnect the hydraulic brake pipe from the suspension strut where applicable.

4 Support the suspension lower arm on a jack.

5 Unscrew the two pinch-bolts which hold the base of the suspension strut (photo).

6 Working at the top of the inner wing within the engine compartment, unscrew and remove the two nuts which secure the strut top mounting (photo).

7 Support the strut assembly and withdraw it from under the ring (photo).

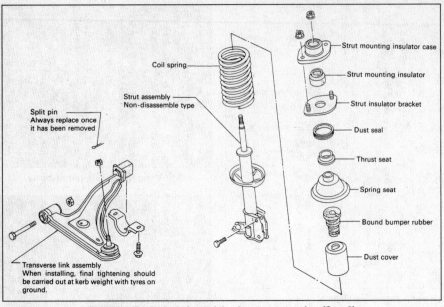

4.4 Lower balljoint on transverse link

16 Offer the strut to its mounting under the wing. Screw on the nuts finger tight.
17 Reconnect the base of the strut to the knuckle.
18 Reconnect the brake pipe to the strut where applicable.
19 Refit the roadwheel and lower the vehicle to the ground.
20 Tighten all nuts and bolts to the specified torques.

Fig. 10.5 Exploded view of the front suspension (Sec 3)

8 Unless coil spring compressors are available do not carry out any further dismantling.
9 Where compressors are available (they can be purchased at most motor accessory stores) fit them to the strut coil spring and compress the spring just sufficiently to be able to turn the strut upper mounting insulator by hand.
10 Unscrew the self-locking nut from the top of the piston rod. Flats are machined on the rod so that an open-end spanner can be used to prevent the rod rotating while the unit is unscrewed.
11 Take off the mounting insulator, the thrust

seat, the dust seal, the spring upper seat, the rebound rubber, coil spring (with compressors) and the dust excluder.
12 Unless the coil spring is to be renewed, the compressors can remain on the spring for reassembly.
13 If the strut is distorted, leaking or has lost its damping qualities, then the strut tube must be renewed, no repair being possible. The renewal of both struts is advised.
14 Reassemble the strut by fitting the spring in its compressed state followed by the upper mounting components in their originally fitted sequence. Apply grease to the underside of the thrust plate.
15 Tighten the piston rod self-locking nut to the specified torque and then gently remove the spring compressors. Make sure that the spring lower end is in full contact with the abutment on the lower seat.

4 Front suspension transverse link - removal and refitting

1 Raise the vehicle and support it on stands placed under the side-members.
2 Remove the roadwheel.
3 Remove the driveshaft (Chapter 8).
4 Remove the split pin and nut from the lower balljoint on the transverse link (photo) and separate the balljoint. It may be necessary to use a balljoint separator to do this.
5 Remove the nuts and bolts from the front and rear transverse link mounting bushes and remove the transverse link.
6 Inspect the balljoint for excessive wear and lateral play, and ensure that it can rotate in its housing. If it is worn then the whole transverse link will have to be renewed.
7 Inspect the rubber mounting bushes and renew any which show signs of wear or age.
8 Refitting is a reversal of this procedure, but note that all nuts and bolts should not be tightened to their final torque until the weight of the vehicle is back on the suspension units.

5 Front axle wheel bearings and knuckle assembly - removal and refitting

1 Remove the driveshaft as described in Chapter 8.
2 With the steering tie-rod disconnected, the lower balljoint separated and the brake caliper tied out of the way, the knuckle and bearing assembly can now be removed from the bottom of the MacPherson strut and transferred to the bench.
3 Prise out the grease seals. Use new seals on reassembly.

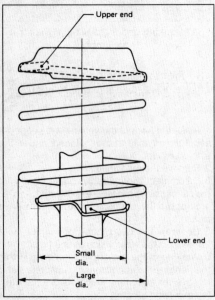

Fig. 10.6 Correct location of front coil spring (Sec 3)

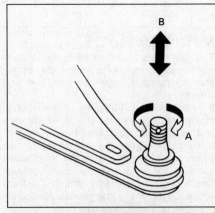

Fig. 10.7 Lower balljoint inspection (Sec 4)

A = Turning torque 4.3 to 30.0 lbf in (5.0 to 35 kgf cm)
B = Axial play (no tolerance allowed)

4 Use pullers to remove the inner and outer bearing races.

5 Inspect the bearings for wear, pitting or scoring and check that they run freely, without any 'rattle'.

6 Bearings should be renewed as a set of inner and outer.

7 Check the hub for any signs of cracking, and inspect the brake disc rotor as described in Chapter 9.

8 Coat each bearing with lithium based grease before pressing them back into the hub using a suitably sized mandrel.

9 Smear some grease onto the grease seals and fit them to the inner and outer bearings, noting that the spring tensioned lip faces outwards.

10 Fit the spacer. If the spacer is being renewed, then it should bear the same identification mark as the old one.

11 If a new knuckle is being fitted, then the size of spacer to use will have to be determined as follows.

12 To calculate the thickness of spacer to use, measure the distance between the inner faces of the two bearings (Fig. 10.13). From this figure subtract 0.0469 in (1.19 mm). The result will be the size of spacer to use. Spacers are available in varying thicknesses from your Nissan dealer.

13 To ensure correct bearing preload on fitment of a new spacer, the turning movement of the hub should be measured after it has been reassembled.

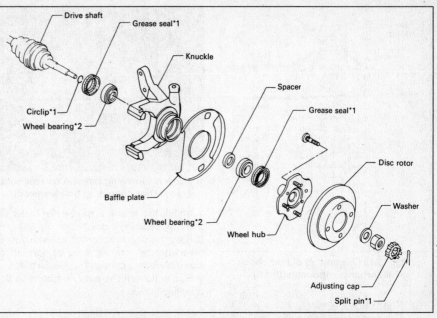

Fig. 10.8 Exploded view of front wheel hub and knuckle (Sec 5)

14 With the spacer fitted, insert the driveshaft outer joint into the knuckle, then fit and tighten the hub nut to the specified torque.

15 Refer to Fig. 10.14 and attach a spring balance to one of the wheel nut studs. Pull the spring balance, gently, at a tangent. The figure on the spring balance should be noted and compared with the figure given in the Specifications. If the bearing preload is too low, fit a thinner spacer, and if it is too high fit a thicker one. Repeat this operation until the correct preload is obtained.

16 Complete reassembly by reversing the removal operations.

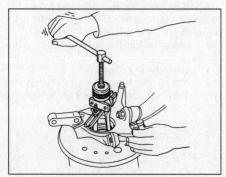

Fig. 10.9 Using a puller to remove the outer bearing (Sec 5)

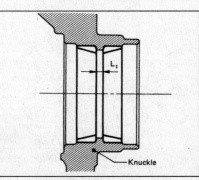

Fig. 10.10 Using a puller to remove the inner bearing (Sec 5)

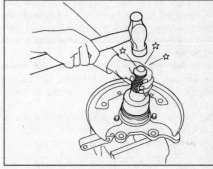

Fig. 10.11 Installing the inner bearing (Sec 5)

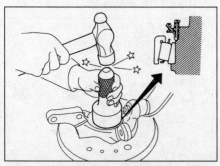

Fig. 10.12 Installing the inner bearing (Note the inset which shows fitment of grease seal) (Sec 5)

Fig. 10.13 Measuring the distance between the two inner faces of the bearings (Sec 5)

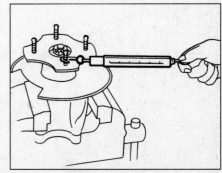

Fig. 10.14 Measuring the torque required to turn wheel hub (Sec 5)

10

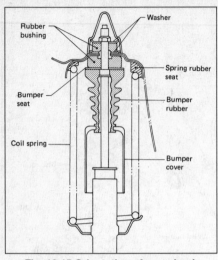

Fig. 10.15 Orientation of rear shock absorber components(Sec 6)

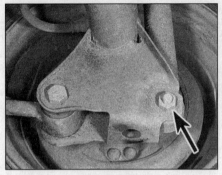

6.3 Lower mounting bracket on rear shock absorber (mounting bolt arrowed)

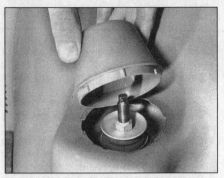

6.4 Top mounting of rear shock absorber

7.6 Typical transverse link mounting

6 Rear shock absorber - removal and refitting

1 Support the rear of the vehicle on axle stands placed under the side-members.
2 Gently jack up the axle tube with a jack positioned under the shock absorber lower mounting, until the weight of the axle is just supported.
3 Remove the nut and bolt from the lower mounting bracket (photo).
4 From inside the luggage compartment, remove the plastic dome (it is a bayonet type fix) to expose the top mounting (photo). Undo the nut and remove the washer and rubber bushing.
5 Lower the jack from under the lower mounting, at the same time supporting the suspension unit. When it comes free remove it from the vehicle.
6 Inspect the coil spring for cracks or deformation, and all rubber parts for hardening or cracking and general wear.

7 Check the shock absorber for leaks and damage, ensuring it is not bent.
8 Refit the shock absorber assembly in the reverse order, making sure all parts of the assembly locate correctly with each other.
9 Finally tighten the nuts and bolts to their specified torque.

7 Rear axle tube - removal and refitting

1 Raise the rear of the vehicle and support it on axle stands placed under the side-members.
2 Remove the roadwheels.
3 Remove the shock absorbers from both sides as described in Section 6.
4 Remove the rear brake drum and brake assembly as described in Chapter 9, and disconnect the hydraulic brake lines and handbrake cable.
5 Leave the backplates attached, and protect the stub axles from damage during the removal operation. If the threads of the stub axle are damaged, the whole axle must be renewed.
6 Support the axle at both ends, then undo the bolts securing the axle to the upper and lower transverse links (photo).

7 Lower the axle and remove it from under the vehicle.
8 Inspect the axle for obvious signs of damage and for cracks, especially around the welded brackets for the transverse links.
9 Inspect the bushes of the transverse links, renewing any that are worn or perished.
10 Inspect the transverse links for any signs of bending.
11 Inspect the stub axles.
12 Refitting the axle is a reversal of this procedure. Refer to Chapter 9 for reassembly of, and bleeding the brake system.

8 Rear wheel bearings - removal and refitting

1 Raise the vehicle onto axle stands positioned under the side-members, and remove the rear wheels.

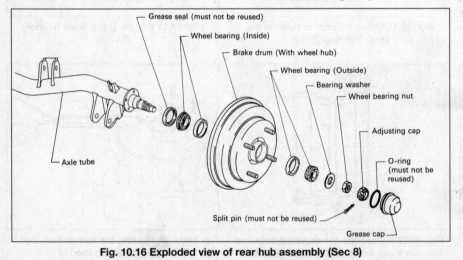

Fig. 10.16 Exploded view of rear hub assembly (Sec 8)

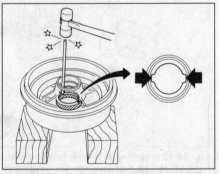

Fig. 10.17 Removing the rear bearings (Sec 8)

8.2 Removing the grease cap from the rear hub . . .

8.3 . . . and the spacer and taper bearing

8.4 Brake backplate mounting bolts

2 Remove the grease cap (photo), the split pin and nut retainer, and undo the nut.

3 The spacer and outer bearing race may now be lifted out (photo), or if it is stuck it will come out as the drum is removed. Be ready to catch the bearing.

4 With the drum removed if necessary, the brake back plate may be removed by disconnecting the hydraulic lines and handbrake cable and removing the four bolts securing the back plate to the axle (photo).

5 The inner bearing race will still be located in the drum. Remove the inner grease seal by prising it out then support the drum on blocks and tap out the inner bearing, using the cut outs in the drum.

6 Inspect the bearings for cracking, pitting, 'rattle', roughness or out of round and renew as necessary. The bearings should always be renewed as a pair, inner and outer.

7 Inspect the drum for cracks and scoring. Refer to Chapter 9, Specifications for resurfacing tolerances.

8 As examined before, if there are any defects in the stub axle, the whole axle tube will have to be replaced.

9 Press new bearings into the drum using a mandrel of suitable size.

10 Fit a new inner bearing, coating each liberally with high melting point lithium based grease.

11 Install the drum, then the outer bearing and washer, followed by the nut, finger tight

only until the adjustment procedure described in Section 9 has been carried out.

12 Complete reassembly, connecting up the brake line and cable if they were removed. Bleed the rear brakes with reference to Chapter 9.

13 When installing the grease cap, always use a new O-ring seal.

14 Refit the roadwheels and remove the vehicle from the axle stands.

9 Rear wheel bearings - adjustment

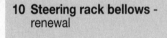

1 Raise the vehicle onto axle stands placed under the side-members, and remove the rear wheels.

2 Remove the grease cap and split pin and nut retainer.

3 Tighten the wheel hub nut to the prescribed torque.

4 Turn the hub in both directions several times to seat the bearings.

5 Re-tighten the wheel bearing nut to the specified torque.

6 Loosen the nut through 90°.

7 Fit the nut retainer, aligning the split pin holes. It is permissible to tighten the wheel hub nut by as much as 15° to achieve this. *Caution: do not overtighten, or wheel bearing seizure may occur.*

8 Check that the drum/hub turns smoothly without drag. There must be no endfloat. If there is, and the adjustment has been made correctly, suspect worn bearings.

9 Bend the ends of the split pin around the nut retainer.

10 Fill the grease cap one third full with multi-purpose grease, check that the O-ring is in good condition and tap the cup squarely into position.

10 Steering rack bellows - renewal

1 The steering rack bellows should be inspected periodically for splits. Have an assistant turn the steering to full lock while doing this, otherwise the split will not be immediately apparent.

2 Unscrew the nut from the balljoint taper pin and, using an extractor, separate the balljoint from the eye of the steering arm (photos).

3 Release the locknut and then unscrew the balljoint from the tie-rod, counting the number of turns required to remove it (photo).

4 Release the bellows securing clips and pull the bellows from the rack housing and off the tie-rod (photo).

5 If the bellows have been split for some time and dirt has entered, wipe away all the old lubricant and smear the rack (extended) and the rack end balljoint with a suitable grease.

10

10.2A Steering rod balljoint split pin and nut

10.2B Using a balljoint separator

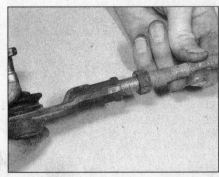

10.3 Removing the balljoint from the steering rod

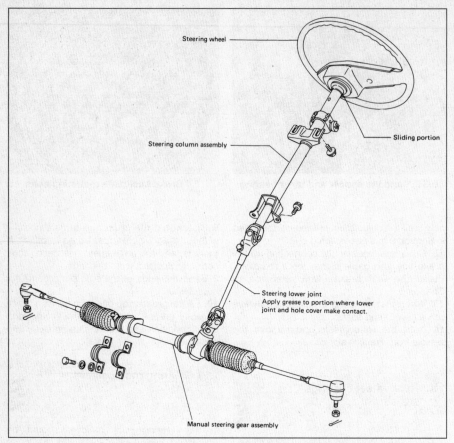

Steering wheel

Steering column assembly

Sliding portion

Steering lower joint
Apply grease to portion where lower
joint and hole cover make contact.

Manual steering gear assembly

Fig. 10.18 Manual steering column and rack (Sec 10)

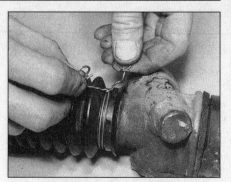

10.4 Bellows securing clips

3 Extract the split pins and unscrew the castellated nuts from the tie-rod end balljoints. With a suitable tool, disconnect the balljoints from the steering arms on the knuckles.

4 Support the transmission on a jack with a block of wood as an insulator.

5 Disconnect the exhaust downpipe from the manifold and also disconnect the exhaust system bracket just ahead of the steering gear.

6 Unbolt and remove the engine rear mounting.

7 Unscrew and remove the bolts from the steering gear mounting clamps.

8 Remove the steering shaft lower joint, as described in Section 18.

9 Withdraw the steering gear from under the front wing, moving it in the direction of the arrow as shown in the diagram (Fig. 10.19).

10 Refitting is a reversal of removal.

11 Fill and bleed the system, as described in Section 15 and finally check the front wheel alignment as described in Section 21.

6 Slide on the new bellows and fit the securing clips.

7 Screw the balljoint onto the tie-rod by the same number of turns as was recorded at removal and tighten the locknut. Reconnect the balljoint to the steering arm of the stub axle carrier, use a new split pin.

8 Check the front wheel alignment by referring to Section 21.

11 Manual steering rack -
removal and refitting

1 Raise the front of the vehicle and support it securely using axle stands under the side-members. Apply the handbrake and remove the front roadwheels.

2 Disconnect both tie-rod balljoints from the steering arms on the knuckles.

3 Remove the steering shaft lower joint, as described in Section 18.

4 Unscrew the rack housing mounting nuts and lift the steering gear from the bulkhead (photo).

5 Refitting is a reversal of removal.

6 Tighten all nuts and bolts to the specified torques, and finally check the front wheel alignment as described in Section 21.

12 Power-assisted steering
gear - removal and refitting

1 Raise the front of the vehicle and support it on axle stands by the side-members. Apply the handbrake and remove the front roadwheels.

2 Disconnect the hydraulic hose clamp at the pinion housing on the steering gear to provide access to the union nut on the pipeline. Unscrew the union nut and allow the fluid to drain into a suitable container.

11.4 Steering rack mounting bolts (arrowed)

13 Power-assisted steering
pump - removal and refitting

1 Release the pump drivebelt adjuster link lockbolt and turn the adjuster bolt to release the tension on the belt. Slip the belt from the pulleys.

2 Disconnect the pressure hose from the

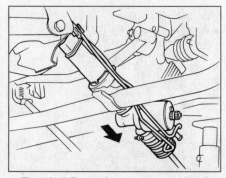

Fig. 10.19 Removing a power-assisted steering rack (Sec 12)

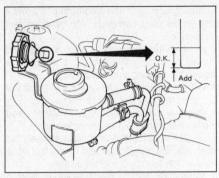

Fig. 10.20 Checking power-assisted steering fluid level (Sec 15)

16.2 Removing the steering wheel cover. Note the horn wire

16.3 Steering wheel retaining nut

pump by unscrewing the banjo union bolt. Allow the fluid to drain into a suitable container.

3 Take off the return hose clamp.

4 Unbolt and remove the pump.

5 If the connecting lines are to be removed, unscrew the union nuts and hose clips.

6 Refitting and reconnection are reversals of disconnection and removal.

7 Tension the pump drivebelt, as described in Chapter 2.

8 Fill and bleed the system, as described in Section 15.

14 Steering gear - overhaul

1 It is not recommended that the manual or power-assisted steering gear or the power steering pump are overhauled.

2 Due to the precise nature of the assembly work and the need for special tools for measuring turning torque, it is preferable to purchase a new or factory-reconditioned unit when the original one becomes worn or develops a fault.

15 Power-assisted steering - fluid level and bleeding

1 At the intervals specified in Section 2 unscrew the power steering pump filler cap when the engine and pump are cold and observe the level of fluid on the dipstick. Add fluid of the correct type to bring the fluid level between the low and high marks.

2 If the system pipelines have been disconnected or new components fitted then, after reassembly, the system must be bled.

3 Fill the pump reservoir with fluid.

4 Raise the front of the vehicle until the roadwheels are off the floor.

5 Turn the steering from lock to lock ten times and then top up the fluid in the reservoir so that it is at the correct level on the dipstick.

6 Start the engine and turn the steering wheel to left and right lock until the fluid becomes hot to touch (60 to 80°C - 140 to 176°F).

7 Switch off the engine and top up the reservoir, if necessary.

8 Start the engine and run for five seconds. Switch off and top up the fluid, if necessary.

9 If air is still present in the system, which will be indicated by the steering wheel being stiff to turn, repeat the operations as previously described. When turning the steering from lock to lock during bleeding, do not hold it at full lock for more than fifteen seconds while the engine is running.

16 Steering wheel - removal and refitting

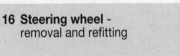

1 Set the front roadwheels in the straight-ahead position, disconnect the battery.

2 Pull the cover from the centre of the steering wheel by gripping the top of it. If the cover has not been removed since new it will require a firm pull to remove it (photo). Disconnect the horn wire.

3 Hold the steering wheel stationary and unscrew the retaining nut (photo).

4 Mark the steering wheel in relation to the inner column then remove it. If anything more than a gentle thump with the palms of the hands is required to remove the wheel from the splined steering shaft, a puller will have to be used. Tapped holes are incorporated in the steering wheel hub for attaching a puller.

5 Apply a little grease to the shaft splines and petroleum jelly to the horn contact ring before refitting the steering wheel. Make sure that the

previously made marks are correctly aligned. Tighten the nut to the specified torque.

6 Refit the cover and re-connect the battery lead.

17 Steering lock - removal and refitting

1 Remove the steering wheel as described in Section 16.

2 Remove the column shrouds (photo).

3 Disconnect the wiring from the ignition switch.

4 The steering lock is secured with two cross-head screws and two shear type screws (photo). Unscrew the cross-head screws and drill out the shear type screws. Remove the steering lock.

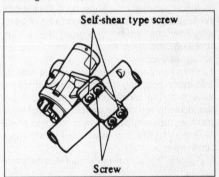

Self-shear type screw

Screw

Fig. 10.21 Correct location of steering column lock screws (Sec 17)

10

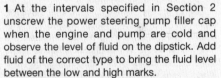

17.2 Steering column shrouds

17.4 Steering column lock securing screws

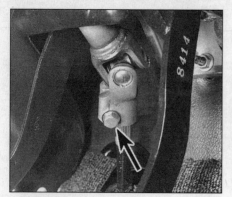

18.2A Steering column lower pinch bolt (arrowed)

5 To refit the lock align it with the hole in the outer column, locate the clamp plate, and insert the screws finger tight.

6 Check that the lock operates correctly then tighten the cross-head screws and tighten the shear type screws until the heads break off.

7 Re-connect the wiring then refit the shrouds and steering wheel.

18 Steering shaft lower joint - removal and refitting

1 To provide better access remove the steering column aperture dust excluding cover from the bulkhead. Set the steering in the straight-ahead position.

2 Unscrew the pinch-bolts from both universally-jointed couplings, prise the jaws of the couplings open just enough to be able to withdraw the lower joint from the upper coupling and then from the steering gear pinion shaft (photos).

3 When refitting the joint, connect it first to the upper coupling and then to the pinion. Note that the pinch-bolt cut-out must be aligned with the upper coupling clamp jaws and that the jaws of the lower coupling must be aligned with the mark on the steering pinion spacer.

4 Tighten the pinch-bolts to the specified torque.

19.7 Steering column upper mounting bracket bolts

18.2B Undoing the pinch-bolt on steering gear input pinion

19 Steering column - removal and refitting

1 Remove the steering wheel (Section 16).

2 Remove the shaft lower joint (Section 18).

3 Remove the shrouds from the upper steering column. Disconnect the battery.

4 Extract the screws, disconnect the wiring harness plugs and remove the steering column switch.

5 Remove the heater ducts.

6 Remove the nuts from the column dust excluder on the bulkhead.

7 Unscrew the upper and lower column mounting bracket bolts and withdraw the column from under the facia panel. Recover the spacer plates noting their location (photo).

8 Check the column length L (Fig. 10.22). If it does not conform, renew the assembly.

Refitting

9 Offer the column into position making sure that the sliding plates are correctly located. Fit the bolts finger tight at this stage.

10 Fit the lower joint (Section 18). again leaving the pinch-bolts finger tight.

11 Check that none of the brackets or couplings are under stress and then tighten the column bolts to the specified torque.

20 Steering column - overhaul

1 The steering column shaft can be removed from the column jacket tube if the bearings

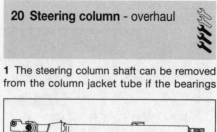

Fig. 10.22 Steering column length (Sec 19)

L = 22.57 to 22.63 in (573.2 to 574.8 mm)

require greasing. If the bearings are worn a new jacket tube, complete with bearings, will be required.

2 Remove the steering column, as described in the preceding Section, and unlock the steering lock using the ignition key.

3 With a pair of circlip pliers, extract the circlip from the upper end of the column.

4 Remove the plain and wave washers and then pull the shaft out of the jacket tube.

5 Grease the bearings and bushes, push the shaft into the jacket tube and locate the wave washer followed by the plain washer.

6 Make sure that the circlip which is located below the upper bearings, and the one which is to be fitted above the plain washer both have their rounded edges towards the bearing. New circlips should always be used at reassembly.

21 Steering angles and front wheel alignment - general

1 Accurate front wheel alignment is essential to good steering and for even tyre wear. Before considering the steering angles, check that the tyres are correctly inflated, that the front wheels are not buckled, the hub bearings are not worn and that the steering linkage is in good order, without slackness or wear at the joints.

2 Wheel alignment consists of four factors:

Camber, is the angle at which the roadwheels are set from the vertical when viewed from the front or rear of the vehicle. Positive camber is the angle (in degrees) that the wheels are tilted outwards at the top from the vertical.

Castor, is the angle between the steering axis and a vertical line when viewed from each side of the vehicle. Positive castor is indicated when the steering axis is inclined towards the rear of the vehicle at its upper end.

Steering axis inclination, is the angle, when viewed from the front or rear of the vehicle, between the vertical and an imaginary line drawn between the upper and lower front suspension strut mountings.

Toe is the amount by which the distance between the front inside edges on the roadwheel rim differs from that between the rear inside edges. If the distance between the front edges is less than that at the rear, the wheels are said to toe-in. If the distance between the front inside edges is greater than that at the rear, the wheels toe-out.

3 Owing to the need for precision gauges to measure the small angles of the steering and suspension settings. It is preferable that checking of camber and castor is left to a service station having the necessary equipment. Camber and castor are set during production of the vehicle, and any deviation from the specified angle will be due to accident damage or gross wear in the suspension mountings.

4 To check the front wheel alignment, first make sure that the lengths of both tie-rods are equal when the steering is in the straight-ahead position. The tie-rod lengths can be adjusted for length if necessary by releasing the locknuts from the balljoint ends and rotating the rods. Flats are provided on the rods in order to hold them still with an open-ended spanner when the locknut is undone.

5 Obtain a tracking gauge. These are available in various forms from accessory stores, or one can be fabricated from a length of steel tubing suitably cranked to clear the sump and bellhousing and having a setscrew and locknut at one end.

6 With the gauge, measure the distances between the two wheel inner rims (at hub height) at the rear of the wheel. Push the vehicle forward to rotate the wheel through 180° (half a turn) and measure the distance between the wheel inner rims, again at hub height, at the front of the wheel. This last measurement should differ from the first by the appropriate toe-in which is given in the Specifications. The vehicle must be on level ground.

7 Where the toe-in is found to be incorrect, release the tie-rod balljoint locknut and turn the tie-rods equally. Only turn them a quarter of a turn at a time before re-checking the alignment. Do not grip the threaded part of the tie-rod during adjustment, but use an open-ended spanner on the flats provided. It is important not to allow the tie-rods to become unequal in length during adjustment, otherwise the alignment of the steering wheel will become incorrect and tyre scrubbing will occur on turns.

8 On completion, tighten the locknuts without disturbing the setting. Check that the balljoint is at the centre of its arc of travel.

22 Wheels and tyres - general care and maintenance

1 Wheels and tyres should give no real problems in use provided that a close eye is kept on them with regard to excessive wear or damage. To this end, the following points should be noted.

2 Ensure that tyre pressures are checked regularly and maintained correctly. Checking should be carried out with the tyres cold and not immediately after the vehicle has been in use. If the pressures are checked with the tyres hot, an apparently high reading will be obtained owing to heat expansion. Under no circumstances should an attempt be made to reduce the pressures to the quoted cold reading in this instance, or effective underinflation will result.

3 Underinflation will cause overheating of the tyre owing to excessive flexing of the casing, and the tread will not sit correctly on the road surface. This will cause a consequent loss of adhesion and excessive wear, not to mention the danger of sudden tyre failure due to heat build-up.

4 Overinflation will cause rapid wear of the centre part of the tyre tread coupled with reduced adhesion, harsher ride, and the danger of shock damage occurring in the tyre casing.

5 Regularly check the tyres for damage in the form of cuts or bulges, especially in the sidewalls. Remove any nails or stones embedded in the tread before they penetrate the tyre to cause deflation. If removal of a nail *does* reveal that the tyre has been punctured, refit the nail so that its point of penetration is marked. Then immediately change the wheel and have the tyre repaired by a tyre dealer. Do *not* drive on a tyre in such a condition. In many cases a puncture can be simply repaired by the use of an inner tube of the correct size and type. If in any doubt as to the possible consequences of any damage found, consult your local tyre dealer for advice.

6 Periodically remove the wheels and clean any dirt or mud from the inside and outside surfaces. Examine the wheel rims for signs of rusting, corrosion or other damage. Light alloy wheels are easily damaged by 'kerbing' whilst parking, and similarly steel wheels may become dented or buckled. Renewal of the wheel is very often the only course of remedial action possible.

7 The balance of each wheel and tyre assembly should be maintained to avoid excessive wear, not only to the tyres but also to the steering and suspension components. Wheel imbalance is normally signified by vibration through the vehicle's bodyshell, although in many cases it is particularly noticeable through the steering wheel. Conversely, it should be noted that wear or damage in suspension or steering components may cause excessive tyre wear. Out-of-round or out-of-true tyres, damaged wheels and wheel bearing wear/maladjustment also fall into this category. Balancing will not usually cure vibration caused by such wear.

8 Wheel balancing may be carried out with the wheel either on or off the vehicle. If balanced on the vehicle, ensure that the wheel-to-hub relationship is marked in some way prior to subsequent wheel removal so that it may be refitted in its original position.

9 General tyre wear is influenced to a large degree by driving style harsh braking and acceleration or fast cornering will all produce more rapid tyre wear. Interchanging of tyres may result in more even wear, but this should only be carried out where there is no mix of tyre types on the vehicle. However, it is worth bearing in mind that if this is completely effective, the added expense of replacing a complete set of tyres simultaneously is incurred, which may prove financially restrictive for many owners.

10 Front tyres may wear unevenly as a result of wheel misalignment. The front wheels should always be correctly aligned according to the settings specified by the vehicle manufacturer.

11 Legal restrictions apply to the mixing of tyre types on a vehicle. Basically this means that a vehicle must not have tyres of differing construction on the same axle. Although it is not recommended to mix tyre types between front axle and rear axle, the only legally permissible combination is crossply at the front and radial at the rear. When mixing radial ply tyres, textile braced radials must always go on the front axle, with steel braced radials at the rear. An obvious disadvantage of such mixing is the necessity to carry two spare tyres to avoid contravening the law in the event of a puncture.

12 In the UK, the Motor Vehicles Construction and Use Regulations apply to many aspects of tyre fitting and usage. It is suggested that a copy of these regulations is obtained from your local police if in doubt as to the current legal requirements with regard to tyre condition, minimum tread depth, etc.

Fault Finding commences overleaf

Fault finding - front suspension

Vehicle wanders

☐ Incorrect wheel alignment
☐ Worn transverse link balljoints

Heavy or stiff steering

☐ Incorrect front wheel alignment
☐ Incorrect tyre pressures

Excessive pitching or rolling on corner or during braking

☐ Faulty strut
☐ Weak or broken coil spring

Tyre squeal when cornering

☐ Incorrect front wheel alignment
☐ Incorrect tyre pressures

Wheel wobble or vibration

☐ Roadwheels out of balance
☐ Roadwheel buckled
☐ Incorrect front wheel alignment
☐ Faulty strut
☐ Weak coil spring

Abnormal tyre wear

☐ Incorrect tyre pressures
☐ Incorrect front wheel alignment
☐ Worn hub bearing

Poor roadholding and wander

☐ Faulty shock absorber
☐ Weak coil spring
☐ Worn or incorrectly adjusted hub bearing
☐ Worn bushes on link mountings

Fault finding - manual steering

Stiff action

☐ Lack of rack lubrication
☐ Seized tie-rod end balljoint
☐ Seized suspension lower balljoint (transverse link)

Free movement at steering wheel

☐ Wear in tie-rod balljoint
☐ Wear in rack teeth

Knocking when traversing uneven surface

☐ Incorrectly adjusted rack slipper

Fault finding - power-assisted steering

The symptoms and reasons applicable to manual steering gear will apply, plus the following:

Stiff action or no return action

☐ Slipping pump drivebelt
☐ Air in fluid
☐ Steering column out of alignment
☐ Castor angle incorrect due to damage or gross wear in bushes and
☐ mountings

Steering effort on both locks unequal

☐ Leaking seal in steering gear
☐ Clogged fluid passage within gear assembly

Noisy pump

☐ Loose pulley
☐ Kinked hose
☐ Clogged filter in fluid reservoir
☐ Low fluid level

Chapter 11 Bodywork and fittings

For modifications. and information applicable to later models. see Supplement at end of manual

Contents

Degrees of difficulty

Easy, suitable for novice with little experience	Fairly easy, suitable for beginner with some experience	Fairly difficult, suitable for competent DIY mechanic	Difficult, suitable for experienced DIY mechanic	Very difficult, suitable for expert DIY or professional

1 General description

The bodywork on all Micra models is of a unitary welded steel construction, with an emphasis on weight saving.

The whole bodyshell is dipped against corrosion.

All models in the range are well equipped, and all the usual optional extras are available.

2 Maintenance - bodywork and underframe

The general condition of a vehicle's bodywork is the one thing that significantly affects its value. Maintenance is easy, but needs to be regular. Neglect, particularly after minor damage, can lead quickly to further deterioration and costly repair bills. It is important also to keep watch on those parts of the vehicle not immediately visible, for instance the underside, inside all the wheel arches, and the lower part of the engine compartment.

The basic maintenance routine for the bodywork is washing - preferably with a lot of water, from a hose. This will remove all the loose solids which may have stuck to the vehicle. It is important to flush these off in such a way as to prevent grit from scratching the finish. The wheel arches and underframe need washing in the same way, to remove any accumulated mud, which will retain moisture and tend to encourage rust. Paradoxically enough, the best time to clean the underframe and wheel arches is in wet weather, when the mud is thoroughly wet and soft. In very wet weather, the underframe is usually cleaned of large accumulations automatically, and this is a good time for inspection.

Periodically, except on vehicles with a wax-based underbody protective coating, it is a good idea to have the whole of the underframe of the vehicle steam-cleaned, engine compartment included, so that a thorough inspection can be carried out to see what minor repairs and renovations are necessary. Steam-cleaning is available at many garages, and is necessary for the removal of the accumulation of oily grime, which sometimes is allowed to become thick in certain areas. If steam-cleaning facilities are not available, there are some excellent grease solvents available which can be brush-applied; the dirt can then be simply hosed off. Note that these methods should not be used on vehicles with wax-based underbody protective coating, or the coating will be removed. Such vehicles should be inspected annually, preferably just prior to Winter, when the underbody should be washed down, and any damage to the wax coating repaired. Ideally, a completely fresh coat should be applied. It would also be worth considering the use of such wax-based protection for injection into door panels, sills, box sections, etc, as an additional safeguard against rust damage, where such protection is not provided by the vehicle manufacturer.

After washing paintwork, wipe off with a chamois leather to give an unspotted clear finish. A coat of clear protective wax polish will give added protection against chemical

11

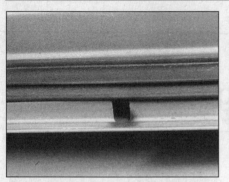

2.4A Drain hole in underside of door

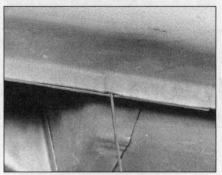

2.4B Clearing a drain hole in the sill

pollutants in the air. If the paintwork sheen has dulled or oxidised, use a cleaner/polisher combination to restore the brilliance of the shine. This requires a little effort, but such dulling is usually caused because regular washing has been neglected. Care needs to be taken with metallic paintwork, as special non-abrasive cleaner/polisher is required to avoid damage to the finish. Always check that the door and ventilator opening drain holes and pipes are completely clear, so that water can be drained out (photos). Brightwork should be treated in the same way as paintwork. Windscreens and windows can be kept clear of the smeary film which often appears, by the use of proprietary glass cleaner. Never use any form of wax or other body or chromium polish on glass.

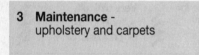

3 Maintenance - upholstery and carpets

Mats and carpets should be brushed or vacuum-cleaned regularly, to keep them free of grit. If they are badly stained, remove them from the vehicle for scrubbing or sponging, and make quite sure they are dry before refitting. Seats and interior trim panels can be kept clean by wiping with a damp cloth. If they do become stained (which can be more apparent on light-coloured upholstery), use a little liquid detergent and a soft nail brush to scour the grime out of the grain of the material. Do not forget to keep the headlining clean in the same way as the upholstery. When using liquid cleaners inside the vehicle, do not over-wet the surfaces being cleaned. Excessive damp could get into the seams and padded interior, causing stains, offensive odours or even rot.

HAYNES HINT *If the inside of the vehicle gets wet accidentally, it is worthwhile taking some trouble to dry it out properly, particularly where carpets are involved. Do not leave oil or electric heaters inside the vehicle for this purpose.*

4 Minor body damage - repair

Note: *For more detailed information about bodywork repair, Haynes Publishing produce a book by Lindsay Porter called "The Car Bodywork Repair Manual". This incorporates information on such aspects as rust treatment, painting and glass-fibre repairs, as well as details on more ambitious repairs involving welding and panel beating.*

Repairs of minor scratches in bodywork

If the scratch is very superficial, and does not penetrate to the metal of the bodywork, repair is very simple. Lightly rub the area of the scratch with a paintwork renovator, or a very fine cutting paste, to remove loose paint from the scratch, and to clear the surrounding bodywork of wax polish. Rinse the area with clean water.

Apply touch-up paint to the scratch using a fine paint brush; continue to apply fine layers of paint until the surface of the paint in the scratch is level with the surrounding paintwork. Allow the new paint at least two weeks to harden, then blend it into the surrounding paintwork by rubbing the scratch area with a paintwork renovator or a very fine cutting paste. Finally, apply wax polish.

Where the scratch has penetrated right through to the metal of the bodywork, causing the metal to rust, a different repair technique is required. Remove any loose rust from the bottom of the scratch with a penknife, then apply rust-inhibiting paint to prevent the formation of rust in the future. Using a rubber or nylon applicator, fill the scratch with bodystopper paste. If required, this paste can be mixed with cellulose thinners to provide a very thin paste which is ideal for filling narrow scratches. Before the stopper-paste in the scratch hardens, wrap a piece of smooth cotton rag around the top of a finger. Dip the finger in cellulose thinners, and quickly sweep it across the surface of the stopper-paste in the scratch; this will ensure that the surface of the stopper-paste is slightly hollowed. The scratch can now be painted over as described earlier in this Section.

Repairs of dents in bodywork

When deep denting of the vehicle's bodywork has taken place, the first task is to pull the dent out, until the affected bodywork almost attains its original shape. There is little point in trying to restore the original shape completely, as the metal in the damaged area will have stretched on impact, and cannot be reshaped fully to its original contour. It is better to bring the level of the dent up to a point which is about 3 mm below the level of the surrounding bodywork. In cases where the dent is very shallow anyway, it is not worth trying to pull it out at all. If the underside of the dent is accessible, it can be hammered out gently from behind, using a mallet with a wooden or plastic head. Whilst doing this, hold a suitable block of wood firmly against the outside of the panel, to absorb the impact from the hammer blows and thus prevent a large area of the bodywork from being "belled-out".

Should the dent be in a section of the bodywork which has a double skin, or some other factor making it inaccessible from behind, a different technique is called for. Drill several small holes through the metal inside the area - particularly in the deeper section. Then screw long self-tapping screws into the holes, just sufficiently for them to gain a good purchase in the metal. Now the dent can be pulled out by pulling on the protruding heads of the screws with a pair of pliers.

The next stage of the repair is the removal of the paint from the damaged area, and from an inch or so of the surrounding "sound" bodywork. This is accomplished most easily by using a wire brush or abrasive pad on a power drill, although it can be done just as effectively by hand, using sheets of abrasive paper. To complete the preparation for filling, score the surface of the bare metal with a screwdriver or the tang of a file, or alternatively, drill small holes in the affected area. This will provide a really good "key" for the filler paste.

To complete the repair, see the Section on filling and respraying.

Repairs of rust holes or gashes in bodywork

Remove all paint from the affected area, and from an inch or so of the surrounding "sound" bodywork, using an abrasive pad or a wire brush on a power drill. If these are not available, a few sheets of abrasive paper will do the job most effectively. With the paint removed, you will be able to judge the severity of the corrosion, and therefore decide whether to renew the whole panel (if this is possible) or to repair the affected area. New body panels are not as expensive as most people think, and it is often quicker and more satisfactory to fit a new panel than to attempt to repair large areas of corrosion.

Remove all fittings from the affected area, except those which will act as a guide to the original shape of the damaged bodywork (eg headlight shells etc). Then, using tin snips or a hacksaw blade, remove all loose metal and any other metal badly affected by corrosion. Hammer the edges of the hole inwards, in order to create a slight depression for the filler paste.

Wire-brush the affected area to remove the powdery rust from the surface of the remaining metal. Paint the affected area with rust-inhibiting paint, if the back of the rusted area is accessible, treat this also.

Before filling can take place, it will be necessary to block the hole in some way. This can be achieved by the use of aluminium or plastic mesh, or aluminium tape.

Aluminium or plastic mesh, or glass-fibre matting, is probably the best material to use for a large hole. Cut a piece to the approximate size and shape of the hole to be filled, then position it in the hole so that its edges are below the level of the surrounding bodywork. It can be retained in position by several blobs of filler paste around its periphery.

Aluminium tape should be used for small or very narrow holes. Pull a piece off the roll, trim it to the approximate size and shape required, then pull off the backing paper (if used) and stick the tape over the hole; it can be overlapped if the thickness of one piece is insufficient. Burnish down the edges of the tape with the handle of a screwdriver or similar, to ensure that the tape is securely attached to the metal underneath.

Bodywork repairs - filling and respraying

Before using this Section, see the Sections on dent, deep scratch, rust holes and gash repairs.

Many types of bodyfiller are available, but generally speaking, those proprietary kits which contain a tin of filler paste and a tube of resin hardener are best for this type of repair. A wide, flexible plastic or nylon applicator will be found invaluable for imparting a smooth and well-contoured finish to the surface of the filler.

Mix up a little filler on a clean piece of card or board - measure the hardener carefully (follow the maker's instructions on the pack), otherwise the filler will set too rapidly or too slowly. Using the applicator, apply the filler paste to the prepared area; draw the applicator across the surface of the filler to achieve the correct contour and to level the surface. As soon as a contour that approximates to the correct one is achieved, stop working the paste - if you carry on too long, the paste will become sticky and begin to "pick-up" on the applicator. Continue to add thin layers of filler paste at 20-minute intervals, until the level of the filler is just proud of the surrounding bodywork.

Once the filler has hardened, the excess can be removed using a metal plane or file. From then on, progressively-finer grades of

abrasive paper should be used, starting with a 40-grade production paper, and finishing with a 400-grade wet-and-dry paper. Always wrap the abrasive paper around a flat rubber, cork, or wooden block - otherwise the surface of the filler will not be completely flat. During the smoothing of the filler surface, the wet-and-dry paper should be periodically rinsed in water. This will ensure that a very smooth finish is imparted to the filler at the final stage.

At this stage, the "dent" should be surrounded by a ring of bare metal, which in turn should be encircled by the finely "feathered" edge of the good paintwork. Rinse the repair area with clean water, until all of the dust produced by the rubbing-down operation has gone.

Spray the whole area with a light coat of primer - this will show up any imperfections in the surface of the filler. Repair these imperfections with fresh filler paste or bodystopper, and once more smooth the surface with abrasive paper. Repeat this spray-and-repair procedure until you are satisfied that the surface of the filler, and the feathered edge of the paintwork, are perfect. Clean the repair area with clean water, and allow to dry fully.

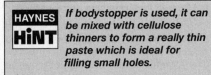

> **HAYNES HiNT**
> If bodystopper is used, it can be mixed with cellulose thinners to form a really thin paste which is ideal for filling small holes.

The repair area is now ready for final spraying. Paint spraying must be carried out in a warm, dry, windless and dust-free atmosphere. This condition can be created artificially if you have access to a large indoor working area, but if you are forced to work in the open, you will have to pick your day very carefully. If you are working indoors, dousing the floor in the work area with water will help to settle the dust which would otherwise be in the atmosphere. If the repair area is confined to one body panel, mask off the surrounding panels; this will help to minimise the effects of a slight mis-match in paint colours. Bodywork fittings (eg chrome strips, door handles etc) will also need to be masked off. Use genuine masking tape, and several thicknesses of newspaper, for the masking operations.

Before commencing to spray, agitate the aerosol can thoroughly, then spray a test area (an old tin, or similar) until the technique is mastered. Cover the repair area with a thick coat of primer; the thickness should be built up using several thin layers of paint, rather than one thick one. Using 400-grade wet-and-dry paper, rub down the surface of the primer until it is really smooth. While doing this, the work area should be thoroughly doused with water, and the wet-and-dry paper periodically rinsed in water. Allow to dry before spraying on more paint.

Spray on the top coat, again building up the thickness by using several thin layers of paint. Start spraying at one edge of the repair area, and then, using a side-to-side motion, work until the whole repair area and about 2 inches of the surrounding original paintwork is covered. Remove all masking material 10 to 15 minutes after spraying on the final coat of paint.

Allow the new paint at least two weeks to harden, then, using a paintwork renovator, or a very fine cutting paste, blend the edges of the paint into the existing paintwork. Finally, apply wax polish.

5 Major body damage - repair

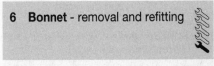

This should be left to your dealer or a local body repair specialist, who have the necessary body jigs and presses for realignment.

Failure to detect and straighten bent underframes can lead to poor roadholding and steering.

6 Bonnet - removal and refitting

1 Open the bonnet and have an assistant support its weight.
2 Mark the position of the hinges on the underside of the bonnet with a soft pencil.
3 Unscrew the hinge bolts (photo) and then lift the bonnet from the vehicle.
4 Refitting is a reversal of removal, but before fully tightening the bolts, gently close the bonnet and check its alignment. Adjust as necessary before fully tightening the bolts.
5 Now close the bonnet. If it does not shut smoothly and positively adjust the bonnet lock and striker, as described in Section 8.

11

6.3 Removing the bonnet hinge bolts

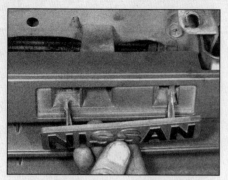

7.1 Removing the Nissan motif

7.2A Releasing the clip . . .

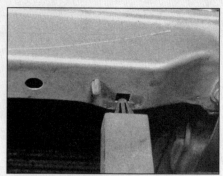

7.2B . . . at the top right and left side . . .

7.2C . . . and the centre

8.3 Bonnet lock retaining bolt locations

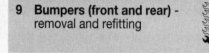

9 Bumpers (front and rear) - removal and refitting

1 The bumpers at the front and rear are bolted to the bodyshell.
2 To remove them, raise the front or rear of the vehicle as required, for ease of access, and support it on axle stands.
3 Disconnect any electrical components and then unbolt and remove the bumpers.
4 Refitting is a reversal of removal.

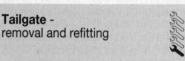

10 Tailgate - removal and refitting

1 Open the tailgate and disconnect the lead to the rear window demister. Also, disconnect the leads to the tailgate wiper motor, which are reached from behind the rear combination light, or by removing the interior trim in the luggage compartment (photo).
2 Remove the bolts securing the tailgate stay arms to the tailgate supporting the tailgate afterwards (photo).
3 To facilitate feeding the electrical cables back through the tailgate during refitting, attach a piece of string to the end of the cables before they are pulled out. The string will then be in place of the cables within the tailgate.
4 Remove the tailgate hinge bolts (photo).
5 Carefully remove the tailgate, feeding the

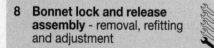

7 Radiator grille - removal and refitting

1 Open the bonnet and using a screwdriver prize out the 'Nissan' motif (photo).
2 Use the screwdriver to depress the plastic clips at the top edge of the grille. There are three of these (photos).
3 The bottom edge is held by locating dowels. Lift the grille out.
4 Refitting is a reversal of removal.

8 Bonnet lock and release assembly - removal, refitting and adjustment

1 Open the bonnet and support it on its strut.

2 Unscrew the three lock retaining bolts, pull the lock from its mounting bracket and unhook the release cable from it.
3 The control lever and cable may be removed after unscrewing the lever fixing screws under the facia panel and withdrawing the cable through its bulkhead grommet.
4 Refining is a reversal of removal, but set the lock bolts finger tight so that when the bonnet is closed the striker enters the lock slot centrally.
5 Close the bonnet and check that there is no up and down movement when the front of the bonnet is depressed with the hand. If there is, move the lock downwards to eliminate any free play. Fully tighten the lock fixing bolts. If necessary, adjust the rubber corner stops so that the bonnet is supported firmly when shut. Apply a little grease to the lock lever end and pivot.

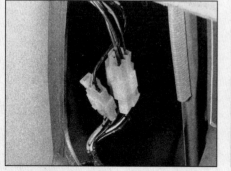

10.1 Electrical connectors to tailgate

10.2 Tailgate stay bolts . . .

10.4 . . . and the hinge bolts

11.2A Tailgate lock . . .

11.2B . . . and striker

electrical cables up and out of the left-hand pillar. Once the cables are removed, tape the ends of the string to the tailgate.

6 Refitting is the reverse of removal.

7 When refitting the tailgate, attach the string to the cables and pull them back through the tailgate cavity.

Note: *The tailgate stays should be handled*

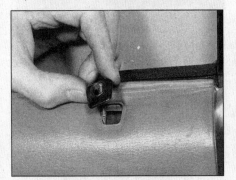

13.1 Remove the armrest screws . . .

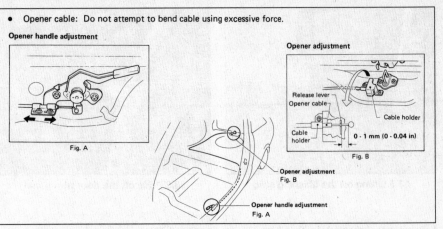

● Opener cable: Do not attempt to bend cable using excessive force.

Opener handle adjustment

Fig. A

Opener adjustment

Release lever
Opener cable
Cable holder
Cable holder
0 - 1 mm (0 - 0.04 in)
Fig. B

Opener adjustment
Fig. B

Opener handle adjustment
Fig. A

Fig. 11.1 Components of the tailgate remote release mechanism (Sec 12)

with care to prevent scratches which may cause gas leakage.

11 Tailgate lock - removal, refitting and adjustment

1 The tailgate lock is contained in the tailgate, with the striker on the floor pan of the luggage compartment.

2 To remove either component, remove the securing bolts. The remote release mechanism is held by two screws (photos).

3 Refitting is a reversal of removal.

Adjustment

4 Ensure that the tailgate is central in its aperture.

5 If necessary, adjust the tailgate by loosening the hinge bolts and centralising the tailgate. Then adjust the striker so it is in the centre of the lock.

12 Tailgate remote release mechanism - general and adjusting

1 The tailgate remote release mechanism cable is operated by a lever by the driver's seat. It is held by two bolts.

2 The cable is routed to the tailgate lock under the carpet.

3 Adjust the release lever end as shown in Fig. 11.1, so that there is between zero and 1 mm slack between the cable end and the release lever.

13 Front door trim - removal and refitting

1 Undo the screws and remove the armrest (photo).

2 Prise off the plastic surround from the door release handle.

3 Unscrew the door lock plunger knob and remove the guide plate (photos).

4 Remove the window regulator handle. Do this by using a hook made from wire to pull the spring clip from the handle, then pull the handle from the driveshaft (photos).

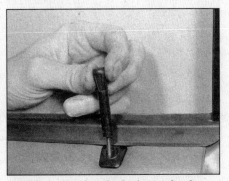

13.3A . . . the door lock plunger knob . . .

13.3B . . . and guide plate

13.4A Removing the door window handle

13.4B Using wire to remove the retaining clip (handle removed to show clip and wire)

11

13.5 Lifting off the finishing strip

13.6 Prise off the door trim panel

13.8 Don't forget the plastic sheet

5 Remove the embellishing plate from around the rear view mirror and prise up the finishing strip (photo).
6 The door trim panel may now be removed by carefully prising it away from the door. It is held at intervals by plastic poppers (photo).
7 Refitting is a reversal of removal. Note, however, that it will be necessary to fit the spring clip to the window regulator handle before fitting the handle.
8 The plastic sheet which is stuck to the door with mastic should always be refitted as it prevents damp entering the door (photo).

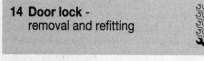

14 Door lock -
removal and refitting

1 Remove the trim panel, as described in the preceding Section.
2 Unscrew the lock plunger knob and the screws which hold the lock assembly to the door edge (photo).
3 Disconnect the control rods from the lock and withdraw the lock through the aperture in the door inner panel.
4 The door exterior handle can be removed by unscrewing its two fixing nuts by passing a tool through the hole in the upper part of the door inner panel. The lock cylinder can be

removed after prising out its retaining clip (photo).
5 Refitting is a reversal of removal, but adjust the door exterior handle by turning the stepped bush on the control rod as required, and also adjust the door striker as necessary.
6 Shims are available for use behind the striker.

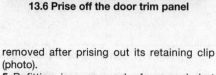

15 Front door window -
removal and refitting

1 Remove the door trim panel, as previously described (Section 13).

14.2 Door lock retaining screws

2 Unscrew the window regulator fixing screws. Lower and swivel the regulator and release its lifting arms from the channel at the base of the glass (photos).
3 Release the screw from the glass guide channel.
4 Lower the glass fully and remove the two weatherseal strips from the glass slot. These are held by spring clips.
5 Pull the glass upwards, tilt it and remove it from the door.
6 If a new window is being fitted, tap the base channel onto it using a wooden or plastic-faced hammer.
7 Refit by reversing the removal operations. Adjust the position of the glass guide channel before tightening its screw so that the window moves up and down smoothly.

14.4 Door lock cylinder viewed from inside

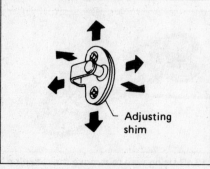

**Fig. 11.2 Front door striker adjustment
(Sec 14)**

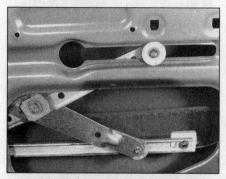

15.2A Window regulator scissors

15.2B Lower channel fixing nut

16 Rear windows (3-door) - removal and refitting

1 Undo and remove the screws securing the rear latch (photo).
2 Remove the screws from the two front hinges (photo) and remove the window.
3 Refitting is a reversal of removal.

17 Front door - removal and refitting

1 The door hinges are of bolt-on type (photo).
2 Open the door wide and support its lower edge on jacks or blocks with pads of rag to prevent damage to the paintwork.
3 Disconnect the check strap either by removing the fixing screws or by driving out the roll pin (photo).
4 Mark the position of the hinges on the body with a soft pencil and then support the weight of the door and remove the hinge bolts.
5 Lift the door from the vehicle.
6 Refitting is a reversal of removal. Provided the hinges are positioned within their original marked areas the door should close satisfactorily. Adjustment may be carried out by releasing the hinge bolts and moving the door.
7 The striker on the door pillar may also be adjusted to ensure smooth positive closure (photo).
8 Later models incorporate a hinge reinforcement plate to help prevent door sag.

18 Windscreen and tailgate window - renewal

Both the windscreen and the tailgate window are sealed using a primer and sealant, which requires temperature and humidity to be at a certain level for complete curing. It is recommended that this be left to your local dealer, or auto glass replacement specialist.

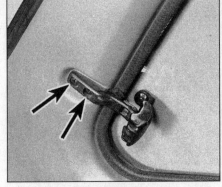
16.1 Rear window latch securing screws

16.2 Rear window hinge screws

17.1 Front door hinge

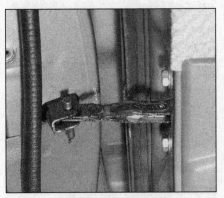
17.3 Door check strap

19 Interior trim and mouldings - general

1 Most of the interior trim and mouldings are of plastic construction and care should be exercised when removing or refitting it.
2 Clips are used extensively to fix the trim, with self-tapping screws in certain positions (photos).
3 Removal of the headlining is best left to an expert.

20 Exterior trim and mouldings - general

1 The exterior body trim is either clipped in position or held by double-sided tape.
2 The side and rear guard mouldings are secured by double-sided tape. To remove a moulding, the use of an electrically-operated heat gun will be found to be the most effective.

17.7 Striker plate

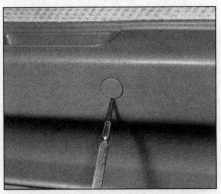
19.2A Typical screw cover being levered out

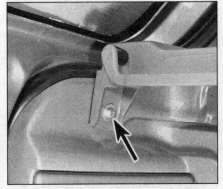
19.2B Self-tapping screws

11

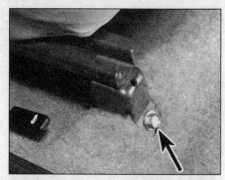

21.1 Front seat runner retaining bolt (front)

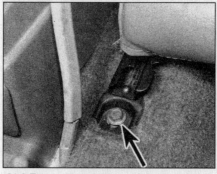

21.2 Front seat runner retaining bolt (rear)

21.4 Seat adjustment mechanism

21 Front seat - removal and refitting

1 Slide the seat fully rearwards and undo the bolts securing the runners to the floor pan (photo).
2 Slide the seat forward and repeat the operation at the rear of the runners (photo).
3 Remove the seat.
4 The adjusting mechanism should be greased periodically (photo).
5 Refitting is a reversal of removal.

22 Rear seat - removal and refitting

1 Grip the front edge of the seat cushion and pull it upwards to release the tongues from the retaining recesses (photo).
2 Pull the cushion forwards and remove it from the car.
3 Either a single or double backrest is fitted. To remove the backrest release it from the upper clip, fold it forwards, then unbolt the pivot brackets.
4 Refitting is a reversal of removal. The upper retaining bracket may be adjusted within the elongated screw holes (photo).

23 Facia panel - removal and refitting

1 Remove the instrument panel, speedometer cable, radio and facia mounted switches as described in Chapter 12.
2 Remove the choke cable (Chapter 3), steering wheel (Chapter 10) and the heater controls and ducting (Section 31 and 34).
3 Remove the plastic covers (photo) which conceal the top mounting nuts and remove them and the side mounting bolts (photo).
4 Before withdrawing the facia panel ensure all electrical leads are disconnected.
5 Refitting is a reversal of removal.

24 Sunroof - removal and refitting

1 The sunroof consists of a glass roof panel and a sunshade plate attached under the glass.
2 To remove the sunshade plate, hold the plate while unscrewing the retaining bolts. Pull the hooks of the plate out of their holders.
3 To remove the sunroof (always having first removed the sunshade plate), tilt the roof and push in the two buttons on the handle while pushing the sunroof upwards.
4 Raise the roof vertical then slide it to the left to disengage it from the hinges.
5 Lift the two air deflectors at the front

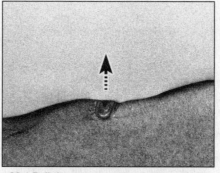

22.1 Pull the rear seat squab upwards to release it

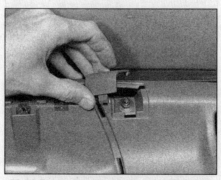

23.3A Facia panel top nuts are concealed beneath plastic covers

corners of the aperture if the car is to be used with the sunroof removed. Store the sunroof in the special bag in the rear compartment.
6 Refitting is a reversal of removal. The sunroof is correctly engaged with the front hinges when the red marks are no longer visible.

25 Seat belts - general

1 The condition of the seat belts should be checked regularly for fraying or cuts. If damaged, they should be renewed.
2 The retracting mechanism may be reached

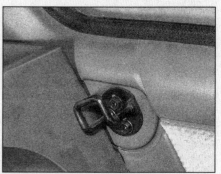

22.4 Upper retaining bracket for seat back

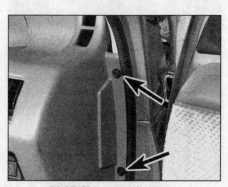

23.3B Side mounting bolts

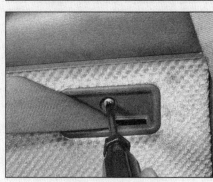

25.2A Removing the trim . . .

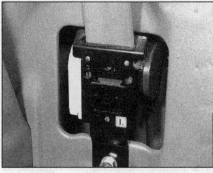

25.2B . . . to reveal the retracting mechanism

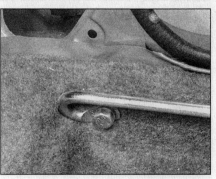

25.3 Lower anchorage point

by removing the trim panel in the passenger compartment (photo).

3 The lower anchorage point is bolted to the floor pan (photo), as are the inboard anchorages.

4 Do not alter the attachment points, and replace all washers and spacers in their original positions when refitting.

26 Rear view mirrors -
removal and refitting

Interior mirror

1 Remove the securing screw (photo).
2 The base is secured to the roof rail by three screws (photo).

Door mounted mirror

3 Undo the screw and remove the adjusting handle (photo).
4 Prise off the large cover plate (photo).
5 Prise off the front cover plate (photo).
6 Remove the three bolts holding the mirror to the door (photo) and remove the mirror.
7 The adjusting action may be tightened by doing up the screws on the captive ball (photo).
8 The mirror glass may be changed if it is cracked, but this is an extremely fiddly job and it is better to replace the whole unit.
9 Refitting is a reversal of removal.

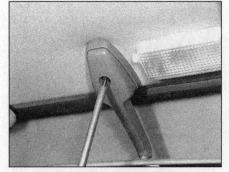

26.1 Remove the screw

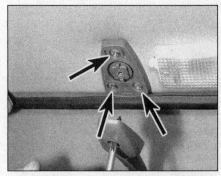

26.2 There are three screws in the base

26.3 Remove the screw from the handle

26.4 Prise off the cover plate . . .

26.5 . . . and front cover

26.6 Remove the three bolts (arrowed)

26.7 Tighten the two screws

11

27.1 Remove the plastic covers and screws . . .

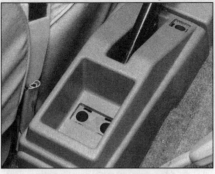

27.3 . . . and lift the console

28.2 Removing the retaining screw

27 Centre console - removal and refitting

1 Prise off the plastic cover (photo) and remove the screws.
2 There is another cover and screw at the front end.
3 Lift the console from around the handbrake cover (photo).
4 Refit in the reverse order.

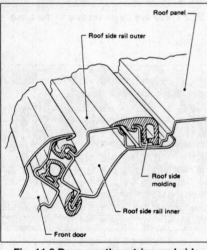
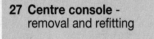

Fig. 11.3 Door weather strips and side moulding (Sec 29)

Roof panel
Roof side rail outer
Roof side molding
Roof side rail inner
Front door

28 Ashtray - removal and refitting

1 Snap out the centre part of the ashtray.
2 Undo the securing screw (photo) and prise the surround from the trim panel.
3 Refit in the reverse order.

29 Door weather strips and finishers - general

1 Should the weather strips or edge finishers become perished they can be renewed.
2 New weather strips may be purchased in lengths from your dealer.
3 They are fixed in place either by plastic caps, adhesive or are a push fit over the seam edges which they cover.
4 When refitting the weather strip, it is usual to start at the centre bottom of the door, and work around, pushing or clipping the strip in place until the ends meet.
5 Re-check the strip is pushed fully home all round the edges before cutting to a snug fit.

30 Heating and ventilation system - description

1 The heater incorporates a matrix to which

hot coolant from the engine cooling system is fed.
2 A booster, or blower motor, is used to force air through the matrix, where it is heated, before being ducted to the car interior.
3 By altering the distribution flaps, hot or cold air may be directed to the feet or to the windscreen, or both.
4 Fresh air ventilation is supplied through facia mounted grilles, air being drawn in through the grille at the base of the windscreen. Stale air is exhausted through grilles on the rear pillars.

31 Heater - removal and refitting

Control panel and lever assembly

1 Pull off the plastic knobs from the ends of the control levers (photos).
2 Prise out the panel front and disconnect the cigar lighter (photo), remove the panel.
3 Remove the cable clips and unhook the cables at the distribution flap ends (photo).
Note: *There are three such cables.*
4 Disconnect the electrical lead to the blower motor.
5 Remove the screw securing the control lever assembly and then slide it to the right to disengage the rear clips. Pull the unit forward

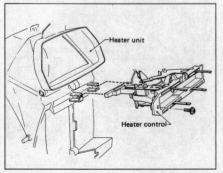

Fig. 11.4 Removing the heater control lever assembly (Sec 29)

Heater unit
Heater control

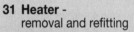

31.1 Remove the control lever knobs

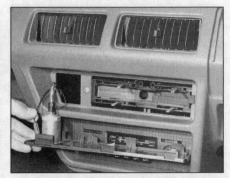

31.2 Prise out the panel and disconnect the cigar lighter

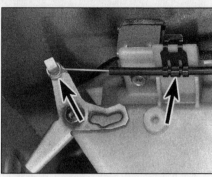

31.3 Remove the cable clips and unhook the cable ends (arrowed)

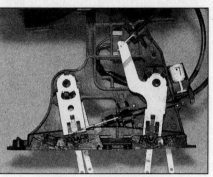

31.5 Control lever assembly

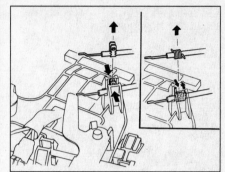

Fig. 11.5 Control cable clips at control lever end (Sec 32)

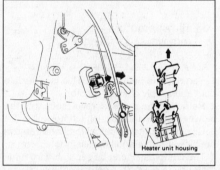

Fig. 11.6 Control cable clips at central flap end (Sec 32)

sufficiently to unhook the control cables, and remove it (photo).

6 Refitting is a reversal of removing, but see Section 32 for control cable adjustment.

32 Heater control cables - adjustment

1 The control cables are adjusted by altering their positions in the cable fixing clips, at the control flap ends.

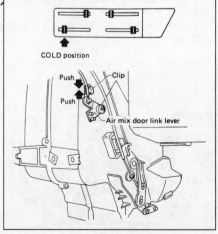

Fig. 11.9 Adjusting the temperature control cable (Sec 32)

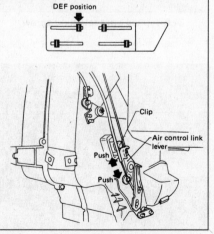

Fig. 11.7 Adjusting intake door central cable (Sec 32)

2 When fitting new cables, fit the control lever ends first, setting the outer sheath in the cable fixing clip so that each lever has full and free movement.

3 Refer to Figs. 11.5 to 11.10 and set the control flap ends of the cables.

4 Later models may have a water cock added to the system.

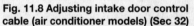

Fig. 11.10 Adjusting the air control cable (Sec 32)

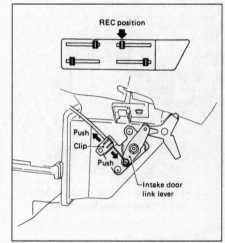

Fig. 11.8 Adjusting intake door control cable (air conditioner models) (Sec 32)

5 When adjusting the water cock control rod (refer to Fig. 11.11) disconnect the temperature control cable from the air mix door lever before the adjustment.

6 To adjust the rod, push the door lever and pull the rod in the direction of the arrows, before measuring the gap.

7 Reconnect the temperature control cable on completion.

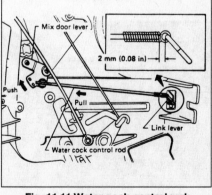

Fig. 11.11 Water cock control rod adjustment (Sec 32)

11

33.1 Remove the heater duct

33.2 Undoing the three securing screws

33.3 Removing the blower motor

33.4 Remove the central nut to separate the impeller from the motor

34.2 The heater hoses on the engine compartment rear bulkhead

33 Blower motor -
removal and refitting

1 Remove the heater duct. This is a flexible duct and simply pulls off (photo).
2 Remove the three screws securing the blower motor in the housing (photo).
3 Disconnect the electrical lead and remove the blower motor and impeller (photo).
4 The compressor can be separated from the motor by removing the central nut (photo).
5 Refitting is a reversal of removal.

34 Heater (complete unit) -
removal and refitting

1 Drain the cooling system, as described in Chapter 2.
2 Disconnect the heater hoses at the rear bulkhead of the engine compartment (photo).
3 Remove the facia panel as described in Section 23.
4 Remove the heater control panel as described in Section 31.
5 Disconnect the electrical lead to the resistor (photo).
6 Remove the fixing screws from the ducting (photo) and remove the ducting.
7 Remove the nuts and bolts securing the heater unit to the body (photos).

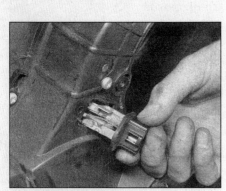

34.5 Removing the resistor

34.6 Typical duct retaining screw

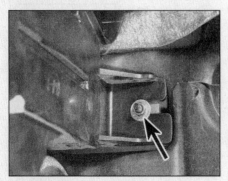

34.7A Heater unit retaining nut . . .

34.7B . . . and bolt, at the top

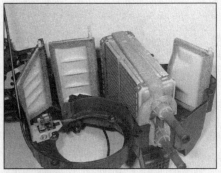

34.9 Heater unit removed and partly disassembled

34.10 Ducting behind the facia panel

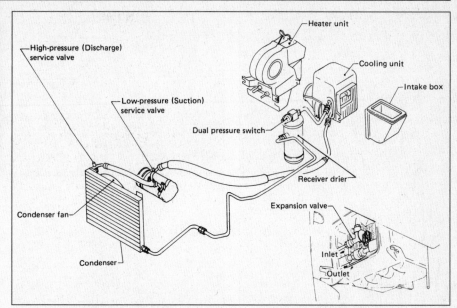

Fig. 11.12 Components of the air conditioning system (Sec 35)

8 Manoeuvre the heater unit from the vehicle.
9 The casing may be split by removing the securing screws, revealing the individual components (photo).
10 The ducting may be removed from the facia panel by removing the retaining screws (photo).
11 Refitting is a reversal of removal.
12 Refill the cooling system on completion, as described in Chapter 2.

35 Air conditioner -
operation and precautions

1 An air conditioner with combined heater is an option on certain models.
2 The refrigerant fluid used in the system is odourless and non-poisonous.
3 Leaks are not dangerous unless the fluid or vapour comes into contact with a naked flame when poisonous gas is created.
4 Refrigerant fluid is dangerous to the eyes and skin and contact should be avoided.
5 If overhaul operations require the removal of any part of the system, try and move the obstructing component within the limits of its flexible discharged connecting hoses. If this is not sufficient then have the system discharged by your dealer or a competent refrigeration engineer. He should also be employed to recharge the system on completion. It is most important that the refrigerant lines and components are kept free from internal moisture and your dealer will use a vacuum pump to ensure this after the circuit has been broken.
6 To operate the air conditioner, push the A/C switch to ON and the fan control lever to a setting between 1 and 3. The air conditioner warning lamp will come on.
7 Two further settings are available - RECIRC and FRESH. The RECIRC setting should be selected for rapid cooling in very hot or humid conditions.

8 To obtain the best results from your air conditioner, observe the following points.
9 If the vehicle has been parked in the sun for a long time with the windows closed, open them fully and drive along for two or three minutes after switching on the air conditioner.
10 Under normal conditions, keep all windows and ventilators closed when the air conditioner is working.
11 During the summer, if the air conditioner has not been used for a week, turn the fan control lever on and off several times at three second intervals with the engine idling.
12 During the winter, run the system for ten minutes at monthly intervals.
13 If the vehicle is being steam cleaned, avoid using the steam on the system components, particularly the condenser.
14 Periodically brush or hose flies and dirt from the condenser which might otherwise restrict its airflow.

36 Air conditioner components
- removal and refitting

1 As already explained in the preceding Section, have the system discharged by your dealer before carrying out any of the following operations.

Condenser

2 Disconnect the battery.
3 Remove the radiator grille (Section 7).
4 Disconnect the refrigerant pipelines from the condenser and cap them.

5 Remove the condenser cooling fan.
6 Disconnect the radiator mountings and support the radiator, not allowing it to hang on its hoses.
7 Disconnect the condenser mountings.
8 Push the radiator towards the engine and lift out the condenser.

Compressor

9 Disconnect the battery.
10 Raise the front of the vehicle and support it on axle stands.
11 Remove the compressor drivebelt (refer to Chapter 2).
12 Disconnect the compressor clutch harness.
13 Disconnect the flexible hoses from the compressor and cap them.
14 Remove the compressor after disconnecting its mounting and adjuster bolts.
15 Keep the compressor in its 'in car' attitude, otherwise oil could enter the low pressure chambers. Should this happen, the compressor pulley must be turned through several revolutions when refitted to the vehicle in order to expel the oil. Failure to do this could result in internal damage once the air conditioning system is operated.

Evaporator

16 Disconnect the battery.
17 Disconnect the refrigerant lines from the evaporator and cap the pipes.
18 Remove the instrument panel as described in Chapter 12.
19 Remove the mounting screws and withdraw the evaporator.

11

Notes

Chapter 12 Electrical system

For modifications, and information applicable to later models, see Supplement at end of manual

Contents

Degrees of difficulty

Easy, suitable for novice with little experience	**Fairly easy,** suitable for beginner with some experience	**Fairly difficult,** suitable for competent DIY mechanic	**Difficult,** suitable for experienced DIY mechanic	**Very difficult,** suitable for expert DIY or professional

Specifications

System type .... 12 volt negative earth

Battery
Type .... Maintenance-free
Capacity .... 30 amp hr

Alternator
Rating .. .. 35, 40 or 50 amp
Output voltage .... 14.1 to 14.7 volt
Minimum brush wear limit .... 7.0 mm (0.28 in)

Starter motor
Type .... Pre-engaged
Minimum brush wear limit .... 11.5 mm (0.453 in)
Clearance between pinion front edge and pinion stopper -
manual transmission .... 0.5 to 2.0 mm (0.020 to 0.079 in)
Difference in height of pinion assembly - automatic transmission .... 0.5 to 2.0 mm (0.020 to 0.079 in)

Wiper blades .... Champion X4503

Fuses (typical)*	**Amps**
Headlamps	15
Stop/tail lamp	15
Horn/hazard warning lights	15
Air conditioner	15
Rear screen demister	15
Heater	10
Wash/wipe	20
Radiator fan motor	15
Engine control	15

Before replacing any fuse, be sure to check the fuse specifications listed on the fuse box cover. Never use a fuse of higher amperage rating than that specified.

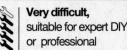

12

Bulbs

	Wattage
Headlamp (sealed beam)	65/55
Headlamp (halogen, semi-sealed)	60/55
Front combination light:	
Turn signal	21
Side light	5
Front side turn signal light	5
Rear combination light:	
Turn signal	21
Stop/tail light	21/5
Reversing light	21
Rear foglight	21
Number plate light	5
Interior light	5
Luggage compartment light	10

Torque wrench settings

	lbf ft	kgf m
Alternator bracket bolt	7.0 to 9.0	1.0 to 1.2
Alternator adjustment bolt	12.0 to 15.0	1.6 to 2.0
Alternator pulley nut	36.0 to 47.0	5.0 to 6.5
Alternator tie-bolts	2.9 to 4.0	0.40 to 0.55
Starter motor tie-bolts	3.6 to 5.1	0.50 to 0.70
Solenoid attachment bolts	2.9 to 5.8	0.40 to 0.80

1 General description

The major components of the negative earth system consist of a 12 volt battery, an alternator (driven from the crankshaft pulley), and a starter motor.

The battery supplies a steady amount of current for the ignition, lighting and other electrical circuits and provides a reserve of power when the current consumed by the electrical equipment exceeds that being produced by the alternator.

The alternator has its own regulator which ensures a high output if the battery is in a low state of charge and the demand from the electrical equipment is high, and a low output if the battery is fully charged and there is little demand from the electrical equipment.

When fitting electrical accessories to cars with a negative earth system it is important, if they contain silicon diodes or transistors, that they are connected correctly, otherwise serious damage may result to the components concerned. Items such as radios, tape players, electronic ignition systems, electronic tachometer, automatic dipping, etc., should all be checked for correct polarity.

2 Battery - charging

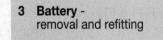

1 The battery is of the maintenance-free type and requires no periodic maintenance, apart from cleaning, and occasionally applying petroleum jelly to the terminals to minimise corrosion.
2 The recommended method of charging the battery is by running the engine.
3 If the engine cannot be started, then charge the battery for at least 4 hours using a 6 amp DC charger, and then try to start the engine.

4 If the battery still will not start the engine, it needs renewing.
5 The specific gravity of the electrolyte may be taken by removing the blind plug on the top of the battery. *On no account use the blind plug to fill the battery with distilled water.*

3 Battery - removal and refitting

1 Open the bonnet, then disconnect the negative and then the positive leads.
2 Unscrew the nuts which hold the battery retaining strap in place (photo).
3 Remove the retaining strap and lift out the battery, being careful not to tilt it.
4 Refitting is a reversal of removing, but make sure the battery is correctly positioned for connecting up positive (+) and negative (-) leads. Reconnect the negative lead **last**.
5 The battery tray is held in place by four bolts (photo).

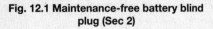

Fig. 12.1 Maintenance-free battery blind plug (Sec 2)

3.2 Battery retaining strap

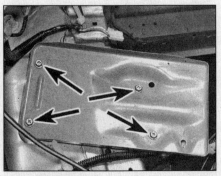

3.5 Battery tray retaining bolts

5.2 Wiring connections on the rear of the alternator

4 Alternator - description, maintenance and precautions

1 The alternator is mounted on the crankcase at the timing belt end of the engine.
2 The unit is driven by a belt from the crankshaft pulley. A voltage regulator is integral with the brush holder plate.
3 Keep the drivebelt correctly tensioned (see Chapter 2) and the electrical connections tight.
4 Keep the outside of the alternator free from grease and dirt.
5 It is important that the battery leads are always disconnected if using electrical welding equipment, the alternator must be disconnected otherwise serious damage can be caused.
6 Do not stop the engine by pulling a lead from the battery.

5 Alternator - removal and refitting

1 Disconnect the battery.
2 Disconnect the leads from the back of the alternator (photo).
3 Loosen the alternator mounting and adjuster bracket bolts, and push the alternator in so that the drivebelt may be slipped off the pulley.

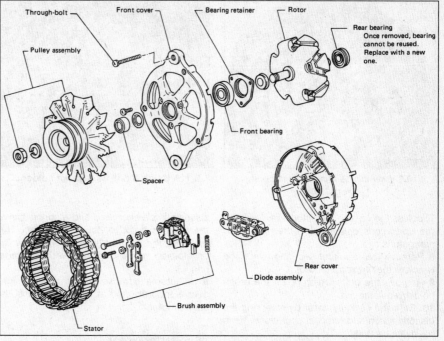

Fig. 12.2 Exploded view of the alternator (Sec 6)

4 Remove the adjuster bracket and mounting bolt and remove the alternator from the engine.
5 Refitting is a reversal of this procedure, but ensure that any spacers and/or washers go back in their original positions.

6 Alternator - overhaul

1 In the event of the charge (ignition) warning lamp not going out after the engine has started or if the battery is being overcharged, or undercharged, the following operations may be carried out to rectify worn brushes of a faulty voltage regulator. If more extensive overhaul is required, or if the alternator has had a long service life, it is recommended that a new or factory-rebuilt unit is obtained.
2 Remove the alternator and clean away the external dirt.
3 Mark the relative position of the rear cover to the front (drive end) cover by scribing a line on them. Unscrew the tie-bolts.

4 Pull off the rear cover with the stator.
5 Unscrew the fixing nuts and separate the rear cover from the stator.
6 If the brush length is less than the specified minimum the brushes must be renewed. To do this, the brush leads must be unsoldered. The new brushes must be attached quickly to prevent the heat leaking away and damaging adjacent components (photo).

6.6 View inside alternator showing brush holder

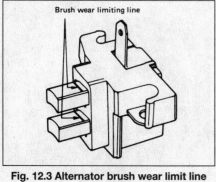

Fig. 12.3 Alternator brush wear limit line (Sec 6)

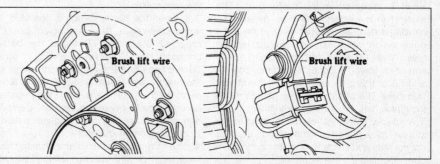

Fig. 12.4 Using a brush lift wire (Sec 6)

12

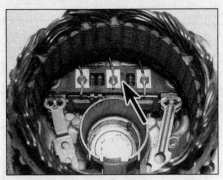

6.8 View inside alternator showing regulator

6.11A Using a drill as a brush holder . . .

6.11B . . . through this hole

7 Unless the voltage regulator is faulty ignore the operations described in the next three paragraphs.
8 Remove the regulator securing rivets and unsolder the terminals (photo).
9 Remove the bolts which retain the brush holder/regulator unit.
10 Refit the new regulator by reversing the disconnection and removal operations. Peen the rivets securely.
11 Before reassembling the rear cover/brush holder assembly to the motor/front cover, the brushes must be held in the raised position in order to be able to locate them on the slip rings. Do this by passing a thin rod through the hole provided in the alternator rear cover (photo).
12 Align the marks made on the front and rear covers and join the sections of the alternator together.
13 Fit the tie-bolts, remove the temporary brush lift rod.
14 If for any reason the alternator pulley must be removed, the pulley retaining nut can be unscrewed if the rotor shaft is prevented from rotating by inserting a splined socket in the shaft recess or by gripping the rotor in a vice with the alternator dismantled.

7 Starter motor - description

1 The starter motor is of pre-engaged type.
2 When the starter switch is operated, current flows from the battery to the solenoid switch which is mounted on the starter body. The plunger in the solenoid moves inwards, so causing a centrally pivoted lever to push the drive pinion into mesh with the starter ring gear. When the solenoid plunger reaches the end of its travel, it closes an internal contact and full starting current flows to the starter field coils. The armature is then able to rotate the crankshaft, so starting the engine.
3 A special freewheel clutch is fitted to the starter drive pinion so that as soon as the engine fires and starts to operate on its own it does not drive the starter motor.
4 When the starter switch is released, the solenoid is de-energised and a spring moves the plunger back to its rest position. This operates the pivoted lever to withdraw the drive pinion from engagement with the starter ring.
5 On automatic transmission models, an idler gear is incorporated at the drive end of the starter motor.

8 Starter motor - testing in situ

1 If the starter motor fails to turn the engine when the switch is operated there are five possible causes:
(a) The battery is faulty
(b) The electrical connections between the switch, solenoid battery and starter motor are somewhere failing to pass the necessary current from the battery through the starter to earth
(c) The solenoid switch is faulty
(d) The starter motor is mechanically or electrically defective
(e) The starter motor pinion and/or flywheel ring gear is badly worn and in need of replacement
2 To check the battery, switch on the headlight. if they dim after a few seconds the battery is in a discharged state. If the lights glow brightly, operate the starter switch and see what happens to the lights. If they dim then you know that power is reaching the starter motor but failing to turn it. If the starter turns slowly when switched on, proceed to the next check.
3 If, when the starter switch is operated, the lights stay bright, then insufficient power is reaching the motor. Remove the battery connections, starter/solenoid power connections and the engine earth strap and thoroughly clean them and refit them. Smear petroleum jelly around the battery connections to prevent corrosion. Corroded connections are the most frequent cause of electric system malfunctions.
4 When the above checks and cleaning tasks have been carried out, but without success, you will possibly have heard a clicking noise each time the starter switch was operated. This was the solenoid switch operating, but it does not necessarily follow that the main contacts were closing properly (if no clicking has been heard from the solenoid, it is certainly defective). The solenoid contact can be checked by putting a voltmeter or bulb across the main cable connection of the starter side of the solenoid and earth. When the switch is operated, there should be a reading or lighted bulb. If there is no reading or lighted bulb, the solenoid unit is faulty and should be renewed.
5 If the starter motor operates but doesn't turn the engine over then it is most probable that the starter pinion and/or flywheel ring gear are badly worn, in which case the starter motor will normally be noisy in operation.
6 Finally, if it is established that the solenoid is not faulty and 12 volts are getting to the starter, then the motor is faulty and should be removed for inspection.

9 Starter motor - removal and refitting

1 Disconnect the battery.
2 Disconnect the leads from the starter motor and solenoid terminals (photo).
3 Unscrew the starter motor fixing bolts and lift the unit from the engine.
4 Refitting is a reversal of removal.

9.2 Starter motor electrical connections

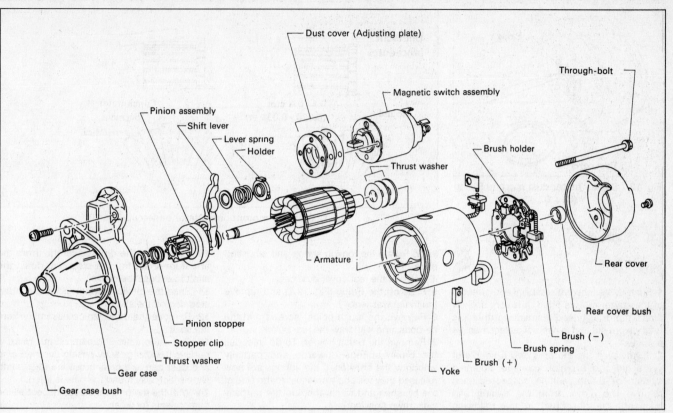

Fig. 12.5 Exploded view of starter motor for manual transmission (Sec 10)

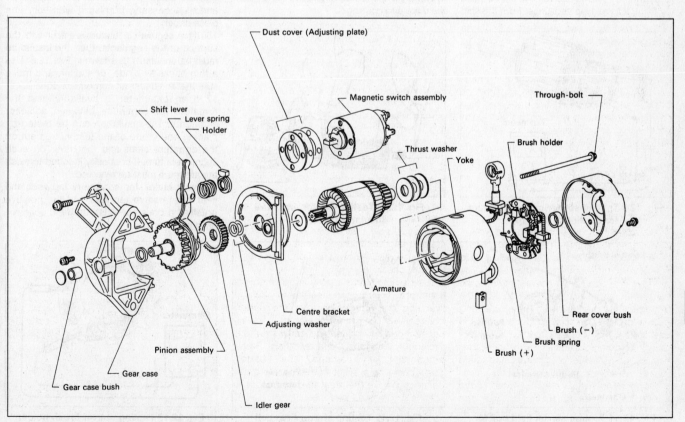

Fig. 12.6 Exploded view of starter motor for automatic transmission (Sec 10)

12

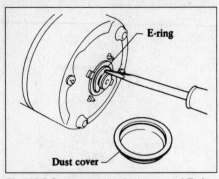

Fig. 12.7 Starter motor dust cap and E-ring (Sec 10)

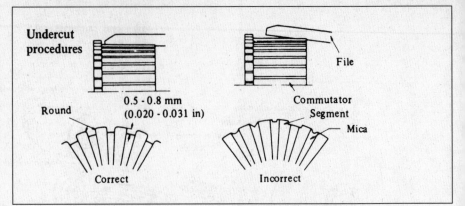

Fig. 12.8 Starter motor commutator undercut (Sec 10)

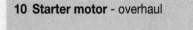

10 Starter motor - overhaul

1 Such is the inherent reliability and strength of the starter motors fitted, it is very unlikely that a motor will need dismantling until it is totally worn out and in need of replacement as a whole.

2 If, however, the motor is only a couple of years old and a pinion carriage, solenoid system or brush fault is suspected then remove the motor from the engine and dismantle as described in the following paragraphs.

3 Extract the screws and remove the solenoid by tilting it to release its plunger from the shift lever. Retain the torsion spring and adjusting plate.

4 Prise off the rear cover dust cap.

5 Prise off the E-ring (Fig. 12.7) and remove the thrust washers.

6 Remove the brush holder screws and the tie-bolts, and withdraw the rear cover.

7 Remove the brush holder. To do this, pull the brush springs upwards and partially withdraw the brushes. If the springs are now released they will apply pressure to the side of the brushes and retain them in the partially withdrawn position.

8 Withdraw the yoke.

9 Withdraw the armature and shift lever from the drive end housing.

10 To remove the drive assembly from the armature shaft, tap the stop ring down the shaft to expose the circlip.

11 Prise the circlip from its groove, pull the stop ring off the shafts.

12 Remove the drive pinion assembly from the shaft.

13 On automatic transmission models remove the idler gear by prising out the E-ring and dust cap and driving out the idler shaft. Note which way round the gear is fitted.

14 With the motor dismantled, inspect all the components for wear.

15 If the commutator appears dirty or burned, clean it with a solvent-soaked rag and, if necessary, burnish it with very fine glass paper.

16 If the segment insulators are flush with the surface of the segments, then the insulators must be undercut, as shown in Fig. 12.8. Use a thin hacksaw blade, or similar, and make sure that the undercut corners are square.

17 If an ohmmeter is available, test the armature for continuity between adjacent segments. The insulation can be tested by placing one probe of the test instrument on the armature shaft and the other on each segment in turn. If continuity is found to exist, the armature must be renewed.

18 Now check for continuity between the field coil positive terminal and the positive brush. If it does not exist, the field coils will have to be renewed.

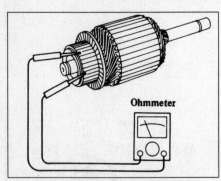

Fig. 12.9 Testing starter motor armature for continuity (Sec 10)

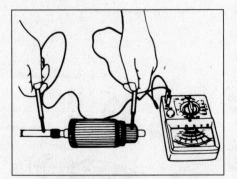

Fig. 12.10 Testing starter armature insulation (Sec 10)

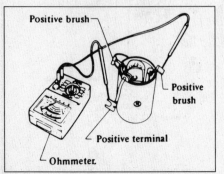

Fig. 12.11 Testing starter field coil for continuity (Sec 10)

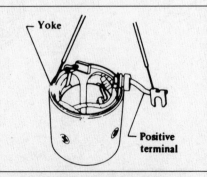

Fig. 12.12 Testing starter field coil insulation (Sec 10)

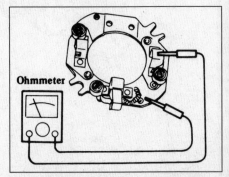

Fig. 12.13 Testing starter brush holder insulation (Sec 10)

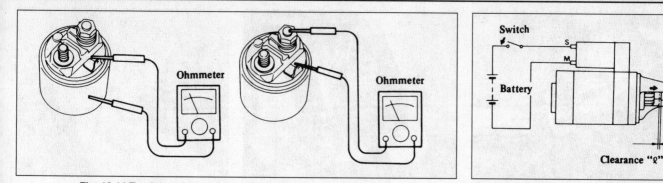

Fig. 12.14 Testing starter solenoid switch for continuity (Sec 10)

Fig. 12.15 Starter pinion setting diagram –
manual transmission (Sec 10)

Clearance 0.5 to 2.0 mm (0.020 to 0.079 in)

19 Check the insulation by connecting one probe of the test instrument to the field coil positive terminal and the yoke. If continuity exists, the field coils must be renewed.

20 Renewal of the starter motor field coils is a job best left to your dealer or auto-electrical agent due to the need for a pressure screwdriver and other equipment.

21 Check the brushes for wear. If they have worn down to the minimum specified length, renew them by removing the old brush lead and soldering on the new. Carry out the work quickly to avoid the spread of heat to the field coils, and do not allow the solder to seep down the lead or its flexibility will be impaired.

22 The brush holder can be checked for insulation breakdown by placing one probe of the tester on the positive side of the brush holder and the other one on the negative (baseplate) side. If continuity is indicated, renew the brush holder.

23 The solenoid switch can be checked for continuity by connecting the test instrument between the S terminal and the switch body. If no continuity is indicated, renew the switch.

24 Now place the probes of the tester on the S and M terminals of the switch. If no continuity is indicated, renew the switch.

25 Finally check the teeth of the drive pinion and idler gear, (where applicable). If they are worn or chipped renew the component. Test the pinion/clutch assembly for correct operation. It should turn smoothly in the drive direction and lock when turned in the reverse direction.

26 Reassemble by reversing the dismantling procedure. Lightly grease the friction surfaces, bushes, bearings and pivots as work proceeds.

27 On automatic transmission models, make sure that the idler gear is fitted the right way round with its collar opposite the groove in the pinion.

28 The pinion projection should now be checked by connecting the solenoid to a 12V battery to actuate it.

29 *On manual transmission models*, the clearance between the face of the pinion and the stop plate should be as specified in the Specifications at the beginning of this Chapter. If it is not, change the adjustment plate under the solenoid switch for one of different thickness. The plates are available in thickness of 0.5 mm (0.020 in) and 0.8 mm (0.031 in).

30 *On automatic transmission models*, with the solenoid actuated, measure the projection of the front face of the idler gear. Now measure again when the idler gear is pulled out by hand. The difference between the two measurements should be within the specified tolerance. If it is not, change the adjusting plate for one of suitable thickness.

11 Fuses, fusible links and relays - general

Fuses

1 The fusebox (photo) is located inside the vehicle under the right-hand side of the facia panel on RHD models, left-hand side on LHD models.

2 Place the fingers under the fusebox cover and pull it off.

3 The fuses are of 10 to 20A rating according to the circuit which is protected.

4 A blown fuse can be detected visually and should be renewed with one of the same amperage.

5 If the new fuse blows immediately, suspect a short circuit, probably faulty insulation, which should be rectified at once.

6 Never substitute a fuse of higher amperage, or a piece of wire or foil as a means of preventing a fuse blowing, this could lead to a fire or severely damage the components of the circuit.

Fusible links

7 These are designed to melt in the event of a

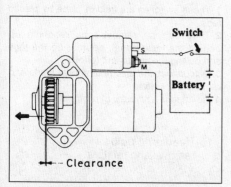

Fig. 12.16 Starter pinion setting diagram –
automatic transmission (Sec 10)

*Clearance difference = 0.5 to 2.0 mm
(0.020 to 0.079 in)*

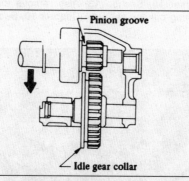

Fig. 12.17 Starter pinion-to-idler gear
relationship – automatic transmission
(Sec 10)

12

11.1 Fuse box

11.7 Fusible link on battery terminal

12.3 Typical switch unit attachment screws

13.1 Courtesy lamp

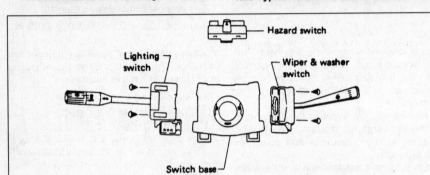
Fig. 12.18 Components of the combination switch (Sec 12)

Hazard switch
Lighting switch
Wiper & washer switch
Switch base

short in a major current carrying circuit (photo).

8 The links must never be taped up or placed in contact with adjacent wiring, plastic or rubber parts.

9 Before renewing a melted fusible link, rectify the cause or have a thorough check carried out on the vehicle wiring harness.

10 The circuits which the fusible links supply are shown in the wiring diagrams at the end of the manual.

Relays

11 The number and purpose of the relays fitted depends upon the particular model vehicle and its equipment.

12 The flasher unit is located under the facia panel next to the steering column.

13 The ignition and accessory relays are located on top of the fusebox.

14 At the front corners of the engine

compartment relays may be located which actuate the following:
Air conditioner
Air conditioner condenser fan
Horn
Headlamp dimmer
Rear foglamp
Automatic choke
Transmission switch

15 On the engine compartment rear bulkhead a relay may be located which actuates the windscreen wiper (intermittent).

12 Steering column combination switch - removal and refitting

1 Remove the steering wheel as described in Chapter 10, Section 16. Also remove the steering column shrouds (Chapter 10, Section 17).

2 The combination switch assembly consists of four basic units which can be removed and fitted independently of each other. They are: lighting switch, wash/wipe switch, hazard switch and the switch base.

3 Each unit may be removed by unscrewing the retaining screws (photo) and disconnecting the electrical leads.

4 To remove the switch base, remove the switch clamp screw, push the unit down, and turn it clockwise, then lift it off the column.

5 Refitting the switch base or any units is a reversal of removal.

13 Courtesy lamp - removal and refitting

1 The courtesy lamp is fitted above the windscreen by the rear view mirrors (photo).

2 Snap off the cover to replace a bulb.

3 Remove the securing screw to release the base plate. Make sure the electrical supply lead does not disappear inside the roof panel while the base plate is removed.

4 Refitting is a reversal of removing.

14 Facia panel mounted switches - removal and refitting

1 These switches are held in place by plastic tabs.

2 They can be removed by reaching up behind the facia panel, depressing the tags and pulling the switch out (photo).

3 Disconnect the electrical supply leads and remove the switch.

4 Refitting is a reversal of removal.

15 Headlamp bulbs - removal and refitting

1 The headlamp bulb may be changed from inside the engine compartment.

2 Lift the bonnet and then pull off the electrical connector (photo).

14.2 Showing the rear of a facia switch

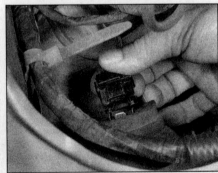
15.2 Remove the connector

15.3 Remove the dust cover

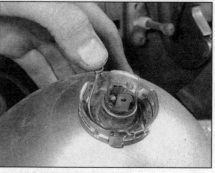

15.4 Release the spring clip

15.5 Lift out the bulb

3 Lift off the dust cover (photo).
4 Unhook the spring retainer (photo).
5 Lift out the bulb (photo).
Note: *Do not handle halogen bulbs, as deposits from fingers will shorten the bulb's life.*
6 Refit in the reverse order.

16 Headlamp unit - removal and refitting

1 Remove the front combination light unit described in Section 18.
2 Remove the front radiator grille as described in Chapter 11.

3 Remove the headlamp retaining bolt (photo).
4 Unhook the tensioning spring (photo) and remove the headlamp unit.

17 Headlamp beam adjustment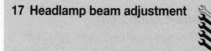

1 Although adjustment screws are provided for setting the headlamp beam, it is recommended that this operation be left to your local dealer or garage who has the necessary equipment.

18 Combination light - removal, refitting and bulb changing

Front combination light

1 Remove the top retaining screw (photo).
2 Pull the unit out at the top, and unhook it from the plastic retaining clip at the bottom (photo).
3 Depress the plastic catch and pull off the connector (photo).
4 Prise open the lens, revealing the bulb, which is of the bayonet type fixing (photo).
5 Refit in the reverse order.

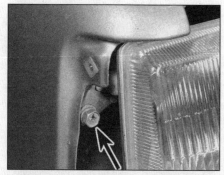

16.3 Remove the headlamp retaining bolt

16.4 Unhook the tensioning spring

18.1 Remove the top securing screw

18.2 Unhook the bottom end from the retaining clip

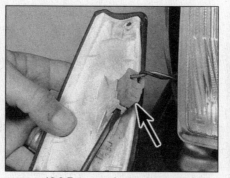

18.3 Remove the connector

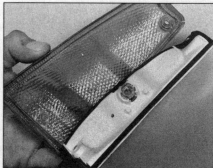

18.4 Prise off the lens

12

18.6 Remove the two screws

18.7 Pull off the lens

18.10 Remove the plastic panel

Front marker and direction indicator lights

6 Remove the two retaining screws (photo).
7 Pull off the lens (photo).
8 The bulbs are a bayonet fix.
9 Refit in the reverse order.

Rear combination lights

10 The bulbs in the rear combination light unit may be changed in situ by removing the plastic cover in the luggage compartment (photo).
11 This will reveal the back of the unit. The bulbholders twist and pull out and the bulbs are a bayonet fix (photo).
12 To remove the light unit, undo the two nuts from the inboard edge of the unit by reaching inside the luggage compartment, and pull the unit outwards (photo).
13 The outboard edge has locating lugs to hold it in place (photo).
14 Refit in the reverse order.

Number plate light

15 The rear number plate light can be reached by removing the trim covering the inside of the tailgate.
16 Twist and pull the lamp unit from its housing (photo).
17 Twist off the lamp cover (photo). The bulb is a push fit in the holder.
18 Refit in the reverse order.

19 Instrument panel - removal and refitting

1 The term 'instrument panel' refers to that part of the complete facia assembly which is immediately above the steering column, and houses the speedometer and gauges. Instructions for removing the complete facia panel will be found in Chapter 11.
2 If preferred, remove the steering wheel as described in Chapter 10, Section 16, for better access; otherwise, remove the column shrouds.
3 Remove the screws holding the instrument panel hood, and take off the hood (photos).

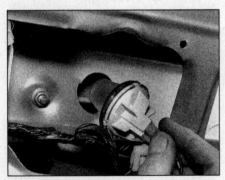

18.11 Removing the bulbholders

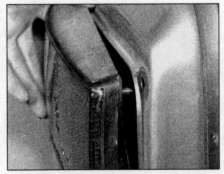

18.12 Removing the lens cover

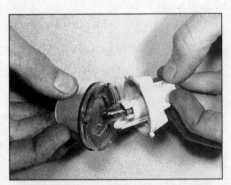

18.13 Outboard edge has locating lugs

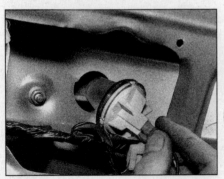

18.16 Removing the rear number plate light from the tailgate

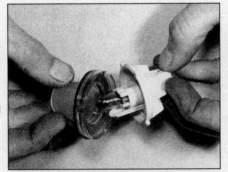

18.17 Separating the cover from the holder

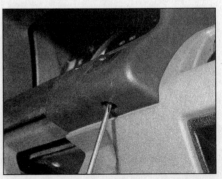

19.3 Instrument panel shroud screws

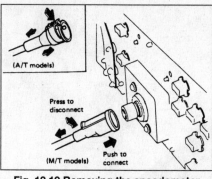

Fig. 12.19 Removing the speedometer cable (Sec 19)

19.4 Removing the instrument panel to facia screws

19.5 Pull out the speedometer cable

4 Remove the screws holding the instrument panel to the facia (photo).

5 Pull the panel forward gently and then disconnect the speedometer cable (photo). Do this by depressing the plastic clip and pulling the cable from its housing. It is a push fit on refitting.

6 The panel will now come further forward allowing the electrical connectors to be disconnected, and the panel removed (photo).

7 The perspex cover may be removed by depressing the plastic clips (photo).

8 Further clips hold the panel surround (photo).

9 The instruments themselves (photo) may be removed by pulling off the plastic backing sheet (photo) and removing the nuts (photo).

10 The instrument bulbs are a push fit in the holders, and can be pulled out for renewal

(photos). The holders are a bayonet fit in the instrument panel. Note that it is usually possible to remove these bulbs and holders

from the rear without it being necessary to remove the instrument panel.

11 Refitting is a reversal of this procedure.

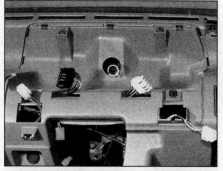

19.6 Instrument panel removed

19.7 Removing the perspex cover . . .

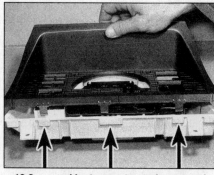

19.8 . . . and instrument panel surround

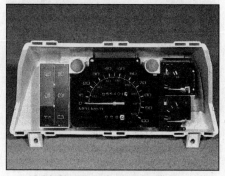

19.9A Showing the instruments . . .

19.9B . . . plastic locking sheet . . .

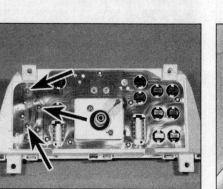

19.9C . . . and instrument securing nuts

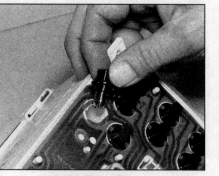

19.10A The bulbs . . .

19.10B . . . are a push fit

12

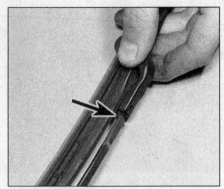

20.4 Removing windscreen wiper blade

20.7 Removing the arm from drive spindle

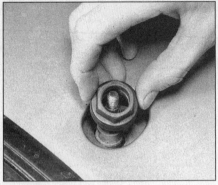

21.2 Removing the wiper drive spindle nut

21.3A Air intake grille screws . . .

20 Windscreen wiper blades and arms - removal and refitting

1 The wiper blades should be renewed as soon as they cease to wipe the glass cleanly.
2 The complete blade assembly or just the rubber insert are available as replacements.
3 Pull the wiper arm from the glass until it locks.
4 Depress the small tab and slide the blade off the arm (photo).
5 Refitting is a reversal of removal.
6 Before removing a wiper arm, it is

worthwhile sticking a strip of masking tape on the glass against the edge of the wiper blade as a guide to wiper arm setting when refitting.
7 Lift up the cap to expose the nut which holds the wiper arm to the driving spindle (photo).
8 Unscrew the nut and pull the arm/blade assembly from the spindle splines.
9 Refit by reversing the removal operations.
10 Wet the glass and operate the wipers to check their arc of travel. If it is incorrect, remove the arm and move it a spline or two in the required direction.

21.3B . . . and location tabs

21.4A Prise the link arms . . .

21 Windscreen wiper motor and linkage - removal and refitting

1 Remove the wiper arms as described in Section 20 and disconnect the battery.
2 Remove the wiper drive spindle nut from both spindles (photo).
3 Remove the air intake grille held by screws (photo) at its rear edge and locating tabs (photo) on its front edge.
4 Prise off the wiper link arms (photos).
5 Unbolt the motor from the engine bulkhead (photo).
6 Refitting is a reversal of these operations.

21.4B . . . from the other components . . .

21.4C . . . of the wiper linkage

21.5 Unbolting the motor from the bulkhead

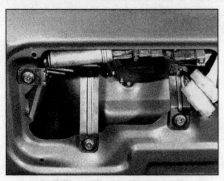

22.6 The tailgate wiper motor

24.2 The horn is situated behind the headlamp

25.1 Heated rear screen elements and electrical connection

22 Tailgate wiper motor - removal and refitting

1 The tailgate wiper motor is of direct drive type, without linkages.
2 The wiper arm/blade is removed as described for the windscreen wiper in Section 20.
3 Open the tailgate and remove the trim panel by carefully prising out the clips. Disconnect the battery.
4 Disconnect the wiper motor wiring.
5 Prise off the cap and unscrew the drive spindle nut.
6 Unbolt and remove the wiper motor (photo).
7 Refitting is a reversal of removal.

23 Washer system - general

1 All models are equipped with a windscreen washer.
2 The washer reservoir is located within the engine compartment.
3 On vehicles with a tailgate washer, the fluid reservoir with its electric pumps serves both the windscreen and tailgate.
4 Where a headlamp washer system is fitted, a separate fluid reservoir is used.
5 The windscreen wiper/washer is controlled

by a stalk switch on the steering column.
6 The tailgate wiper/washer is controlled by a double action rocker switch.
7 The headlamp washer switch is of single action rocker type.
8 The washer jets which are located within the slots of the air intake grille are adjusted by inserting a pin in their nozzles and repositioning them to give a satisfactory spray pattern.

24 Horn - removal and refitting

1 Remove the headlamp unit as described in Section 16.
2 Unbolt the horn from the bracket and disconnect the wiring (photo).
3 If the horn emits a weak sound it may be possible to improve it by adjusting the screw on the rear of the unit.
4 Refitting is a reversal of removal.

25 Heated rear window - general

1 Care should be taken to avoid damage to the element for the heated rear window or tailgate (photo).
2 Avoid scratching with rings on the fingers

when cleaning, and do not allow luggage to rub against the glass.
3 Do not stick labels over the element on the inside of the glass.
4 If the element grids do become damaged, a special conductive paint is available from most motor factors to repair it.
5 Do not leave the heated rear window switch on unnecessarily as it draws a high current from the electrical system.

26 Idle speed control system - description and testing

1 This system is designed to increase the engine idle speed whenever the headlamps, heated rear window, heater blower or radiator fan are switched on, which can cause the engine speed to drop due to the increased retarding effect of the alternator.
2 The main component of the system is an electronic control unit located under the front passenger seat (photo). This unit monitors the ignition signal (engine idling speed) and the moment when electrical accessories are switched on. When a certain level of electrical demand is reached, the unit opens a solenoid valve in the carburettor fuel mixture by-pass passage to admit additional mixture, which maintains the specified engine idle speed (photo).

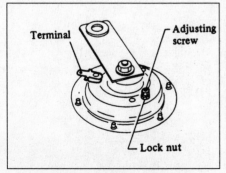

Fig. 12.20 Adjusting screw on the horn (Sec 24)

Terminal — Adjusting screw

Lock nut

26.2A Idle speed control unit

26.2B Idle speed control system solenoid at carburettor

12

27.1 Prise off the surround

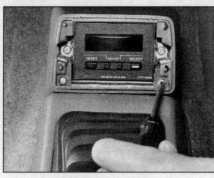

27.2 Undo the screws . . .

27.3 . . . and electrical connector

3 To check the system, switch on one of the electrical accessories referred to in paragraph 1. The engine idling speed should increase by between 50 and 200 rpm.

4 If this does not happen, connect a voltmeter between terminal number 10 of the control unit and earth and switch on the ignition.

5 Turn on the heated rear window or the headlamps. The indicated voltage should be 12V. Turn off the accessories and OV should be indicated.

6 Now connect the voltmeter between terminal number 6 and earth. Increase the engine speed to above 3300 rpm, when 12V should be indicated. Reduce the engine speed to below 3300 rpm, when OV should be indicated.

7 Check the solenoid valve by disconnecting and reconnecting the battery negative lead. A 'clicking' sound should be heard.

8 If the components do not perform as described, renew them.

27 Digital clock - removal and refitting

1 Prise off the surround (photo).
2 Undo the securing screws (photo).

3 Disconnect the electrical lead (photo) and lift the clock from the housing.
4 Refitting is a reversal of this procedure.

28 Cigar lighter - removal and refitting

1 The cigar lighter is contained within the heater control panel.
2 Prise out the heater control panel front as described in Chapter 11.
3 Disconnect the electrical lead and unscrew the cigar lighter from the panel.
4 Refit in the reverse order.

Fault finding - electrical system

No voltage at starter motor

- [ ] Battery discharged
- [ ] Battery defective internally
- [ ] Battery terminals loose or earth lead not securely attached to body
- [ ] Loose or broken connections in starter motor circuit
- [ ] Starter motor switch or solenoid faulty

Voltage at starter motor - faulty motor

- [ ] Starter brushes badly worn, sticking, or brush wires loose
- [ ] Commutator dirty, worn or burnt
- [ ] Starter motor armature faulty
- [ ] Field coils earthed

Starter motor noisy or rough in engagement

- [ ] Pinion or flywheel gear teeth broken or worn
- [ ] Starter motor retaining bolts loose

Alternator not charging*

- [ ] Drivebelt loose and slipping, or broken
- [ ] Bushes worn, sticking, broken or dirty
- [ ] Brush springs weak or broken

If all appears to be well but the alternator is still not charging, take the car to an automobile electrician for checking of the alternator

Battery will not hold charge for more than a few days

- [ ] Battery defective internally
- [ ] Electrolyte level too low or electrolyte too weak due to leakage
- [ ] Plate separators no longer fully effective
- [ ] Battery plates severely sulphated
- [ ] Drivebelt slipping
- [ ] Battery terminal connections loose or corroded
- [ ] Alternator not charging properly
- [ ] Short in lighting circuit causing continual battery drain

Ignition light fails to go out, battery runs flat in a few days

- [ ] Drivebelt loose and slipping, or broken
- [ ] Alternator faulty

Fuel gauge gives no reading

- [ ] Fuel tank empty
- [ ] Electric cable between tank sender unit and gauge earthed or loose
- [ ] Fuel gauge case not earthed
- [ ] Fuel gauge supply cable interrupted
- [ ] Fuel gauge unit broken

Fuel gauge registers full all the time

- [ ] Electric cable between tank unit and gauge broken or disconnected

Horn operates all the time

- [ ] Horn push either earthed or stuck down
- [ ] Horn cable to horn push earthed

Horn fails to operate

- [ ] Blown fuse
- [ ] Cable or cable connection loose, broken or disconnected
- [ ] Horn has an internal fault

Horn emits intermittent or unsatisfactory noise

- [ ] Cable connections loose
- [ ] Horn incorrectly adjusted

Lights do not come on

- [ ] If engine not running, battery discharged
- [ ] Light bulb filament burnt out or bulbs broken
- [ ] Wire connections loose, disconnected or broken
- [ ] Light switch shorting or otherwise faulty

Lights come on but fade

- [ ] If engine not running, battery discharged

Lights give very poor illumination

- [ ] Lamp glasses dirty
- [ ] Reflector tarnished or dirty
- [ ] Lamps badly out of adjustment
- [ ] Incorrect bulb with too low wattage fitted
- [ ] Existing bulbs old and badly discoloured
- [ ] Electrical wiring too thin not allowing full current to pass

Lights work erratically, flashing on and off, especially over bumps

- [ ] Battery terminals or earth connections loose
- [ ] Lights not earthing properly
- [ ] Contacts in light switch faulty

Wiper motor fails to work

- [ ] Blown fuse
- [ ] Brushes badly worn
- [ ] Wire connections loose, disconnected or broken
- [ ] Armature worn or faulty
- [ ] Field coils faulty

Wiper motor works very slowly and takes excessive current

- [ ] Commutator dirty, greasy or burnt
- [ ] Drive to spindles bent or unlubricated
- [ ] Drive spindle binding or damaged
- [ ] Armature bearings dry or misaligned
- [ ] Armature body worn or faulty

Wiper motor works slowly and takes little current

- [ ] Brushes badly worn
- [ ] Commutator dirty, greasy or burnt
- [ ] Armature badly worn or faulty

Wiper motor works but wiper blades remain static

- [ ] Linkage disengaged or faulty
- [ ] Drive spindle damaged or worn
- [ ] Wiper motor gearbox parts badly worn

12

Notes

Chapter 13 Supplement:
Revisions and information on later models

Contents

13

Degrees of difficulty

| **Easy,** suitable for novice with little experience | ⚒ | **Fairly easy,** suitable for beginner with some experience | ⚒ | **Fairly difficult,** suitable for competent DIY mechanic | ⚒ | **Difficult,** suitable for experienced DIY mechanic | ⚒ | **Very difficult,** suitable for expert DIY or professional | ⚒ |

1 Introduction

This Supplement contains information which is additional to, or a revision of, material in the first 12 Chapters.

The Sections in this Supplement follow the same order as the Chapters to which they relate. The Specifications are all grouped together for convenience, but they too follow Chapter order.

It is recommended that before any particular operation is undertaken, reference is made to both the relevant Section of this Supplement and to the main Chapter, so that any changes to procedures or components can be noted before work commences.

Since first publication of this manual, the Micra range received a minor facelift and an increase in the number of models available in June 1985, followed by the introduction of the 'Colette' versions in February 1986, 5-door models in April 1987, and the announcement of the 'S-series' models in March 1988, with a general revision of model names and an uprating of specification. In March 1989, the range received another facelift, with a further uprating of specification, and was extended by the introduction of the 1.2 models; all engines were now fitted with electronic ignition. In January 1991, some 1.2 models had catalytic converters fitted as standard equipment, while in January 1992, the range was revised and specifications uprated for the last time before the (K10-series) models covered in this manual were replaced by a new Micra model in 1993.

The vehicles used in the preparation of this Supplement and appearing in many of the photographs were a 1988 GSX, a GS and a 1989 1.2 GS with automatic transmission; also used was a 1992 1.2 SLX with a catalytic converter.

2 Specifications

Note: *The Specifications given below are supplementary to, or revisions of, those at the beginning of preceding Chapters.*

General dimensions, weights and capacities

Dimensions - mm (in)
Overall length - June 1985 to October 1988	3760 (148.0)
Overall length - 1.2 Super S	3737 (147.1)
Overall length - all other models, November 1988-on	3735 (147.0)
Overall width - 1.2 Super S	1590 (62.6)
Overall height - 'Canvastop' models	1440 (56.7)

Kerb weights - kg (lb)
3-door, manual transmission	630 to 710 (1389 to 1565)
3-door, automatic transmission	675 to 740 (1490 to 1631)
5-door, manual transmission	705 to 725 (1554 to 1598) 5-door, automatic transmission

Engine - 1.0 models

General
Designation	MA10 S
Compression ratio:	
Models with four-speed manual transmission	9.5 :1
All other models	10.3:1
Compression pressure - models with five-speed manual or automatic transmission - @ 350 rev/min:	
Standard	210 lbf/in^2 (14.8 kgf/cm^2)
Minimum	178 lbf/in^2 (12.5 kgf/cm^2)
Power output:	
Models with four-speed manual transmission	50 bhp (37 kW) @ 6000 rev/min
All other models	55 bhp (41 kW) @ 6000 rev/min

Cylinder block
Cylinder bore diameter	
Grade 1	68.000 to 68.010 mm (2.6772 to 2.6776 in)
Grade 2	68.010 to 68.020 mm (2.6776 to 2.6780 in)
Grade 3	68.020 to 68.030 mm (2.6780 to 2.6783 in)
Grade 4	68.030 to 68.040 mm (2.6783 to 2.6787 in)
Grade 5	68.040 to 68.050 mm (2.6787 to 2.6791 in)
Oversize 0.20 mm (0.0079 in)	68.200 to 68.250 mm (2.6850 to 2.6870 in)
Main bearing bore internal diameter:	
Grade 0	49.000 to 49.004 mm (1.9291 to 1.9293 in)
Grade 1	49.004 to 49.008 mm (1.9293 to 1.9294 in)
Grade 2	49.008 to 49.012 mm (1.9294 to 1.9296 in)
Grade 3	49.012 to 49.016 mm (1.9296 to 1.9298 in)

Crankshaft

Main journal diameter:

Grade 0 .... 44.966 to 44.970 mm (1.7703 to 2.7705 in)
Grade 1 .... 44.962 to 44.966 mm (1.7701 to 1.7703 in)
Grade 2 .... 44.958 to 44.962 mm (1.7700 to 1.7701 in)
Grade 3 .... 44.954 to 44.958 mm (1.7698 to 1.7700 in)
Undersize 0.25 mm (0.0098 in) .... 44.700 to 44.720 mm (1.7598 to 1.7606 in)

Main bearing shell thickness:

Grade 0 (Black colour code) .... 2.000 to 2.004 mm (0.0787 to 0.0789 in)
Grade 1 (Brown colour code) .... 2.002 to 2.006 mm (0.0788 to 0.0790 in)
Grade 2 (Green colour code) .... 2.004 to 2.008 mm (0.0789 to 0.0791 in)
Grade 3 (Yellow colour code) .... 2.006 to 2.010 mm (0.0790 to 0.0791 in)
Grade 4 (Blue colour code) .... 2.008 to 2.012 mm (0.0791 to 0.0792 in)
Grade 5 (Pink colour code) .... 2.010 to 2.014 mm (0.0791 to 0.0793 in)
Grade 6 (Red or purple colour code) .... 2.012 to 2.016 mm (0.0792 to 0.0794 in)
Undersize 0.25 mm (0.0098 in) .... 2.125 to 2.129 mm (0.0837 to 0.0838 in)

Crankpin diameter:

Undersize 0.25 mm (0.0098 in) .... 39.710 to 39.720 mm (1.5634 to 1.5638 in)
Maximum main journal and crankpin taper .... 0.02 mm (0.0008 in)

Pistons

Clearance in block - November 1988 on .... 0.010 to 0.030 mm (0.0004 to 0.0012 in)

Piston skirt diameter - up to November 1988:

Grade 1 .... 67.967 to 67.977 mm (2.6759 to 2.6763 in)
Grade 2 .... 67.977 to 67.987 mm (2.6763 to 2.6767 in)
Grade 3 .... 67.987 to 67.997 mm (2.6767 to 2.6770 in)
Grade 4 .... 67.997 to 68.007 mm (2.6770 to 2.6774 in)
Grade 5 .... 68.007 to 68.017 mm (2.6774 to 2.6778 in)
Oversize 0.20 mm (0.0079 in) .... 68.167 to 68.217 mm (2.6837 to 2.6857in)

Piston skirt diameter - November 1988 on:

Grade 1 .... 67.980 to 67.990 mm (2.6764 to 2.6768 in)
Grade 2 .... 67.990 to 68.000 mm (2.6768 to 2.6772 in)
Grade 3 .... 68.000 to 68.010 mm (2.6772 to 2.6776 in)
Grade 4 .... 68.010 to 68.020 mm (2.6776 to 2.6780 in)
Grade 5 .... 68.020 to 68 030 mm (2 6780 to 2.6783 in)
Oversize 0.20 mm (0.0079 in) .... 68.180 to 68.230 mm (2.6842 to 2.6862 in)

Note: *Skirt diameter is measured 9 mm (0.35 in) above the base of the skirt, at right-angles to the gudgeon pin axis.*

Piston rings

End gap:

2nd .... 0.15 to 0.34 mm (0.0059 to 0.0134 in)
Oil control .... 0.20 to 0.69 mm (0.0079 to 0.0272 in)
End gap wear limit - all rings .... 0.80 mm (0.0315 in)

Torque wrench settings

	lbf ft	kgf m
Clutch pressure plate bolts	16 to 22	2.2 to 3.0
Sump pan bolts - January 1985-on	3.6 to 5.1	0.5 to 0.7
Crankshaft rear oil seal housing/retainer bolts	2.9 to 3.6	0.4 to 0.5

Engine - 1.2 models

Note: *Specifications are given only where different from those given for the MA10 S engine, including those above.*

General

Designation .... MA12 S
Bore .... 71.0 mm (2.80 in)
Stroke .... 78.0 mm (3.07 in)
Capacity .... 1235 cc (75.36 cu in)
Compression ratio 9.0:1

Compression pressure - @ 350 rev/min:

Standard .... 181 lbf/in² (12 kgf/cm²)
Minimum .... 172 lbf/in² (10.0 kgf/cm²)
Power output .... 60 bhp (44 kW) @ 6000 rev/min

Cylinder block

Cylinder bore diameter:

Grade 1 .... 71.000 to 71.010 mm (2 7953 to 2.7957in)
Grade 2 .... 71.010 to 71.020 mm (2.7957 to 2.7961 in)
Grade 3 .... 71.020 to 71.030 mm (2.7961 to 2.7965in)
Grade 4 .... 71.030 to 71.040 mm (2 7965 to 2.7968in)
Grade 5 .... 71.040 to 71.050 mm (2.7968 to 2.7972in)
Oversize 0.20 mm (0.0079 in) .... 71.200 to 71.250 mm (2.8031 to 2.8051in)

13

Pistons

Piston skirt diameter:
Grade1	70.980 to 70.990 mm (2.7945 to 2.7949 in)
Grade 2	70.990 to 71.000 mm (2.7949 to 2.7953 in)
Grade 3	71.000 to 71.010 mm (2.7953 to 2.7957in)
Grade 4	71.010 to 71.020 mm (2.7957 to 2.7961in)
Grade 5	71.020 to 71.030 mm (2.7961 to 2.7965in)
Oversize 0.20 mm (0.0079 in)	71.180 to 71.230 mm (2.8024 to 2.8043in)

Camshaft

Cam lobe height:
Height	33.98 to 34.23 mm (1.3378 to 1.3476 in)
Exhaust	33.94 to 34.19 mm (1.3362 to 1.3461 in)

Cooling system

Coolant - 1.2 models

Capacity - total, including heater and expansion tank	9.7 Imp pt (5.5 litre)

Fuel, exhaust and emission control systems

General

Recommended fuel - minimum octane rating:
1.0 models with four-speed manual transmission	90 RON, unleaded or leaded (nearest UK equivalent, unleaded Premium)
All other 1.0 models up to April 1990*	97 RON, unleaded or leaded (UK equivalents, unleaded Super/Superplus or four-star)
All other 1.0 models, April 1990 onwards	95 RON, unleaded or leaded (UK equivalent, unleaded Premium)
1.2 models without catalytic converters	91 RON, unleaded or leaded (nearest UK equivalent, unleaded Premium)
1.2 models with catalytic converters	91 RON, unleaded **only** (nearest UK equivalent, unleaded Premium)

Note: *At the time of writing, exact equivalents to the manufacturer's recommendations may not be available in the UK*
Petrols currently on sale are four-star (97 RON leaded), unleaded Premium (95 RON) and unleaded Super/Superplus (97 RON).
*For these models to run on unleaded Premium (95 RON), the ignition timing must first be retarded by 3°.

Carburettor

Type
1.0 models with manual transmission, January 1985 to October 1988	Hitachi DCZ 306-81 A
1.0 models with automatic transmission, January 1985 to October 1988	Hitachi DCZ 306-82A
1.0 models with manual transmission, November 1988 on	Hitachi DCZ 306-91A
1.0 models with automatic transmission, November 1988 on	Hitachi DCZ 306-92A
1.2 models with manual transmission, without catalytic converters	Hitachi DCZ 306-94
1.2 models with automatic transmission, without catalytic converters	Hitachi DCZ 306-95
1.2 models with manual transmission and catalytic converters	Hitachi DCZ 306-96
1.2 models with automatic transmission and catalytic converters	Hitachi DCZ 306-97

Idling speed - models with automatic transmission, position 'N' selected:
1.0 models with automatic transmission, up to January 1985	900 ± 50 rev/min
All other models	800 ± 50 rev/min
CO content - @ idling speed - models with catalytic converters	0.5% maximum

Jet sizes:
	Primary	Secondary
Main jet - 1.2 models without catalytic converters	93	130
Main jet - 1.2 models with catalytic converters	91	130
Main air bleed - 1.2 models	70	80
Slow air bleed - 1.2 models	170	80

Carburettor settings

Vacuum break adjustment - 1.2 models with catalytic converters:
Clearance R1 (Fig.13.11)	1.10 ± 0.15 mm (0.0433 ± 0.0059 in)
Clearance R2 (Fig.13.12)	1.60 ± 0.15 mm (0.0630 ± 0.0059 in)
Dashpot/stop lever contact engine speed - all applicable models, November 1988 on	1900 to 2100 rev/min
Primary throttle valve-to-inner wall clearance ('A', Fig. 3.8) - all 1.2 models with manual transmission	0.47 ± 0.07 mm (0.0185 ± 0.0028 in)

Float heights - all 1.0 models November 1988 on, all 1.2 models:
Fuel inlet needle valve closed ('H', Fig. 3.17)	11.5 to 12.5 mm (0.4528 to 0.4921 in)
Fuel inlet needle valve fully open ('h', Fig.3.18)	46.5 to 47.5 mm (1.8307 to 1.8701 in)

Torque wrench settings

	lbf ft	kgf m
Air/fuel ratio solenoid screws	1.1 to 2.9	0.15 to 0.40
EGR control valve retaining nuts	13 to 17	1.8 to 2.3
Exhaust gas sensor	30 to 37	4.1 to 5.1
Exhaust downpipe-to-primary catalytic converter nuts	26 to 30	3.6 to 4.1
Secondary catalytic converter flange bolts	32 to 41	4.4 to 5.6
Exhaust system intermediate-to-rear pipe flange bolts	32 to 41	4.4 to 5.6
Exhaust system intermediate silencer mounting bolts:		
Early models	12 to 15	1.6 to 2.1
January 1985 to June 1987	2.2 to 3.6	0.3 to 0.5
Exhaust system U-bolt nuts	12 to 15	1.6 to 2.1
Exhaust system heat shield screws	3.6 to 51	0.5 to 0.7
Exhaust system rubber mounting bolts and nuts:		
Early models	5.8 to 8.7	0.8 to 1.2
January 1985 to June 1987, front mounting bolt only	12 to 15	1.6 to 2.1
All, November 1988 on	9 to 12	1.3 to 1.6

Ignition system

System type

All 1.0 models November 1988-on, and all 1.2 models without catalytic converters	Electronic, incorporating distributor (with IC ignition unit and conventional mechanical and vacuum advance/retard) and ignition coil
1.2 models with catalytic converters	Fully-electronic, incorporating distributor (with crank angle sensor), ignition coil and power transistor, ignition timing controlled by ECC control unit

Coil - all 1.0 models November 1988 on, and all 1.2 models

Primary resistance - approximate:
1.0 models, and 1.2 models without catalytic converters	1.0 to 1.2 ohm
1.2 models with catalytic converters	Not available

Secondary resistance - approximate:
1.0 models, and 1.2 models without catalytic converters	7.6 to 11.4 k ohm

Ignition timing - @ idling speed

Note: *For all models except those with catalytic converters, the normal timing check is with the vacuum disconnected; for these models, the 'vacuum connected' entry is given for reference only. For models with catalytic converters, both specifications are required; note that it is the boost pressure sensor vacuum hose that is to be disconnected - refer to the appropriate text for details.*

Vacuum disconnected:
1.0 models with four-speed manual transmission	2° ± 1° ATDC
other 1.0 models up to April 1990*	5° ± 1° BTDC
All other 1.0 models, April 1990 onwards	4° ± 1° BTDC
1.2 models without catalytic converters	0° ± 1° (ie, TDC)
1.2 models with catalytic converters	3° ATDC

Vacuum connected:
1.0 models with four-speed manual transmission	12° ± 5° BTDC
All other 1.0 models up to April 1990*	12° ± 5°BTDC
All other 1.0 models, April 1990 onwards	11° ± 5° BTDC
1.2models withoutcatalyticconverters	0° ± 1° (ie, TDC)
1.2 models with catalytic converters	10° ± 2 ° BTDC

*For these models to run on unleaded Premium (95 RON), the ignition timing must first be retarded by 3°.

HT leads

Resistance - approximate	10 to 20 k ohms per metre

Clutch

Clutch pedal free play

Clutch pedal free play	12.5 to 17.5 mm (0.49 to 0.69 in)

Torque wrench setting

	lbf ft	kgf m
Pressure plate bolts	16 to 22	2.2 to 3.0

Manual transmission - five-speed, January 1985 on

Ratios

1st	3.412 : 1
2nd	1.958 : 1
3rd	1.323 : 1
4th	1.028 : 1
5th	0.850 : 1
Reverse	3.385 : 1
Final drive	4.050 : 1 or 3.810 : 1

13

Automatic transmission

General

Type:	Model	Code number
1.0 models up to 1984	RL3F01B	15X00
1.0 models, January 1985 to October 1988	RL3F01A	15X04
1.0 models, November 1988 on	RL3F01A	15X72
1.2	RL3F01A	
Description - RL3F01 A	As noted in Chapter 7, but water-cooled	

Ratios .... Refer to Chapter 7

Torque wrench setting	lbf ft	kgf m
Fluid cooler banjo union bolts	22 to 36	3.0 to 5.0

Driveshafts

Lubrication

Quantity of grease required for each driveshaft	60 to 90 g (2.12 to 3.17 oz)	

Joint bellows setting length

Inboard joint	82.5 mm (3.25 in)
Outboard joint	85.5 mm (3.37 in)

Torque wrench setting	lbf ft	kgf m
Driveshaft nut -- November 1988 on (one-piece wheel bearings)	108 to 152	15.0 to 21.0

Braking system

Brake pedal - January 1985 on

Depressed height (engine running, force of 110 lb/50 kg)	At least 95 mm (3.74 in)

Suspension and steering - all models, November 1988 on

Roadwheels

Type	Pressed-steel
Size	5J-13

Tyres

Size	155/70 R 13 75S or 175/60 R 13 76H

Torque wrench settings	lbf ft	kgf m
Rear suspension upper and lower link mounting bolts	57 to 72	7.9 to 9.9
Rear suspension stabiliser bar mounting bolts	29 to 37	4.0 to 5.1
Rear hub nut	137 to 188	19.0 to 26.0

Bodywork and fittings - 1985 on

Torque wrench settings	lbf ft	kgf m
Front bumper:		
Reinforcement bar-to-body bolts	6.7 to 8.7	0.93 to 1.2
Plastic trim side bolts	2.7 to 3.7	0.38 to 0.51
Rear bumper:		
Reinforcement bar-to-body bolts	6.7 to 8.7	0.93 to 1.2
Plastic trim side bolts	2.7 to 3.7	0.38 to 0.51

---

3 Engine

Sump pan - general

1 On engines built during 1985, reinforcing strips were fitted to the sump pan mountings, as shown in Fig. 13.1.

2 From January 1986 onwards, the reinforcing strips and the side gaskets were no longer fitted, the seal being made by a modified sump pan and liquid sealing compound; a Nissan dealer should be able to recommend a suitable product. Carefully clean and degrease the mating surfaces so that oil leaks do not occur on reassembly, and locate the end sealing strips correctly before refitting the sump pan. Follow the sealant manufacturer's instructions as to the size of bead to be applied, whether to one or both mating surfaces, and note the length of time required for the sealant to cure.

3 Note the revised torque wrench setting for the sump bolts on later models.

Pistons - renewal

4 After manufacture, the cylinder bores and piston skirts are measured and classified into five grades, which must be carefully matched together to ensure the correct piston/cylinder

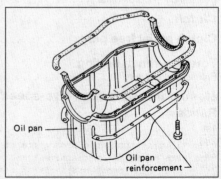

Fig. 13.1 Engine oil sump pan reinforcing strips – 1985 models (Sec 3)

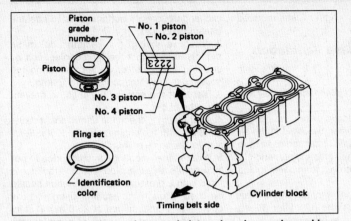

Fig. 13.2 Cylinder bore, piston and piston ring size grade markings (Sec 3)

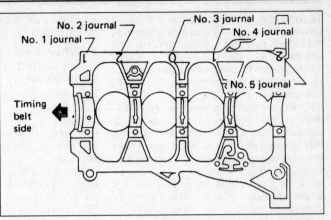

Fig. 13.3 Cylinder block main bearing bore size grade markings (Sec 3)

clearance. Only the first three grades are employed in production engines.

5 The selection of replacement pistons requires very accurate and painstaking measurement if it is to be successful; if you are at all in doubt as to your ability to carry out this work, take the cylinder block and original pistons to a competent Nissan dealer or engine-reconditioning specialist.

6 If it is decided that a piston is to be renewed, and careful measurement reveals the cylinder bore to be within the specified limits (even after any honing has been carried out) for the grade marked on the top of the cylinder block (Fig. 13.2), a piston of the corresponding grade can be selected.

7 If honing has enlarged the bore to Grade 4 or 5 diameter but the bore's out-of-round and taper remain sufficiently within limits for the exercise to be viable, the new bore grade should be stamped on the cylinder block, and the corresponding piston (and rings) should be selected.

8 As noted in Chapter 1, if the degree of wear

in any cylinder is such that reboring is required (to the specified oversize), all four cylinders must be rebored at the same time, and new pistons and rings must be fitted. If reboring is carried out, the grading system becomes irrelevant, as replacements are supplied (by Nissan) in one oversize only.

Piston rings - renewal

9 The piston rings are similarly classified into three grades, but Grade 1 (identified by a yellow paint mark next to the ring end gap) is only fitted to a combination of Grade 1 piston and bore.

10 In all other cases, the rings are selected by measuring their installed end gaps (Chapter 1, Section 11) and choosing the grade according to the measurements obtained.

11 If the cylinders are rebored, new (oversize) rings must be fitted with the new pistons.

Crankshaft main bearing shells - renewal

12 After manufacture, the cylinder block main bearing bores and crankshaft main bearing journals are measured and classified into grades, the grade numbers being stamped into the cylinder block and crankshaft (Figs. 13.3 and 13.4). The main bearing shells are graded into seven thicknesses, each identified by a colour code marked on the shells. When the crankshaft is fitted, main bearing shells are selected according to the chart given below.

13 The selection of replacement shells requires very accurate and painstaking measurement if it is to be successful; if you are at all in doubt as to your ability to carry out this work, take the cylinder block, crankshaft and original shells to a competent Nissan dealer or engine reconditioning specialist.

14 If it is decided that the shells are to be renewed, and careful measurement reveals the crankshaft main bearing journals to be within the specified limits for the grade marked, and if each journal's out-of-round and taper remain sufficiently within limits for

the exercise to be viable, shells of the corresponding grade can be selected. Matching the grade numbers noted to the following chart, select the new bearing shells.

Crankshaft (main journal grade) no.	Block (main bearing bore ID grade) no.	Bearing shell grade (colour code)
0	0	Grade 0 (Black)
0	1	Grade 1 (Brown)
0	2	Grade 2 (Green)
0	3	Grade 3 (Yellow)
1	0	Grade 1 (Brown)
1	1	Grade 2 (Green)
1	2	Grade 3 (Yellow)
1	3	Grade 4 (Blue)
2	0	Grade 2 (Green)
2	1	Grade 3 (Yellow)
2	2	Grade 4 (Blue)
2	3	Grade 5 (Pink)
1, 2 (ie 3)	0	Grade 3 (Yellow)
1, 2 (ie 3)	1	Grade 4 (Blue)
1, 2 (ie 3)	2	Grade 5 (Pink)
1, 2 (ie 3)	3	Grade 6 (Red/Purple)

15 The bearing's running clearance should be checked using an American product called 'Plastigage'. This consists of a fine thread of perfectly-round plastic, which is compressed between the bearing shell and the journal. When the shell is removed, the plastic is deformed, and can be measured with a special card gauge supplied with the kit. The running clearance is determined from this gauge. Plastigage is sometimes difficult to obtain in this country, but enquiries at one of the larger specialist chains of quality motor factors should produce the name of a stockist in your area. The procedure for using Plastigage is as follows.

16 With the main bearing upper shells in place, carefully lay the crankshaft in position. Do not use any lubricant; the crankshaft journals and bearing shells must be perfectly clean and dry.

17 Cut several lengths of the appropriate size Plastigage (they should be slightly shorter than the width of the main bearings), and place one length on each crankshaft journal axis.

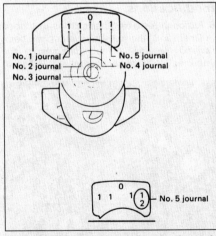

Fig. 13.4 Crankshaft main bearing journal size grade markings – on crankshaft timing belt end (Sec 3)

Note: Inset shows marking used for a grade 3-size journal

13

18 With the main bearing lower shells in position, refit the main bearing cap, tightening the bolts in the sequence shown in Chapter 1 and to the specified torque wrench setting. Take care not to disturb the Plastigage, and don't rotate the crankshaft at any time during this operation.

19 Remove the main bearing cap. Don't disturb the Plastigage or rotate the crankshaft. Compare the width of the crushed Plastigage on each journal to the scale printed on the Plastigage envelope to obtain the main bearing running clearance.

20 If the clearance is not as specified, the bearing shells may be the wrong grade (or excessively worn if the original shells are being re-used). Before deciding that different grade shells are needed, make sure that no dirt or oil was trapped between the bearing shells and the cap or cylinder block when the clearance was measured. If the Plastigage was wider at one end than at the other, the journal may be tapered.

21 Carefully scrape away all traces of the Plastigage material from the crankshaft and bearing shells, using your fingernail or other object which is unlikely to score the shells.

22 As noted in Chapter 1, if the degree of wear on any journal is such that regrinding is required (to the specified undersize), all four journals must be reground at the same time, and new shells must be fitted. If regrinding is carried out, the grading system becomes irrelevant, as replacements are supplied (by Nissan) in one undersize only.

23 When fitting the bearing shells, be careful to locate them exactly as described and shown in Chapter 1, Section 20, paragraph 4 (and photos).

24 Regardless of year, model and whether the crankshaft is standard or reground, the thrustwasher fitted on each side of No 4 upper main bearing are supplied in only one thickness.

Main bearing cap - refitting

25 When refitting the main bearing cap (Chapter 1, Section 20), apply a dab of sealant (a Nissan dealer should be able to recommend a suitable product) to the areas shown in Fig. 13.5.
26 Follow the sealant manufacturer's instructions as to the length of time required for the sealant to cure.

Positive Crankcase Ventilation (PCV) system - all engines

Note: Refer also to Chapter 1, Section 24 and Fig. 1.23.

27 The system incorporates a small, rectangular, foam air filter, mounted in the air filter housing. This smaller filter serves to stop dirt passing into the crankcase, and to prevent the air filter element from being fouled excessively with oil.

28 To reach the PCV filter, remove the air filter cover (Chapter 3); the PCV filter will be found next to the breather hose union.

29 At the annual (or equivalent) check of the system, remove the air filter cover and withdraw the PCV filter; clean it in a suitable solvent, and renew it if split or otherwise damaged. Refit the filter and cover.

30 At the two-yearly (or equivalent) interval, renew the filter as a matter of course, irrespective of its apparent condition.

4 Engine (1.2 models)

General

1 These vehicles are powered by the 1235 cc MA12 S engine. Apart from its different bore and stroke dimensions, revised to give the increased capacity, this engine is essentially the same as the 988 cc MA10 unit described in Chapter 1. Note, however, the differences mentioned in the Specifications Section of this Chapter.

5 Cooling system

Radiator - automatic transmission models

1 The radiator on later automatic transmission models incorporates a heat exchanger along its bottom edge, to cool the transmission fluid.

2 When removing the radiator on these models, disconnect the fluid cooler lines by undoing the worm-drive clips securing the hoses to the radiator connections (photo).

3 Blank off the ends of the lines, to prevent the entry of dirt.

4 After refitting, check the cooler connections for leaks with the engine running. **Note:** Refer also to Section 9 of this Chapter.

5 Where the cooling system does not incorporate an expansion tank, the radiator is fitted with a pressure cap. The system should be filled through the radiator filler, and the coolant level maintained at 25.0 mm (1.0 in) below the bottom of the filler neck (engine cold).

6 Fuel, exhaust and emission control systems - models without catalytic converters

Carburettor - modifications

1 Revised versions of the Hitachi carburettor are fitted to later models.

2 Overhaul and adjustment procedures remain basically the same as described in Chapter 3, but using the specifications given in this Supplement.

Fuel pump (1987 on) - fuel return hose

3 From 1987, the fuel pump cover has been modified to include a fuel return line to the fuel tank for excess fuel (photo).

4 On earlier models, the return hose was fitted to the carburettor (see Fig. 3.2 in Chapter 3).

5 Fuel pump removal and overhaul procedures remain as described in Chapter 3.

Exhaust system (1985-on) - modifications

6 Although remaining basically as described in Chapter 3, the exhaust system has been revised several times, particularly the intermediate silencer mounting. Refer to

Fig. 13.5 Main bearing cap sealant application points (Sec 3)

5.2 Automatic transmission fluid cooler connections at base of radiator

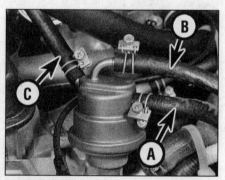

6.3 Fuel pump hoses – 1987 on models

A Fuel inlet – from tank
B Fuel return – to tank
C Fuel feed to – carburettor

Fig. 13.21 for details of a typical (later-model) layout, and to the Specifications at the start of this Chapter for revised torque wrench settings (where applicable).

Unleaded fuel

7 All (non-catalytic converter-equipped) Micra models can use either unleaded or leaded petrol as desired; the manufacturer's recommended **minimum** octane ratings are given in the Specifications at the start of this Chapter, with their equivalents in terms of the petrols currently on sale in the UK. Where unleaded Premium is specified as the equivalent, 'Super/Superplus'-grade unleaded petrol may also be used if wished, with no ill-effects.

8 No Micra model requires 'adjustment' (ie, to the ignition timing) to allow it to use the specified grade of unleaded petrol. However, 1.0 models with either five-speed manual or automatic transmissions built up to April 1990 must have the ignition timing retarded by 3° if they are to be run on the 'Premium-grade'. (95 RON) unleaded usually on sale in UK filling stations. After this date, these engines were modified to accept unleaded 95 RON fuel without adjustment. A Nissan dealer will have the information required to identify exactly any car's date of manufacture, from its vehicle identification number.

9 Note that 1.2 models, and 1.0 models with four-speed manual transmissions, may use 91 RON 'Regular' or 'Normal'-grade unleaded petrol, which is not yet available in the UK. If you are taking such a vehicle abroad, seek the advice of a Nissan dealer (or one of the motoring organisations) to ensure that you are aware of the grades of petrol that you are likely to encounter, and be sure that you are aware of the different (and sometimes confusingly contradictory) names used for these grades, compared with the UK terms with which you are familiar.

7 Fuel, exhaust and emission control systems - models with catalytic converters

Air filter housing - removal and refitting

1 Removal and refitting of the housing cover and filter element are as described in Chapter 3.

2 To remove the complete housing assembly, remove the cover and element, then disconnect the cold air intake trunking from the bonnet lock platform and unscrew the retaining screws so that the housing can be lifted slightly; take care not to stretch or damage any of the hoses.

3 Working methodically and referring to the accompanying illustrations for guidance when required, disconnect all the hoses and vacuum pipes connected to the housing components, and withdraw the housing.

4 Refitting is the reverse of the removal procedure; ensure that all hoses are correctly reconnected, securely fastened and clipped (where clips or ties are provided) clear of other components, then check that the assembly sits properly on the carburettor inlet before tightening the screws securely.

Air filter automatic air temperature control system

Description

5 The flap valve air temperature control system allows cold air from the outside of the vehicle and warm air from the exhaust

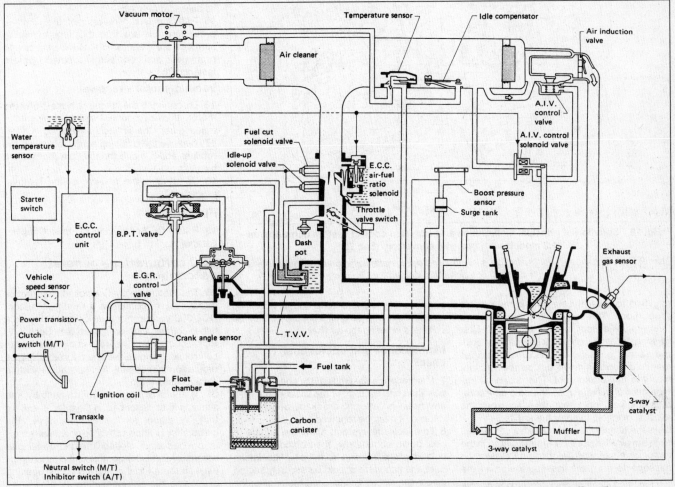

Fig. 13.6 ECC fuel/ignition system and emission control systems – 1.2 models with catalytic converters (Sec 7)

13

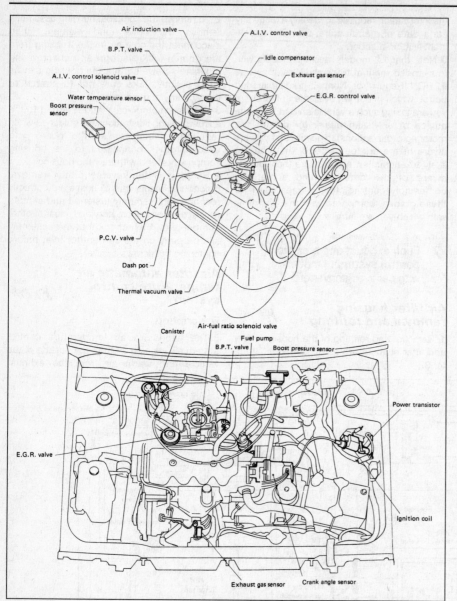

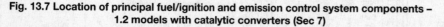

Fig. 13.7 Location of principal fuel/ignition and emission control system components – 1.2 models with catalytic converters (Sec 7)

Note: Engine compartment illustration is of left-hand drive model location of some (bulkhead-mounted) components reversed for UK

manifold to enter the air filter in the correct proportions. The system is controlled by a temperature sensor mounted in the air filter housing; when the engine is started from cold, the sensor passage is open to allow inlet manifold depression to act on the vacuum motor in the intake duct. This draws a flap-type control valve across the cold air intake, thus allowing only (warmed) air from the exhaust manifold to enter the air filter.

6 As the temperature of the exhaust-warmed air in the air filter rises, a bi-metallic strip in the temperature sensor deforms and closes the passage to shut off the depression in the vacuum motor; the flap is lowered gradually across the hot air intake until, when the

engine is fully warmed up to normal operating temperature, only cold air from the front of the vehicle is entering the air filter.

Maintenance and operational check

7 Maintenance is limited to checking the condition and security of the vacuum hoses, if any hose is leaking, cracked, perished or trapped, it must be renewed.

8 To check the system, allow the engine to cool down completely, then disconnect the cold air intake trunking from the air filter intake duct; the flap valve should be securely seated across the hot air intake. Start the engine; the flap should immediately rise to close off the

cold air intake, and should then lower steadily as the engine warms up until it is eventually seated across the hot air intake again.

9 To check the temperature sensor, disconnect the vacuum pipe from the vacuum motor when the engine is running. With the engine cold, full inlet manifold depression should be felt sucking at the pipe end; none at all when the engine is fully warmed up.

10 To check the vacuum motor, disconnect the cold air intake trunking from the air filter intake duct; the flap valve should be securely seated across the hot air intake. Disconnect the vacuum pipe, and suck hard at the vacuum motor stub; the flap should rise to shut off the cold air intake.

11 If either component is faulty, it must be renewed, but always check the hoses carefully first, to ensure that the fault is not due to a leaky hose.

Temperature sensor - renewal

12 Either remove the air filter housing completely (see paragraphs 2 and 3 above), or remove its retaining screws and raise the housing sufficiently for the sensor vacuum hoses to be disconnected from underneath.

13 Remove the air filter element (Chapter 3).

14 Release and withdraw the sensor, noting its sealing grommet.

15 Refitting is the reverse of the removal procedure; ensure that the sensor mating surfaces are clean, and that the sensor and grommet are correctly located before fastening the sensor.

Vacuum motor - renewal

16 Disconnect the vacuum hose from the motor, then disconnect the cold air intake trunking from the air filter intake duct.

17 Remove the retaining screw, withdraw the retainer and remove the vacuum motor from the duct.

18 Refitting is the reverse of the removal procedure.

Fuel pump

19 Refer to Section 6 of this Chapter, paragraphs 3 to 5.

ECC carburettor - general description

20 The Electronically-Controlled Carburettor (ECC) system combines a modified Hitachi DCZ 306 carburettor (see Chapter 3) with a fully electronic ignition system (see Section 8, Part B, of this Chapter) under the same control unit, to give the fine degree of engine regulation necessary for operation with a catalytic converter.

21 The fuel system is fundamentally the same as that described in Chapter 3, except that in place of the power valve, the carburettor is fitted with a solenoid valve; this is opened and closed rapidly under the control of the ECC control unit, to richen or weaken the air/fuel mixture ratio by opening or closing the compensating air bleed and main jet.

22 The electrical side of the system consists of the ECC control unit and all the sensors that provide it with information; the basic method of operation is as follows - note that the ignition system is controlled by the same unit, and is described in Section 8 of this Chapter.

23 The principal information required by the control unit is provided by the boost pressure sensor and the (distributor) crank angle sensor. The boost pressure sensor is connected by a hose to the inlet manifold; variations in manifold pressure are converted into graduated electrical signals, which are used by the control unit to determine the load on the engine. Information on engine speed and crankshaft position comes from the crank angle sensor (see Section 8 of this Chapter).

24 Additional information to refine air/fuel mixture control comes from ancillary sensors. The coolant temperature sensor gives the engine temperature. The throttle valve switch, which is linked to the throttle valve spindle, opens when the throttle is fully closed (ie, in the idle position) and closes when the throttle is in any other position. The ignition switch shows when the engine is being started, the reversing light/neutral and clutch switches (manual transmission) or inhibitor switch (automatic transmission) show when the transmission is in gear and the clutch is engaged. A vehicle speed sensor, mounted in the speedometer, transmits information on vehicle speed. Finally, the exhaust gas sensor, screwed into the exhaust manifold in front of the primary catalytic converter, sends the control unit information on the amount of oxygen in the exhaust gases, allowing it to control the air/fuel mixture strength.

25 The exhaust gas sensor provides the control unit with constant feedback, which enables it to adjust the mixture continuously - 'closed loop' control to provide the best possible conditions for the catalytic

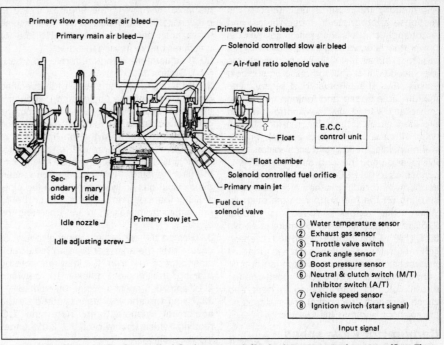

Fig. 13.8 Electrically-Controlled Carburettor air/fuel mixture control system (Sec 7)

converters to operate. Until the sensor is fully warmed up it gives no feedback so, when the engine is started from cold, the control unit uses pre-programmed values (open-loop control) to determine the correct air/fuel ratio solenoid valve operating rate. When the sensor reaches its normal operating temperature, its tip (which is sensitive to oxygen) sends the control unit a varying voltage depending on the amount of oxygen in the exhaust gases; if the intake air/fuel mixture is too rich, the exhaust gases are low in oxygen, so the sensor sends a low-voltage signal - the voltage rising as the mixture weakens and the amount of oxygen rises in

the exhaust gases. Peak conversion efficiency of all major pollutants occurs if the intake air/fuel mixture is maintained at the chemically-correct ratio for the complete combustion of petrol of 14.7 parts (by weight) of air to 1 part of fuel (the 'stoichiometric' ratio). The sensor output voltage alters in a large step at this point, the control unit using the signal change as a reference point, and correcting the intake air/fuel mixture accordingly by altering the rate at which the air/fuel ratio solenoid valve opens and closes.

26 All these signals are compared by the control unit with set values pre-programmed (mapped) into its memory; based on this

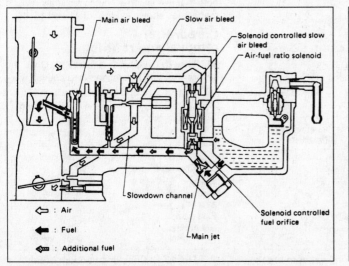

Fig. 13.9 Electronically-Controlled Carburettor air/fuel ratio solenoid valve 'On' to richen mixture (Sec 7)

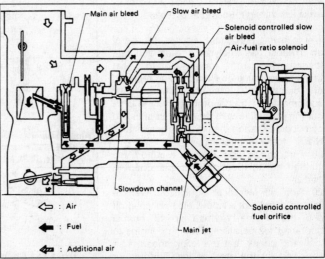

Fig. 13.10 Electronically-Controlled Carburettor air/fuel ratio solenoid valve 'Off' to weaken mixture (Sec 7)

13

information, the control unit selects the response appropriate to those values, and accordingly controls the ignition coil (via the power transistor, varying the ignition timing as required), the air/fuel ratio solenoid valve, the idle speed control and anti-dieseling solenoid valves, and the exhaust gas sensor. The mixture, idle speed and ignition timing are constantly varied by the control unit, to provide the best settings for cranking, starting (with either a hot or cold engine), engine warm-up, idle, cruising and acceleration.

27 In addition, the anti-dieseling valve is connected to the ECC system, to improve fuel economy and reduce exhaust emissions by shutting off the fuel supply on the overrun. When the engine speed is about 2150 rev/min, engine temperature is above 60°C (140°F), the throttle switch and reversing light/neutral and clutch switches (manual transmission) or inhibitor switch (automatic transmission) are in the 'OFF' positions (ie, throttle closed, transmission in gear and clutch engaged), the control unit switches off the solenoid, and thus the fuel supply.

Carburettor - idle speed and mixture adjustment

Note: *If the CO level reading is incorrect (or if any other symptom is encountered which causes you to suspect the presence of a fault), always check first that the air filter element is clean, that the spark plugs are in good condition and correctly gapped, that the engine breather and vacuum hoses are clear and undamaged, that there are no leaks in the air intake trunking, the carburettor or the manifolds, and that the throttle cable is correctly adjusted (Chapter 3). If the engine is running very roughly, check the valve clearances and compression pressures (Chapter 1). Check also that all wiring is in good condition, with securely fastened connectors, that the fuel filter has been renewed at the recommended intervals, and that the exhaust system is entirely free of air leaks which might upset the operation of the catalytic converter.*

The following procedure requires the use of an exhaust gas analyser and an accurate tachometer, and may require that tamperproof plugs be extracted and replaced on completion. Owners without such equipment, or who doubt their ability to carry out the procedure with the required standard of accuracy, should take the vehicle to a Nissan dealer for attention.

28 First check, and adjust if required, the ignition timing (Section 8 of this Chapter, Part B).

29 With all electrical equipment (vehicle lights, heated rear window, etc.) switched off and the engine warmed up to normal operating temperature, allow the engine to idle, and check that the idling speed is as specified (at the start of this Chapter, or Chapter 3). To ensure that the idling speed is stable, clear excess fuel from the inlet

manifold by running the engine quickly to between 2000 and 3000 rev. min two or three times, then allowing the ending to idle for 2 minutes before making the check.

30 If adjustment is required, refer to Chapter 3, Section 10.

31 If the idling speed is within the specified range, switch off the engine and disconnect the air/fuel ratio solenoid valve wiring from the carburettor. Trace the Exhaust Air Induction (AIV) system pipe from the left-hand end of the exhaust manifold around to the air filter housing, and disconnect the hose linking it to the filter housing. Plug the hose, and insert the exhaust gas analyser probe into the pipe, sealing the opening around the probe to prevent air from leaking in and upsetting the reading.

32 Restart the engine and allow it to idle; to ensure that the analyser reading is correct, clear excess fuel from the inlet manifold by running the engine quickly to between 2000 and 3000 rev/min two or three times.

33 Using the analyser as instructed by the equipment manufacturer, note the CO reading, which should be 5.0 ± 2.0% under these conditions.

34 If the reading is incorrect, check for air leaks at all vacuum hoses and pipes, and at the carburettor and manifold joint surfaces; correct any faults found, then start the procedure again at paragraph 28 above. If no fault is found, turn the idle mixture screw (Chapter 3, Section 10) until a reading of 5.0 ± 1.0% is obtained. Where the idle mixture screw is sealed by a tamperproof plug, this must be extracted by drilling into its centre (be careful not to drill too far, or you may damage the head of the screw) so that a suitable tool

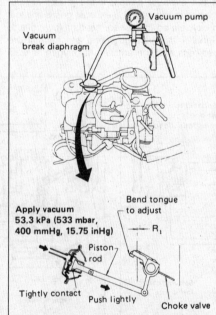

Apply vacuum 53.3 kPa (533 mbar, 400 mmHg, 15.75 inHg)

Fig. 13.11 Checking vacuum break clearance R1 – 1.2 models with catalytic converters (Sec 7)

can be inserted to prise it out. If the correct reading cannot be obtained, the carburettor must be overhauled and/or renewed to cure the fault.

35 If the reading is correct but the engine runs roughly, check for air leaks at all vacuum hoses and pipes, and at the carburettor and manifold joint surfaces; correct any faults found.

36 Once the CO reading is correct and the engine is running smoothly, switch off and reconnect the air/fuel ratio solenoid valve wiring and the Exhaust Air Induction (AIV) system pipe and hose.

37 Restart the engine and allow it to idle; to ensure that the analyser reading is correct, clear excess fuel from the inlet manifold by running the engine quickly to between 2000 and 3000 rev/min two or three times.

38 Recheck the idle speed and adjust if necessary, then insert the exhaust gas analyser probe into the exhaust tailpipe and note the CO reading; under these conditions, the reading should be no more than the maximum value given in the Specifications at the start of this Chapter.

39 On completion, switch off the engine and disconnect all test equipment, then check that all disturbed vacuum hoses and wiring have been correctly reconnected and are securely fastened. If a tamperproof plug was removed, tap a new one into place to seal the adjusting screw.

Carburettor - adjustments

40 Although the carburettor appears much more difficult to service than that described in Chapter 3, this is only due to the presence of the additional components such as solenoid valves, wiring and vacuum hoses.

41 Essentially, it is the same carburettor and adjusting procedures are unchanged; note, however, the different values given in the Specifications Section of this Chapter.

42 If checking the vacuum break adjustment, note that this is carried out in a slightly revised manner, as shown in Figs. 13.11 and 13.12.

Carburettor - removal and refitting

43 Refer to Chapter 3, Section 12. Once the air filter housing is removed (see above), work

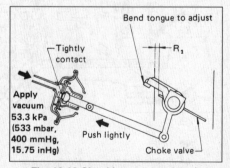

Apply vacuum 53.3 kPa (533 mbar, 400 mmHg, 15.75 inHg)

Fig. 13.12 Checking vacuum break clearance R2 – 1.2 models with catalytic converters (Sec 7)

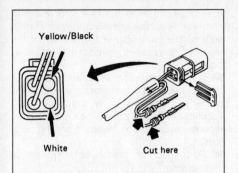

Fig. 13.13 Releasing air/fuel ratio solenoid valve's wiring from multi-plug block connector (Sec 7)

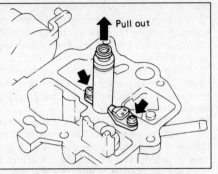

Fig. 13.14 Remove screws (arrowed) to withdraw air/fuel ratio solenoid valve (Sec 7)

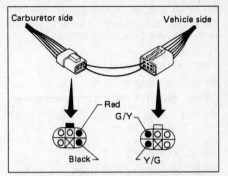

Fig. 13.15 Connect anti-dieseling solenoid valve wiring as shown so that engine can run while throttle valve switch adjustment is checked (Sec 7)

methodically (taking notes as necessary and referring to the accompanying illustrations for guidance when required) to disconnect all the wiring, hoses and vacuum pipes connected to the carburettor or preventing its removal.

44 Refitting is the reverse of the removal procedure; ensure that all hoses are correctly reconnected, securely fastened and clipped (where clips or ties are provided) clear of other components.

ECC components - removal and refitting

ECC control unit

45 This component is mounted under the front passenger seat, secured in a mounting bracket by three screws, and protected by a plastic cover.

46 To remove the unit, disconnect the battery earth terminal, slide the seat fully forwards or backwards as required, then unclip the cover and unscrew the securing screws. Disconnect the wiring and withdraw the unit.

47 Refitting is the reverse of the removal procedure.

Air/fuel ratio solenoid valve

48 Remove the carburettor and withdraw the top cover (Chapter 3).

49 Release the solenoid valve's wiring from the multi-plug block connector, and cut the wires as shown in Fig. 13.13. Tie a length of string to the ends of the wires, then pull them

out of the carburettor harness sleeve, leaving the string in place.

50 Remove its two retaining screws and withdraw the solenoid valve (Fig. 13.14); remove and discard the wiring sealing grommet.

51 On refitting, slide a new grommet into place on the wiring, and apply a smear of silicone grease to the O-ring at each end of the solenoid valve. Tighten the screws to the specified torque wrench setting. Use the string to draw the new solenoid valve's wires into the carburettor harness sleeve.

52 Reassemble and refit the carburettor, then slide new rubber seals on to the multi-plug end of the solenoid valve's wires, crimp new terminal ends on to the wires and secure them in the connector.

Boost pressure sensor

53 This component is mounted on the engine compartment bulkhead, secured by two screws.

54 To remove the sensor, disconnect its vacuum hose and wiring, then remove the screws and withdraw it.

55 Refitting is the reverse of the removal procedure; note that, as no fuel vapour trap is fitted, it is essential that the sensor vacuum hose is routed so that it falls steadily from the sensor to the manifold, so that any fuel droplets are not trapped in the sensor or hose, but can drain into the inlet port.

56 Note the sealed vacuum delay valve/surge tank in the vacuum hose; if this is

thought to be faulty, it can be renewed only as part of the complete hose assembly.

Crank angle sensor

57 Refer to Section 8 of this Chapter, Part B.

Coolant temperature sensor

58 This component is screwed into the left-hand end of the inlet manifold. Removal and refitting is as described in Section 10 of Chapter 2.

Throttle valve switch - removal and refitting

59 This component is secured by two screws on a mounting bracket adjacent to the throttle linkage. It may be necessary to remove the air filter housing to reach the switch.

60 To remove the unit, disconnect the battery earth terminal and the switch wiring, remove the screws and withdraw the switch.

61 On refitting, adjust the switch as described below.

Throttle valve switch - adjustment

62 With the engine switched off, disconnect the carburettor wiring, and use two spare lengths of wire to connect the anti-dieseling solenoid valve wiring as shown in Fig. 13.15.

63 Check that continuity does not exist between the throttle valve switch wire terminals, as shown in Fig. 13.16. Connect an accurate tachometer to the engine, start the engine and increase speed to approximately 2000 rev/min; check that continuity now exists.

64 Decrease speed to 900 to 1600 rev/min for manual transmission models, 1050 to 1750 rev/min for automatic transmission models; the switch should open so that the circuit is broken.

65 If adjustment is required, switch off the engine and remove the carburettor, then check the primary and secondary throttle valve plate interlock clearance 'G' (Chapter 3, Section 11 and Fig. 3.12). At this point when the switch opens, the clearance should be 0.32 ± 0.07 mm (0.0126 ± 0.0028 in) for manual transmission models, or 0.38 ± 0.07 mm (0.0150 ± 0.0028 in) for automatic transmission models.

66 If adjustment is required, bend the plate shown in Fig. 13.17.

13

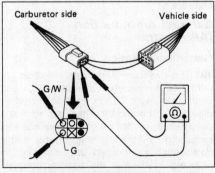

Fig. 13.16 Checking throttle valve switch operation (Sec 7)

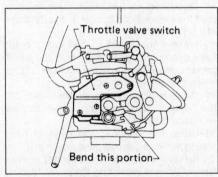
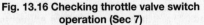

Fig. 13.17 Adjusting primary and secondary throttle valve plate interlock clearance (Sec 7)

67 When the setting is correct, refit the carburettor and recheck the switch operation as described in paragraphs 62 to 64.

Reversing light/neutral switch (manual transmission)

68 Refer to Chapter 6, Section 10.

Clutch switch (manual transmission)

69 This component is mounted on the clutch pedal bracket, secured by two locknuts as described for the stop-lamp switch in Section 18 of Chapter 9.

Inhibitor switch (automatic transmission)

70 Refer to Chapter 7, Section 6.

Vehicle speed sensor

71 This component is mounted in the speedometer assembly (Chapter 12, Section 19) and does not appear to be available as a separate item. If it is thought to be faulty, seek the advice of a Nissan dealer.

Exhaust gas sensor - operational check

72 Before suspecting the sensor of being faulty, ensure that the engine oil and coolant levels, the valve clearances and compression pressures are correct, that the battery, fuses, fuel and ignition system components, hoses and wiring are in good condition, and that the oil filler cap and dipstick are securely fastened. Correct any faults found; if the sensor is still thought to be faulty, or if you are checking it as part of routine maintenance, proceed as follows.

73 To check the sensor operation, first slide the front passenger seat fully forwards or backwards as required, so that the ECC control unit's plastic cover can be removed and the green Light-Emitting Diode (LED) in the unit's rear face can be seen.

74 Connect a tachometer following the equipment manufacturer's instructions, then start the engine and warm it up to normal operating temperature.

75 When the engine is fully warmed up, run it at 2500 rev/min for approximately 5 minutes with all electrical equipment switched off, so that there is no load on the engine. Have an assistant maintain the engine speed at approximately 2000 rev/min, and check that the LED cycles on and off more than five times in any 10-second period: Switch off the engine, disconnect the tachometer and refit all disturbed components.

76 If the LED flashed as described, the system is in good order; if not, take the vehicle to a Nissan dealer for the complete ECC system to be checked carefully on proper test equipment. If no other fault can be found, the exhaust gas sensor must be renewed.

Exhaust gas sensor - removal and refitting

77 When handling the sensor, note that it is fragile, take care not to drop it, and do not allow it to contact fuel or silicone substances.

78 Start the engine and run it until it reaches normal operating temperature, then switch off and disconnect the battery. Disconnect the sensor wiring.

79 Using a suitable spanner (and wearing heavy gloves to protect your hands from the hot exhaust system and sensor), unscrew the sensor and withdraw it.

80 On refitting, apply anti-seize compound to the threads of the sensor. The sensor must be tightened securely, to the specified torque wrench setting; this will require the use of a deep socket, slotted to allow for the sensor wiring.

Inlet manifold - removal and refitting

Note: *The following procedure describes the removal of the manifold with the carburettor. Access to some of the components concerned is, however, much better if the carburettor is first removed separately (see above); if this is done, the following procedure should be amended as required.*

81 Disconnect the battery negative lead.

82 Remove the air filter housing (see above).

83 Either drain the cooling system completely (Chapter 2) or to below the level of the manifold, which usually requires the draining-off of about 1 litre (1.8 pints) of coolant, or clamp the coolant hoses connected to the inlet manifold to minimise coolant loss, and be prepared to catch the coolant that will be released from the manifold and cylinder head.

84 Disconnect all coolant hoses from the manifold, as described in Chapter 3.

85 Disconnect the brake vacuum servo unit hose from the manifold (Chapter 9).

86 Making notes as required, and referring to the accompanying illustrations for guidance when necessary, disconnect all the crankcase breather hoses, EGR system components, vacuum hoses and other pipes connected to the manifold or preventing its removal.

87 Releasing their clips, unplug the connectors to disconnect the carburettor, coolant temperature sensor and other component wiring from the manifold.

88 Disconnect the throttle cable (Chapter 3).

89 Disconnect the fuel feed and return hoses from the carburettor (Chapter 3, and Section 6 of this Chapter).

90 Make a final check that all components have been removed or disconnected which prevent access to the manifold fasteners, or which prevent its removal.

91 Unscrew the nuts securing the manifold to the cylinder head, and withdraw it; remove and discard the gasket.

92 Clean the manifold and cylinder head mating surfaces carefully, and check that they are flat and unmarked. **Note:** *Do not use any form of silicone sealant on the manifold joints or pipe unions; pieces of sealant may break off and foul the catalytic converters.*

93 On refitting, always fit a new manifold gasket, and tighten the manifold retaining nuts evenly to the specified torque wrench setting. The remainder of the procedure is a reversal of removal, noting the following points.

94 Adjust the throttle cable, and reconnect the fuel feed and return pipes. Use the notes made on dismantling to ensure that all vacuum hoses and other pipes are correctly reconnected, securely fastened and properly routed.

95 Reconnect all disconnected electrical components.

96 Reconnect all disturbed coolant hoses, refill the cooling system, and check the level when the engine is restarted and has warmed up fully (Chapter 2).

Exhaust manifold - removal and refitting

97 Disconnect the exhaust gas sensor wiring, the Exhaust Air Induction (AIV) system pipe from the left-hand end of the exhaust manifold, and the Exhaust Gas Recirculation (EGR) system pipe from its right-hand end. Unbolt the manifold heat shield if better access is required to the manifold nuts.

98 Unbolt the primary catalytic converter from the manifold (see below) and unfasten the exhaust downpipe mountings so that the converter and downpipe can be lowered clear of the manifold.

99 Unscrew the nuts securing the manifold to the cylinder head and withdraw it, taking care not to damage the fragile exhaust gas sensor; remove and discard the gasket.

100 Clean the manifold and cylinder head mating surfaces carefully, and check that they are flat and unmarked.

101 On refitting, always fit a new manifold gasket, and tighten the manifold retaining nuts evenly to the specified torque wrench setting. The remainder of the procedure is a reversal of removal, referring to the relevant text for details. Clean the EGR and EIV pipe unions and threads carefully, then tighten them securely to ensure that they are gas-tight.

Note: *Do not use any form of silicone sealant on the manifold joints or pipe unions; pieces of sealant may break off and foul the catalytic converters.*

Exhaust Air Induction (AIV) system

General description

102 This system reduces emission or unburned hydrocarbon particles (HC) and carbon monoxide (CO) by passing filtered air directly into the exhaust manifold, so that a considerable proportion of these substances remaining in the exhaust gases after combustion are burned up, either in the manifold itself or in the primary catalytic converter.

103 The system consists of the AIV control solenoid valve, the AIV control valve itself, and

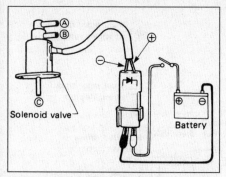

Fig. 13.18 Checking Exhaust Air Induction (AIV) system control solenoid valve (Sec 7)

a reed-type Air Induction valve; refer to Fig. 13.6 for details.

104 The system functions by using the pressure variations in the exhaust gases to draw air through from the filter housing, so that there is no need for a separate air pump; air will flow into the exhaust only when its pressure is below atmospheric. The Air Induction valve can allow gases to flow only one way, so there is no risk of hot exhaust gases flowing back into the filter.

105 To ensure that the system does not upset the smooth running of the engine under normal driving conditions, it is linked by the AIV control solenoid valve to the ECC control unit, so that it only functions when engine temperature is above 15°C (59°F) on start-up, or below 60°C (140°F) immediately after. In normal running, the system only functions when engine temperature is about 70°C (158°F), engine speed is below 950 rev/min and vehicle speed below 2 mph (4 km/h) with the throttle valve switch off.

Maintenance and operational check

106 Maintenance is limited to checking the condition and security of the vacuum hoses, if any hose is leaking, cracked, perished or trapped, it must be renewed.

107 To check the system, first disconnect the hose from the pipe, and suck on or blow down the hose to check that air cannot flow through the valve.

108 Connect a hand-operated vacuum pump to the control valve hose, apply vacuum, and then suck on or blow down the hose to check that air can now flow through the valve. If not, check the control and air induction valves for wear or damage, renewing them if necessary.

109 With the engine running, disconnect the hose from the control solenoid valve to the control valve, and ensure that intake manifold vacuum can be felt at the hose end when the conditions outlined in paragraph 105 apply.

110 If the control solenoid valve is thought to be faulty, disconnect its wiring and check the resistance of its windings; a reading of 30 to 40 ohms should be obtained. Connect a fully-charged battery across its wires; the solenoid should be heard to click open.

111 To check the control solenoid valve's operation, connect a fully-charged battery

across its wires as shown in Fig. 13.18, then use a hand-operated vacuum pump to check that there is free flow between ports B and C when the valve is off, and between ports A and B when it is on.

112 If any component is faulty, it must be renewed, but always check the hoses carefully first, to ensure that the fault is not due to a leaky hose.

AIV control solenoid valve - removal and refining

113 Remove the air filter housing (see above) and disconnect the battery earth lead.

114 Disconnect the solenoid wiring, then disconnect its vacuum hoses one by one, labelling each to ensure that it can be correctly reconnected.

115 Unbolt the solenoid from its bracket, and withdraw it.

116 Refitting is the reverse of the removal procedure; ensure that the vacuum hoses are correctly reconnected.

AIV control valve - removal and refitting

117 Remove the air filter housing (see above); if not already done, disconnect the valve's vacuum hose.

118 Remove its retaining screws and withdraw the valve from the underside of the filter housing, noting its sealing ring.

119 Refitting is the reverse of the removal procedure; renew the sealing ring if no longer serviceable, and ensure that all disturbed hoses are correctly reconnected.

Air induction valve - removal and refitting

120 Remove its retaining screws and withdraw the valve cover from the side of the air filter housing, then remove the valve itself.

121 Refitting is the reverse of the removal procedure; ensure that the valve is seated correctly on its seal before refitting the cover and tightening the screws.

Exhaust Gas Recirculation (EGR) system

General description

122 This system reintroduces small amounts of exhaust gas into the combustion cycle, to reduce the generation of oxides of nitrogen (NOx); refer to Fig. 13.6 for details.

123 The volume of exhaust gas reintroduced is governed by carburettor depression. This is controlled by engine temperature through the Thermal Vacuum Valve (TVV) and by exhaust gas pressure through the Back Pressure Transducer (BPT valve). When the engine temperature is above 60°C (140°F) and exhaust gas pressure is high, exhaust gases are allowed to flow through a metal pipe from the exhaust manifold right-hand end, via the opened Exhaust Gas Recirculation (EGR) control valve mounted on the inlet manifold, into the inlet tract.

Maintenance and operational check

124 Maintenance is limited to checking the condition and security of the vacuum hoses; if any hose is leaking, cracked, perished or trapped, it must be renewed. Check at regular intervals that the pipe unions are securely fastened.

125 To check the system, observe closely the movement of the EGR control valve's diaphragm as follows - note that the diaphragm is visible only through the apertures in the underside of the valve, so a torch and small mirror may be useful.

126 With the engine fully warmed up to normal operating temperature and idling, briefly open and close the throttle; the diaphragm should move upwards as the manifold vacuum changes. When the engine is idling smoothly again, press upwards (very carefully, so that it is not distorted or damaged) on the diaphragm; the idle speed should drop significantly (approximately 100 rpm).

127 If the EGR control valve does not respond as described, disconnect the hose from the thermal vacuum valve to the back pressure transducer, and check that full inlet manifold depression can be felt sucking on the hose end. If all is well, reconnect the hose and repeat the check on the EGR control valve hose.

128 If no vacuum can be felt at all, remove the thermal vacuum valve (see below), attach lengths of hose to its unions, and use a hand-operated vacuum pump to check that the valve opens when the valve body is immersed in a container of water that is heated to 60°C (140°F); do not allow water to enter the valve itself during this test. If the valve is faulty, it must be renewed.

129 If the back pressure transducer is thought to be faulty, it can be tested only by the substitution of a known good component; if the transducer is proven faulty, it must be renewed.

130 If all other components of the system are in good order, but the EGR control valve does not respond as described, it must be cleaned. Pull off the hose from the valve, then unbolt the valve and remove it. Clean away all carbon using a wire brush and a pointed tool, but take care not to damage the valve seat. Renew the valve gasket to prevent induction leaks. Refit the valve and reconnect the hose, then recheck the system's performance; if there is no improvement, the valve must be renewed.

Thermal vacuum valve - removal and refitting

131 This component is screwed into the right-hand underside of the inlet manifold. Drain the cooling system to below the level of the manifold, which usually requires the draining-off of about 1 litre (1.8 pints) of coolant (Chapter 2).

132 Disconnect its vacuum hoses one by one, labelling each to ensure that it can be correctly reconnected.

13

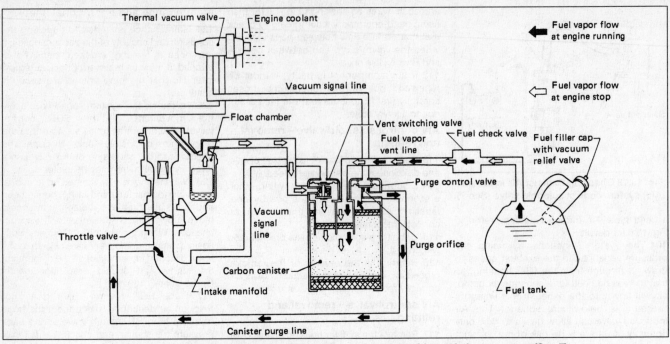

Fig. 13.19 Evaporative Emissions Control system – 1.2 models with catalytic converters (Sec 7)

Note: *See also Fig. 13.6*

133 Unscrew the valve and withdraw it.

134 Refitting is the reverse of the removal procedure; apply a smear of sealant to its threads to prevent leaks, then tighten the valve securely and ensure that its vacuum hoses are correctly reconnected. Refill the cooling system, and check the level when the engine is restarted and has warmed up fully (Chapter 2).

Back pressure transducer - removal and refitting

135 This component is rubber-mounted, secured by three screws, to a mounting bracket on the left-hand side of the inlet manifold.

136 To remove the unit, disconnect its vacuum hoses one by one, labelling each to ensure that it can be correctly reconnected. Unfasten its screws and remove it.

137 Refitting is the reverse of the removal procedure; ensure that its vacuum hoses are correctly reconnected.

EGR control valve - removal and refitting

138 The valve is secured by two nuts to the top right-hand side of the inlet manifold.

139 To remove the unit, disconnect its vacuum hose, unscrew the nuts and withdraw it, noting the washers. Remove and discard the gasket; this should always be renewed, as should that beneath the valve spacer, if this is ever disturbed.

140 Refitting is the reverse of the removal procedure; tighten the nuts to the specified torque wrench setting, and ensure that the vacuum hose is securely reconnected.

Evaporative Emission Control system

General description

141 This system is fitted to minimise the escape into the atmosphere of unburned hydrocarbons (fuel vapour). The system consists of a charcoal canister and a Thermal Vacuum Valve (TVV) mounted in the engine compartment, with a fuel check valve located next to the fuel tank and filler tube, as well as the hoses connecting these components; refer to Figs. 13.6 and 13.19 for details.

142 The fuel tank filler cap is sealed, incorporating a vacuum relief valve to allow air to pass only into the fuel tank to replace the fuel used while the engine is running. The charcoal canister collects the petrol vapours generated in the tank and carburettor when the vehicle is parked, and stores them until they can be cleared from the canister into the inlet tract, to be burned by the engine during normal combustion.

143 The system's operation is governed by carburettor depression, which is controlled by engine temperature through the Thermal Vacuum Valve (TVV) to act on the canister's purge control valve. When engine temperature is above 60°C (140°F), fuel vapours are allowed to flow into the inlet tract. The system of valves is designed to ensure that the engine runs correctly when it is cold and/or idling, and to protect the catalytic converter from the effects of an over-rich mixture.

Maintenance and operational check

144 No special maintenance operations are required, other than a general check of the security and condition of the system's components at the intervals given in Section 3 of this Chapter.

145 To check the operation of the thermal vacuum valve, refer to paragraphs 127 and 128 above.

146 To check the operation of the fuel check valve, blow through from the fuel tank end; considerable resistance should be felt, with only part of the airflow being allowed to pass. Now blow through from the engine end; no resistance should be felt, with the full airflow being allowed to pass.

147 To check the operation of the filler cap vacuum relief valve, wipe the cap clean and suck hard through it; slight resistance should be felt at first, with better airflow (accompanied by clicking from the valve) as you suck harder.

148 If any of the components are found to be worn, damaged or faulty, they must be renewed.

Thermal vacuum valve - removal and refitting

149 This is the same component used in the EGR system; refer to paragraphs 131 to 134 above.

Charcoal canister - removal and refitting

150 This component is mounted on the engine compartment bulkhead, behind the air filter housing.

151 Disconnect the canister's vacuum hoses one by one; either note the manufacturer's colour-coding, or label each hose to ensure that it can be correctly reconnected. Unfasten the canister and remove it.

152 Refitting is the reverse of the removal procedure; ensure that its vacuum hoses are correctly reconnected.

Fuel check valve - removal and refitting

153 The location of the fuel check valve varies according to model and year, but can be traced from the fuel tank along the filler neck. Release any clamps or ties securing the hoses, and unfasten the clips to disconnect the hoses from the valve.

154 Refitting is the reverse of the removal procedure; renew any clamps, ties or clips damaged during removal.

Catalytic converters - general information and precautions

155 The exhaust gases of any internal combustion engine (however efficient or well-tuned) which burns petrol consists largely (approximately 99%) of nitrogen (N_2), carbon dioxide (CO_2), oxygen (O_2) and other inert gases and water vapour (H_2O). The remaining 1% is made up of the noxious materials which are currently seen (CO_2 apart) as the major polluters of the environment; carbon monoxide (CO), unburned hydrocarbons (HC), oxides of nitrogen (NO_x) and some solid matter, including a small lead content.

156 Left to themselves, most of these pollutants are thought eventually to break down naturally (CO and NO, for example, break down in the upper atmosphere to release CO_2) having first caused ground-level environmental problems, but the massive increase world-wide in the use of motor cars and the current popular concern for the environment has caused the introduction in most countries of legislation, in varying stages of severity, to combat the problem.

157 The device most commonly used to clean up car exhausts is the catalytic converter. It is fitted into the car's exhaust system, and uses precious metals (platinum and palladium or rhodium) as catalysts to speed up the reaction between the pollutants and the oxygen in the car's exhaust gases, CO and HC being oxidised to form CO_2 and H_2O and (in the three-way type of catalytic converter) NO_x being reduced to N_2. The catalytic converter is not a filter in the physical sense; its function is to promote a chemical reaction, but it is not itself affected by that reaction.

158 The converter consists of an element (or 'substrate') of ceramic honeycomb, coated with a combination of precious metals in such a way as to produce a vast surface area over which the exhaust gases must flow; the whole usually being mounted in a stainless-steel box. A simple 'oxidation' (or 'two-way') catalytic converter can deal with CO, HC and NO_x. Three-way catalytic converters are further sub-divided into 'open-loop' (or 'uncontrolled') converters which can remove 50 to 70% of pollutants, and 'closed-loop' (also known as 'controlled' or 'regulated')

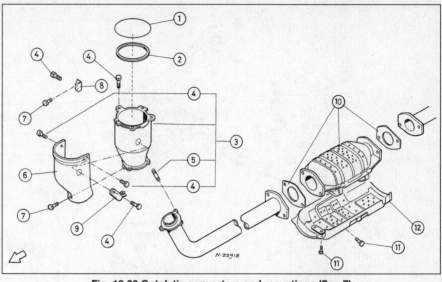

Fig. 13.20 Catalytic converters and mountings (Sec 7)

1 Sealing ring	6 Heat shield	10 Secondary catalytic
2 Converter cap	7 (Hexagon-headed screw	converter
3 Primary catalytic converter	8 Left-hand support bracket	11 Bolt
4 Bolt	9 Right-hand support	12 Heat shield
5 Stud	bracket	

converters which can remove over 90% of pollutants. Micra models are fitted with two closed-loop converters, one under the exhaust manifold and the second further down the exhaust system.

159 A catalytic converter is a reliable and a simple device, which needs no maintenance in itself, but there are some facts of which an owner should be aware if the converters are to function properly for their full service life.

(a) *DO NOT use leaded petrol in a car equipped with catalytic converters - the lead will coat the precious metals, reducing their converting efficiency, and will also seriously affect the operation of the exhaust gas sensor. Opinions vary as to how much leaded fuel is necessary to affect a converter's performance, and whether it can recover even if only unleaded petrol is used afterwards; the best course of action is, therefore, to assume the worst, and to ensure that NO leaded petrol is used at any time.*

(b) *Always keep the ignition and fuel systems well-maintained in accordance with the manufacturer's schedule (see Routine maintenance at the beginning of this manual) - particularly, ensure that the air cleaner filter element, the fuel filter and the spark plugs are renewed a the correct interval if the intake air/fuel mixture is allowed to become too rich due to neglect, the unburned surplus will enter and burn in the catalytic converters, overheating their elements and eventually destroying the converters.*

(c) *If the engine develops a misfire, do not drive the car at all (or at least as little as*

possible) *until the fault is cured the misfire will allow unburned fuel to enter the converters, which will result in their overheating, as noted above. For the same reason, do not persist if the engine ever refuses to start (either trace the problem and cure it yourself, or have the car checked immediately by a qualified mechanic), and never allow the car to run out of petrol.*

(d) *DO NOT push- or tow-start the car - this will soak the catalytic converters in unburned fuel, causing them to overheat when the engine does start see (b) above.*

(e) *DO NOT switch off the ignition at high engine speeds - if the ignition is switched off at anything above idle speed, unburned fuel will enter the (very hot) catalytic converters, with the possible risk of its igniting on the elements and damaging the converters.*

(f) *Try to avoid repeated successive cold starts which are then followed by short journeys - if the converters are never allowed to reach their proper working temperature, they will gather unburned fuel, allowing some to pass into the atmosphere and the rest to soak the elements in unburned fuel, causing them to overheat when the engine starts see (b) above.*

(g) *DO not use fuel or engine oil additives - these may contain substances harmful to the catalytic converters.*

(h) *DO NOT continue to use the car if the engine burns oil to the extent of leaving a visible trail of blue smoke - the unburned carbon deposits will clog the converter passages and reduce their efficiency; in severe cases, the element will overheat.*

13

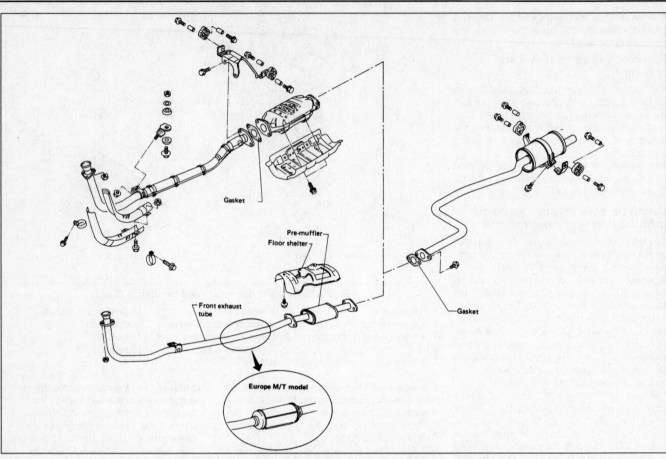

Fig. 13.21 Exhaust system components (typical) – all later models (Sec 7)

(l) *Remember that the catalytic converter operates at very high temperatures - hence the heat shields on the car's underbody and the casing will become hot enough to ignition combustible materials which brush against it DO NOT, therefore, park the car in dry undergrowth, over long grass or piles of dead leaves.*

(j) *Remember that a catalytic converter is FRAGILE - do not strike it with tools during servicing work, take great care when working on the exhaust system. Ensure that the (secondary) converter is well clear of any jacks or other lifting gear used to raise the car. Do not drive the car over rough ground, road humps, etc., in such a way as to 'ground' the exhaust system.*

(k) *In some cases, particularly when the car is and/or is used for stop/start driving, a sulphurous smell (like that of rotten eggs) may be noticed from the exhaust. This is common to many catalytic converter-equipped cars, and seems to be due to the small amount of sulphur found in some petrols reacting with hydrogen in the exhaust to produce hydrogen sulphide (H_2S) gas; while this gas is toxic, it is not produced in sufficient amounts to*

be a problem. Once the car has covered a few thousand miles, the problem should disappear in the meanwhile, a change of driving style or of the brand of petrol used may effect a solution.

(l) *The catalytic converters, used on a well-maintained and well-driven car, should last for between 50 000 and 100 000 miles - from this point on, careful checks should be made at all specified service intervals of the CO level, to ensure that the converter is still operating efficiently - if the converter is no longer effective, it must be renewed.*

Catalytic converters - removal and refitting

Primary converter

160 Unfasten the exhaust downpipe front mounting, and either unhook or unbolt the next mounting along.

161 Unbolt the converter and manifold heat shields if required to reach the converter's retaining nuts and bolts.

162 Unscrew the nuts securing the exhaust downpipe to the converter, and lower the exhaust system onto a suitable support; pack the downpipe with rag, to prevent any dirt and foreign matter from dropping in and fouling the secondary converter.

163 Unbolt the converter from the manifold and withdraw it, noting the presence of the sealing ring(s).

164 On reassembly, use a wire brush or similar to carefully clean the mating surfaces of the manifold, converter and downpipe; renew the sealing ring(s) if there is any doubt about their condition. **Note:** *Do **not** use any form of silicone or other sealant on the joints; pieces of sealant may break off and foul the catalytic converters.*

165 Ensuring that the sealing ring(s) are correctly installed, fit the converter to the manifold, and tighten the bolts evenly and securely.

166 Connect the downpipe to the converter, and tighten the nuts to the specified torque wrench setting.

167 Refit the heat shields (if removed) and reassemble the exhaust system mountings. Start the engine and warm it up to normal operating temperature, then check for leaks. Recheck the security of all disturbed fasteners once the engine has cooled down again.

Secondary converter

168 Undo the converter's front and rear flange bolts. Prise away the rear part of the system until the converter can be withdrawn; collect any gaskets fitted.

169 On refitting, clean the mating surfaces

carefully, fit new gaskets (where applicable), and tighten the bolts to the specified torque wrench setting.

170 When working on any other part of the system, note that the underbody of the vehicle is protected by heat shields from the very high operating temperatures of a catalytic converter; these may have to be unbolted before the exhaust system itself can be removed from the vehicle.

Unleaded fuel

171 Micra models with catalytic converters **must** use unleaded petrol **only**; the manufacturer's recommended **minimum** octane rating is given in the Specifications at the start of this Chapter, with the equivalent in terms of the petrol currently on sale in the UK. Note that 'Super/Superplus'-grade unleaded petrol may also be used if wished, with no ill-effects.

172 Note that these models may use 91 RON 'Regular' or 'Normal' grade unleaded petrol, which is not yet available in the UK. If you are taking such a vehicle abroad, seek the advice of a Nissan dealer (or of one of the motoring organisations) to ensure that you are aware of the grades of petrol that you are likely to encounter, and be sure that you are aware of the different (and sometimes confusingly contradictory) names used for these grades, compared with the UK terms with which you are familiar.

8 Ignition system

PART A:
MODELS WITHOUT CATALYTIC CONVERTERS

Electronic ignition - general description

1 The electronic ignition system fitted to all 1.0 models built from November 1988 onwards, and to all 1.2 models without catalytic converters, incorporates a distributor which uses and IC (Integrated Circuit) ignition unit to replace the contract breaker points and condenser described in Chapter 4. In all other respects the distributor is conventional, employing mechanical and vacuum advance/retard mechanisms.

2 The spark is generated by the magnetic influence of the regulator's shaped projections as they approach and pass the poles of the IC ignition unit/baseplate. This allows a stronger spark to be generated, and eliminates the regular maintenance required by contact breaker systems.

3 In all other respects, the system is as described in Chapter 4.

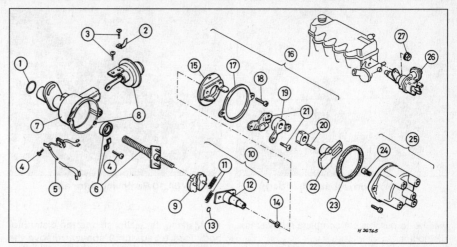

Fig. 13.22 Exploded view of the distributor – all 1.0 models November 1988 on, and all 1.2 models without catalytic converters (Sec 8A)

1 Sealing O-ring	10 Advance/retard mechanism
2 Earth terminal	assembly
3 Screw	11 Advance/retard mechanism
4 Screw	springs
5 IC ignition unit wires	12 Reluctor shaft
6 Distributor driveshaft, bush	13 E-clip
and retainer assembly	14 Screw
7 Distributor body	15 Baseplate
8 Vacuum capsule assembly	16 IC ignition unit assembly
9 Advance/retard mechanism	17 Baseplate locating ring
weight assembly	18 Screw

19 IC ignition unit
20 Reluctor and roll pin
21 Magnet and mounting
screws
22 Rotor arm
23 Gasket
24 Carbon brush
25 Distributor cap assembly
26 Distributor assembly
27 Clamp nut

⚠️ **Warning: The voltages produced by the electronic ignition system are considerably higher than those produced by conventional systems. Extreme care must be taken when working on the system with the ignition switched on. Persons with surgically-implanted cardiac pacemaker devices should keep well clear of the ignition circuits, components and test equipment.**

Routine maintenance 🔧🔧

4 Maintenance is considerably simplified by the elimination of all tasks relating to the contact breaker points, while the ignition timing check is merely to ensure that all is in order; the ignition timing, once set, should not vary unless the distributor or its device is disturbed.

5 At the specified interval, check the condition of the spark plug HT leads (Chapter 4, Section 10) and the distributor cap and rotor arm (Chapter 4, Sections 7 and 10).

6 Spark plug maintenance remains as described in Chapter 4.

Distributor - removal and refitting

7 Refer to Chapter 4, Section 6, but note the anti-chatter bush at the drive end (photos).

Distributor overhaul 🔧🔧🔧🔧

8 Remove the distributor (see paragraph 7 above) and clean away all external dirt. Check carefully the cost and availability of replacement parts before starting work; depending on the degree of wear, the simplest and most economical solution may

8A.7A Removing distributor

8A.7B Note distributor driveshaft anti-chatter bush

13

8A.9 Note driveshaft offset dog

8A.10 Removing rotor arm

8A.11 Removing reluctor

well be to purchase a complete replacement distributor.

9 Remove the two screws and withdraw the distributor cap, noting the gasket. With the rotor arm aligned with No 1 cylinder cap contact, note and mark (using a felt-tipped marker pen, paint or similar) the position of the driveshaft's offset dog in the distributor body, and of the reluctor against the IC ignition unit (photo).

10 Pull off the rotor arm (photo).

11 Carefully mark (see paragraph 9 above) the relationship of the reluctor to its shaft, then very carefully prise the reluctor off the shaft and collect the roll pin (photo).

12 Noting carefully their connections, disconnect the IC ignition unit wires (photo).

13 Marking its relationship to the distributor body (see paragraph 9 above), remove the retaining screws and withdraw the IC ignition unit and magnet (photos); store the magnet in a plastic bag, to keep it clean of metal particles.

14 Remove the two screws to withdraw the baseplate locating ring from the distributor body; if any alignment marks are visible, note them as an aid to correct reassembly (photo).

15 Extract the retaining E-clip to disconnect its link rod from the baseplate, remove the external fixing screws (noting the earth terminal on one), then withdraw the vacuum capsule from the distributor body (photo). Withdraw the baseplate, noting how its pivot pin is aligned with the vacuum capsule

passage in the distributor body; if any alignment marks are visible, note them as an aid to correct reassembly.

16 Checking that the driveshaft is still aligned (and marked) as described in paragraph 9 above, mark carefully the relationship of the reluctor shaft to the main distributor driveshaft. Remove the screw from inside the end of the reluctor shaft and extract the E-clips, then carefully withdraw the reluctor shaft from the driveshaft and advance/retard mechanism; take care not to stretch or distort the springs.

17 Using different colours, identify the springs and weights so that they can be refitted in their original locations. Remove the springs (taking care not to stretch or distort

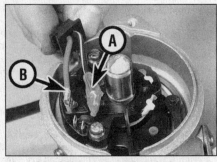

8A.12 Note connections before disconnecting wires from IC ignition unit

A Insulated connector   B Bared connector

8A.13A Remove fixing screws . . .

8A.13B . . . to release IC ignition unit . . .

8A. 13C . . . and the magnet

8A.14 Remove screws (arrowed) to release locating ring and baseplate

8A.15 Prise off circlip to release vacuum unit link rod from baseplate

them) and weight assembly, storing them carefully.

18 Using a slim screwdriver, remove the single screw from inside the distributor body, withdraw the retainer plate and pull out the driveshaft. If the driveshaft bush in the distributor body is worn, it can be renewed only as part of the complete driveshaft assembly.

19 Clean all components thoroughly, and check for signs of wear or damage; renew any component that is unfit for further use. Check the distributor cap and rotor arm carefully, as described in Chapter 4 (photo).

20 Refitting is the reverse of the removal procedure, noting the following points.

21 Using high-melting-point grease, lubricate the bearing surfaces of the distributor body and driveshaft, and of the advance/retard mechanism pivots and weights; also lubricate the mechanism springs, and the bearing surfaces of the reluctor shaft and driveshaft, and of the baseplate.

22 As components are refitted, ensure that the marks or notes made on removal are realigned correctly.

23 When refitting the reluctor shaft, refer also to Fig. 13.23 to ensure that it is correctly aligned.

24 When refitting the baseplate, refer also to Fig. 13.24 to ensure that it is correctly aligned.

25 On refitting the reluctor, secure it by inserting the roll pin as shown in Fig. 13.25. Check that the air gap between each reluctor projection and each of the IC ignition unit/baseplate poles is between 0.30 and 0.45 mm (0.0118 and 0.0177 in), as shown in Fig. 13.26; rotate the driveshaft to ensure that the gap is correct for all positions. If adjustment is required, slacken the IC ignition unit retaining screws and move the unit until the air gap is correct.

26 Refit the rotor arm and distributor cap, refit the distributor to the engine, and check the ignition timing on restarting.

Ignition timing - adjustment

27 The ignition timing check can only be carried out dynamically as described in Sections 8 and 9 of Chapter 4, referring to the Specifications Section of this Chapter for the timing settings.

Fault finding - ignition system

28 The components of electronic ignition systems are normally very reliable; most faults are far more likely to be due to loose or dirty connections, or to 'tracking' of HT voltage due to dirt, dampness or damaged insulation than to the failure of any of the system's components. **Always** check thoroughly all wiring before condemning an electrical component, and work methodically to eliminate all other possibilities before deciding that a particular component is faulty.

29 The basic checks of the ignition system, and the tests of the coil windings (note the coil resistances given in the Specifications

8A.19 Interior of distributor cap, showing HT lead contacts and (centre) carbon brush

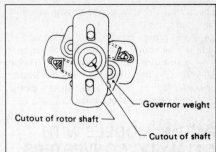

Fig. 13.23 Correct alignment of reluctor shaft on advance/retard (governor) mechanism – models without catalytic converters (Sec 8A)

Governor weight
Cutout of rotor shaft
Cutout of shaft

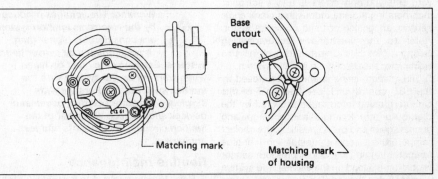

Fig. 13.24 Baseplate-to-distributor body alignment marks – models without catalytic converters (Sec 8A)

Base cutout end
Matching mark
Matching mark of housing

Section of this Chapter) are as described in Chapter 4.

30 When testing for a spark at the HT leads, **do not** hold the lead away from the block as described in Chapter 4; not only is there a high risk of a powerful electric shock, but the coil or IC ignition unit will be damaged. Similarly, **never** try to 'diagnose' misfires by pulling off one HT lead at a time. Instead, either use a securely-earthed spark plug or proprietary 'spark jumper', or connect a timing light and turn the engine over on the starter motor; if the light flashes, voltage is reaching the spark plugs, so these should be checked first. If the light does not flash, check the HT leads themselves, followed by the

distributor cap, carbon brush and rotor arm (Chapter 4).

31 If the HT side of the circuit is sound, but there is still no spark, the fault must lie in the LT circuit.

32 To check the power supply, disconnect the green wire from the ignition coil's positive terminal, then use a voltmeter to check that there is full battery voltage available between the end of the wire and a good earth point. If not, check back through the wiring to the ignition switch and battery until the fault is found and rectified.

33 To check the earth, disconnect the blue wire from the ignition coil's negative terminal and from the distributor IC ignition unit, then

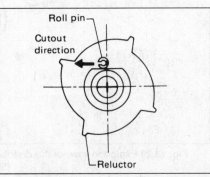

Roll pin
Cutout direction
Reluctor

Fig. 13.25 Fit roll pin as shown to secure reluctor – models without catalytic converters (Sec 8A)

Fig. 13.26 Measuring reluctor-to-IC ignition unit/baseplate air gap models without catalytic converters slacken screws arrowed to adjust (Sec 8A)

13

check that the wire is not broken or short-circuited to earth.

34 If the power supply, coil, wiring and HT side are all sound, then the fault must be in the distributor IC ignition unit. Before condemning this wrongly, have the system checked by an expert at a Nissan dealer, using the proper test equipment.

PART B: MODELS WITH CATALYTIC CONVERTERS

Electronic ignition - general description

1 The ignition system fitted to all 1.2 models with catalytic converters is fully-electronic, incorporating a distributor (with a crank angle sensor), an ignition coil and power transistor. Refer to the illustrations accompanying Section 7 of this Chapter as well as this Section for details of the complete system.

2 The ignition timing is entirely controlled by the ECC control unit (see Section 7 of this Chapter), using information provided by the distributor crank angle sensor (signalling engine speed and piston position), the coolant temperature sensor (signalling engine temperature) and the boost pressure sensor (signalling the load on the engine). The system also includes the ignition switch and power supply, as well as components such as the reversing light/neutral and clutch switches (manual transmission) or inhibitor switch (automatic transmission).

3 All these signals are compared by the control unit, using digital techniques, with set values pre-programmed (mapped) into its memory; based on this information, the control unit selects the ignition timing appropriate to those values, and controls the ignition coil accordingly, its signals being amplified by the power transistor.

4 The spark is triggered in the distributor by the rotation of a rotor plate between a light-emitting diode (LED) and a photo diode. The plate has 360 slits cut in its periphery at 1° intervals, to correspond with each degree of crankshaft rotation. Within this row of slits is a series of four slits, corresponding to 180° of crankshaft rotation, to give the engine speed signal; one of these slits is significantly larger than the others, to identify No 1 cylinder. The passage of these slits causes interruptions in the light sent from the LED to the photo diode, which causes pulses to be generated in the photo diode. These pulses are shaped into usable digital on-off signals by the wave-forming circuit, and sent to the ECC control unit.

5 This allows a stronger and more accurately-controlled spark to be generated, and eliminates not only the regular maintenance required by contact breaker systems, but also the variations in ignition timing which can result from wear in the mechanical components (advance/retard mechanism, etc.) of conventional electronic systems.

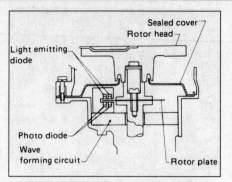

Fig. 13.27 Cross-section through distributor/crank angle sensor – 1.2 models with catalytic converters (Sec 8B)

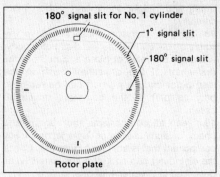

Fig. 13.28 Distributor/crank angle sensor rotor plate slits – 1.2 models with catalytic converters (Sec 8B)

⚠️ *Warning: The voltages produced by the electronic ignition system are considerably higher than those produced by conventional systems. Extreme care must be taken when working on the system with the ignition switched on. Persons with surgically-implanted cardiac pacemaker devices should keep well clear of the ignition circuits, components and test equipment.*

Routine maintenance

6 Refer to paragraphs 4 to 6 of Part A of this Section.

Distributor - removal and refitting

7 Disconnect the battery earth terminal.

8 Disconnect the wiring connector from the distributor.

9 Position the engine so that No 1 cylinder is at TDC on the compression stroke (Chapter 1, Section 5).

10 Remove the distributor cap as described in Chapter 4, and check that the rotor arm is pointing towards the cap's No 1 terminal.

11 Mark the relationship of the distributor body to the cylinder head, using a scriber or similar.

12 Unscrew the distributor clamp nut and withdraw the distributor. Do not disturb the crankshaft setting while the distributor is removed, or rotate the distributor shaft.

13 Remove the distributor body sealing O-ring; this must be renewed whenever it is disturbed.

14 On reassembly, first check that No 1

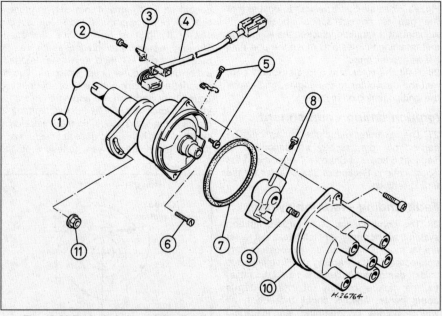

Fig. 13.29 Exploded view of the distributor – 1.2 models with catalytic converters (Sec 8B)

1 Sealing O-ring	5 Screw	9 Carbon brush
2 Screw	6 Screw	10 Distributor cap assembly
3 Earth terminal	7 Gasket	11 Clamp nut
4 Distributor wiring	8 Rotor arm assembly	

cylinder is at TDC, then rotate the rotor arm to align with the distributor cap's No 1 terminal. Fit a new sealing O-ring to the distributor body, and lubricate it with a smear of engine oil.

15 Aligning the marks made on removal, refit the distributor. If necessary, rotate the rotor arm very slightly to help the distributor drive dogs locate in the camshaft slots; they are offset, and so will fit only one way. Refit the clamp nut.

16 Refit the distributor cap, ensuring it is correctly located, then reconnect the HT leads.

17 Reconnect the distributor wiring and battery.

18 Check, and adjust if necessary, the ignition timing.

Distributor - overhaul

19 Remove the distributor (see paragraphs 7 to 13 above), and clean away all external dirt.

20 Remove and check the distributor cap (Chapter 4).

21 Unscrew the retaining screw and withdraw the rotor arm; renew it if its contact surfaces are burned or eroded, and check it for signs of tracking (Chapter 4).

22 This is as far as the distributor should be dismantled, as no more individual replacement parts are available. If the unit is worn or faulty, it must be renewed complete. Before condemning it wrongly, have it checked by an expert at a Nissan dealer, using the proper test equipment.

Ignition timing - adjustment

23 The ignition timing check can only be carried out dynamically, as described in Sections 8 and 9 of Chapter 4, referring to the Specifications Section of this Chapter for the timing settings.

24 With the strobe light and tachometer connected following the equipment manufacturer's instructions, and all electrical equipment (vehicle lights, heated rear window, etc.) switched off, start the engine and warm it up to normal operating temperature.

25 Allow the engine to idle, and check that the idling speed is as specified (at the start of this Chapter, or Chapter 3). To ensure that the idling speed is stable, clear excess fuel from the inlet manifold by running the engine quickly to between 2000 and 3000 rev/min two or three times, then allowing the engine to idle for 2 minutes before making the check.

26 Aim the stroke light at the timing marks, and check that the pulley mark is aligned with the appropriate (vacuum connected) timing mark on the timing belt lower cover scale.

27 If adjustment is required, disconnect the vacuum hose from the boost pressure sensor and plug it. Slacken the distributor clamp nut

and turn the distributor (as shown in Chapter 4, Fig. 4.4) until the pulley mark is aligned as exactly as possible at the (vacuum disconnected) timing setting note that this will mean guessing the correct position approximately halfway between the scale's '0' and end marks. When the setting is correct, tighten the clamp nut, unplug and reconnect the vacuum hose, then repeat the procedure to recheck the timing, working from paragraph 25 onwards.

28 When the timing is correct, switch off the engine and disconnect the test equipment.

Ignition coil - removal and refitting

29 The coil is a moulded plastic unit, secured by two screws and nuts in a mounting bracket on the engine compartment left-hand inner wing panel.

30 To remove the coil, disconnect the battery earth lead and the coil wiring and distributor HT lead, then unscrew the nuts and withdraw the coil.

31 Refitting is the reverse of the removal procedure.

32 While the coil windings can be checked as described in Chapter 4, Section 11, no resistances are quoted by Nissan. If the readings obtained are thought to be incorrect, they can be verified only by comparison with a known good one.

Power transistor - removal and refitting

33 The power transistor is secured by two screws to the coil's mounting bracket (see paragraph 29 above).

34 To remove the transistor, disconnect the battery earth lead and the coil wiring, then remove the screws and withdraw the transistor.

35 Refitting is the reverse of the removal procedure.

36 No information is available to help the DIY mechanic test the transistor. If it is thought to be faulty, it can be checked only by substituting a known good unit.

Fault finding - ignition system

37 The general comments made in Part A of this Section, paragraph 28 to 34, apply equally to this system, but note that in this case, the control unit is also at risk if the system is triggered with an open (ie, not properly earthed) HT circuit; control units are very much more expensive to replace, so take care!

38 If you are in any doubt as to your skill and ability to test an ignition system's components and to understand what is happening, or if you do not have the required equipment, take the vehicle immediately to a good Nissan dealer; it is better to pay the

labour charges involved in having the vehicle checked by an expert than to risk damage to the system or to yourself.

Engine will not start

39 If the engine either will not turn over at all, or only turns very slowly, check the battery and starter motor. Connect a voltmeter across the battery terminals (meter positive probe to battery positive terminal), disconnect the ignition coil HT lead from the distributor cap and earth it, then note the voltage reading obtained while turning over the engine on the starter for (no more than) ten seconds. If the reading obtained is less than approximately 9.5 volts, check the battery, starter motor and charging system (Chapter 12).

40 If the engine turns over at normal speed but will not start, check the HT circuit by connecting a timing light and turning the engine over on the starter motor; if the light flashes, voltage is reaching the spark plugs, so these should be checked first. If the light does not flash, check the HT leads themselves, followed by the distributor cap, carbon brush and rotor arm (Chapter 4).

41 If there is a spark, check the fuel system for faults (Section 7).

42 If the HT circuit appears to be in good condition, the feed to the ignition coil can be checked as described in Part A, paragraph 32, while the coil itself can be checked roughly as described in paragraph 32 of this Part. Note, however, that the control unit regulates the coil's earth; **DO NOT** attempt to 'test' the control unit with anything other than the correct test equipment, which will be available only at a good Nissan dealer. If any of the wires are to be checked which lead to the control unit, always unplug the relevant connector from the unit first, so that there is no risk of its being damaged by the application of incorrect voltages from test equipment.

43 If all components have been checked for signs of obvious faults such as dirty or poorly-fastened connections, damp or 'tracking', and have been tested as far as is possible but the system is still thought to be faulty, the vehicle must be taken to a good Nissan dealer for testing on the correct equipment.

Engine misfires

44 Refer to paragraphs 37 to 38 above, but note that the possible causes of partial failures which might result in a misfire are far too numerous to be eliminated without the correct test equipment. Once the ignition system components have been checked for obvious faults such as dirty or poorly-fastened connections, damp, or 'tracking', and have been tested as far as is possible, take the vehicle to a good Nissan dealer for the full fuel/ignition system to be tested on the correct equipment.

13

9.1 Automatic transmission fluid cooler pipe (arrowed) at transmission casing

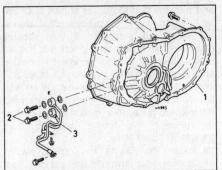

Fig. 13.30 Automatic transmission fluid cooler connections at transmission – 1985 on models (Sec 9)

1 *Transmission casing*   3 *Fluid pipes*
2 *Banjo union bolts*

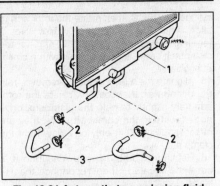

Fig. 13.31 Automatic transmission fluid cooler connections at radiator – 1985 on models (Sec 9)

1 *Radiator*   3 *Flexible hoses*
2 *Worm-drive clips*

9 Automatic transmission

Fluid cooler

1 Post-1985 automatic transmission models are fitted with water-cooled fluid coolers (photo).
2 The fluid cooler is integral with the cooling system radiator, the automatic transmission fluid being fed and returned to the cooler via the two banjo unions on the transmission casing, and two pipe lines.
3 The connections at the radiator end are by flexible hoses, secured with worm-drive clips.
4 When removing the transmission unit, as described in Chapter 7, disconnect the cooler pipes at the transmission housing banjo unions, blanking off the open ends to prevent ingress of dirt.
5 Similarly, when removing the radiator, as described in Chapter 2, disconnect and blank off the unions at the radiator.
6 The fluid is not under pressure, and only a small amount of fluid will be lost.
7 On reconnecting the pipes at the transmission housing banjo unions, tighten the unions to the specified torque, and check for leaks with the engine running.

10 Braking system

Brake master cylinder

1 The manufacturer may fit master cylinders from various suppliers, and the internal diameter of these cylinders differ, according to source.

2 It is important, therefore, when ordering repair kits, to know which make of master cylinder is fitted to your vehicle, in order that the correct kits are obtained.

Rear wheel cylinder

3 The comments made in the preceding paragraphs about different suppliers applies also to the rear wheel cylinder.
4 Although externally similar, the internal seals and piston are different, and there is no interchangeability between makes.
5 When ordering repair kits, quote the manufacturer's name.

Brake pedal (1985-on)

6 Note the revised brake pedal depressed height given in the Specifications section of this Supplement.

Rear brake drums (1988 on)

7 The rear brake drums on later models are detachable from the hub/bearing assembly on which they are mounted. Refer to Section 11 of this supplement.

11 Suspension and steering

Front hub bearings (1988 on) - description and renewal

1 Later models are fitted with one-piece bearings instead of the separate inner and outer bearings used previously.
2 To renew a bearing, first raise the front of the car and support it on axle stands. Remove the roadwheel.
3 Prise off the grease cap (if fitted), extract the split pin and take off the nut retainer. Unscrew and remove the locknut and thrustwasher.

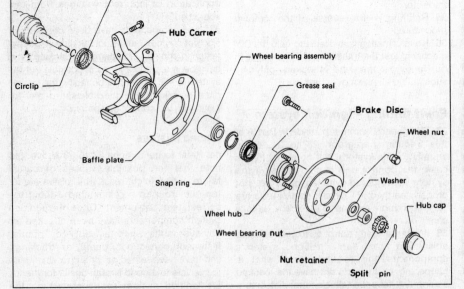

Fig. 13.32 Exploded view of front wheel hub and hub carrier – 1988 on models (Sec 11)

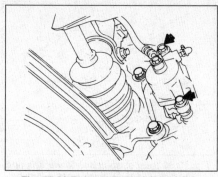

Fig. 13.33 Remove bolts (arrowed) to release brake caliper from hub carrier (Sec 11)

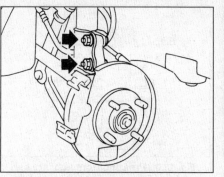

Fig. 13.34 Remove bolts (arrowed) to release hub carrier from suspension strut (Sec 11)

11.4A Unscrewing a caliper mounting bolt

4 Unbolt the brake caliper and tie it up to the strut coil spring to avoid straining the hydraulic hose (photos).
5 Take off the disc pads and springs, and then remove the brake disc (photos).
6 Using a suitable balljoint 'splitter' tool, disconnect the tie-rod end balljoint from the steering arm of the hub carrier (photo).
7 Push or tap the driveshaft out of the hub carrier.
8 Unscrew and remove the bolts from the clamp at the base of the suspension strut (photo).
9 Using the balljoint 'splitter' tool, separate the suspension arm balljoint from the hub carrier. Remove the hub carrier (photos).

11.4B Withdrawing caliper, leaving pads in place

11.5A Removing a brake pad . . .

11.5B. . . and the spring clip

11.5C Withdrawing brake disc

11.6 Disconnecting a tie-rod end balljoint

11.8 Unfastening strut bottom clamp bolts

11.9A Disconnect suspension arm balljoint . . .

11.9B . . . to release hub carrier

13

11.11 Hub carrier oil seal

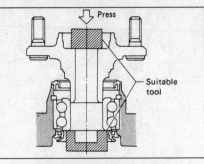

Fig. 13.35 Pressing front hub into hub carrier – note support for bearing inner track (Sec 11)

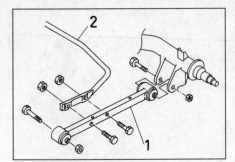

Fig. 13.36 Rear suspension lower link and stabiliser bar mountings (Sec 11)

1 Lower link   2 Stabiliser bar

10 If a press is not available, use a tubular drift to drive out the hub from the carrier.

11 Prise out the oil seal (photo).

12 Extract the bearing circlip.

13 Press the bearing out of the hub carrier by applying pressure to the inboard side of the bearing. If a press is not available, use a bolt, nut and distance pieces to draw it out. The action of removal will destroy the bearing, so it must not be used again.

14 When fitting the new bearing, apply pressure to the outer track only.

15 Fill the lips of a new inboard seal with grease, and fit it squarely in position.

16 Fit the bearing circlip and the outboard oil seal, the lips again filled with grease.

17 Press the hub into the carrier. It is essential that the inboard side of the inner track of the bearing is supported during pressing or drawing in of the hub (Fig. 13.35).

18 Bolt the hub carrier to the base of the suspension strut.

19 Engage the driveshaft with the hub carrier.

20 Reconnect the suspension arm balljoint and the tie-rod end balljoint.

21 Fit the brake disc and the brake caliper.

22 Fit the thrustwasher, screw on the nut and tighten to specified torque. Fit the nut retainer, a new split pin and the grease cap (if fitted) (photos).

23 Fit the roadwheel and lower the car.

Rear suspension stabiliser bar - description

24 Models produced since 1985 have provision for the fitting of a rear stabiliser bar, which is an item of optional equipment.

25 The stabiliser bar is bolted between the two lower links. In order to achieve this, the lower link profile has been changed from round section to square section (photo).

26 When refitting a stabiliser bar, tighten the mounting bolts to the specified torque given in the Specifications section of this Supplement.

Steering wheel (later models) - removal and refitting

27 On later models, the steering wheel centre cover horn push arrangement may differ slightly from that described in Chapter 10, Section 16.

28 In general, to remove the horn push, undo the screws securing the 'Nissan' motif to the steering wheel. The screws are accessible from the underside of the steering wheel.

29 Remove the motif, and then undo the screws securing the horn push to the steering wheel. These are recessed into the plastic moulding of the horn push (photo).

11.22A Fitting thrustwasher . . .

11.22B . . . tightening driveshaft nut . . .

11.22C . . . fitting nut retainer . . .

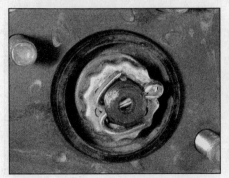

11.22D . . . fit split pin as shown to secure nut

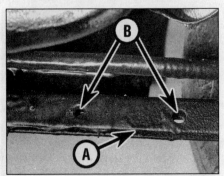

11.25 Holes (B) in square-section lower link (A) for stabiliser bar

11.29 Removing a screw from (later model) horn push

11.37A Tighten rear hub nut to specified-torque wrench setting . . .

11.37B . . . then refit hub grease cap

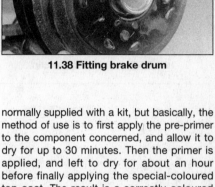

11.38 Fitting brake drum

30 The remainder of the procedure is as adjusted in Chapter 10, Section 16.

Rear hub bearings (1988 on) - description and renewal

31 The rear hub bearings on later models are of sealed type, and can only be renewed as a complete hub/bearing assembly.
32 To renew a bearing, raise the car, support it on axle stands and remove the roadwheel.
33 Extract the fixing screws and pull off the brake drum. Remove the grease cap, the split pin and the nut retainer.
34 Unscrew and remove the hub nut. This is very tight, so use a long socket bar, and make sure that the car cannot be displaced from its axle stands. Remove the thrustwasher.
35 Withdraw the hub/bearing assembly. If it is tight, use a three-legged puller.
36 While the brake drum is off, do not depress the brake pedal.
37 Fit the new hub/bearing assembly, then the thrustwasher, and tighten the nut to the specified torque. Fit the nut retainer (where used) and a new split pin, then tap in the grease cap squarely (photos).
38 Refit the brake drum and the roadwheel (photo).
39 Remove the axle stands and jack, and lower the car to the ground.

12 Bodywork and fittings

Minor body damage - repair of plastic components

1 With the use of more and more plastic body components by the vehicle manufacturers (eg bumpers. spoilers, and in some cases major body panels), rectification of more serious damage to such items has become a matter of either entrusting repair work to a specialist in this field, or renewing complete components. Repair of such damage by the DIY owner is not really feasible, owing to the cost of the equipment and materials required

for effecting such repairs. The basic technique involves making a groove along the line of the crack in the plastic, using a rotary burr in a power drill. The damaged part is then welded back together, using a hot-air gun to heat up and fuse a plastic filler rod into the groove. Any excess plastic is then removed, and the area rubbed down to a smooth finish. It is important that a filler rod of the correct plastic is used, as body components can be made of a variety of different types (eg polycarbonate, ABS, polypropylene).
2 Damage of a less serious nature (abrasions, minor cracks etc) can be repaired by the DIY owner using a two-part epoxy filler repair material. Once mixed in equal proportions, this is used in similar fashion to the bodywork filler used on metal panels. The filler is usually cured in twenty to thirty minutes, ready for sanding and painting.
3 If the owner is renewing a complete component himself, or if he has repaired it with epoxy filler, he will be left with the problem of finding a suitable paint for finishing which is compatible with the type of plastic used. At one time, the use of a universal paint was not possible, owing to the complex range of plastics encountered in body component applications. Standard paints, generally speaking, will not bond to plastic or rubber satisfactorily. However, it is now possible to obtain a plastic body parts finishing kit which consists of a pre-primer treatment, a primer and coloured top coat. Full instructions are

normally supplied with a kit, but basically, the method of use is to first apply the pre-primer to the component concerned, and allow it to dry for up to 30 minutes. Then the primer is applied, and left to dry for about an hour before finally applying the special-coloured top coat. The result is a correctly-coloured component, where the paint will flex with the plastic or rubber, a property that standard paint does not normally possess.

Radiator grille (1987 to 1988) - removal and refitting

4 The procedure is as described in Chapter 11, Section 7, but the left hand clip (viewed from the front of the car) is now located beneath a plastic cover which is removed in the same manner as the 'Nissan' motif.

Radiator grille (1989 on) - removal and refitting

5 The grille incorporates two holes for insertion of a screwdriver to turn the headlamp adjusting screws (photos).
6 To remove the grille, open the bonnet and release the upper clips (photo).
7 Twist the lower plastic retainers through 90°, close the bonnet and withdraw the grille (photos).
8 When refitting, secure the lower clips in the grille before offering up the assembly to the car.

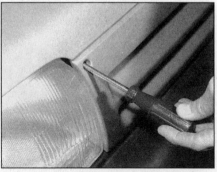

12.5A Headlamps are adjusted through hole in grille . . .

12.5B . . . to turn adjuster as shown

13

12.6 Radiator grille upper clip

12.7A Release lower clips as described . . .

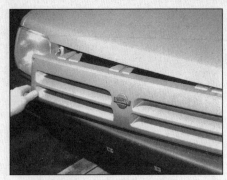

12.7B . . . to withdraw grille

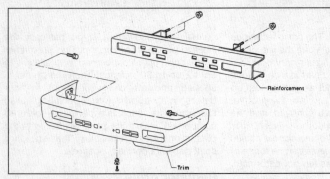

Fig. 13.37 Front bumper – 1985 to 1988 models (Sec 12)

Fig. 13.38 Rear bumper – 1985 to 1988 models (Sec 12)

Bumpers - 1985 to 1988

9 The bumpers fitted to models after the 1985 facelift consist of a plastic compound trim fitted over a steel reinforcement bar.

12.12 Bumper trim securing screw and bracket

10 The reinforcement bar is bolted to the frame, and the trim is clipped to the reinforcement bar.
11 When refitting a bumper, tighten the mounting bolts and nuts to the torque figures given in the Specifications at the start of this Supplement.

Bumpers - 1989 on

12 The bumpers on the later models are of similar construction, and incorporate a spoiler (air dam). Although still bolted to the body as on earlier versions, additional screws are used to secure some edges (photo).

Tailgate exterior handle - removal and refitting

13 Open the tailgate and remove the interior cover panel.
14 Remove the two nuts securing the handle to the tailgate skin.
15 Lift off the handle.
16 Refit in reverse order.

Front door and door components (5-door models) - removal and refitting

17 The front doors on 5-door models are narrower than those on 3-door models, but the procedure for removal and refitting of the door, door trim, locks and handles is as described in Chapter 11. Note that the armrest is secured by two screws, and not three.

Rear door interior trim panel - removal and refitting

18 Unscrew and remove the door lock plunger knob.
19 Prise out and remove the moulding from around the interior handle (photo).
20 Remove the window regulator handle, as described in Chapter 11, Section 13.
21 Prise back the plastic covers on the armrest, remove the screws, then lift off (photo).

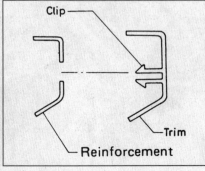

Fig. 13.39 Bumper trim-to-reinforcement clip (Sec 12)

12.19 Removing rear door interior handle moulding

12.21 Removing rear door armrest screws

12.26 Rear door exterior handle nuts

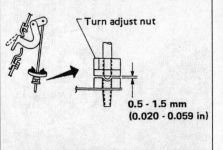

Fig. 13.40 Rear door exterior handle link
rod adjustment (Sec 12)

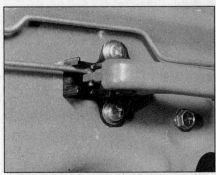

12.30 Rear door interior handle securing
screws and link rod

22 Carefully prise out the clips securing the trim panel to the door, using a wide-bladed screwdriver.
23 Peel back the plastic sheeting from the door. It is important that this sheet is kept intact and refitted, to prevent moisture penetrating the fibre door trim panel.
24 Refitting is a reversal of removal.

Rear door exterior handle - removal and refitting

25 Remove the interior trim panel as described in the preceding paragraphs.
26 Remove the two nuts securing the handle to the door, accessible through the upper door aperture (photo).
27 Unhook the link rod between the handle and the door lock, and lift off the handle.
28 Refit in reverse order, and turn the adjuster on the link rod to give the clearance shown in Fig. 13.40.

Rear door interior handle - removal and refitting

29 Remove the door interior trim panel, as described in paragraphs 18 to 24.
30 Remove the two securing screws and lift off the handle at the same time disconnecting the link rod (photo).
31 Refit in the reverse order.

Rear door lock plunger mechanism - removal and refitting

32 Remove the door interior trim panel, as described in paragraphs 18 to 23.

33 Undo the screw securing the bellcrank to the door (photo).
34 Unhook the bellcrank from the link rod, and remove it from the door.
35 Refit in reverse order.

Rear door lock - removal and refitting

36 Remove the interior trim panel described in paragraphs 18 to 23.
37 Unhook the control rods from the exterior handle, lock plunger and interior handle.
38 Remove the three retaining screws and lift out the lock assembly (photos).
39 Refitting is a reversal of removal, but it will be found easier to reconnect the exterior handle link rod if the handle is first removed. The adjuster on the link rod will then have to be turned to give the clearance shown in Fig. 13.40.

Rear door window and quarter-light - removal and refitting

40 Remove the door interior trim panel, as described in paragraphs 18 to 23.
41 Lower the window to gain access to the two bolts securing the window to the lift mechanism (photo).
42 Remove the two bolts, and carefully lower the window into the bottom of the door.
43 Prise off the door weatherstrip moulding from the bottom of the window aperture, and pull out the rubber channelling in the door window recess.

12.33 Remove central screw to remove
bellcrank

44 Remove the rear window guide channel, held by a screw at the top and a bolt at its lower end.
45 The window can now be lifted out of the door.
46 The rear quarter-light is removed by pulling it forward and out of the door.
47 Refitting is a reversal of removal. Adjust the guide channel and glass position as necessary to obtain smooth operation.

Rear door window lift mechanism - removal and refitting

48 Remove the rear door window as described in paragraphs 40 to 45.
49 Remove the bolts securing the window regulator and lift mechanism to the door inner

12.38A Remove retaining screws . . .

12.38B . . . to release rear door lock

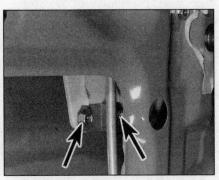

12.41 Door window glass-to-lift
mechanism securing bolts (arrowed)

13

12.49A Door window regulator securing bolts . . .

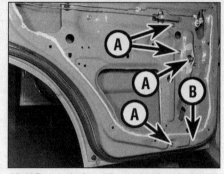

12.49B . . . window lift mechanism bolts (A) and plastic clip (B)

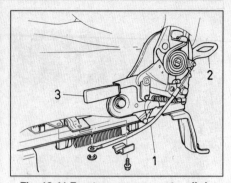

Fig. 13.41 Front passenger seat walk-in device mechanism – 3-door models (Sec 12)

1 Operating cable   *3 Operating lever*
2 Release handle

skin. There is also a plastic clip at the bottom of the door which has to be released (photos).
50 Carefully manoeuvre the mechanism out of the lower aperture in the door, being careful not to bend it excessively.
51 Refitting is a reversal of removal, adjusting the securing bolts to give smooth operation of the lift mechanism.

Rear door – removal and refitting

52 The procedure for removing the rear door is similar to that described for the front door in Chapter 11, Section 17.

Front passenger seat (3-door models) – walk-in device

53 In addition to the normal tilt mechanism

operating handle mounted on the side of the front passenger seat, there is a cable-operated release handle at the rear of the seat, enabling rear seat passengers to more readily tilt the seatback forward.
54 This cable is non-adjustable, and if it stretches or breaks, it should be renewed.
55 Access to the mechanism is by removal of the cover panel, held by two screws (photo).
56 The cable is held on its spigots by C-clips (photo).
57 To keep the mechanism operating smoothly, grease all moving parts at regular intervals.

Head restraints - general

58 Later models are fitted with adjustable, removable head restraints on the front seats.

59 Adjustment and removal is achieved by depressing the catch at the side of the head restraint socket in the seat back (photo).

Glovebox lid and lock - removal and refitting

60 Open the glovebox lid, and remove the screws from the lid back panel (photo).
61 Lift up the back panel and remove the screws from the stay bracket (photo).
62 Drop the back panel down again, and remove the screws from the hinge inside the glovebox (photo).
63 Remove the lid, and lift the back panel from the stay bracket.

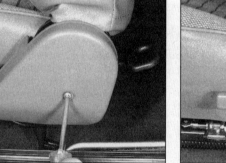

12.55 Removing walk-in device cover screw

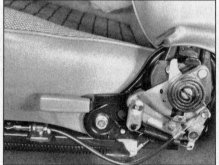

12.56 Walk-in device – cover removed

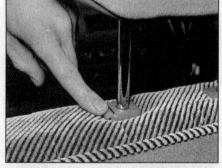

12.59 Depress catch to adjust height of head restraints

12.60 Removing a glovebox lid panel screw

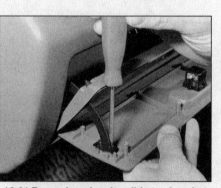

12.61 Removing glovebox lid stay bracket screws

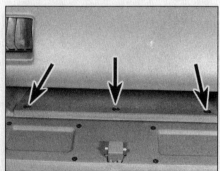

12.62 Glovebox lid hinge screws (arrowed)

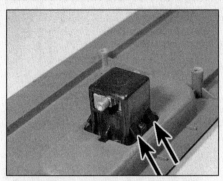

12.64A Release plastic clips (arrowed) . . .

12.64B . . . to remove glovebox lid lock assembly

12.66 Parcel shelf securing screw (arrowed)

64 The lock assembly is held in the lid by plastic clips (photos).
65 Refit in the reverse order, feeding the stay bracket through the back panel before fitting the lid.

Parcel shelf - removal and refitting

66 Remove the screw securing the shelf to the bracket at its outboard edge (photo) and the two screws securing it at its inboard edge.
67 Pull the shelf forwards to release it from the clip at the back (photo).
68 Refit in reverse order.

Interior trim panels - general

69 The location of the interior trim panel

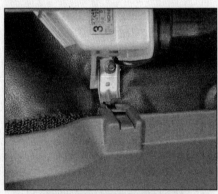

12.67 Parcel shelf retaining clip

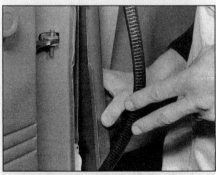

12.70 Pull back door edge capping to release 'B' pillar trim panel on 5-door models

fixing screws and clips for both 3 and 5-door models is shown in Fig. 13.42.
70 On 5-door models the 'B' pillar trim panels are held in place by the door edge capping, which when pulled back allows the trim to be removed (photo).

Stone chip guard - removal and refitting

71 Some models are fitted with a stone chip guard in front of the rear wheel arches.
72 The guard, which is made of a plastic

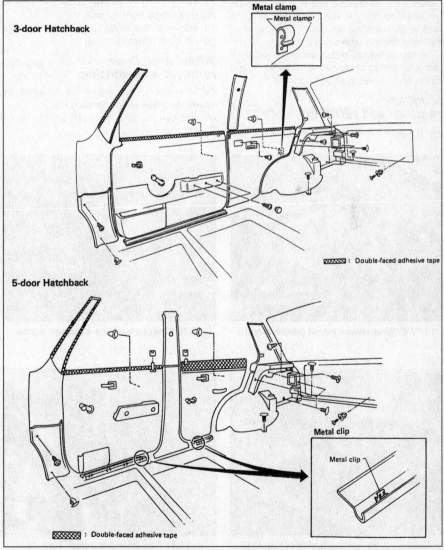

Fig. 13.42 Interior trim panel fasteners (Sec 12)

13

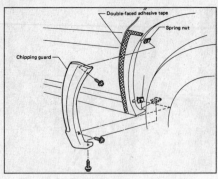

Fig. 13.43 Stone chip guard fasteners (Sec 12)

12.72 Removing a stone chip guard retaining screw

12.75 Mudflap securing screws (arrowed)

material, is held in position by three screws and double-sided adhesive tape (photo).

73 When removing a stone guard, the application of gentle heat will ease the removal of the guard from the adhesive tape.

74 Similarly, the application of heat will increase the adhesion property of the old tape on refitting, but if the tape has lost its tackiness, it will be necessary to remove all traces of the old tape using a solvent (caution - some solvents may cause paintwork damage) and to apply new double-sided tape to the area shown in Fig. 13.43).

Mudflaps - removal and refitting

75 Remove the screws securing the mudflap to the wheel arch, and lift off the mudflap (photo).

76 Refit in reverse order.

Engine splash panels - removal and refitting

77 The protective panels under the engine are secured by bolts (photo).

78 Remove the bolts and lift down the panels. Refit in reverse order.

Wheel arch liners - removal and refitting

79 The wheel arch liners are secured by screws and plastic washers (photo).

80 Remove the screws and lift out the liners. Refit in reverse order.

Fuel filler lid - removal and refitting

81 All models are fitted with a lockable fuel filler lid.

82 The lock is secured to the lid by a spring clip, which when released allows the lock to be removed (photos).

83 The lid is secured to the bodywork by two screws (photo).

Grab rails - removal and refitting

84 The grab rails, located above the door openings inside the car, can be removed after prising back the flap at each end of the rail and extracting the screws (photo).

12.77 Engine splash panel retaining bolts

12.79 Wheel arch liner securing screw

12.82A Remove spring clip . . .

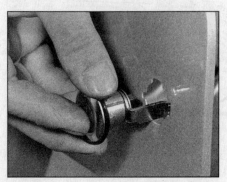

12.82B . . . to release fuel filler flap lock

12.83 Fuel filler flap hinge screws (arrowed)

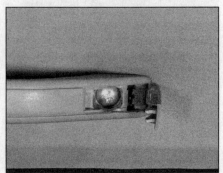

12.84 Grab rail securing screw

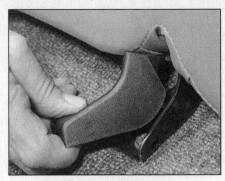

12.85 Remove plastic cover . . .

12.86 . . . to reach rear seat cushion hinge screws

12.87 Rear seat belt quick-release centre buckle

Split-type rear seat - removal and refitting

85 Prise off the plastic hinge covers at the front edge of the seat cushion (photo).
86 Unscrew and remove the hinge screws (photo).
87 Release the seat backs, and fold them down until the seat belt can be disconnected at the quick-release centre buckle (photo).
88 Fold the seat backs fully forward, and then remove the rear seat assembly from the car.
89 Refitting is a reversal of removal.

Exterior rear view mirror (1989-on) - glass renewal

90 To renew a cracked glass insert a lever

12.93A Remove screw . . .

12.93B . . . to release exterior mirror trim plate

between the mirror frame and the edge of the glass, and lever it out of its spring clips.
91 Fit the new glass by applying even pressure to engage it in its retaining clips.
92 Self-adhesive glasses are available to stick to the original glass, if the glass is discoloured but does not warrant removal.

Exterior rear view mirror (1989 on) - removal and refitting

93 To remove the mirror complete, extract the screw and take off the triangular trim plate (photos).
94 Extract the three fixing screws holding the

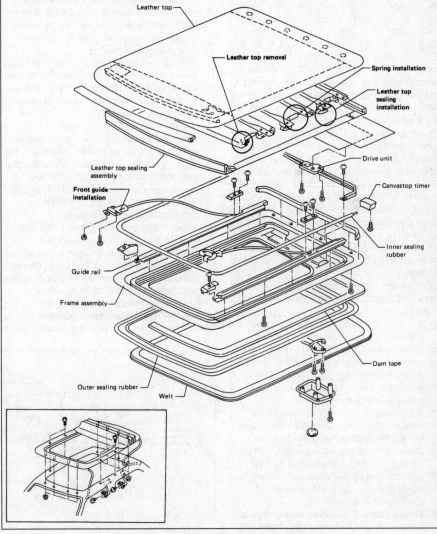

Fig. 13.44 'Canvastop' components (Sec 12)

Leather top
Leather top removal
Spring installation
Leather top sealing installation
Drive unit
Canvastop timer
Leather top sealing assembly
Front guide installation
Inner sealing rubber
Guide rail
Frame assembly
Dam tape
Outer sealing rubber
Welt

13

mirror to the door, and remove the mirror complete.

95 It is not recommended that the mirror is dismantled, as it is adjusted by pre-tensioned cables, which can be damaged if released.

96 Refitting the mirror is a reversal of the removal process.

'Canvastop' - general

97 The full-length sunroof (known as the 'Suntop' or 'Canvastop') is electrically-operated, the operating system consisting of the motor and the roof-mounted switch, a timer/amplifier unit and a relay. The relay is energised, battery voltage is supplied via a brown fusible link, through the relay and a circuit breaker to the timer unit.

98 Apart from the relay (which is mounted in the rear right-hand corner of the engine compartment) and the circuit breaker (located next to the fuses, behind the facia on the driver's side), all other components are mounted in the roof of the passenger compartment, above the headlining; the motor and timer/amplifier unit being at the rear of the vehicle.

99 To open the sunroof, press the switch lightly on the 'AUTO OPEN' side; to close it, check first that the opening is clear of obstructions, and press the switch on the 'CLOSE' side. For one-touch opening, press the switch firmly on the 'AUTO OPEN' side; the sunroof will open fully, but can be stopped at any point by pressing the switch once on the 'CLOSE' side. Do not use one-touch opening if the roof is already mostly open, as this will trigger the circuit breaker and stop the motor from working until it resets itself; if this happens, simply wait until the circuit breaker resets, whereupon normal operation can be resumed.

100 Maintenance is confined to checking for freedom of action and snug fit when shut. If required, lubricate the guide shoes with a good general-purpose grease, but take care not to allow grease to come into contact with the roof material. Check that the seals are in good clean condition and not scratched or damaged.

101 Owners must note the following to ensure the maximum trouble-free life from this feature.

(a) It is normal for the motor to slow down as the sunroof approaches full opening.

(b) If the sunroof stops before it is fully opened in cold weather, this may be due to the material being too hard to fold correctly, do not force the sunroof open if this is suspected.

(c) If the material does not fold correctly on opening at any time, close the sunroof again, correct the folds by hand, and try again.

(d) Never open or close the sunroof with the vehicle travelling at more than 50 mph (80 km/h) and never allow passengers to travel standing up or with any part of themselves in the opening.

(e) Ensure that any collected water, snow or ice is removed from the sunroof before opening it: Check that the deflector is

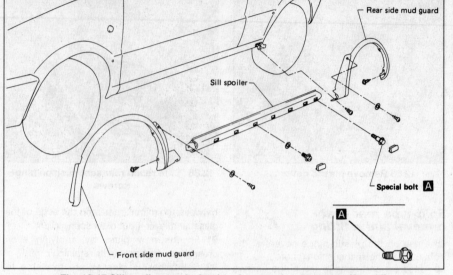

Fig. 13.45 Sill spoilers and wheel arch extension fasteners (Sec 12)

clear of water, particularly after washing the vehicle; sponge it dry if necessary.

(f) Never place heavy objects on the sunroof or its surrounds. If the front edge is ever scratched immediately apply a thin layer of leather wax dressing.

(g) The sunroof should be cleaned frequently, to avoid the material being stained by dirt. Use a sponge, soft brush or soft cloth and a neutral detergent, rinsing with a gentle flow of clean water from directly above until all traces of dirt and detergent are removed. **Never** use a high-pressure jet, pressure washer or similar, do not aim the jet from a hose at the joints of the sunroof with the body (or water will enter the passenger compartment) and **never** use alcohol, petrol, thinners or similar products to clean the material.

(h) If the vehicle is parked in heavy rain, or if it is parked outside for long periods, a proprietary car cover or tarpaulin should be used to protect the roof and body. **Do not** leave the sunroof open for long periods; the material will stiffen in its folds, with a consequent risk of tearing when the sunroof is eventually operated again.

102 If the system fails with the sunroof open,

it can be closed in emergency by switching off the ignition, prising out the access plug at the rear of the roof, and using the crank provided to rotate the motor shaft anti-clockwise until the roof is closed.

103 If the switch is thought to be at fault, it can be removed by disconnecting the battery earth lead and removing the switch's two retaining screws; the switch can then be eased from its housing until the wires can be disconnected. Refitting is the reverse of the removal procedure.

104 If any other failure or problem is encountered, the general inaccessibility of the system's components means that servicing and fault-finding is beyond the capabilities of most owners; the vehicle should be taken to a Nissan dealer for attention.

Sill spoilers and wheel arch extensions - removal and refitting

105 Refer to Fig. 13.45 for details of the mountings of these components.

Tailgate spoiler - removal and refitting

106 Refer to Fig. 13.46 for details of the tailgate spoiler's mountings.

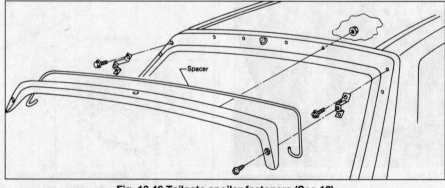

Fig. 13.46 Tailgate spoiler fasteners (Sec 12)

13.8 Electrolyte level marks – conventional battery

13.10 Mitsubishi alternator connections – later models

13.14 Unscrew alternator pulley nut (using an old drivebelt as described in the text) . . .

13 Electrical system

Battery

1 Later type low-maintenance batteries, which can be identified by having a white blind plug, as opposed to yellow on the earlier types (see Chapter 12), now have a facility allowing them to be refilled with distilled water should the electrolyte level drop below the MIN mark on the side of the battery.

2 To refill a battery, first disconnect the battery terminals; negative first, positive last.

3 Remove the perforated part of the cautionary warning label on top of the battery.

4 Using thin-nosed pliers, remove the cell plugs.

5 Fill each cell to the MAX level, using only distilled water; mop up any spillage immediately, as the electrolyte is extremely corrosive.

6 Refit the cell plugs securely, and reconnect the battery in the reverse order of disconnection.

7 More recently, conventional batteries with removable cell plugs and a translucent case through which the electrolyte level can be seen are used.

8 With the conventional type of battery, maintain the electrolyte level between the 'MAX' and 'MIN' marks (photo).

Alternator (Mitsubishi type, 1988-on) - overhaul

9 Later models are equipped with a redesigned alternator.

10 The unit is removed as described in Chapter 12, Section 5 (photo).

11 To dismantle the alternator, first mark the alignment of the front and rear covers and stator using quick drying paint.

12 Unscrew and remove the tie-bolts.

13 Fit an old drivebelt to the pulley, and grip the belt in the jaws of a vice as close as possible to the pulley. This will grip the pulley until the pulley nut is undone.

14 Unscrew the pulley nut, and remove the lockwasher. Note that the pulley is prevented from turning on the shaft solely by the clamping action of the nut - no key is fitted (photo).

15 Remove the small cup from the shaft (photo).

16 Remove the front (drive end) cover (photo).

17 Unscrew and remove the terminal nut and insulator from the rear cover, and take off the cover. If the rear cover bearing must be renewed, extract the three screws and remove the bearing retainer (photos).

18 Remove the cup and spacer from the front end of the shaft. Note the integral fan (photos).

19 Withdraw the rotor from the stator (photo).

20 The brushed can only be renewed as a complete assembly together with the diode pack.

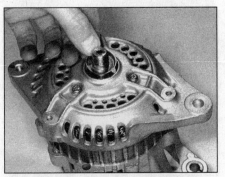

13.15. . . remove small cup from shaft

13.16. . . and withdraw front cover

13.17A Unscrew terminal nut and remove insulator . . .

13.17B . . . to remove rear cover – note bearing retainer

13.18A Remove cup from shaft front end . . .

13

13.18B . . . followed by spacer

13.19 Removing rotor from stator

13.21 Brush holder/diode pack fixing screws (arrowed) – hole in brushes is for . . .

21 To remove the assembly, extract the three internal fixing screws, then unsolder the wiring connections (photo).

22 Reassembly is a reversal of dismantling, but hold the brushes in the retracted state using a small rod or Allen key inserted through the hole in the rear cover and the hole in each brush (photo).

Lighting units and bulb renewal - 1985 on

Headlamp

23 The procedure is as described in Chapter 12, except that later models are fitted with a rubber dust cap over the bulb terminals.

24 When refitting the dust cap, ensure the 'top' or 'arrow' mark (photo) is uppermost, and 'burp' the dust cap free of air, so that it is a good fit on the headlamp.

Front combination light (sidelight) and front direction indicator light

25 On later models these are of slightly different design; the sidelight being in combination with the headlamp, and the front direction indicator light being mounted in the bumper.

26 Bulb and lens renewal is as described in Chapter 12.

Side indicator repeater light

27 Later models have a side indicator repeater light mounted on the front wing.

28 To renew the bulb, twist the unit anti-clockwise to release it from the wing (photo).

29 Twist and pull the lens from the bulbholder (photo).

30 The bulb is a push-fit in the holder.

31 Refit in reverse order.

Rear combination lights

32 The bulb renewal procedure is unchanged from that given in Chapter 12, Section 18.

33 To remove the light unit, first remove all the bulbs, then unscrew the three retaining nuts.

34 The unit is now fastened by adhesive; either butyl sealant or double-sided adhesive tape. These normally require heating (to approximately 30 to 40° C(86 to 104°F) with a hot air gun or similar to break the seal; in the absence of such equipment, use a scalpel or similar to cut through the adhesive. To avoid the risk of breaking the unit, do not rely on pressure alone to push it out of the body.

35 On reassembly, clean off all traces of old adhesive, degrease the mating surfaces thoroughly, then obtain sufficient adhesive material to refix the unit (any Nissan dealer should be able to recommend a suitable product). Follow the adhesive manufacturer's instructions on application; the original Nissan sealant, for example, requires heating (as outlined in the previous paragraph) before the unit is refitted to it.

36 Offer up the unit, entering the studs into their holes and aligning the unit with the surrounding bodywork, press it into place, tighten the retaining nuts carefully, then refit the bulbs and access panel.

13.22. . . rod (Allen key used) to hold brushes retracted on assembly

13.24 Correct positioning of headlamp dust cap – note arrow mark on top

13.28 Side indicator repeater light released from front wing

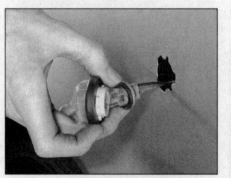

13.29 Releasing side indicator repeater light bulbholder from lens

13.37A Remove centre screw from each fastener . . .

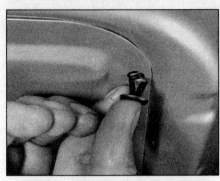

13.37B . . . and extract clips to release tailgate access panel

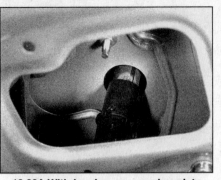

13.38A Withdrawing rear number plate light bulbholder

13.38B Removing bulb from rear number plate light bulbholder

Rear number plate lights (up to 1987)

37 To gain access to light units for bulb changing, first remove the access panel on the inside of the tailgate (photos).
38 The bulbholder is a bayonet fit in the light unit, and can be removed by twisting and pulling it from the unit (photos).
39 To remove the complete unit, undo the two nuts securing the unit to the tailgate, and gently prise it away (photo).
40 Refit in the reverse order.

Rear number plate lights (1987 on)

41 There are two light units, one at each side of the number plate.
42 To renew a bulb, first remove the trim panel from the inside of the tailgate.
43 Although the bulbholders can be reached and removed by twisting and pulling them from the tailgate skin, because of the limited access we found it easier to undo the two nuts securing the unit to the tailgate, then lift off the unit and remove the bulbholder from the unit (photos).
44 Refit in the reverse order.

Rear foglight and reflector unit

45 The rear foglight and reflector units are mounted in the rear bumper.
46 The righthand unit is the foglight, and the left-hand unit is the reflector.
47 To remove both units, undo the two retaining screws (photo).
48 This will release both the lens and light unit (photos).

13.39 Rear number plate light unit retaining nut (arrowed) – up to 1987

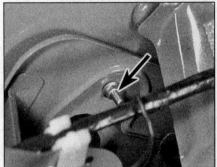

13.43A Rear number plate light unit retaining nut (arrowed) . . .

13.43B . . . removing rear number plate light unit . . .

13.43C . . . withdrawing rear number plate light bulbholder – 1987 on

49 To remove the complete unit, disconnect the electrical connector (photo).

50 The bulb is a bayonet fit in the holder.
51 Refit in the reverse order.

13.47 Remove retaining screws

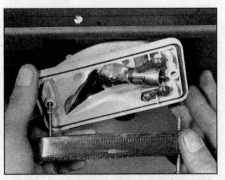

13.48 . . . to release rear foglight lens and light unit . . .

13.49 . . . disconnect wiring at connector (arrowed) to release unit

13

13.52 Luggage compartment lamp lens removed

13.53 Luggage compartment lamp unit removed to show wiring connections

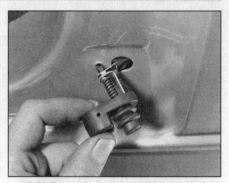

13.56 Removing courtesy lamp switch

Luggage compartment lamp

52 To renew the bulb, prise off the lens cover. The bulb is of the festoon type, held between two spring contacts (photo).

53 To remove the complete lamp unit, undo the two securing screws and disconnect the leads at the rear of the unit (photo).

54 Refit in reverse order.

Courtesy light switches - all models

55 The courtesy light is operated by switches mounted in each door pillar.

56 To remove a switch, remove the retaining screw and carefully lift out the switch, pulling the electrical lead and connector from the hole in the door pillar (photo).

57 Disconnect the electrical lead, transfer the rubber cover to the new microswitch, and refit in the reverse order.

Instrument panel (1987 on) - general

58 On later models, an analogue clock replaces the digital clock fitted to earlier models.

59 The analogue clock is mounted in the instrument panel.

Instrument panel (1987 on) - removal and refitting

60 Disconnect the battery, and then remove the screws and take off the steering column upper and lower shrouds (photos).

61 Extract the screws from under the lower edge of the instrument panel hood, then pull the hood towards you but expect the securing clips at the rear edge to be reluctant to release. Prise out the hood-mounted switches, and then disconnect their wiring plugs before removing the hood (photos).

62 Extract the instrument panel fixing screws, pull the panel towards you, then disconnect the speedometer drive cable and wiring plugs. Remove the panel (photos).

63 Refitting is a reversal of removal.

Radio (standard equipment) - removal and refitting

64 Remove the ashtray from the facia panel by pulling it forwards and tilting it downwards to release it from its housing.

13.60A Remove steering column top shroud . . .

13.60B . . . and withdraw ignition switch bezel . . .

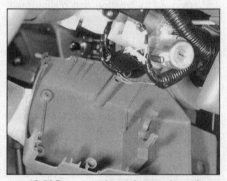

13.60C . . . to release lower shroud

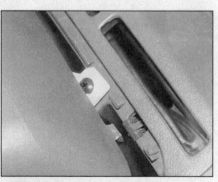

13.61A Instrument panel hood rear edge securing clips

13.61B Removing instrument panel hood-mounted switch . . .

13.61C . . . and disconnecting switch wiring

13.62A Instrument panel – later models front view. . .

13.62B . . . and rear view

13.66 Removing a radio securing screw

65 Extract the screw and take out the metal cover plate from the top of the ashtray recess.
66 Remove the radio securing screws. These are located under the radio (photo).
67 Pull the radio towards you, and disconnect the wiring plugs and aerial lead (photo).

Radio aerial (standard equipment) - removal and refitting

68 Disconnect the aerial from the rear of the radio unit.
69 Undo the screw securing the aerial moulding to the front wing (photo).
70 Pull the aerial upwards, at the same time

feeding the aerial lead through the facia and bodywork (photo).
71 Refit in reverse order.

Dim-dip headlamp lighting system - description

72 From late 1986, all models are equipped with a headlamp dim-dip lighting system.
73 This system is intended to prevent the car being driven at night on sidelights only. When the sidelights are switched on with the ignition also switched on, the headlamp dipped beams will come on automatically, but at one-sixth of their normal brightness.
74 The dim-dip lighting control unit is located on the left-hand inner wing (photo).

Fuses and relays - location

75 On later models, the location of the intermittent wipe relay has been changed. The relay is now situated on the front panel, just to the right of the radiator (photo).
76 On later models, the automatic choke relay is located on the inner right-hand wing (photo).

Lights-on warning buzzer - description

77 If the driver's door is opened while the headlamps are switched on, a warning buzzer will sound until the lighting switch is turned off.
78 The buzzer is located approximately six

13.67 Disconnect wiring plug (A) and aerial lead (B) to remove radio

13.69 Remove aerial securing screw . . .

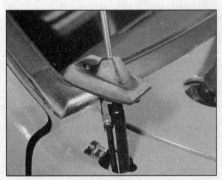

13.70 . . . to release aerial from front wing

13.74 Location of dim-dip lighting control unit on left-hand inner wing

13.75 Location of intermittent wiper relay on engine compartment front panel – later models

13.76 Location of automatic choke relay on right-hand inner wing – later models

13

inches above the fusebox, under the facia panel on the right-hand side of the car.

Front auxiliary lamps - bulb renewal

79 Remove the lens screws and detach the lens, then release the spring clip and withdraw the bulb, disconnecting its wiring. Do not touch the bulb's glass envelope.

80 Refitting is the reverse of the removal procedure.

Front auxiliary lamps - removal and refitting

81 Disconnect the battery earth terminal.

82 Reaching behind the lamp, disconnect its wiring, then unscrew the retaining nuts and withdraw the lamp.

83 Refitting is the reverse of the removal procedure. The lamp can be tilted to the required beam alignment once the pivot bolt has been slackened; tighten the bolt securely on completion.

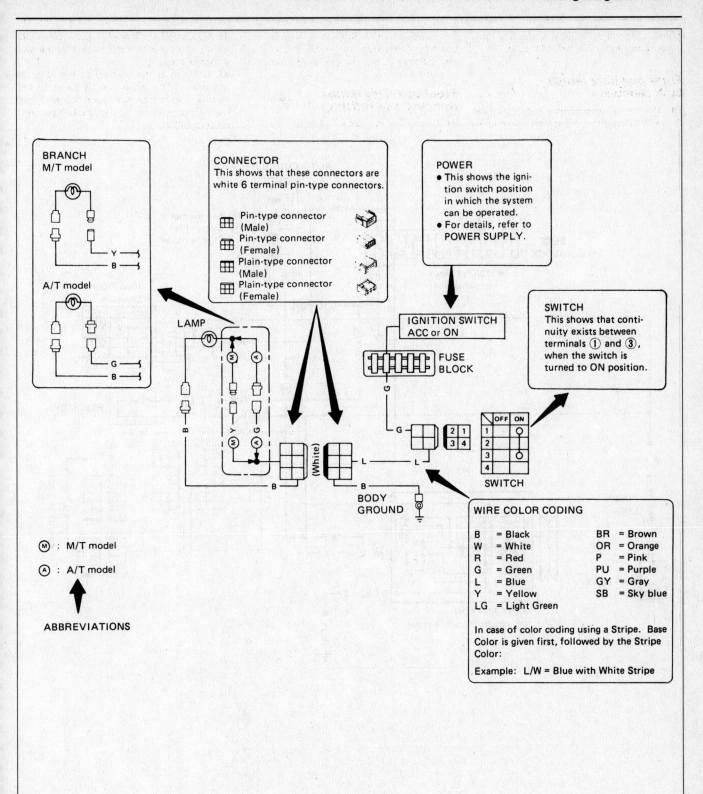

BRANCH
M/T model

A/T model

CONNECTOR
This shows that these connectors are white 6 terminal pin-type connectors.

Pin-type connector (Male)
Pin-type connector (Female)
Plain-type connector (Male)
Plain-type connector (Female)

POWER
• This shows the ignition switch position in which the system can be operated.
• For details, refer to POWER SUPPLY.

LAMP

IGNITION SWITCH
ACC or ON

FUSE BLOCK

SWITCH
This shows that continuity exists between terminals ① and ③, when the switch is turned to ON position.

SWITCH

BODY GROUND

Ⓜ : M/T model

Ⓐ : A/T model

ABBREVIATIONS

WIRE COLOR CODING

B	= Black	BR	= Brown
W	= White	OR	= Orange
R	= Red	P	= Pink
G	= Green	PU	= Purple
L	= Blue	GY	= Gray
Y	= Yellow	SB	= Sky blue
LG	= Light Green		

In case of color coding using a Stripe. Base Color is given first, followed by the Stripe Color:

Example: L/W = Blue with White Stripe

How to use the wiring diagrams

14

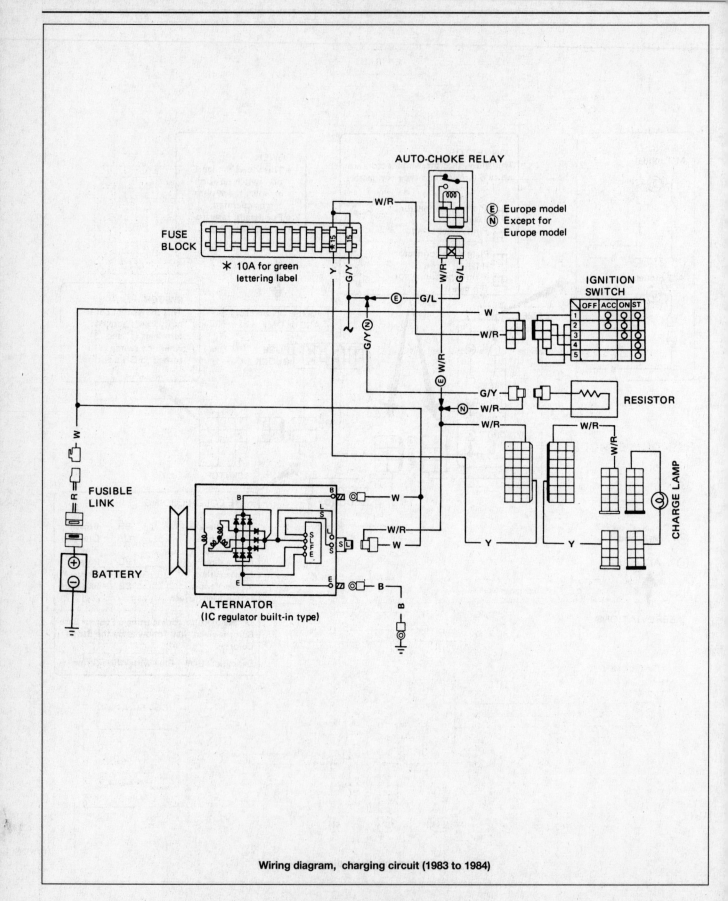

Wiring diagram, charging circuit (1983 to 1984)

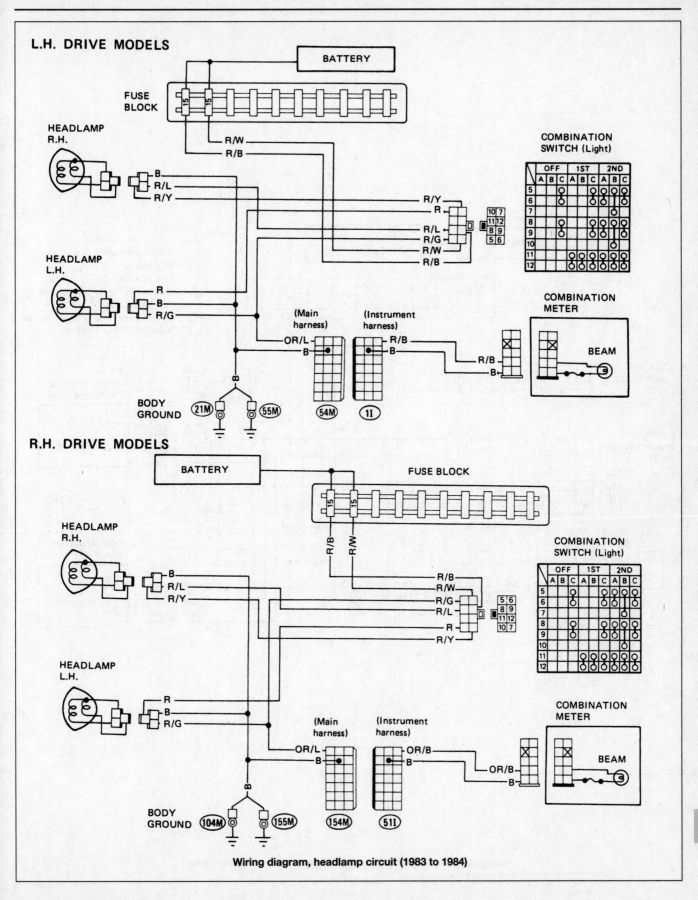

Wiring diagram, headlamp circuit (1983 to 1984)

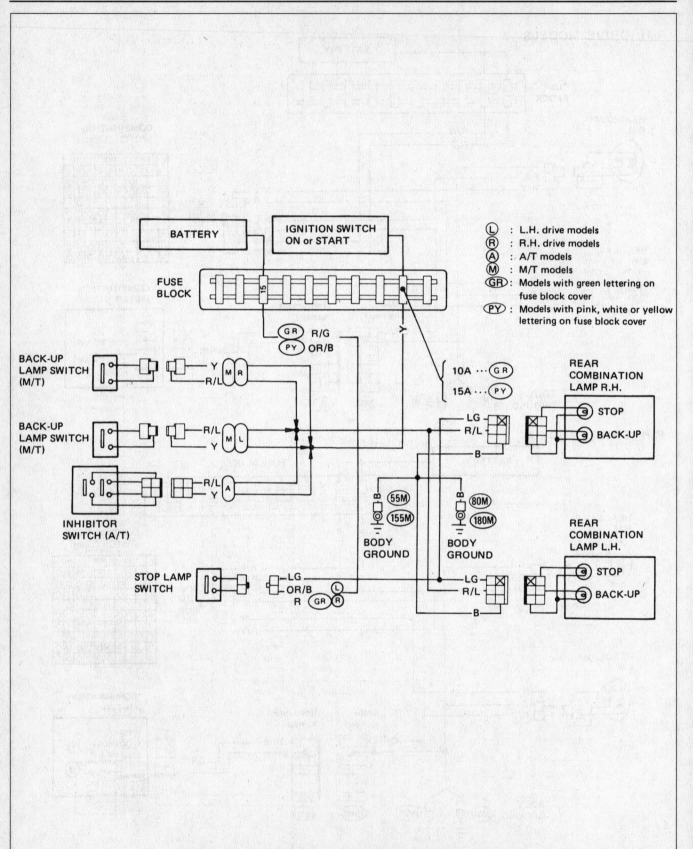

Wiring diagram, reversing light and stoplight circuit (1983 to 1984)

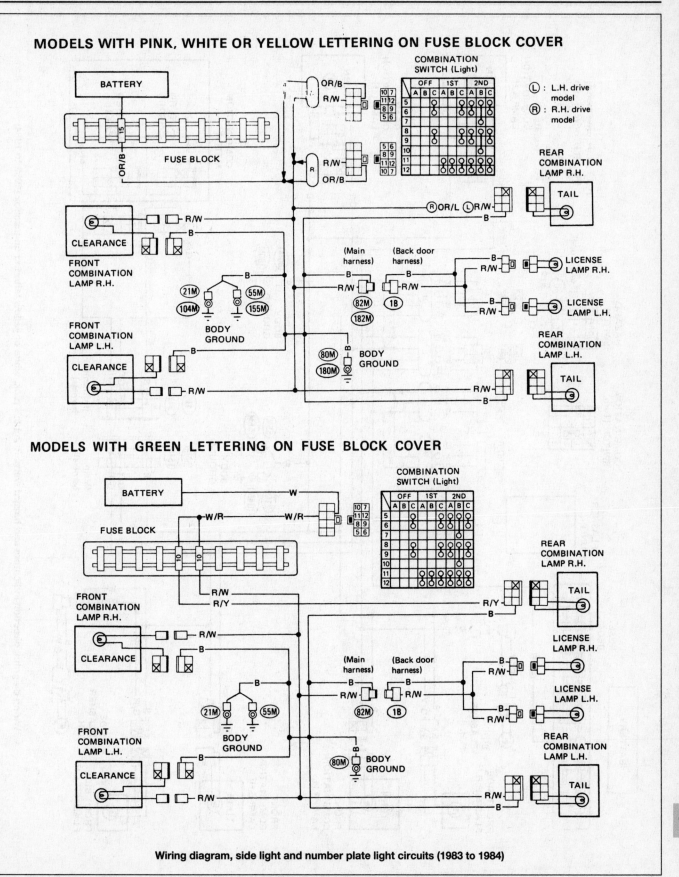

Wiring diagram, side light and number plate light circuits (1983 to 1984)

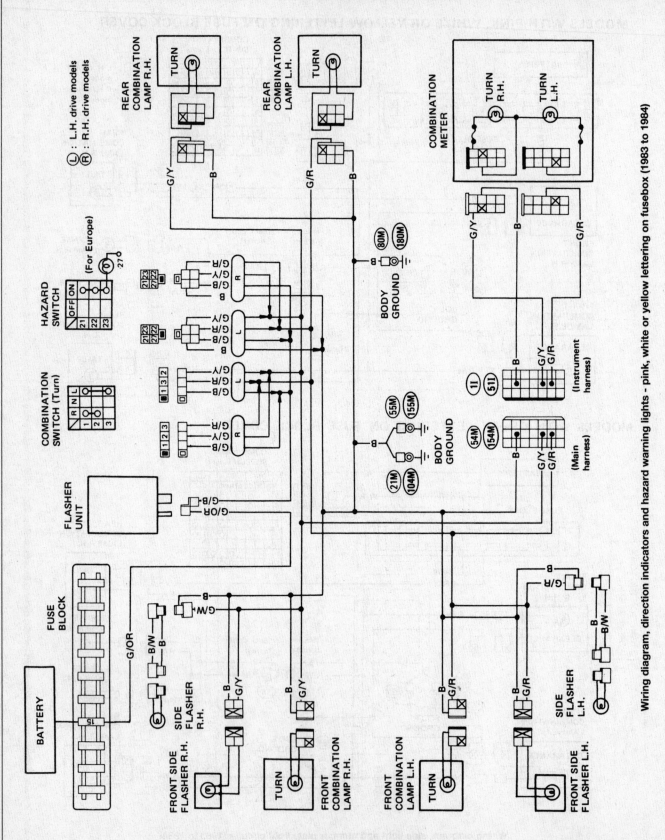

Wiring diagram, direction indicators and hazard warning lights - pink, white or yellow lettering on fusebox (1983 to 1984)

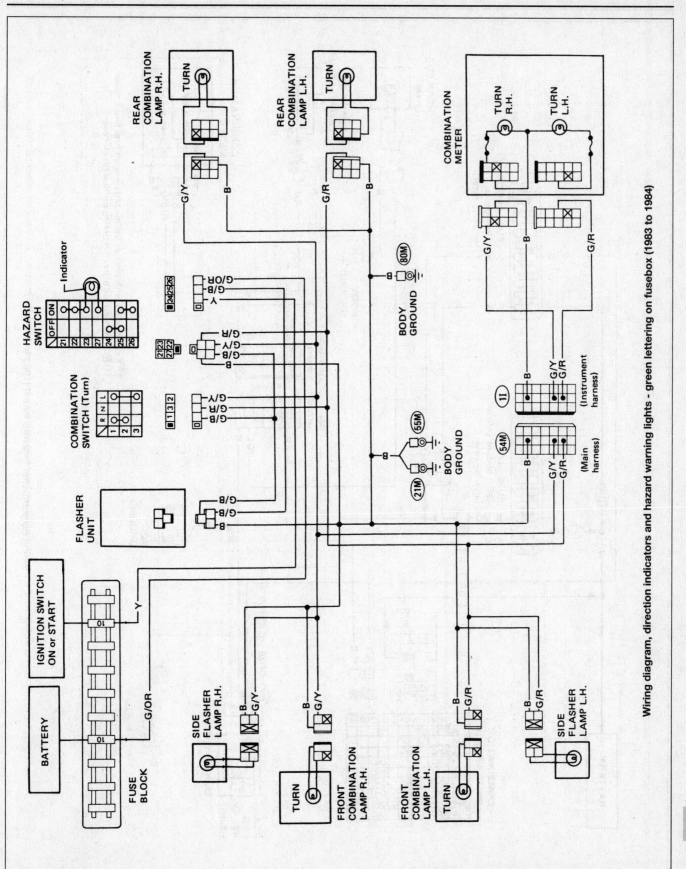

Wiring diagram, direction indicators and hazard warning lights - green lettering on fusebox (1983 to 1984)

14

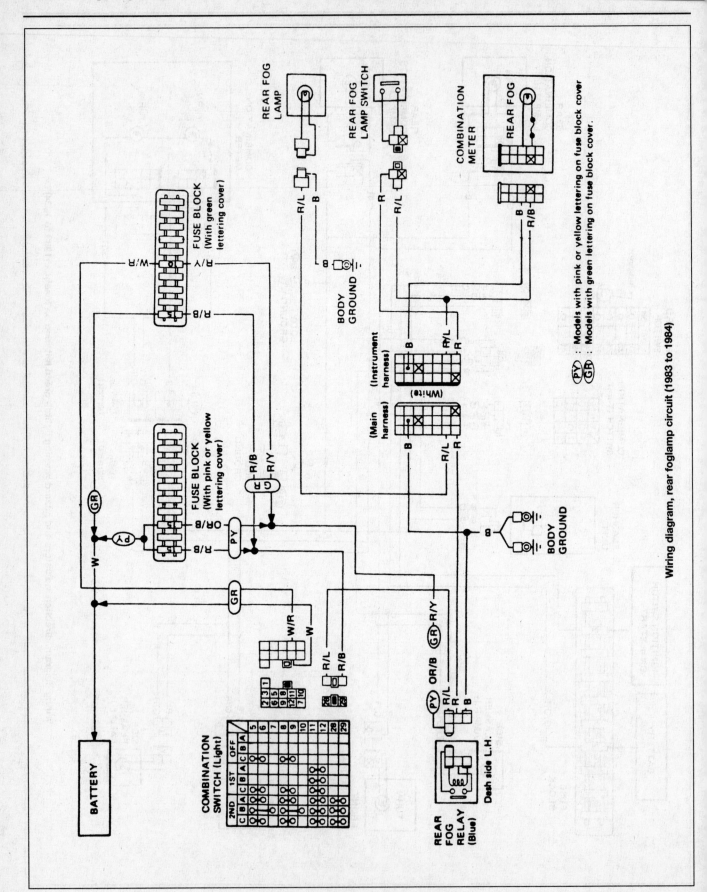

Wiring diagram, rear foglamp circuit (1983 to 1984)

MODELS WITH PINK, WHITE OR YELLOW LETTERING ON FUSE BLOCK COVER

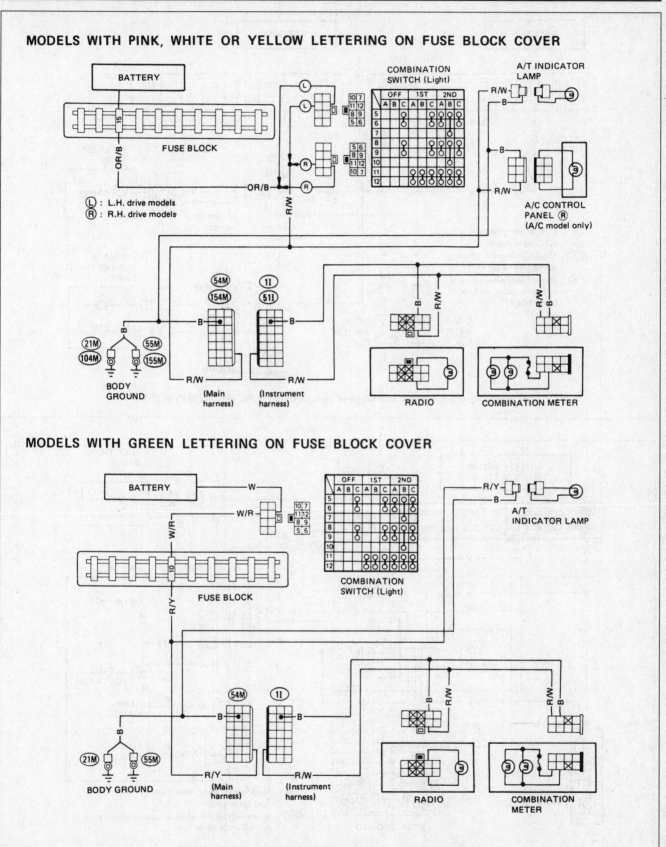

MODELS WITH GREEN LETTERING ON FUSE BLOCK COVER

Wiring diagram, instrument illumination circuit (1983 to 1984)

14

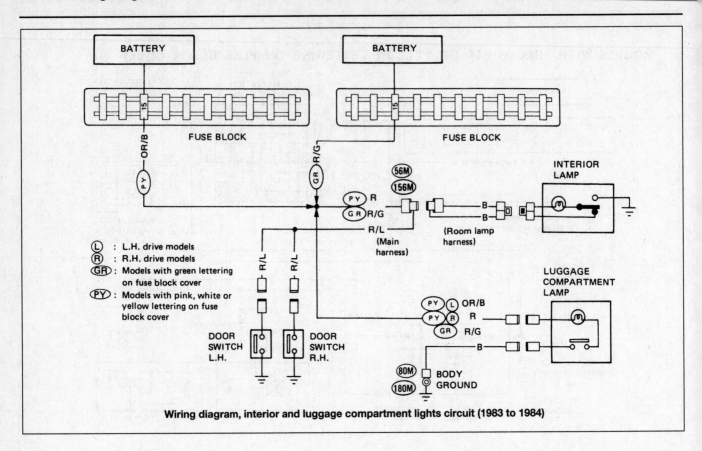

Wiring diagram, interior and luggage compartment lights circuit (1983 to 1984)

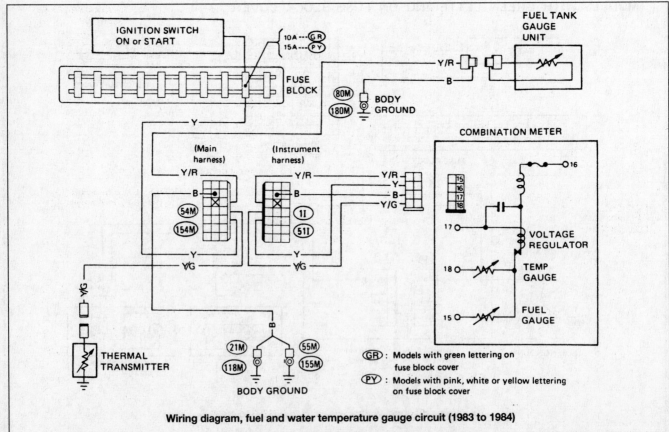

Wiring diagram, fuel and water temperature gauge circuit (1983 to 1984)

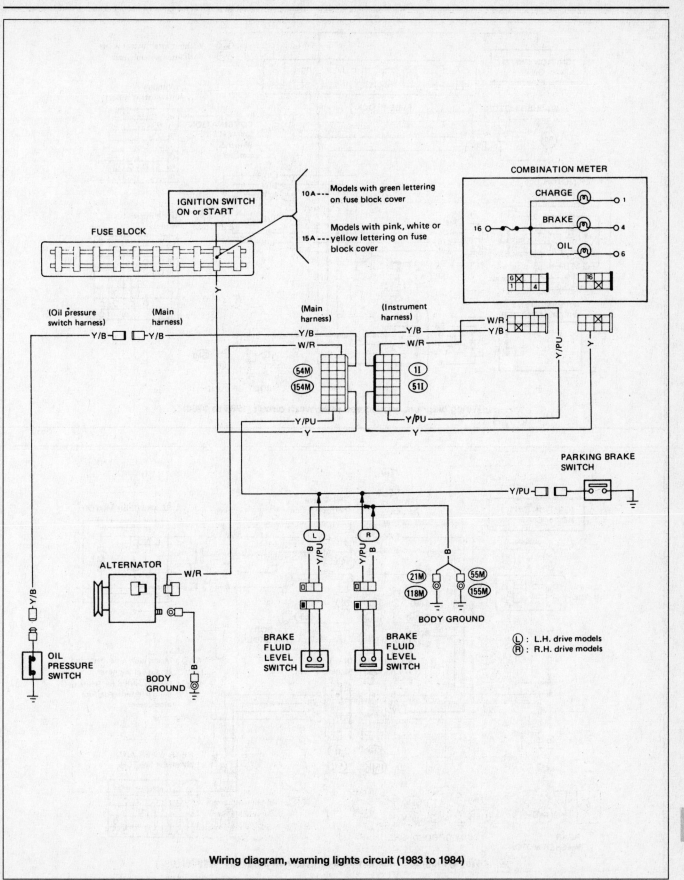

Wiring diagram, warning lights circuit (1983 to 1984)

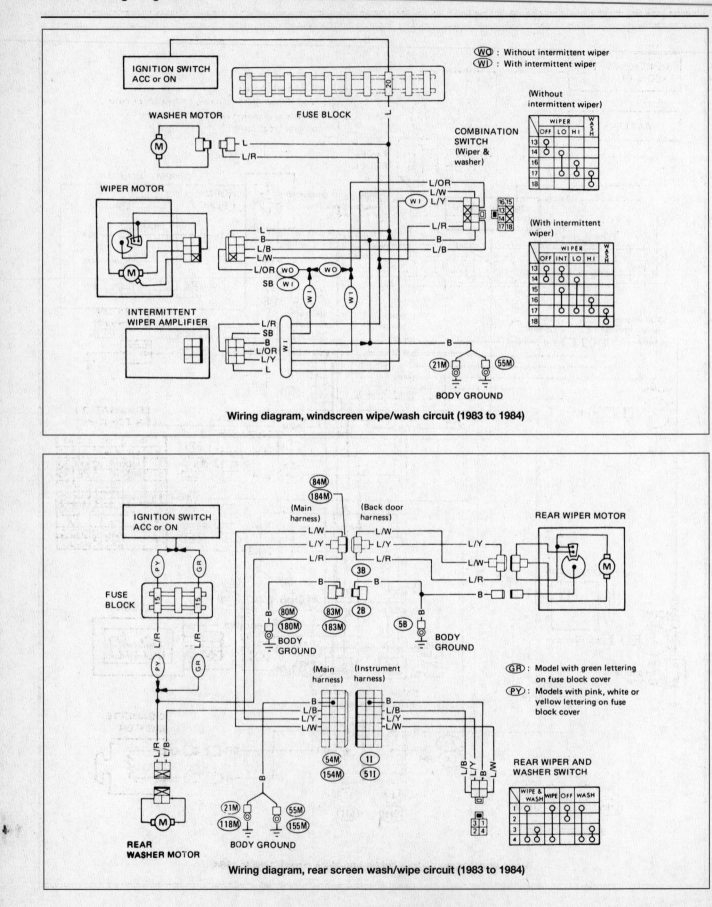

Wiring diagram, windscreen wipe/wash circuit (1983 to 1984)

Wiring diagram, rear screen wash/wipe circuit (1983 to 1984)

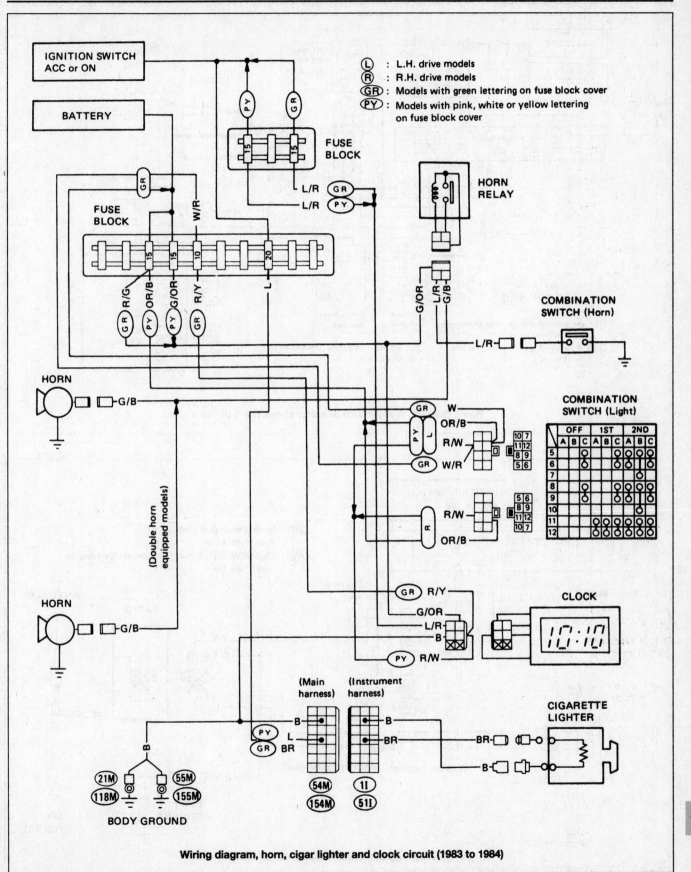

Wiring diagram, horn, cigar lighter and clock circuit (1983 to 1984)

14

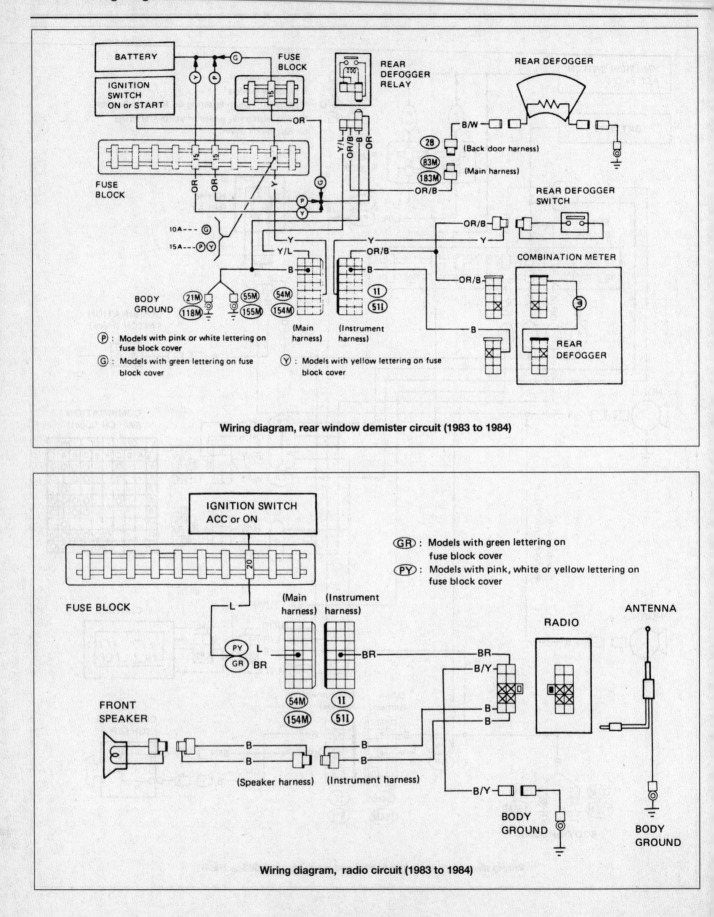

Wiring diagram, rear window demister circuit (1983 to 1984)

Wiring diagram, radio circuit (1983 to 1984)

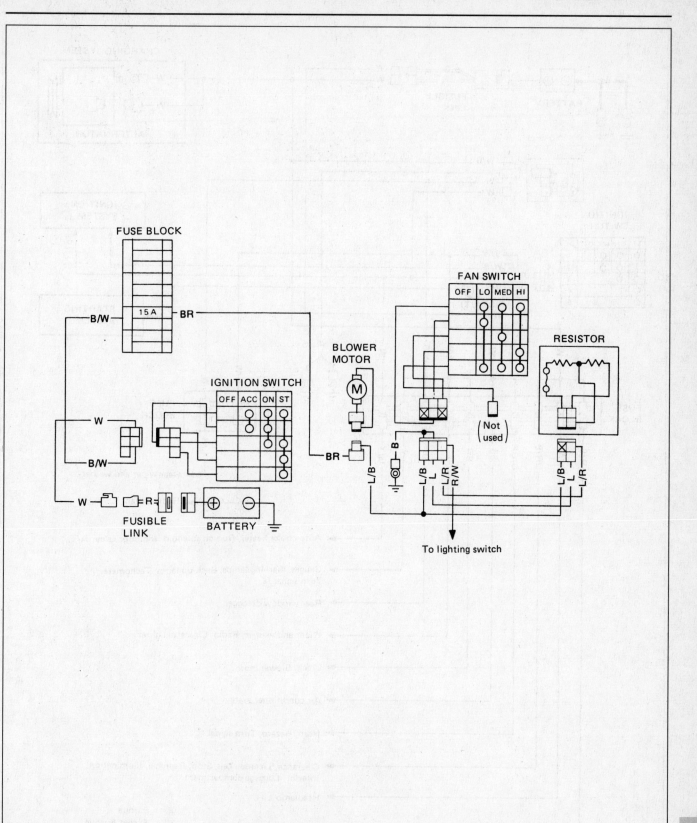

Wiring diagram, heater circuit (1983 to 1984)

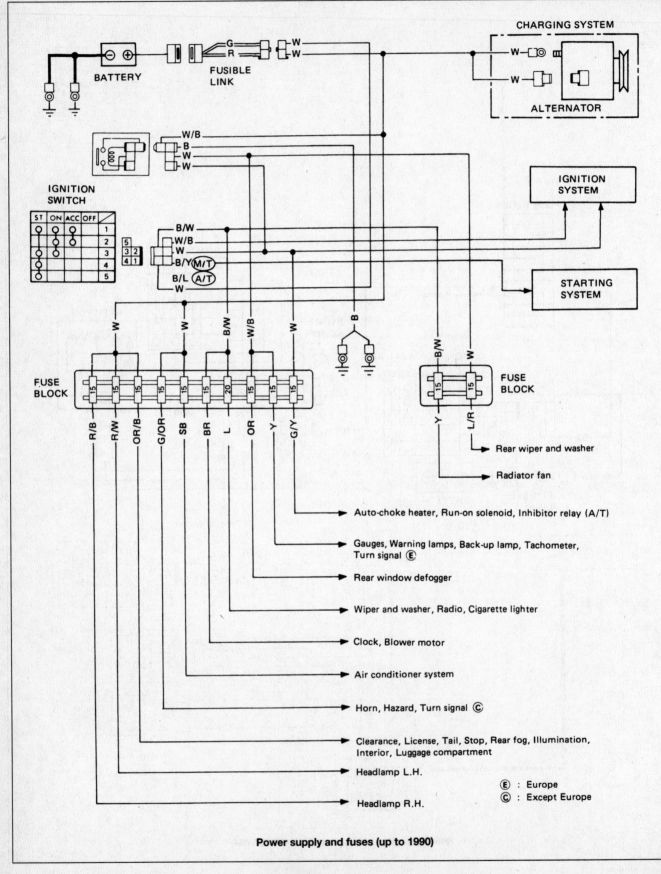

Power supply and fuses (up to 1990)

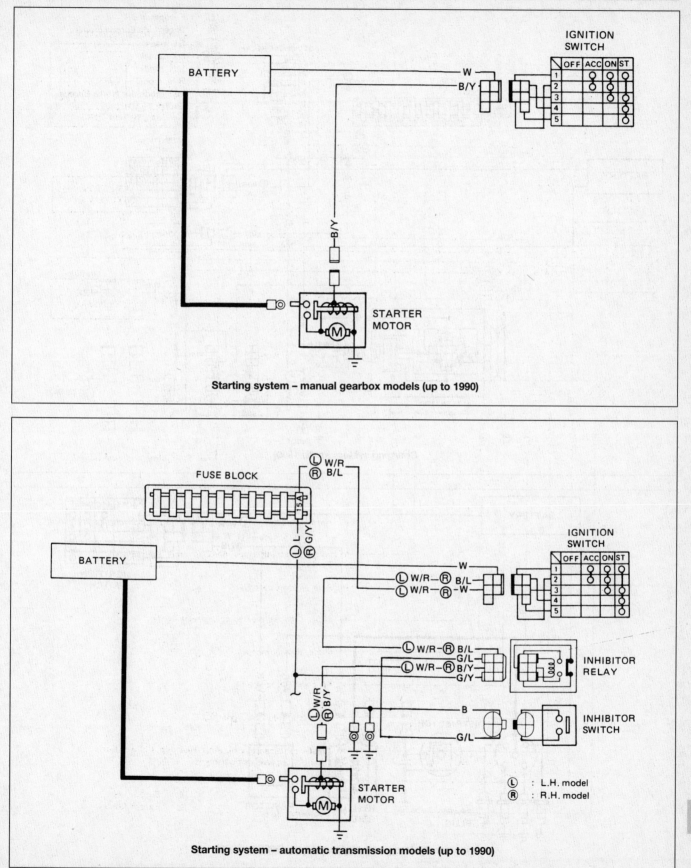

Starting system – manual gearbox models (up to 1990)

Starting system – automatic transmission models (up to 1990)

Ⓛ : L.H. model
Ⓡ : R.H. model

14

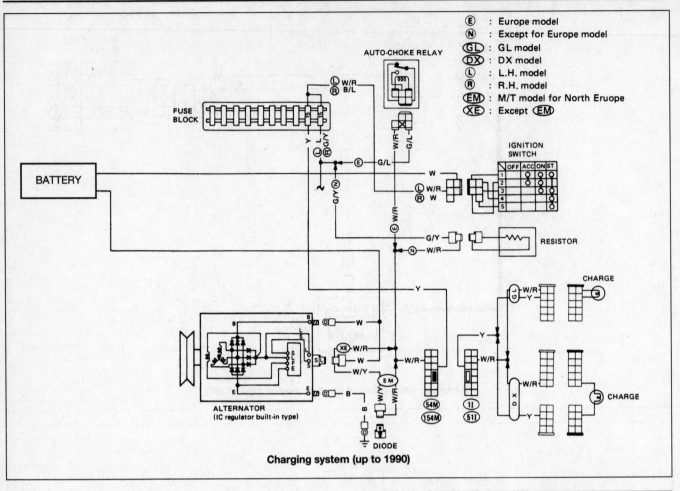

Charging system (up to 1990)

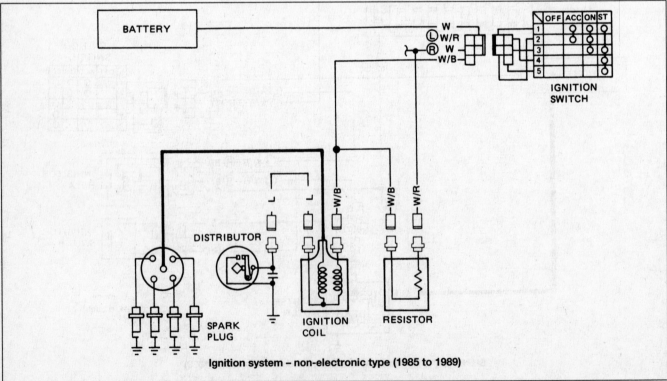

Ignition system – non-electronic type (1985 to 1989)

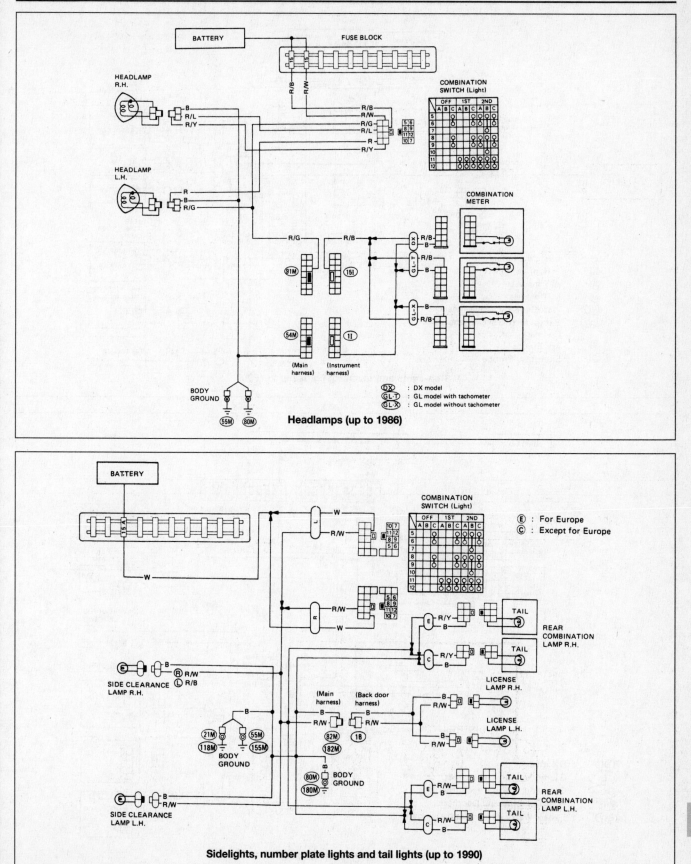

Headlamps (up to 1986)

Sidelights, number plate lights and tail lights (up to 1990)

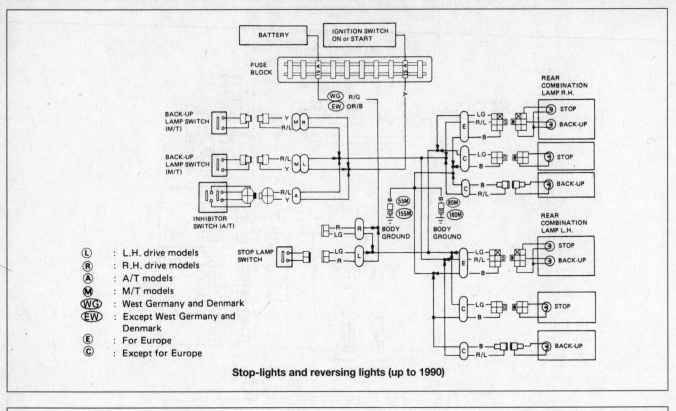

Stop-lights and reversing lights (up to 1990)

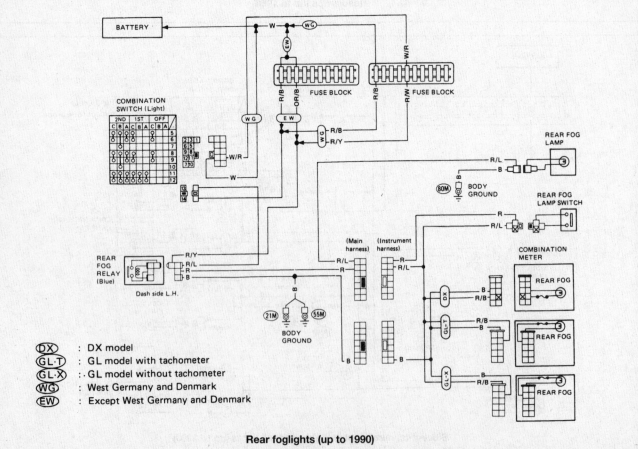

Rear foglights (up to 1990)

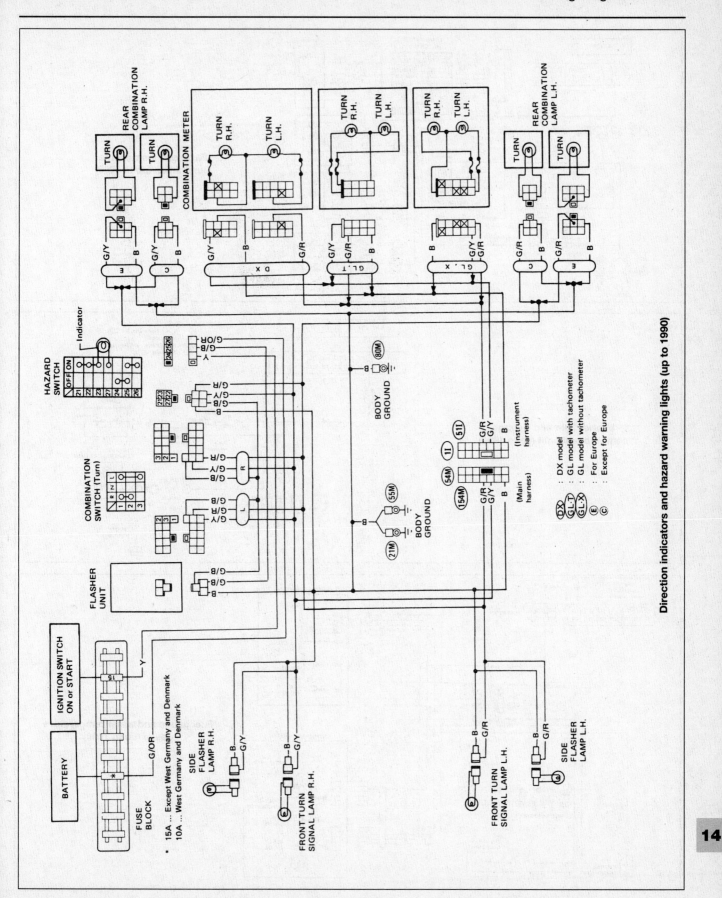

Direction indicators and hazard warning lights (up to 1990)

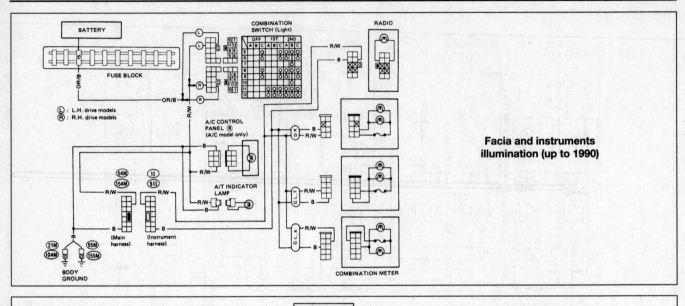

Facia and instruments illumination (up to 1990)

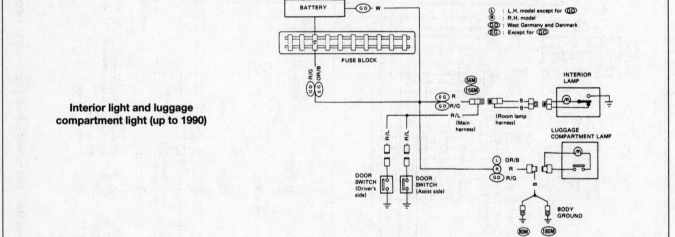

Interior light and luggage compartment light (up to 1990)

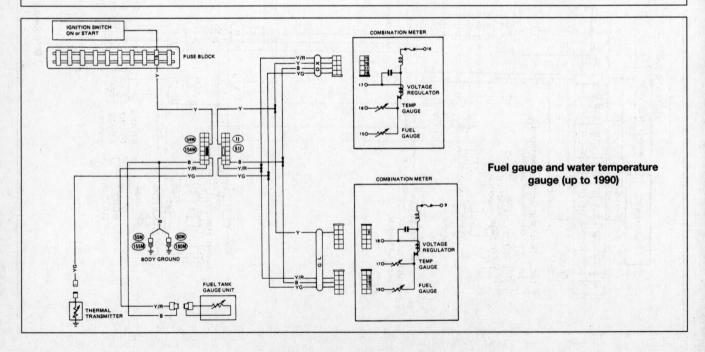

Fuel gauge and water temperature gauge (up to 1990)

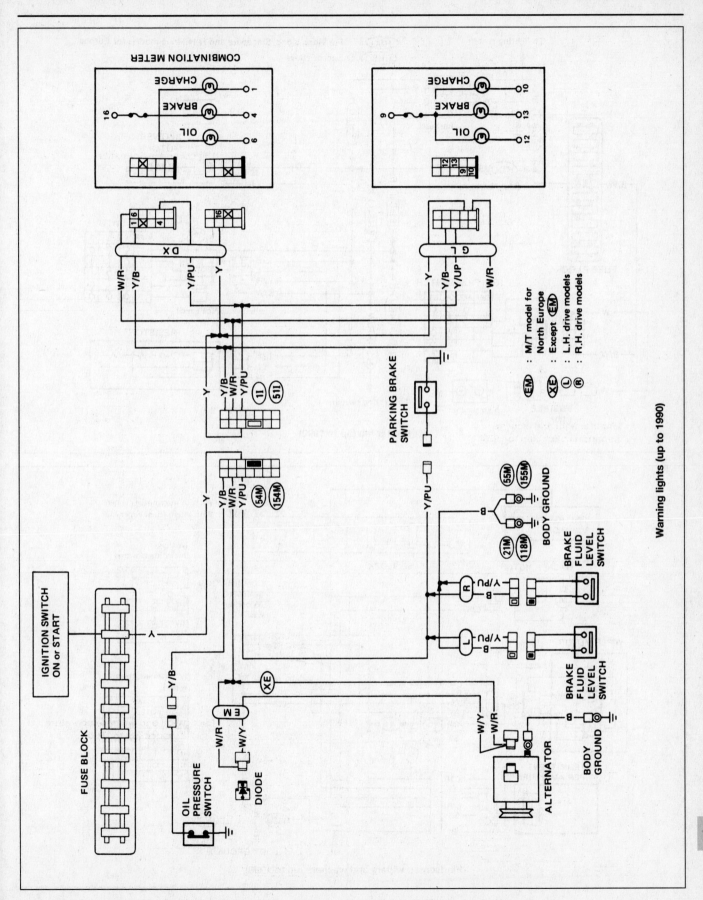

Warning lights (up to 1990)

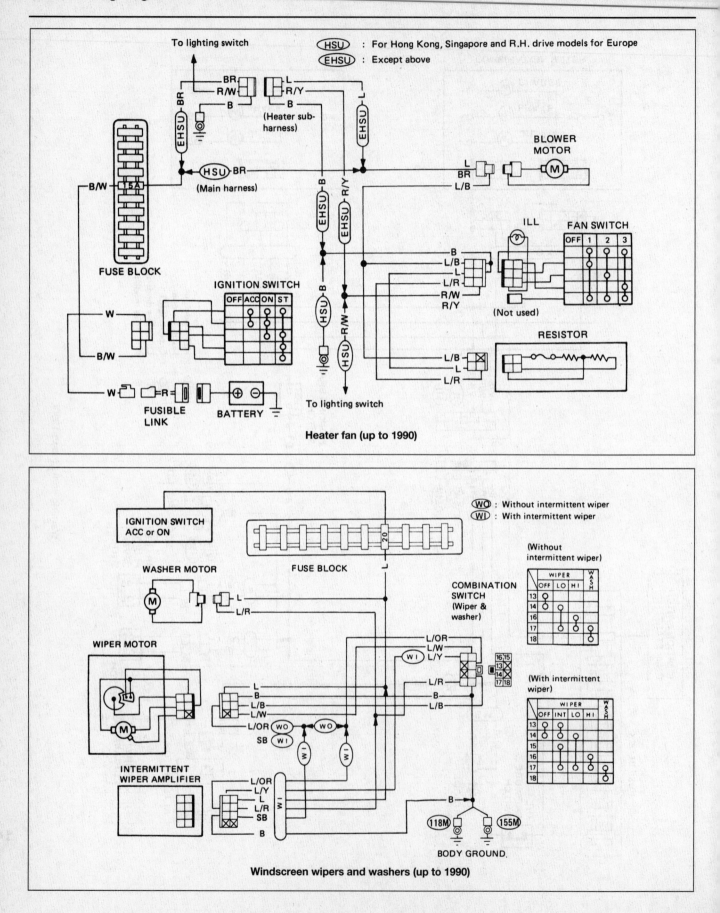

Heater fan (up to 1990)

Windscreen wipers and washers (up to 1990)

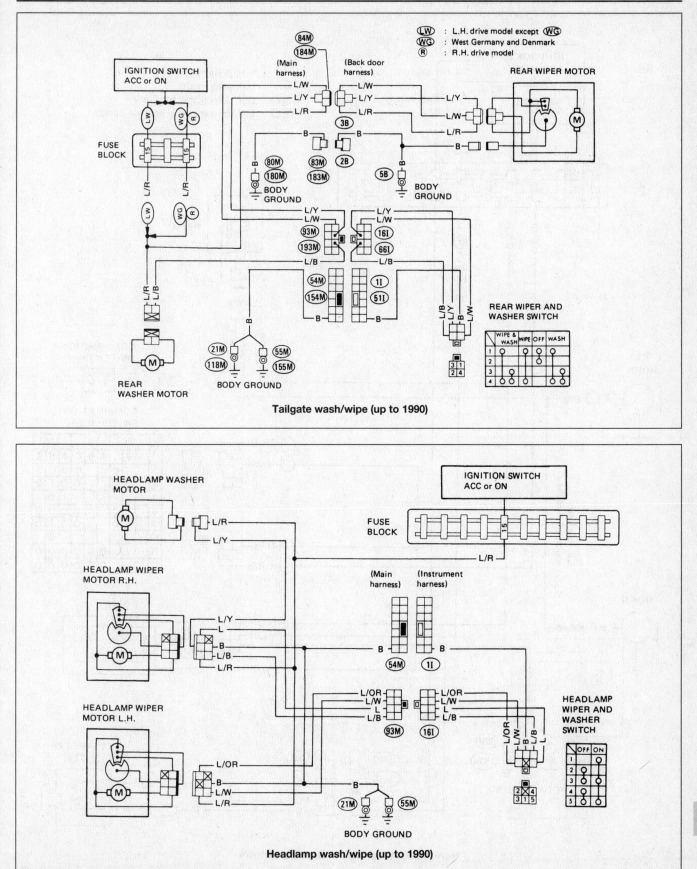

Tailgate wash/wipe (up to 1990)

Headlamp wash/wipe (up to 1990)

14

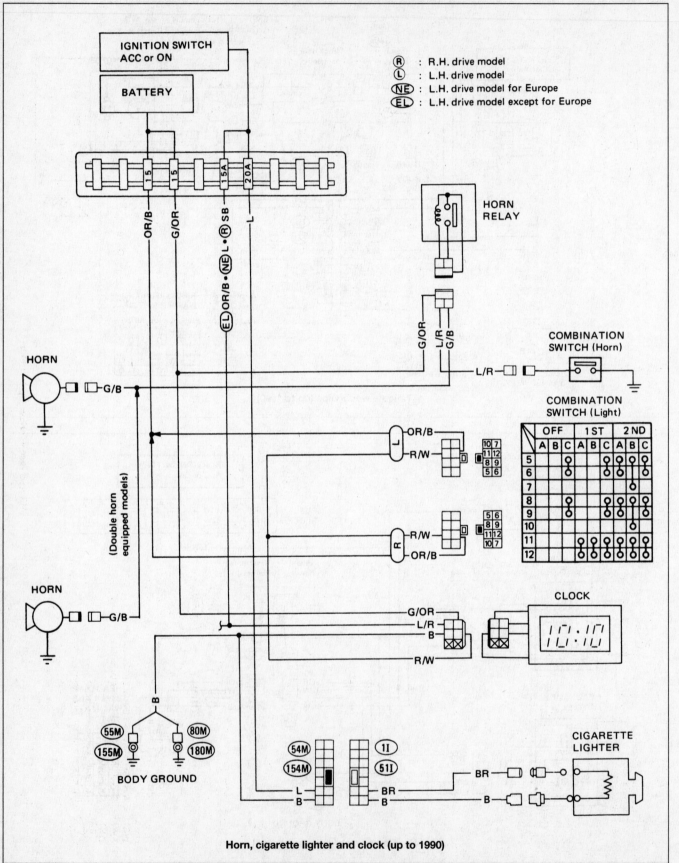

Horn, cigarette lighter and clock (up to 1990)

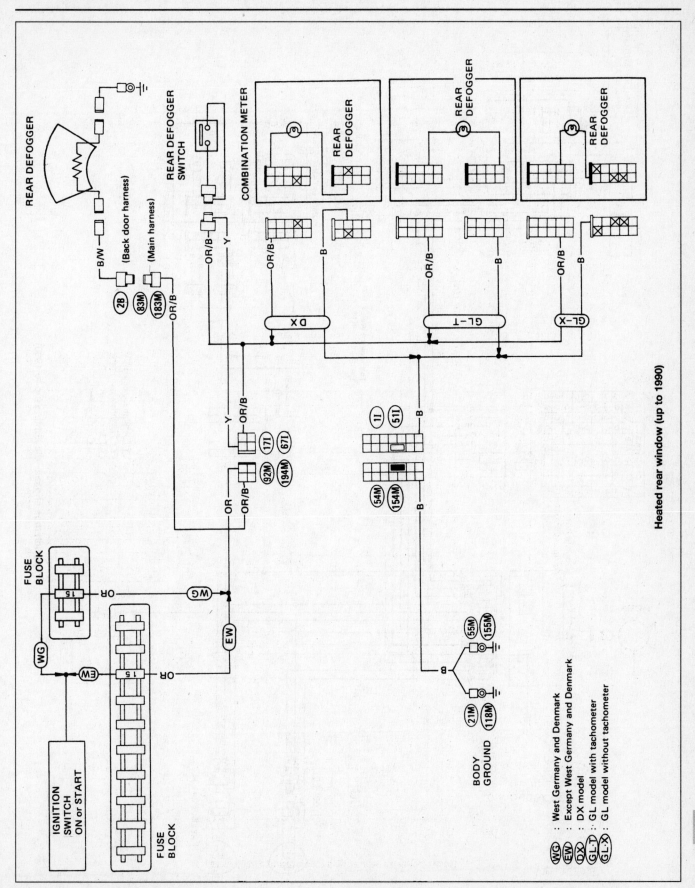

Heated rear window (up to 1990)

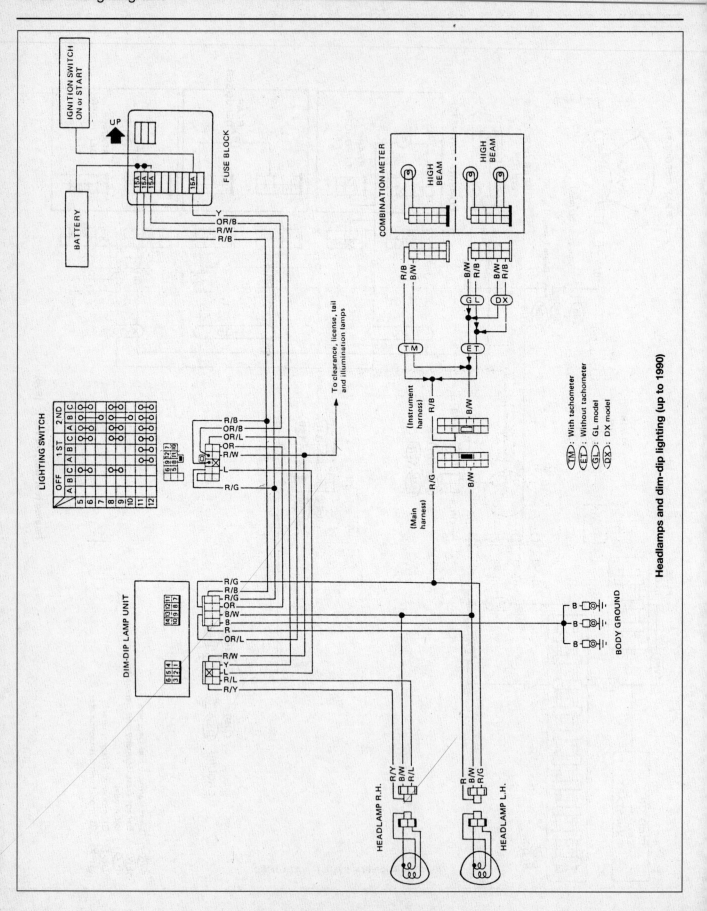

Headlamps and dim-dip lighting (up to 1990)

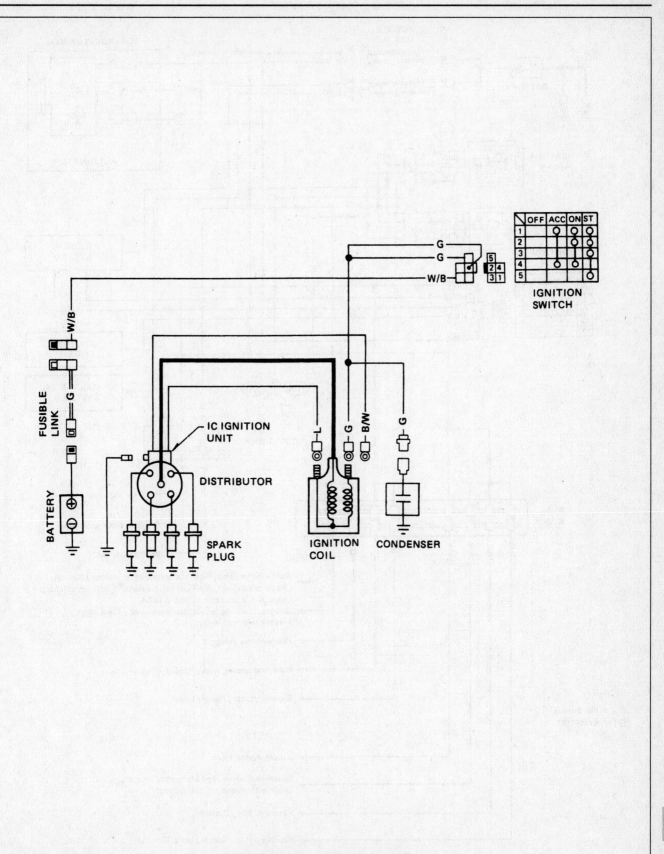

Electronic ignition system (up to 1990)

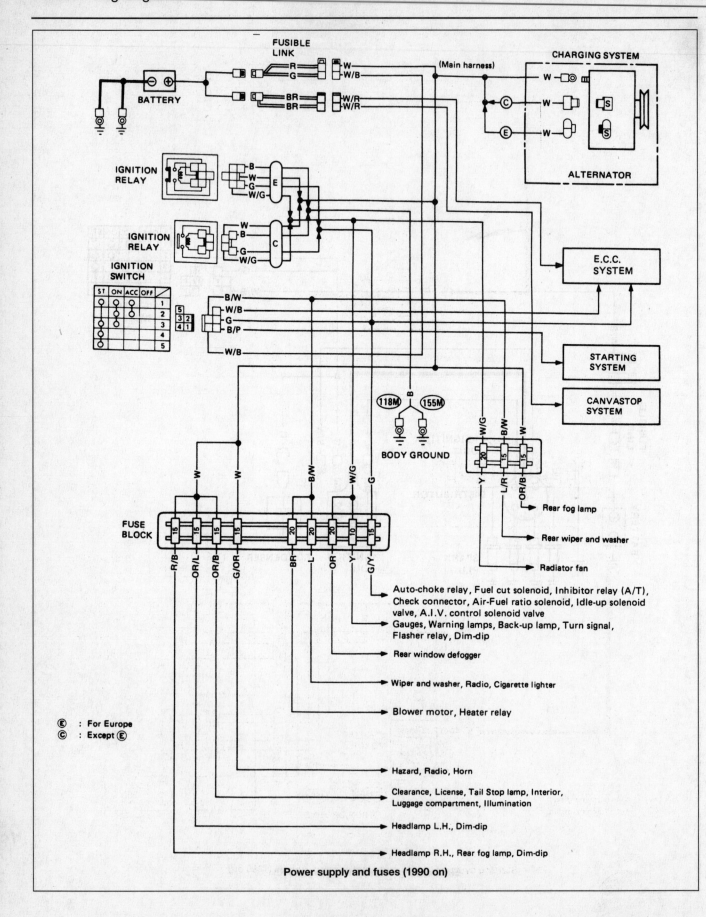

Power supply and fuses (1990 on)

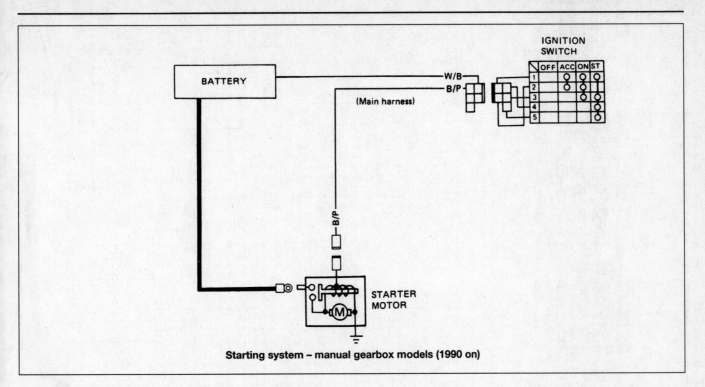

Starting system – manual gearbox models (1990 on)

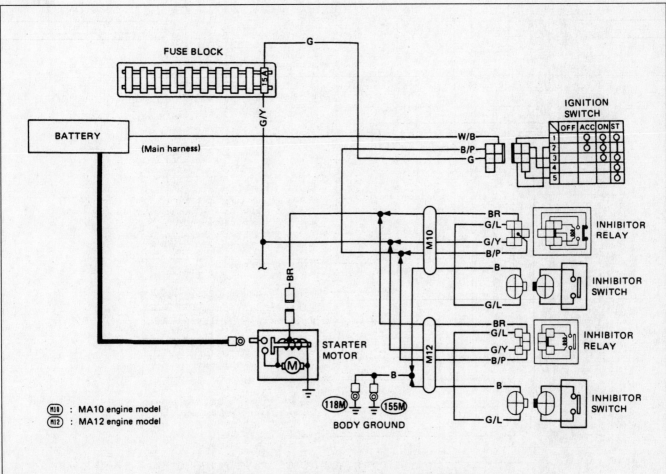

Starting system – automatic transmission models (1990 on)

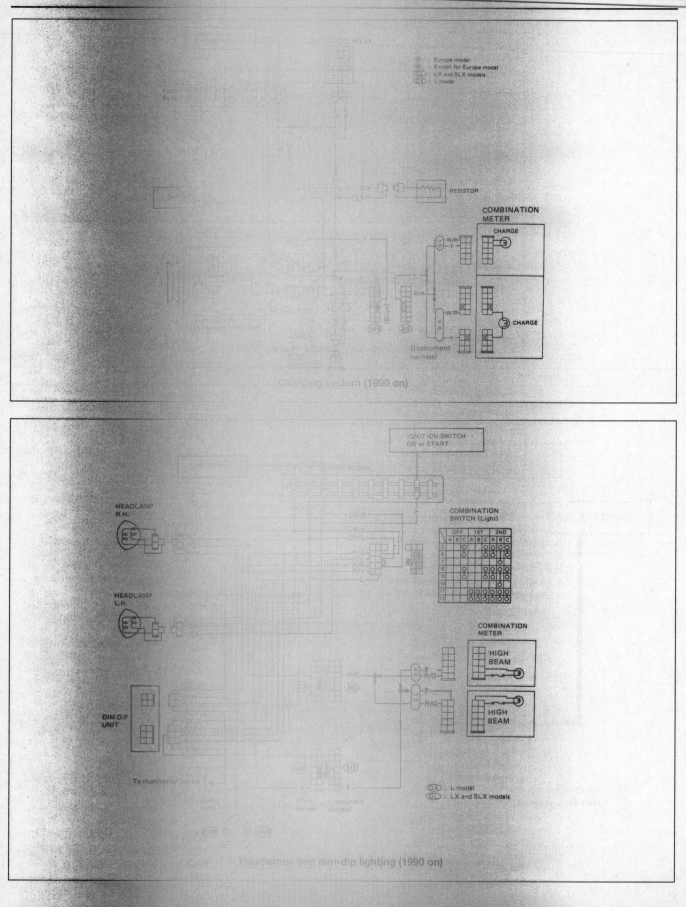

Charging system (1990 on)

Headlamps and dim-dip lighting (1990 on)

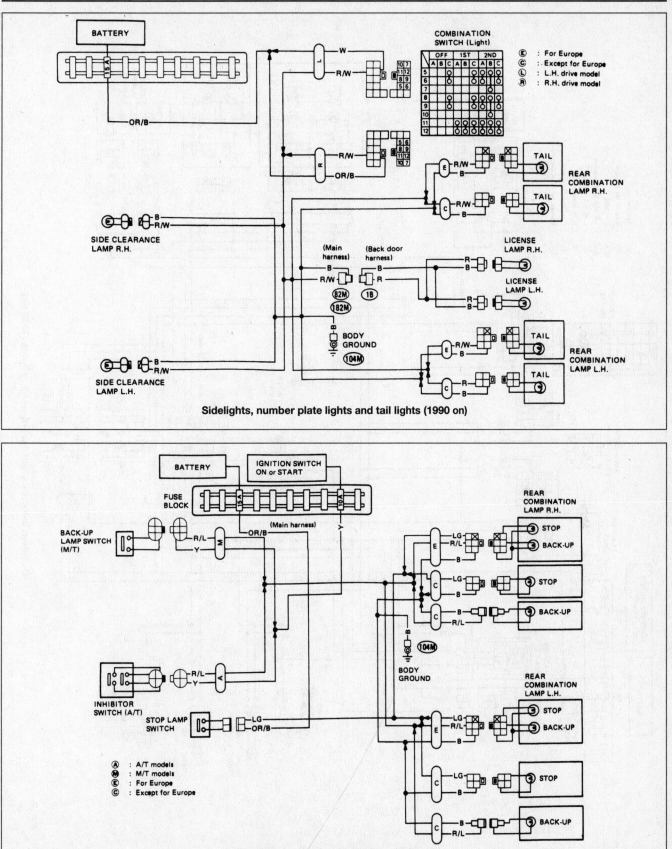

Sidelights, number plate lights and tail lights (1990 on)

Stop-lights and reversing lights (1990 on)

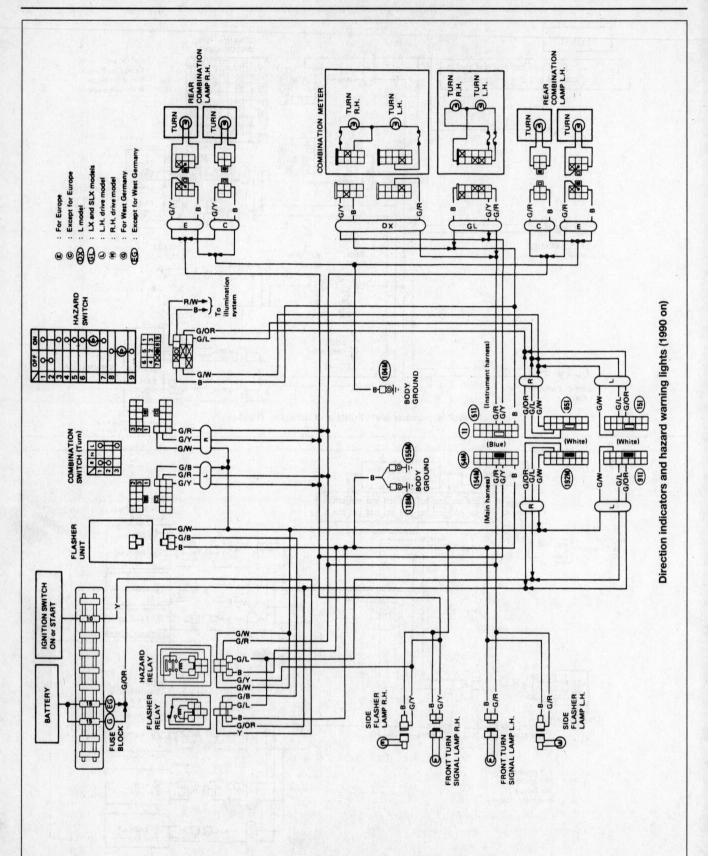

Direction indicators and hazard warning lights (1990 on)

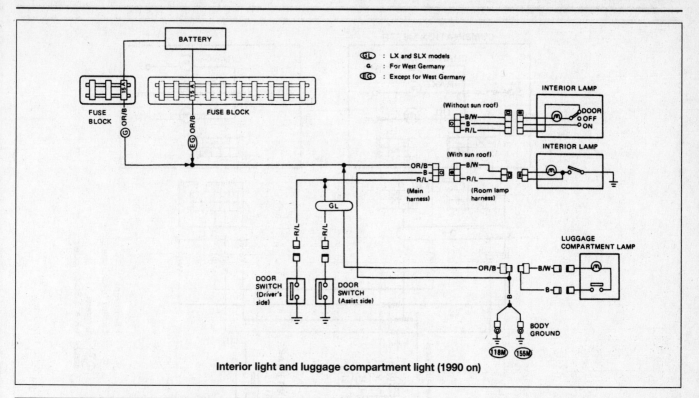

Interior light and luggage compartment light (1990 on)

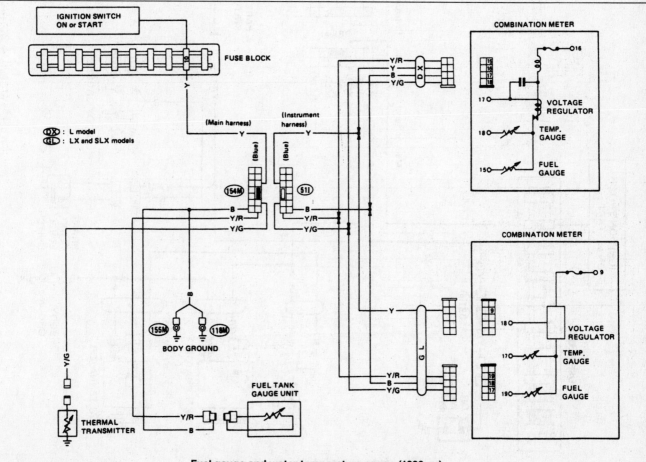

Fuel gauge and water temperature gauge (1990 on)

14

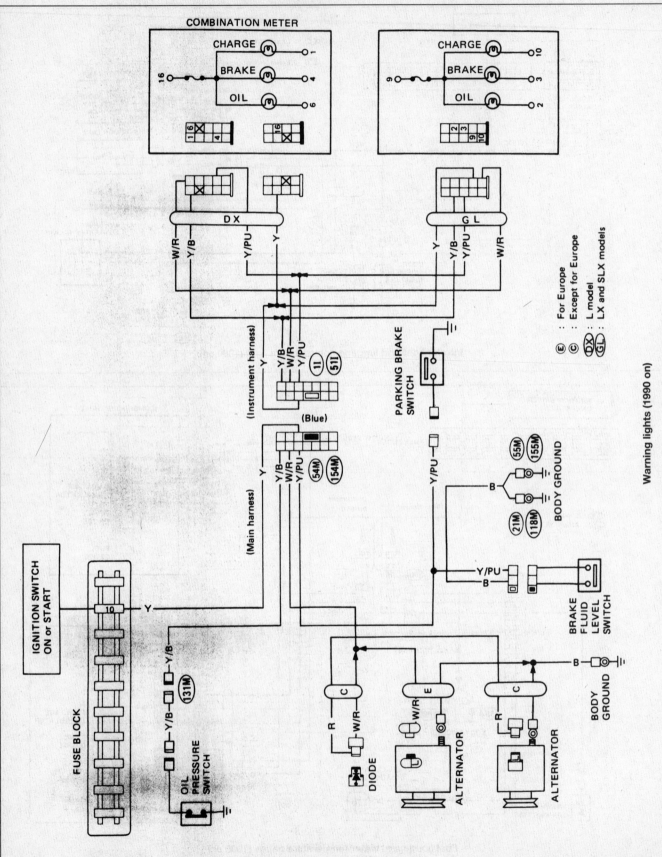

Warning lights (1990 on)

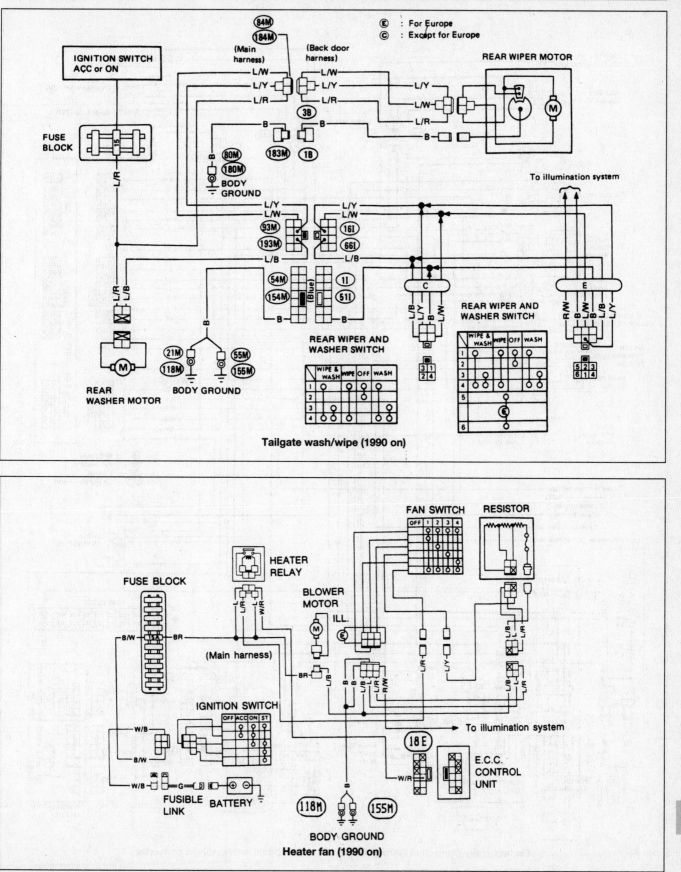

Tailgate wash/wipe (1990 on)

Heater fan (1990 on)

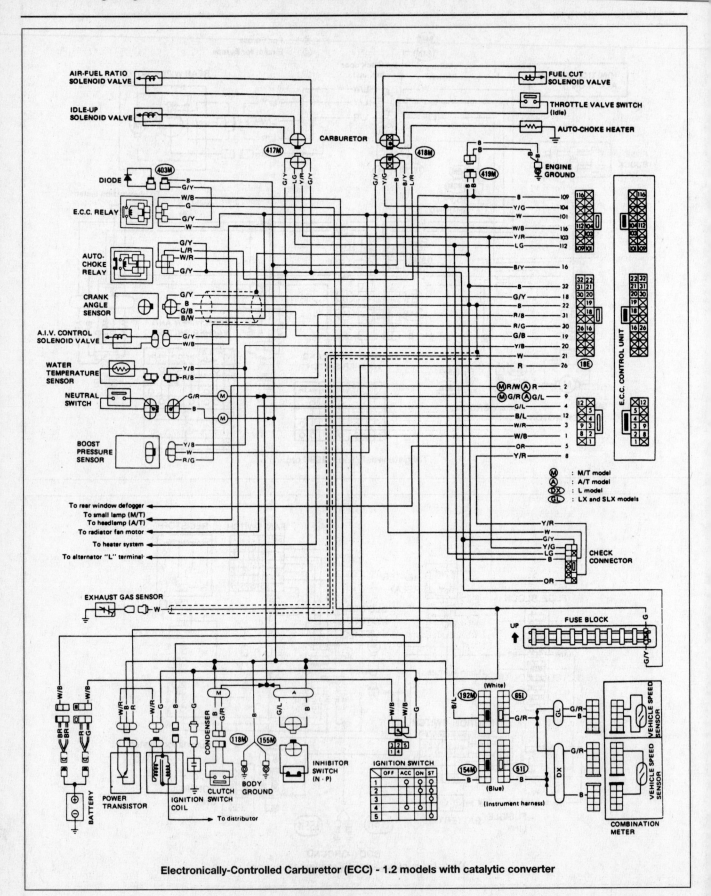

Electronically-Controlled Carburettor (ECC) - 1.2 models with catalytic converter

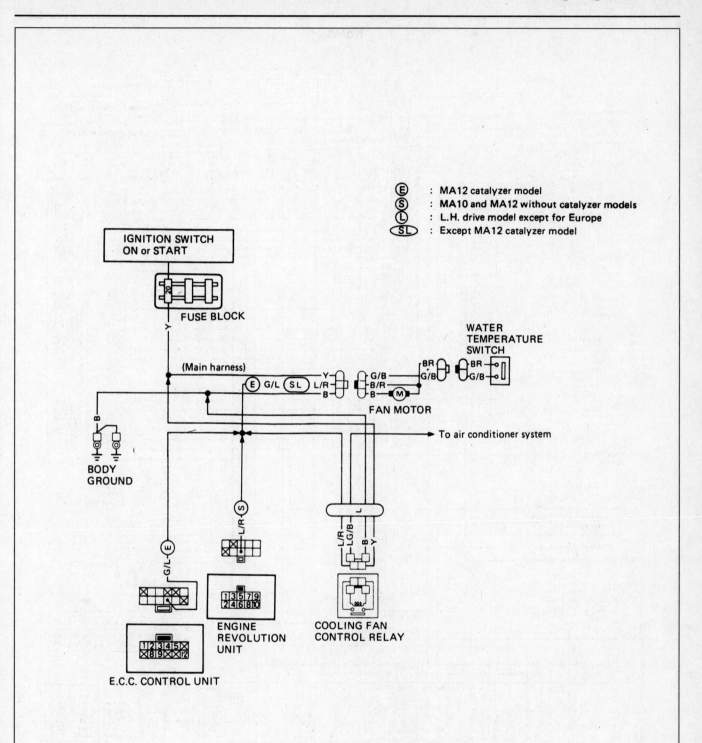

E : MA12 catalyzer model
S : MA10 and MA12 without catalyzer models
L : L.H. drive model except for Europe
SL : Except MA12 catalyzer model

IGNITION SWITCH
ON or START

FUSE BLOCK

WATER
TEMPERATURE
SWITCH

(Main harness)

E G/L SL

BODY
GROUND

FAN MOTOR

To air conditioner system

ENGINE
REVOLUTION
UNIT

COOLING FAN
CONTROL RELAY

E.C.C. CONTROL UNIT

Radiator cooling fan (ECC-equipped models)

14

Notes

This is a guide to getting your vehicle through the MOT test. Obviously it will not be possible to examine the vehicle to the same standard as the professional MOT tester. However, working through the following checks will enable you to identify any problem areas before submitting the vehicle for the test.

Where a testable component is in borderline condition, the tester has discretion in deciding whether to pass or fail it. The basis of such discretion is whether the tester would be happy for a close relative or friend to use the vehicle with the component in that condition. If the vehicle presented is clean and evidently well cared for, the tester may be more inclined to pass a borderline component than if the vehicle is scruffy and apparently neglected.

It has only been possible to summarise the test requirements here, based on the regulations in force at the time of printing. Test standards are becoming increasingly stringent, although there are some exemptions for older vehicles. For full details obtain a copy of the Haynes publication Pass the MOT! (available from stockists of Haynes manuals).

An assistant will be needed to help carry out some of these checks.

The checks have been sub-divided into four categories, as follows:

1 Checks carried out **FROM THE DRIVER'S SEAT**

2 Checks carried out **WITH THE VEHICLE ON THE GROUND**

3 Checks carried out **WITH THE VEHICLE RAISED AND THE WHEELS FREE TO TURN**

4 Checks carried out on **YOUR VEHICLE'S EXHAUST EMISSION SYSTEM**

1 Checks carried out **FROM THE DRIVER'S SEAT**

Handbrake

☐ Test the operation of the handbrake. Excessive travel (too many clicks) indicates incorrect brake or cable adjustment.

☐ Check that the handbrake cannot be released by tapping the lever sideways. Check the security of the lever mountings.

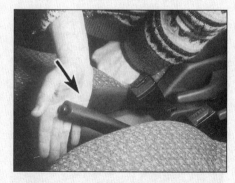

Footbrake

☐ Depress the brake pedal and check that it does not creep down to the floor, indicating a master cylinder fault. Release the pedal, wait a few seconds, then depress it again. If the pedal travels nearly to the floor before firm resistance is felt, brake adjustment or repair is necessary. If the pedal feels spongy, there is air in the hydraulic system which must be removed by bleeding.

☐ Check that the brake pedal is secure and in good condition. Check also for signs of fluid leaks on the pedal, floor or carpets, which would indicate failed seals in the brake master cylinder.

☐ Check the servo unit (when applicable) by operating the brake pedal several times, then keeping the pedal depressed and starting the engine. As the engine starts, the pedal will move down slightly. If not, the vacuum hose or the servo itself may be faulty.

Steering wheel and column

☐ Examine the steering wheel for fractures or looseness of the hub, spokes or rim.

☐ Move the steering wheel from side to side and then up and down. Check that the steering wheel is not loose on the column, indicating wear or a loose retaining nut. Continue moving the steering wheel as before, but also turn it slightly from left to right.

☐ Check that the steering wheel is not loose on the column, and that there is no abnormal

movement of the steering wheel, indicating wear in the column support bearings or couplings.

Windscreen and mirrors

☐ The windscreen must be free of cracks or other significant damage within the driver's field of view. (Small stone chips are acceptable.) Rear view mirrors must be secure, intact, and capable of being adjusted.

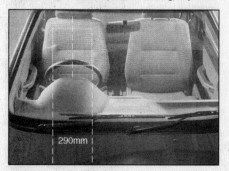

290mm

Seat belts and seats

Note: *The following checks are applicable to all seat belts, front and rear.*

☐ Examine the webbing of all the belts (including rear belts if fitted) for cuts, serious fraying or deterioration. Fasten and unfasten each belt to check the buckles. If applicable, check the retracting mechanism. Check the security of all seat belt mountings accessible from inside the vehicle.

☐ The front seats themselves must be securely attached and the backrests must lock in the upright position.

Doors

☐ Both front doors must be able to be opened and closed from outside and inside, and must latch securely when closed.

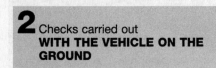

2 Checks carried out WITH THE VEHICLE ON THE GROUND

Vehicle identification

☐ Number plates must be in good condition, secure and legible, with letters and numbers correctly spaced – spacing at (A) should be twice that at (B).

☐ The VIN plate and/or homologation plate must be legible.

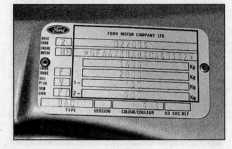

Electrical equipment

☐ Switch on the ignition and check the operation of the horn.

☐ Check the windscreen washers and wipers, examining the wiper blades; renew damaged or perished blades. Also check the operation of the stop-lights.

☐ Check the operation of the sidelights and number plate lights. The lenses and reflectors must be secure, clean and undamaged.

☐ Check the operation and alignment of the headlights. The headlight reflectors must not be tarnished and the lenses must be undamaged.

☐ Switch on the ignition and check the operation of the direction indicators (including the instrument panel tell-tale) and the hazard warning lights. Operation of the sidelights and stop-lights must not affect the indicators - if it does, the cause is usually a bad earth at the rear light cluster.

☐ Check the operation of the rear foglight(s), including the warning light on the instrument panel or in the switch.

Footbrake

☐ Examine the master cylinder, brake pipes and servo unit for leaks, loose mountings, corrosion or other damage.

☐ The fluid reservoir must be secure and the fluid level must be between the upper (**A**) and lower (**B**) markings.

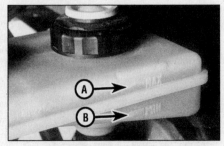

☐ Inspect both front brake flexible hoses for cracks or deterioration of the rubber. Turn the steering from lock to lock, and ensure that the hoses do not contact the wheel, tyre, or any part of the steering or suspension mechanism. With the brake pedal firmly depressed, check the hoses for bulges or leaks under pressure.

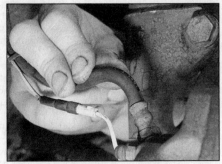

Steering and suspension

☐ Have your assistant turn the steering wheel from side to side slightly, up to the point where the steering gear just begins to transmit this movement to the roadwheels. Check for excessive free play between the steering wheel and the steering gear, indicating wear or insecurity of the steering column joints, the column-to-steering gear coupling, or the steering gear itself.

☐ Have your assistant turn the steering wheel more vigorously in each direction, so that the roadwheels just begin to turn. As this is done, examine all the steering joints, linkages, fittings and attachments. Renew any component that shows signs of wear or damage. On vehicles with power steering, check the security and condition of the steering pump, drivebelt and hoses.

☐ Check that the vehicle is standing level, and at approximately the correct ride height.

Shock absorbers

☐ Depress each corner of the vehicle in turn, then release it. The vehicle should rise and then settle in its normal position. If the vehicle continues to rise and fall, the shock absorber is defective. A shock absorber which has seized will also cause the vehicle to fail.

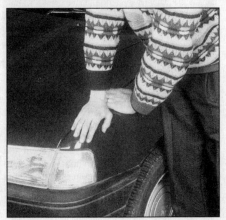

Exhaust system

☐ Start the engine. With your assistant holding a rag over the tailpipe, check the entire system for leaks. Repair or renew leaking sections.

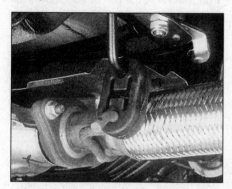

3 Checks carried out
WITH THE VEHICLE RAISED AND THE WHEELS FREE TO TURN

Jack up the front and rear of the vehicle, and securely support it on axle stands. Position the stands clear of the suspension assemblies. Ensure that the wheels are clear of the ground and that the steering can be turned from lock to lock.

Steering mechanism

☐ Have your assistant turn the steering from lock to lock. Check that the steering turns smoothly, and that no part of the steering mechanism, including a wheel or tyre, fouls any brake hose or pipe or any part of the body structure.

☐ Examine the steering rack rubber gaiters for damage or insecurity of the retaining clips. If power steering is fitted, check for signs of damage or leakage of the fluid hoses, pipes or connections. Also check for excessive stiffness or binding of the steering, a missing split pin or locking device, or severe corrosion of the body structure within 30 cm of any steering component attachment point.

Front and rear suspension and wheel bearings

☐ Starting at the front right-hand side, grasp the roadwheel at the 3 o'clock and 9 o'clock positions and shake it vigorously. Check for free play or insecurity at the wheel bearings, suspension balljoints, or suspension mountings, pivots and attachments.

☐ Now grasp the wheel at the 12 o'clock and 6 o'clock positions and repeat the previous inspection. Spin the wheel, and check for roughness or tightness of the front wheel bearing.

☐ If excess free play is suspected at a component pivot point, this can be confirmed by using a large screwdriver or similar tool and levering between the mounting and the component attachment. This will confirm whether the wear is in the pivot bush, its retaining bolt, or in the mounting itself (the bolt holes can often become elongated).

☐ Carry out all the above checks at the other front wheel, and then at both rear wheels.

Springs and shock absorbers

☐ Examine the suspension struts (when applicable) for serious fluid leakage, corrosion, or damage to the casing. Also check the security of the mounting points.

☐ If coil springs are fitted, check that the spring ends locate in their seats, and that the spring is not corroded, cracked or broken.

☐ If leaf springs are fitted, check that all leaves are intact, that the axle is securely attached to each spring, and that there is no deterioration of the spring eye mountings, bushes, and shackles.

☐ The same general checks apply to vehicles fitted with other suspension types, such as torsion bars, hydraulic displacer units, etc. Ensure that all mountings and attachments are secure, that there are no signs of excessive wear, corrosion or damage, and (on hydraulic types) that there are no fluid leaks or damaged pipes.

☐ Inspect the shock absorbers for signs of serious fluid leakage. Check for wear of the mounting bushes or attachments, or damage to the body of the unit.

Driveshafts (fwd vehicles only)

☐ Rotate each front wheel in turn and inspect the constant velocity joint gaiters for splits or damage. Also check that each driveshaft is straight and undamaged.

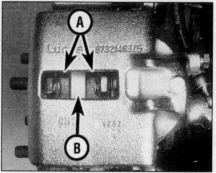

Braking system

☐ If possible without dismantling, check brake pad wear and disc condition. Ensure that the friction lining material has not worn excessively, (A) and that the discs are not fractured, pitted, scored or badly worn (B).

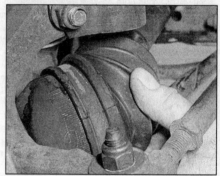

☐ Examine all the rigid brake pipes underneath the vehicle, and the flexible hose(s) at the rear. Look for corrosion, chafing or insecurity of the pipes, and for signs of bulging under pressure, chafing, splits or deterioration of the flexible hoses.

☐ Look for signs of fluid leaks at the brake calipers or on the brake backplates. Repair or renew leaking components.

☐ Slowly spin each wheel, while your assistant depresses and releases the footbrake. Ensure that each brake is operating and does not bind when the pedal is released.

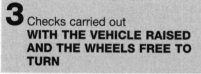

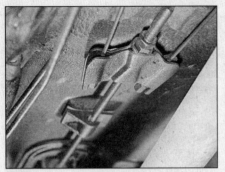

□ Examine the handbrake mechanism, checking for frayed or broken cables, excessive corrosion, or wear or insecurity of the linkage. Check that the mechanism works on each relevant wheel, and releases fully, without binding.

□ It is not possible to test brake efficiency without special equipment, but a road test can be carried out later to check that the vehicle pulls up in a straight line.

Fuel and exhaust systems

□ Inspect the fuel tank (including the filler cap), fuel pipes, hoses and unions. All components must be secure and free from leaks.

□ Examine the exhaust system over its entire length, checking for any damaged, broken or missing mountings, security of the retaining clamps and rust or corrosion.

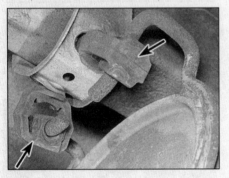

Wheels and tyres

□ Examine the sidewalls and tread area of each tyre in turn. Check for cuts, tears, lumps, bulges, separation of the tread, and exposure of the ply or cord due to wear or damage. Check that the tyre bead is correctly seated on the wheel rim, that the valve is sound and

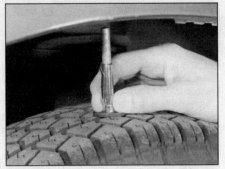

properly seated, and that the wheel is not distorted or damaged.

□ Check that the tyres are of the correct size for the vehicle, that they are of the same size and type on each axle, and that the pressures are correct.

□ Check the tyre tread depth. The legal minimum at the time of writing is 1.6 mm over at least three-quarters of the tread width. Abnormal tread wear may indicate incorrect front wheel alignment.

Body corrosion

□ Check the condition of the entire vehicle structure for signs of corrosion in load-bearing areas. (These include chassis box sections, side sills, cross-members, pillars, and all suspension, steering, braking system and seat belt mountings and anchorages.) Any corrosion which has seriously reduced the thickness of a load-bearing area is likely to cause the vehicle to fail. In this case professional repairs are likely to be needed.

□ Damage or corrosion which causes sharp or otherwise dangerous edges to be exposed will also cause the vehicle to fail.

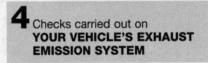

4 Checks carried out on **YOUR VEHICLE'S EXHAUST EMISSION SYSTEM**

Petrol models

□ Have the engine at normal operating temperature, and make sure that it is in good tune (ignition system in good order, air filter element clean, etc).

□ Before any measurements are carried out, raise the engine speed to around 2500 rpm, and hold it at this speed for 20 seconds. Allow

the engine speed to return to idle, and watch for smoke emissions from the exhaust tailpipe. If the idle speed is obviously much too high, or if dense blue or clearly-visible black smoke comes from the tailpipe for more than 5 seconds, the vehicle will fail. As a rule of thumb, blue smoke signifies oil being burnt (engine wear) while black smoke signifies unburnt fuel (dirty air cleaner element, or other carburettor or fuel system fault).

□ An exhaust gas analyser capable of measuring carbon monoxide (CO) and hydrocarbons (HC) is now needed. If such an instrument cannot be hired or borrowed, a local garage may agree to perform the check for a small fee.

CO emissions (mixture)

□ At the time of writing, the maximum CO level at idle is 3.5% for vehicles first used after August 1986 and 4.5% for older vehicles. From January 1996 a much tighter limit (around 0.5%) applies to catalyst-equipped vehicles first used from August 1992. If the CO level cannot be reduced far enough to pass the test (and the fuel and ignition systems are otherwise in good condition) then the carburettor is badly worn, or there is some problem in the fuel injection system or catalytic converter (as applicable).

HC emissions

□ With the CO emissions within limits, HC emissions must be no more than 1200 ppm (parts per million). If the vehicle fails this test at idle, it can be re-tested at around 2000 rpm; if the HC level is then 1200 ppm or less, this counts as a pass.

□ Excessive HC emissions can be caused by oil being burnt, but they are more likely to be due to unburnt fuel.

Diesel models

□ The only emission test applicable to Diesel engines is the measuring of exhaust smoke density. The test involves accelerating the engine several times to its maximum unloaded speed.

Note: *It is of the utmost importance that the engine timing belt is in good condition before the test is carried out.*

□ Excessive smoke can be caused by a dirty air cleaner element. Otherwise, professional advice may be needed to find the cause.

Introduction

A selection of good tools is a fundamental requirement for anyone contemplating the maintenance and repair of a motor vehicle. For the owner who does not possess any, their purchase will prove a considerable expense, offsetting some of the savings made by doing-it-yourself. However, provided that the tools purchased meet the relevant national safety standards and are of good quality, they will last for many years and prove an extremely worthwhile investment.

To help the average owner to decide which tools are needed to carry out the various tasks detailed in this manual, we have compiled three lists of tools under the following headings: *Maintenance and minor repair*, *Repair and overhaul*, and *Special*. Newcomers to practical mechanics should start off with the *Maintenance and minor repair* tool kit, and confine themselves to the simpler jobs around the vehicle. Then, as confidence and experience grow, more difficult tasks can be undertaken, with extra tools being purchased as, and when, they are needed. In this way, a *Maintenance and minor repair* tool kit can be built up into a *Repair and overhaul* tool kit over a considerable period of time, without any major cash outlays. The experienced do-it-yourselfer will have a tool kit good enough for most repair and overhaul procedures, and will add tools from the *Special* category when it is felt that the expense is justified by the amount of use to which these tools will be put.

Maintenance and minor repair tool kit

The tools given in this list should be considered as a minimum requirement if routine maintenance, servicing and minor repair operations are to be undertaken. We recommend the purchase of combination spanners (ring one end, open-ended the other); although more expensive than open-ended ones, they do give the advantages of both types of spanner.

- [ ] *Combination spanners: 10, 11, 12, 13, 14 and 17 mm*
- [ ] *Adjustable spanner - 35 mm jaw (approx)*
- [ ] *Gearbox drain plug key*
- [ ] *Set of feeler gauges*
- [ ] *Spark plug spanner (with rubber insert)*
- [ ] *Spark plug gap adjustment tool*
- [ ] *Brake bleed nipple spanner*

- [ ] *Screwdrivers: Flat blade approx 100 mm long x ...*
- [ ] *Combination pliers*
- [ ] *Hacksaw (junior)*
- [ ] *Tyre pump*
- [ ] *Tyre pressure gauge*
- [ ] *Oil can*
- [ ] *Oil filter removal tool*
- [ ] *Fine emery cloth*
- [ ] *Wire brush (small)*
- [ ] *Funnel (medium size)*

Repair and overhaul tool kit

These tools are virtually essential for anyone undertaking any major repair to a motor vehicle, and are additional given in the *Maintenance and minor repair* list. Included in this list is a comprehensive set of sockets. Although these are expensive, they will be found invaluable as they are so versatile - particularly if various drives are included in the set. We recommend the half-inch square-drive type, as this can be used with most proprietary torque wrenches. If you cannot afford a socket set, even bought piecemeal, then inexpensive tubular box spanners are a useful alternative.

The tools in this list will occasionally need to be supplemented by tools from the *Special* list:

- [ ] *Sockets (or box spanners) to cover range in previous list*
- [ ] *Reversible ratchet drive (for use with sockets) (see illustration)*
- [ ] *Extension piece, 250 mm (for use with sockets)*
- [ ] *Universal joint (for use with sockets)*
- [ ] *Torque wrench (for use with sockets)*
- [ ] *Self-locking grips*
- [ ] *Ball pein hammer*
- [ ] *Soft-faced mallet (plastic/aluminium or rubber)*
- [ ] *Screwdrivers:*
  Flat blade - long & sturdy, short (chubby) and narrow (electrician's) types
  Cross blade - Long & sturdy, and short (chubby) types
- [ ] *Pliers:*
  Long-nosed
  Side cutters (electrician's)
  Circlip (internal and external)
- [ ] *Cold chisel - 25 mm*
- [ ] *Scriber*
- [ ] *Scraper*

- [ ] *Centre-punch*
- [ ] *Pin punch*
- [ ] *Hacksaw*
- [ ] *Brake hose clamp*
- [ ] *Brake bleeding kit*
- [ ] *Selection of twist drills*
- [ ] *Steel rule/straight-edge*
- [ ] *Allen keys*
- [ ] *Selection of files*
- [ ] *Wire brush*
- [ ] *Axle stands*
- [ ] *Jack (strong trolley or hydraulic type)*
- [ ] *Light with extension lead*

Special tools

The tools in this list are those which are not used regularly, are expensive to buy, or which need to be used in accordance with their manufacturers' instructions. Unless relatively difficult mechanical jobs are undertaken frequently, it will not be economic to buy many of these tools. Where this is the case, you could consider clubbing together with friends (or joining a motorists' club) to make a joint purchase, or borrowing the tools against a deposit from a local garage or tool hire specialist. It is worth noting that many of the larger DIY superstores now carry a large range of special tools for hire at modest rates.

The following list contains only those tools and instruments freely available to the public, and not those special tools produced by the vehicle manufacturer specifically for its dealer network. You will find occasional references to these manufacturers' special tools in the text of this manual. Generally, an alternative method of doing the job without the vehicle manufacturers' special tool is given. However, sometimes there is no alternative to using them. Where this is the case and the relevant tool cannot be bought or borrowed, you will have to entrust the work to a franchised garage.

- [ ] *Valve spring compressor (see illustration)*
- [ ] *Valve grinding tool*
- [ ] *Piston ring compressor (see illustration)*
- [ ] *Piston ring removal/installation tool (see illustration)*
- [ ] *Cylinder bore hone (see illustration)*
- [ ] *Balljoint separator*
- [ ] *Coil spring compressors (where applicable)*
- [ ] *Two/three-legged hub and bearing puller (see illustration)*

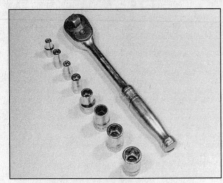

Sockets and reversible ratchet drive

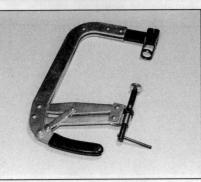

Valve spring compressor

Piston ring compressor

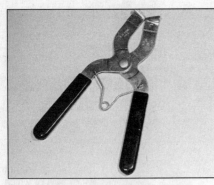

Piston ring removal/installation tool

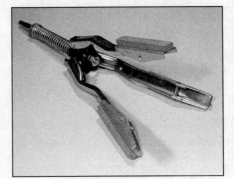

Cylinder bore hone

Three-legged hub and bearing puller

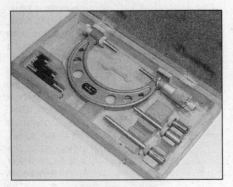

Micrometer set

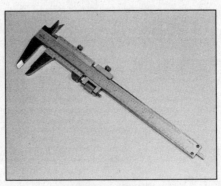

Vernier calipers

Dial test indicator and magnetic stand

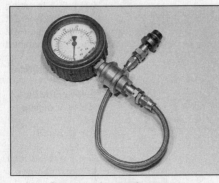

Compression testing gauge

Clutch plate alignment set

Brake shoe steady spring cup removal tool

☐ Impact screwdriver
☐ Micrometer and/or vernier calipers **(see illustrations)**
☐ Dial gauge **(see illustration)**
☐ Universal electrical multi-meter
☐ Cylinder compression gauge **(see illustration)**
☐ Clutch plate alignment set **(see illustration)**
☐ Brake shoe steady spring cup removal tool **(see illustration)**
☐ Bush and bearing removal/installation set **(see illustration)**
☐ Stud extractors **(see illustration)**
☐ Tap and die set **(see illustration)**
☐ Lifting tackle
☐ Trolley jack

Buying tools

For practically all tools, a tool factor is the best source, since he will have a very comprehensive range compared with the average garage or accessory shop. Having said. that, accessory shops often offer excellent quality tools at discount prices, so it pays to shop around.

Remember, you don't have to buy the most expensive items on the shelf, but it is always advisable to steer clear of the very cheap tools. There are plenty of good tools around at reasonable prices, but always aim to purchase items which meet the relevant national safety standards. If in doubt, ask the proprietor or manager of the shop for advice before making a purchase.

Care and maintenance of tools

Having purchased a reasonable tool kit, it is necessary to keep the tools in a clean and serviceable condition. After use, always wipe off any dirt, grease and metal particles using a clean, dry cloth, before putting the tools away. Never leave them lying around after they have been used. A simple tool rack on the garage or workshop wall for items such as screwdrivers and pliers is a good idea. Store all normal spanners and sockets in a metal box. Any measuring instruments, gauges, meters, etc, must be carefully stored where they cannot be damaged or become rusty.

Take a little care when tools are used. Hammer heads inevitably become marked, and screwdrivers lose the keen edge on their blades from time to time. A little timely attention with emery cloth or a file will soon restore items like this to a good serviceable finish.

Working facilities

Not to be forgotten when discussing tools is the workshop itself. If anything more than routine maintenance is to be carried out, some form of suitable working area becomes essential.

It is appreciated that many an owner-mechanic is forced by circumstances to remove an engine or similar item without the benefit of a garage or workshop. Having done this, any repairs should always be done under the cover of a roof.

Wherever possible, any dismantling should be done on a clean, flat workbench or table at a suitable working height.

Any workbench needs a vice; one with a jaw opening of 100 mm is suitable for most jobs. As mentioned previously, some clean dry storage space is also required for tools, as well as for any lubricants, cleaning fluids, touch-up paints and so on, which become necessary.

Another item which may be required, and which has a much more general usage, is an electric drill with a chuck capacity of at least 8 mm. This, together with a good range of twist drills, is virtually essential for fitting accessories.

Last, but not least, always keep a supply of old newspapers and clean, lint-free rags available, and try to keep any working area as clean as possible.

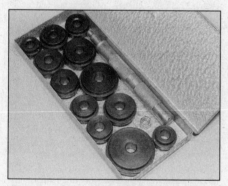

Bush and bearing removal/installation set

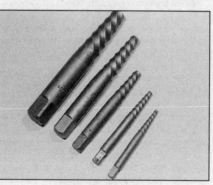

Stud extractor set

Tap and die set

Whenever servicing, repair or overhaul work is carried out on the car or its components, observe the following procedures and instructions. This will assist in carrying out the operation efficiently and to a professional standard of workmanship.

Joint mating faces and gaskets

When separating components at their mating faces, never insert screwdrivers or similar implements into the joint between the faces in order to prise them apart. This can cause severe damage which results in oil leaks, coolant leaks, etc upon reassembly. Separation is usually achieved by tapping along the joint with a soft-faced hammer in order to break the seal. However, note that this method may not be suitable where dowels are used for component location.

Where a gasket is used between the mating faces of two components, a new one must be fitted on reassembly; fit it dry unless otherwise stated in the repair procedure. Make sure that the mating faces are clean and dry, with all traces of old gasket removed. When cleaning a joint face, use a tool which is unlikely to score or damage the face, and remove any burrs or nicks with an oilstone or fine file.

Make sure that tapped holes are cleaned with a pipe cleaner, and keep them free of jointing compound, if this is being used, unless specifically instructed otherwise.

Ensure that all orifices, channels or pipes are clear, and blow through them, preferably using compressed air.

Oil seals

Oil seals can be removed by levering them out with a wide flat-bladed screwdriver or similar implement. Alternatively, a number of self-tapping screws may be screwed into the seal, and these used as a purchase for pliers or some similar device in order to pull the seal free.

Whenever an oil seal is removed from its working location, either individually or as part of an assembly, it should be renewed.

The very fine sealing lip of the seal is easily damaged, and will not seal if the surface it contacts is not completely clean and free from scratches, nicks or grooves. If the original sealing surface of the component cannot be restored, and the manufacturer has not made provision for slight relocation of the seal relative to the sealing surface, the component should be renewed.

Protect the lips of the seal from any surface which may damage them in the course of fitting. Use tape or a conical sleeve where possible. Lubricate the seal lips with oil before fitting and, on dual-lipped seals, fill the space between the lips with grease.

Unless otherwise stated, oil seals must be fitted with their sealing lips toward the lubricant to be sealed.

Use a tubular drift or block of wood of the appropriate size to install the seal and, if the seal housing is shouldered, drive the seal down to the shoulder. If the seal housing is unshouldered, the seal should be fitted with its face flush with the housing top face (unless otherwise instructed).

Screw threads and fastenings

Seized nuts, bolts and screws are quite a common occurrence where corrosion has set in, and the use of penetrating oil or releasing fluid will often overcome this problem if the offending item is soaked for a while before attempting to release it. The use of an impact driver may also provide a means of releasing such stubborn fastening devices, when used in conjunction with the appropriate screwdriver bit or socket. If none of these methods works, it may be necessary to resort to the careful application of heat, or the use of a hacksaw or nut splitter device.

Studs are usually removed by locking two nuts together on the threaded part, and then using a spanner on the lower nut to unscrew the stud. Studs or bolts which have broken off below the surface of the component in which they are mounted can sometimes be removed using a stud extractor. Always ensure that a blind tapped hole is completely free from oil, grease, water or other fluid before installing the bolt or stud. Failure to do this could cause the housing to crack due to the hydraulic action of the bolt or stud as it is screwed in.

When tightening a castellated nut to accept a split pin, tighten the nut to the specified torque, where applicable, and then tighten further to the next split pin hole. Never slacken the nut to align the split pin hole, unless stated in the repair procedure.

When checking or retightening a nut or bolt to a specified torque setting, slacken the nut or bolt by a quarter of a turn, and then retighten to the specified setting. However, this should not be attempted where angular tightening has been used.

For some screw fastenings, notably cylinder head bolts or nuts, torque wrench settings are no longer specified for the latter stages of tightening, "angle-tightening" being called up instead. Typically, a fairly low torque wrench setting will be applied to the bolts/nuts in the correct sequence, followed by one or more stages of tightening through specified angles.

Locknuts, locktabs and washers

Any fastening which will rotate against a component or housing during tightening should always have a washer between it and the relevant component or housing.

Spring or split washers should always be renewed when they are used to lock a critical component such as a big-end bearing retaining bolt or nut. Locktabs which are folded over to retain a nut or bolt should always be renewed.

Self-locking nuts can be re-used in non-critical areas, providing resistance can be felt when the locking portion passes over the bolt or stud thread. However, it should be noted that self-locking stiffnuts tend to lose their effectiveness after long periods of use, and should then be renewed as a matter of course.

Split pins must always be replaced with new ones of the correct size for the hole.

When thread-locking compound is found on the threads of a fastener which is to be re-used, it should be cleaned off with a wire brush and solvent, and fresh compound applied on reassembly.

Special tools

Some repair procedures in this manual entail the use of special tools such as a press, two or three-legged pullers, spring compressors, etc. Wherever possible, suitable readily-available alternatives to the manufacturer's special tools are described, and are shown in use. In some instances, where no alternative is possible, it has been necessary to resort to the use of a manufacturer's tool, and this has been done for reasons of safety as well as the efficient completion of the repair operation. Unless you are highly-skilled and have a thorough understanding of the procedures described, never attempt to bypass the use of any special tool when the procedure described specifies its use. Not only is there a very great risk of personal injury, but expensive damage could be caused to the components involved.

Environmental considerations

When disposing of used engine oil, brake fluid, antifreeze, etc, give due consideration to any detrimental environmental effects. Do not, for instance, pour any of the above liquids down drains into the general sewage system, or onto the ground to soak away. Many local council refuse tips provide a facility for waste oil disposal, as do some garages. If none of these facilities are available, consult your local Environmental Health Department, or the National Rivers Authority, for further advice.

With the universal tightening-up of legislation regarding the emission of environmentally-harmful substances from motor vehicles, most vehicles have tamperproof devices fitted to the main adjustment points of the fuel system. These devices are primarily designed to prevent unqualified persons from adjusting the fuel/air mixture, with the chance of a consequent increase in toxic emissions. If such devices are found during servicing or overhaul, they should, wherever possible, be renewed or refitted in accordance with the manufacturer's requirements or current legislation.

Note: It is antisocial and illegal to dump oil down the drain. To find the location of your local oil recycling bank, call this number free.

Buying spare parts

Spare parts are available from many sources for example: Nissan garages, other garages and accessory shops or motor factors. Our advice concerning spare parts is as follows.

Officially appointed Nissan dealers

The best source for parts which are peculiar to the vehicle and generally not available elsewhere (eg cylinder heads, internal engine or gearbox components, interior trim, etc). They are also the only place where you should buy parts if the vehicle is still under warranty. Non-standard parts may invalidate the warranty.

To be sure of obtaining the correct part, your garage will need to know the vehicle or engine serial number, and if possible, take the old part with you for further identification. Remember, some parts are available on a factory exchange basis, any parts being returned should be clean.

Other garages and accessory shops may often be very good places to buy components such as spark plugs, light bulbs, windscreen wiper blades, oils and greases, needed for the correct maintenance of your vehicle.

Motor factors

Good motor factors carry stock of all the major components with a high turnover such as clutches, brake shoes/pads. exhaust systems, batteries, etc. and some may also run an exchange system for reconditioned parts which can be considerably cheaper than new parts. A word of warning: beware of cheap inferior parts. They may be cheaper and look right, but often wear out quickly, and can cause problems with adjustments and overall running efficiency.

Always use a reputable dealer for your spare parts.

Vehicle identification numbers

There are two plates located on the engine bulkhead. The right-hand one is the vehicle identification plate and the left-hand one the vehicle identification number. There is also a tyre information plate inside the left-hand door pillar.

The engine number is stamped on the machined face of the crankcase just below the distributor (photo).

The manual gearbox number is located on the top housing web and automatic transmission number on the top control central housing.

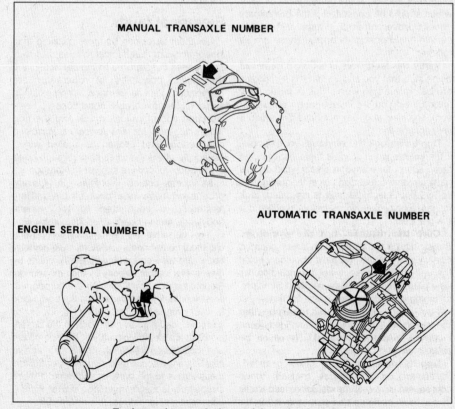

MANUAL TRANSAXLE NUMBER

ENGINE SERIAL NUMBER

AUTOMATIC TRANSAXLE NUMBER

Engine and transmission serial number locations

Engine identification number

Introduction

The vehicle owner who does his or her own maintenance according to the recommended schedules should not have to use this section of the manual very often. Modern component reliability is such that, provided those items subject to wear or deterioration are inspected or renewed at the specified intervals, sudden failure is comparatively rare. Faults do not usually just happen as a result of sudden failure, but develop over a period of time. Major mechanical failures in particular are usually preceded by characteristic symptoms over hundreds or even thousands of miles. Those components which do occasionally fail without warning are often small and easily carried in the vehicle.

With any fault finding, the first step is to decide where to begin investigations. Sometimes this is obvious, but on other occasions a little detective work will be necessary. The owner who makes half a dozen haphazard adjustments or replacements may be successful in curing a fault (or its symptoms), but he will be none the wiser if the fault recurs and he may well have spent more time and money than was necessary. A calm and logical approach will be found to be more satisfactory in the long run. Always take into account any warning signs or abnormalities that may have been noticed in the period preceding the fault – power loss, high or low gauge readings, unusual noises or smells, etc – and remember that failure of components such as fuses or spark plugs may only be pointers to some underlying fault.

The pages which follow here are intended to help in cases of failure to start or breakdown on the road. There is also a Fault Diagnosis Section at the end of each Chapter which should be consulted if the preliminary checks prove unfruitful. Whatever the fault, certain basic principles apply. These are as follows:

Verify the fault. This is simply a matter of being sure that you know what the symptoms are before starting work. This is particularly important if you are investigating a fault for someone else who may not have described it very accurately.

Don't overlook the obvious. For example, if the vehicle won't start, is there petrol in the tank? (Don't take anyone else's word on this particular point, and don't trust the fuel gauge either!) If an electrical fault is indicated, look for loose or broken wires before digging out the test gear.

Cure the disease, not the symptom. Substituting a flat battery with a fully charged one will get you off the hard shoulder, but if the underlying cause is not attended to,the new battery will go the same way. Similarly, changing oil-fouled spark plugs for a new set will get you moving again, but remember that the reason for the fouling (if it wasn't simply an incorrect grade of plug) will have to be established and corrected.

Don't take anything for granted. Particularly, don't forget that a 'new' component may itself be defective (especially if it's been rattling round in the boot for months), and don't leave components out of a fault diagnosis sequence just because they are new or recently fitted. When you do finally diagnose a difficult fault, you'll probably realise that all the evidence was there from the start.

Electrical faults

Electrical faults can be more puzzling than straightforward mechanical failures, but they are no less susceptible to logical analysis if the basic principles of operation are understood. Vehicle electrical wiring exists in extremely unfavourable conditions – heat, vibration and chemical attack and the first things to look for are loose or corroded connections and broken or chafed wires, especially where the wires pass through holes in the bodywork or are subject to vibration.

All metal-bodied vehicles in current production have one pole of the battery 'earthed', ie connected to the vehicle bodywork, and in nearly all modern vehicles it is the negative (–) terminal. The various electrical components – motors, bulb holders, etc – are also connected to earth, either by means of a lead or directly by their mountings. Electric current flows through the component and then back to the battery via the bodywork. If the component mounting is loose or corroded, or if a good path back to the battery is not available, the circuit will be incomplete and malfunction will result. The engine and/or gearbox are also earthed by means of flexible metal straps to the body or subframe; if these straps are loose or missing, starter motor, generator and ignition trouble may result.

Assuming the earth return to be satisfactory, electrical faults will be due either to component malfunction or to defects in the current supply. Individual components are dealt with in Chapter 12. If supply wires are broken or cracked internally this results in an open-circuit, and the easiest way to check for this is to bypass the suspect wire temporarily with a length of wire having a crocodile clip or suitable connector at each end. Alternatively, a 12V test lamp can be used to verify the presence of supply voltage at various points along the wire and the break can be thus isolated.

If a bare portion of a live wire touches the bodywork or other earthed metal part, the electricity will take the low-resistance path thus formed back to the battery: this is known as a short-circuit. Hopefully a short-circuit will blow a fuse, but otherwise it may cause burning of the insulation (and possibly further short-circuits) or even a fire. This is why it is inadvisable to bypass persistently blowing fuses with silver foil or wire.

Spares and tool kit

Most vehicles are supplied only with sufficient tools for wheel changing; the *Maintenance and minor repair* tool kit detailed in *Tools and working facilities*, with the addition of a hammer, is probably sufficient for those repairs that most motorists would consider attempting at the roadside. In addition a few items which can be fitted without too much trouble in the event of a breakdown should be carried. Experience and available space will modify the list below, but the following may save having to call on professional assistance:

- ☐ Spark plugs, clean and correctly gapped
- ☐ HT lead and plug cap – long enough to reach the plug furthest from the distributor
- ☐ Distributor rotor and condenser
- ☐ Drivebelt(s) — emergency type may suffice
- ☐ Spare fuses
- ☐ Set of principal light bulbs
- ☐ Tin of radiator sealer and hose bandage
- ☐ Exhaust bandage
- ☐ Roll of insulating tape
- ☐ Length of soft iron wire
- ☐ Length of electrical flex
- ☐ Torch or inspection lamp (can double as test lamp)
- ☐ Battery jump leads

- ☐ Tow-rope
- ☐ Ignition waterproofing aerosol
- ☐ Litre of engine oil
- ☐ Sealed can of hydraulic fluid
- ☐ Emergency windscreen
- ☐ Wormdrive clips
- ☐ Tube of filler paste

If spare fuel is carried, a can designed for the purpose should be used to minimise risks of leakage and collision damage. A first aid kit and a warning triangle, whilst not at present compulsory in the UK, are obviously sensible items to carry in addition to the above. When touring abroad it may be advisable to carry additional spares which, even if you cannot fit them yourself, could save having to wait while parts are obtained. The items below may be worth considering:

- ☐ Clutch and throttle cables
- ☐ Cylinder head gasket
- ☐ Alternator brushes
- ☐ Tyre valve core

One of the motoring organisations will be able to advise on availability of fuel, etc, in foreign countries.

<table>
<tr><td bgcolor="gray">Engine will not start</td></tr>
</table>

Engine fails to turn when starter operated

- ☐ Flat battery (recharge use jump leads or push start)
- ☐ Battery terminals loose or corroded
- ☐ Battery earth to body defective
- ☐ Engine earth strap loose or broken
- ☐ Starter motor (or solenoid) wiring loose or broken
- ☐ Ignition/starter switch faulty
- ☐ Major mechanical failure (seizure)
- ☐ Starter or solenoid internal fault (see Chapter 12)

Starter motor turns engine slowly

- ☐ Partially discharged battery (recharge, use jump leads, or push start)
- ☐ Battery terminals loose or corroded

- ☐ Battery earth to body defective
- ☐ Engine earth strap loose
- ☐ Starter motor (or solenoid) wiring loose
- ☐ Starter motor internal fault (see Chapter 12)

Starter motor spins without turning engine

- ☐ Flywheel gear teeth damaged or worn
- ☐ Starter motor mounting bolts loose

Engine turns normally but fails to start

- ☐ Damp or dirty HT leads and distributor cap (crank engine and check for spark)
- ☐ No fuel in tank (check for delivery)
- ☐ Fouled or incorrectly gapped spark plugs (remove, clean and regap)
- ☐ Other ignition system fault (see Chapter 4)
- ☐ Other fuel system fault (see Chapter 3)

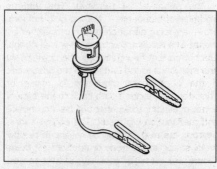

A simple test lamp is useful for checking electrical faults

Carrying a few spares may save you a long walk!

- [ ] Poor compression (see Chapter 1)
- [ ] Major mechanical failure (eg camshaft drive)

Engine fires but will not run

- [ ] Air leaks at carburettor or inlet manifold
- [ ] Fuel starvation (see Chapter 3)
- [ ] Ignition fault (see Chapter 4)

Engine cuts out and will not restart

Engine cuts out suddenly – ignition fault

- [ ] Loose or disconnected LT wires
- [ ] Wet HT leads or distributor cap (after traversing water splash)
- [ ] Coil failure (check for spark)
- [ ] Other ignition fault (see Chapter 4)

Engine misfires before cutting out – fuel fault

- [ ] Fuel tank empty
- [ ] Fuel pump defective or filter blocked (check for delivery)
- [ ] Fuel tank filler vent blocked (suction will be evident on releasing cap)
- [ ] Carburettor needle valve sticking

Crank engine and check for spark. Note use of insulated tool

- [ ] Carburettor jets blocked (fuel contaminated)
- [ ] Other fuel system fault (see Chapter 3)

Engine cuts out – other causes

- [ ] Serious overheating
- [ ] Major mechanical failure (eg camshaft drive)

Engine overheats

Ignition (no-charge) warning light illuminated

- [ ] Slack or broken drivebelt — retension or renew (Chapter 2)

Ignition warning light not illuminated

- [ ] Coolant loss due to internal or external leakage (see Chapter 2)
- [ ] Thermostat defective
- [ ] Low oil level
- [ ] Brakes binding
- [ ] Radiator clogged externally or internally
- [ ] Engine waterways clogged
- [ ] Ignition timing incorrect or automatic advance malfunctioning
- [ ] Mixture too weak

Note: *Do not add cold water to an overheated engine or damage may result*

Low engine oil pressure

Note: *Low oil pressure in a high-mileage engine at tickover is not necessarily a cause for concern. Sudden pressure loss at speed is far more significant. In any event check the gauge or warning light sender before condemning the engine.*

Gauge reads low or warning light illuminated with engine running

- [ ] Oil level low or incorrect grade
- [ ] Defective gauge or sender unit
- [ ] Wire to sender unit earthed
- [ ] Engine overheating
- [ ] Oil filter clogged or bypass valve defective
- [ ] Oil pressure relief valve defective
- [ ] Oil pick-up strainer clogged
- [ ] Oil pump worn or mountings loose
- [ ] Worn main or big-end bearings

Engine noises

Pre-ignition (pinking) on acceleration

- [ ] Incorrect grade of fuel
- [ ] Ignition timing incorrect
- [ ] Distributor faulty or worn
- [ ] Worn or maladjusted carburettor
- [ ] Excessive carbon build-up in engine

Whistling or wheezing noises

- [ ] Leaking vacuum hose
- [ ] Leaking carburettor or manifold gasket
- [ ] Blowing head gasket

Tapping or rattling

- [ ] Incorrect valve clearances
- [ ] Worn valve gear
- [ ] Worn timing chain or belt
- [ ] Broken piston ring (ticking noise)

Knocking or thumping

- [ ] Unintentional mechanical contact (eg fan blades)
- [ ] Worn drivebelt
- [ ] Peripheral component fault (generator, water pump, etc)
- [ ] Worn big-end bearings (regular heavy knocking, perhaps less under load)
- [ ] Worn main bearings (rumbling and knocking, perhaps worsening under load)
- [ ] Piston slap (most noticeable when cold)

A

ABS (Anti-lock brake system) A system, usually electronically controlled, that senses incipient wheel lockup during braking and relieves hydraulic pressure at wheels that are about to skid.

Air bag An inflatable bag hidden in the steering wheel (driver's side) or the dash or glovebox (passenger side). In a head-on collision, the bags inflate, preventing the driver and front passenger from being thrown forward into the steering wheel or windscreen.

Air cleaner A metal or plastic housing, containing a filter element, which removes dust and dirt from the air being drawn into the engine.

Air filter element The actual filter in an air cleaner system, usually manufactured from pleated paper and requiring renewal at regular intervals.

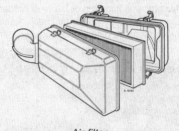

Air filter

Allen key A hexagonal wrench which fits into a recessed hexagonal hole.

Alligator clip A long-nosed spring-loaded metal clip with meshing teeth. Used to make temporary electrical connections.

Alternator A component in the electrical system which converts mechanical energy from a drivebelt into electrical energy to charge the battery and to operate the starting system, ignition system and electrical accessories.

Ampere (amp) A unit of measurement for the flow of electric current. One amp is the amount of current produced by one volt acting through a resistance of one ohm.

Anaerobic sealer A substance used to prevent bolts and screws from loosening. Anaerobic means that it does not require oxygen for activation. The Loctite brand is widely used.

Antifreeze A substance (usually ethylene glycol) mixed with water, and added to a vehicle's cooling system, to prevent freezing of the coolant in winter. Antifreeze also contains chemicals to inhibit corrosion and the formation of rust and other deposits that would tend to clog the radiator and coolant passages and reduce cooling efficiency.

Anti-seize compound A coating that reduces the risk of seizing on fasteners that are subjected to high temperatures, such as exhaust manifold bolts and nuts.

Asbestos A natural fibrous mineral with great heat resistance, commonly used in the composition of brake friction materials.

Asbestos is a health hazard and the dust created by brake systems should never be inhaled or ingested.

Axle A shaft on which a wheel revolves, or which revolves with a wheel. Also, a solid beam that connects the two wheels at one end of the vehicle. An axle which also transmits power to the wheels is known as a live axle.

Axleshaft A single rotating shaft, on either side of the differential, which delivers power from the final drive assembly to the drive wheels. Also called a driveshaft or a halfshaft.

B

Ball bearing An anti-friction bearing consisting of a hardened inner and outer race with hardened steel balls between two races.

Bearing The curved surface on a shaft or in a bore, or the part assembled into either, that permits relative motion between them with minimum wear and friction.

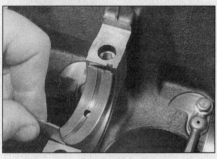

Bearing

Big-end bearing The bearing in the end of the connecting rod that's attached to the crankshaft.

Bleed nipple A valve on a brake wheel cylinder, caliper or other hydraulic component that is opened to purge the hydraulic system of air. Also called a bleed screw.

Brake bleeding Procedure for removing air from lines of a hydraulic brake system.

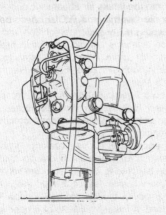

Brake bleeding

Brake disc The component of a disc brake that rotates with the wheels.

Brake drum The component of a drum brake that rotates with the wheels.

Brake linings The friction material which contacts the brake disc or drum to retard the vehicle's speed. The linings are bonded or riveted to the brake pads or shoes.

Brake pads The replaceable friction pads that pinch the brake disc when the brakes are applied. Brake pads consist of a friction material bonded or riveted to a rigid backing plate.

Brake shoe The crescent-shaped carrier to which the brake linings are mounted and which forces the lining against the rotating drum during braking.

Braking systems For more information on braking systems, consult the *Haynes Automotive Brake Manual*.

Breaker bar A long socket wrench handle providing greater leverage.

Bulkhead The insulated partition between the engine and the passenger compartment.

C

Caliper The non-rotating part of a disc-brake assembly that straddles the disc and carries the brake pads. The caliper also contains the hydraulic components that cause the pads to pinch the disc when the brakes are applied. A caliper is also a measuring tool that can be set to measure inside or outside dimensions of an object.

Camshaft A rotating shaft on which a series of cam lobes operate the valve mechanisms. The camshaft may be driven by gears, by sprockets and chain or by sprockets and a belt.

Canister A container in an evaporative emission control system; contains activated charcoal granules to trap vapours from the fuel system.

Canister

Carburettor A device which mixes fuel with air in the proper proportions to provide a desired power output from a spark ignition internal combustion engine.

Castellated Resembling the parapets along the top of a castle wall. For example, a castellated balljoint stud nut.

Castor In wheel alignment, the backward or forward tilt of the steering axis. Castor is positive when the steering axis is inclined rearward at the top.

Catalytic converter A silencer-like device in the exhaust system which converts certain pollutants in the exhaust gases into less harmful substances.

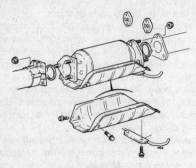

Catalytic converter

Circlip A ring-shaped clip used to prevent endwise movement of cylindrical parts and shafts. An internal circlip is installed in a groove in a housing; an external circlip fits into a groove on the outside of a cylindrical piece such as a shaft.

Clearance The amount of space between two parts. For example, between a piston and a cylinder, between a bearing and a journal, etc.

Coil spring A spiral of elastic steel found in various sizes throughout a vehicle, for example as a springing medium in the suspension and in the valve train.

Compression Reduction in volume, and increase in pressure and temperature, of a gas, caused by squeezing it into a smaller space.

Compression ratio The relationship between cylinder volume when the piston is at top dead centre and cylinder volume when the piston is at bottom dead centre.

Constant velocity (CV) joint A type of universal joint that cancels out vibrations caused by driving power being transmitted through an angle.

Core plug A disc or cup-shaped metal device inserted in a hole in a casting through which core was removed when the casting was formed. Also known as a freeze plug or expansion plug.

Crankcase The lower part of the engine block in which the crankshaft rotates.

Crankshaft The main rotating member, or shaft, running the length of the crankcase, with offset "throws" to which the connecting rods are attached.

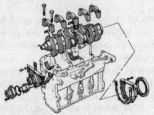

Crankshaft assembly

Crocodile clip See Alligator clip

D

Diagnostic code Code numbers obtained by accessing the diagnostic mode of an engine management computer. This code can be used to determine the area in the system where a malfunction may be located.

Disc brake A brake design incorporating a rotating disc onto which brake pads are squeezed. The resulting friction converts the energy of a moving vehicle into heat.

Double-overhead cam (DOHC) An engine that uses two overhead camshafts, usually one for the intake valves and one for the exhaust valves.

Drivebelt(s) The belt(s) used to drive accessories such as the alternator, water pump, power steering pump, air conditioning compressor, etc. off the crankshaft pulley.

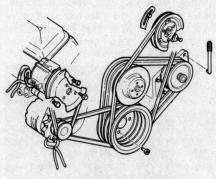

Accessory drivebelts

Driveshaft Any shaft used to transmit motion. Commonly used when referring to the axleshafts on a front wheel drive vehicle.

Drum brake A type of brake using a drum-shaped metal cylinder attached to the inner surface of the wheel. When the brake pedal is pressed, curved brake shoes with friction linings press against the inside of the drum to slow or stop the vehicle.

E

EGR valve A valve used to introduce exhaust gases into the intake air stream.

Electronic control unit (ECU) A computer which controls (for instance) ignition and fuel injection systems, or an anti-lock braking system. For more information refer to the *Haynes Automotive Electrical and Electronic Systems Manual*.

Electronic Fuel Injection (EFI) A computer controlled fuel system that distributes fuel through an injector located in each intake port of the engine.

Emergency brake A braking system, independent of the main hydraulic system, that can be used to slow or stop the vehicle if the primary brakes fail, or to hold the vehicle stationary even though the brake pedal isn't depressed. It usually consists of a hand lever that actuates either front or rear brakes mechanically through a series of cables and linkages. Also known as a handbrake or parking brake.

Endfloat The amount of lengthwise movement between two parts. As applied to a crankshaft, the distance that the crankshaft can move forward and back in the cylinder block.

Engine management system (EMS) A computer controlled system which manages the fuel injection and the ignition systems in an integrated fashion.

Exhaust manifold A part with several passages through which exhaust gases leave the engine combustion chambers and enter the exhaust pipe.

F

Fan clutch A viscous (fluid) drive coupling device which permits variable engine fan speeds in relation to engine speeds.

Feeler blade A thin strip or blade of hardened steel, ground to an exact thickness, used to check or measure clearances between parts.

Feeler blade

Firing order The order in which the engine cylinders fire, or deliver their power strokes, beginning with the number one cylinder.

Flywheel A heavy spinning wheel in which energy is absorbed and stored by means of momentum. On cars, the flywheel is attached to the crankshaft to smooth out firing impulses.

Free play The amount of travel before any action takes place. The "looseness" in a linkage, or an assembly of parts, between the initial application of force and actual movement. For example, the distance the brake pedal moves before the pistons in the master cylinder are actuated.

Fuse An electrical device which protects a circuit against accidental overload. The typical fuse contains a soft piece of metal which is calibrated to melt at a predetermined current flow (expressed as amps) and break the circuit.

Fusible link A circuit protection device consisting of a conductor surrounded by heat-resistant insulation. The conductor is smaller than the wire it protects, so it acts as the weakest link in the circuit. Unlike a blown fuse, a failed fusible link must frequently be cut from the wire for replacement.

G

Gap The distance the spark must travel in jumping from the centre electrode to the side electrode in a spark plug. Also refers to the spacing between the points in a contact breaker assembly in a conventional points-type ignition, or to the distance between the reluctor or rotor and the pickup coil in an electronic ignition.

Adjusting spark plug gap

Gasket Any thin, soft material - usually cork, cardboard, asbestos or soft metal - installed between two metal surfaces to ensure a good seal. For instance, the cylinder head gasket seals the joint between the block and the cylinder head.

Gasket

Gauge An instrument panel display used to monitor engine conditions. A gauge with a movable pointer on a dial or a fixed scale is an analogue gauge. A gauge with a numerical readout is called a digital gauge.

H

Halfshaft A rotating shaft that transmits power from the final drive unit to a drive wheel, usually when referring to a live rear axle.

Harmonic balancer A device designed to reduce torsion or twisting vibration in the crankshaft. May be incorporated in the crankshaft pulley. Also known as a vibration damper.

Hone An abrasive tool for correcting small irregularities or differences in diameter in an engine cylinder, brake cylinder, etc.

Hydraulic tappet A tappet that utilises hydraulic pressure from the engine's lubrication system to maintain zero clearance (constant contact with both camshaft and valve stem). Automatically adjusts to variation in valve stem length. Hydraulic tappets also reduce valve noise.

I

Ignition timing The moment at which the spark plug fires, usually expressed in the number of crankshaft degrees before the piston reaches the top of its stroke.

Inlet manifold A tube or housing with passages through which flows the air-fuel mixture (carburettor vehicles and vehicles with throttle body injection) or air only (port fuel-injected vehicles) to the port openings in the cylinder head.

J

Jump start Starting the engine of a vehicle with a discharged or weak battery by attaching jump leads from the weak battery to a charged or helper battery.

L

Load Sensing Proportioning Valve (LSPV) A brake hydraulic system control valve that works like a proportioning valve, but also takes into consideration the amount of weight carried by the rear axle.

Locknut A nut used to lock an adjustment nut, or other threaded component, in place. For example, a locknut is employed to keep the adjusting nut on the rocker arm in position.

Lockwasher A form of washer designed to prevent an attaching nut from working loose.

M

MacPherson strut A type of front suspension system devised by Earle MacPherson at Ford of England. In its original form, a simple lateral link with the anti-roll bar creates the lower control arm. A long strut - an integral coil spring and shock absorber - is mounted between the body and the steering knuckle. Many modern so-called MacPherson strut systems use a conventional lower A-arm and don't rely on the anti-roll bar for location.

Multimeter An electrical test instrument with the capability to measure voltage, current and resistance.

N

NOx Oxides of Nitrogen. A common toxic pollutant emitted by petrol and diesel engines at higher temperatures.

O

Ohm The unit of electrical resistance. One volt applied to a resistance of one ohm will produce a current of one amp.

Ohmmeter An instrument for measuring electrical resistance.

O-ring A type of sealing ring made of a special rubber-like material; in use, the O-ring is compressed into a groove to provide the sealing action.

Overhead cam (ohc) engine An engine with the camshaft(s) located on top of the cylinder head(s).

Overhead valve (ohv) engine An engine with the valves located in the cylinder head, but with the camshaft located in the engine block.

Oxygen sensor A device installed in the engine exhaust manifold, which senses the oxygen content in the exhaust and converts this information into an electric current. Also called a Lambda sensor.

P

Phillips screw A type of screw head having a cross instead of a slot for a corresponding type of screwdriver.

Plastigage A thin strip of plastic thread, available in different sizes, used for measuring clearances. For example, a strip of Plastigage is laid across a bearing journal. The parts are assembled and dismantled; the width of the crushed strip indicates the clearance between journal and bearing.

Plastigage

Propeller shaft The long hollow tube with universal joints at both ends that carries power from the transmission to the differential on front-engined rear wheel drive vehicles.

Proportioning valve A hydraulic control valve which limits the amount of pressure to the rear brakes during panic stops to prevent wheel lock-up.

R

Rack-and-pinion steering A steering system with a pinion gear on the end of the steering shaft that mates with a rack (think of a geared wheel opened up and laid flat). When the steering wheel is turned, the pinion turns, moving the rack to the left or right. This movement is transmitted through the track rods to the steering arms at the wheels.

Radiator A liquid-to-air heat transfer device designed to reduce the temperature of the coolant in an internal combustion engine cooling system.

Refrigerant Any substance used as a heat transfer agent in an air-conditioning system. R-12 has been the principle refrigerant for many years; recently, however, manufacturers have begun using R-134a, a non-CFC substance that is considered less harmful to the ozone in the upper atmosphere.

Rocker arm A lever arm that rocks on a shaft or pivots on a stud. In an overhead valve engine, the rocker arm converts the upward movement of the pushrod into a downward movement to open a valve.

Rotor In a distributor, the rotating device inside the cap that connects the centre electrode and the outer terminals as it turns, distributing the high voltage from the coil secondary winding to the proper spark plug. Also, that part of an alternator which rotates inside the stator. Also, the rotating assembly of a turbocharger, including the compressor wheel, shaft and turbine wheel.

Runout The amount of wobble (in-and-out movement) of a gear or wheel as it's rotated. The amount a shaft rotates "out-of-true." The out-of-round condition of a rotating part.

S

Sealant A liquid or paste used to prevent leakage at a joint. Sometimes used in conjunction with a gasket.

Sealed beam lamp An older headlight design which integrates the reflector, lens and filaments into a hermetically-sealed one-piece unit. When a filament burns out or the lens cracks, the entire unit is simply replaced.

Serpentine drivebelt A single, long, wide accessory drivebelt that's used on some newer vehicles to drive all the accessories, instead of a series of smaller, shorter belts. Serpentine drivebelts are usually tensioned by an automatic tensioner.

Serpentine drivebelt

Shim Thin spacer, commonly used to adjust the clearance or relative positions between two parts. For example, shims inserted into or under bucket tappets control valve clearances. Clearance is adjusted by changing the thickness of the shim.

Slide hammer A special puller that screws into or hooks onto a component such as a shaft or bearing; a heavy sliding handle on the shaft bottoms against the end of the shaft to knock the component free.

Sprocket A tooth or projection on the periphery of a wheel, shaped to engage with a chain or drivebelt. Commonly used to refer to the sprocket wheel itself.

Starter inhibitor switch On vehicles with an automatic transmission, a switch that prevents starting if the vehicle is not in Neutral or Park.

Strut See MacPherson strut.

T

Tappet A cylindrical component which transmits motion from the cam to the valve stem, either directly or via a pushrod and rocker arm. Also called a cam follower.

Thermostat A heat-controlled valve that regulates the flow of coolant between the cylinder block and the radiator, so maintaining optimum engine operating temperature. A thermostat is also used in some air cleaners in which the temperature is regulated.

Thrust bearing The bearing in the clutch assembly that is moved in to the release levers by clutch pedal action to disengage the clutch. Also referred to as a release bearing.

Timing belt A toothed belt which drives the camshaft. Serious engine damage may result if it breaks in service.

Timing chain A chain which drives the camshaft.

Toe-in The amount the front wheels are closer together at the front than at the rear. On rear wheel drive vehicles, a slight amount of toe-in is usually specified to keep the front wheels running parallel on the road by offsetting other forces that tend to spread the wheels apart.

Toe-out The amount the front wheels are closer together at the rear than at the front. On front wheel drive vehicles, a slight amount of toe-out is usually specified.

Tools For full information on choosing and using tools, refer to the *Haynes Automotive Tools Manual*.

Tracer A stripe of a second colour applied to a wire insulator to distinguish that wire from another one with the same colour insulator.

Tune-up A process of accurate and careful adjustments and parts replacement to obtain the best possible engine performance.

Turbocharger A centrifugal device, driven by exhaust gases, that pressurises the intake air. Normally used to increase the power output from a given engine displacement, but can also be used primarily to reduce exhaust emissions (as on VW's "Umwelt" Diesel engine).

U

Universal joint or U-joint A double-pivoted connection for transmitting power from a driving to a driven shaft through an angle. A U-joint consists of two Y-shaped yokes and a cross-shaped member called the spider.

V

Valve A device through which the flow of liquid, gas, vacuum, or loose material in bulk may be started, stopped, or regulated by a movable part that opens, shuts, or partially obstructs one or more ports or passageways. A valve is also the movable part of such a device.

Valve clearance The clearance between the valve tip (the end of the valve stem) and the rocker arm or tappet. The valve clearance is measured when the valve is closed.

Vernier caliper A precision measuring instrument that measures inside and outside dimensions. Not quite as accurate as a micrometer, but more convenient.

Viscosity The thickness of a liquid or its resistance to flow.

Volt A unit for expressing electrical "pressure" in a circuit. One volt that will produce a current of one ampere through a resistance of one ohm.

W

Welding Various processes used to join metal items by heating the areas to be joined to a molten state and fusing them together. For more information refer to the *Haynes Automotive Welding Manual*.

Wiring diagram A drawing portraying the components and wires in a vehicle's electrical system, using standardised symbols. For more information refer to the *Haynes Automotive Electrical and Electronic Systems Manual*.

Note: *References throughout this index relate to Chapter•page number*

Haynes Manuals – The Complete List

Title	Book No.
ALFA ROMEO	
Alfa Romeo Alfasud/Sprint (74 - 88) up to F	0292
Alfa Romeo Alfetta (73 - 87) up to E	0531
AUDI	
Audi 80 (72 - Feb 79) up to T	0207
Audi 80, 90 (79 - Oct 86) up to D & Coupe (81 - Nov 88) up to F	0605
Audi 80, 90 (Oct 86 - 90) D to H & Coupe (Nov 88 - 90) F to H	1491
Audi 100 (Oct 82 - 90) up to H & 200 (Feb 84 - Oct 89) A to G	0907
Audi 100 & A6 Petrol & Diesel (May 91 - May 97) H to P	3504
Audi A4 (95 - Feb 00) M to V	3575
AUSTIN	
Austin/MG/Rover Maestro 1.3 & 1.6 (83 - 95) up to M	0922
Austin/MG Metro (80 - May 90) up to G	0718
Austin/Rover Montego 1.3 & 1.6 (84 - 94) A to L	1066
Austin/MG/Rover Montego 2.0 (84 - 95) A to M	1067
Mini (59 - 69) up to H	0527
Mini (69 - Oct 96) up to P	0646
Austin/Rover 2.0 litre Diesel Engine (86 - 93) C to L	1857
BEDFORD	
Bedford CF (69 - 87) up to E	0163
Bedford/Vauxhall Rascal (86 - Oct 94) C to M	3015
BMW	
BMW 316, 320 & 320i (4-cyl) (75 - Feb 83) up to Y	0276
BMW 320, 320i, 323i & 325i (6-cyl) (Oct 77 - Sept 87) up to E	0815
BMW 3-Series (Apr 91 - 96) H to N	3210
BMW 3- & 5-Series (sohc) (81 - 91) up to J	1948
BMW 520i & 525e (Oct 81 - June 88) up to E	1560
BMW 525, 528 & 528i (73 - Sept 81) up to X	0632
CITROEN	
Citroën 2CV, Ami & Dyane (67 - 90) up to H	0196
Citroën AX Petrol & Diesel (87 - 97) D to P	3014
Citroën BX (83 - 94) A to L	0908
Citroën C15 Van Petrol & Diesel (89 - Oct 98) F to S	3509
Citroën CX (75 - 88) up to F	0528
Citroën Saxo Petrol & Diesel (96 - 01) N to X	3506
Citroën Visa (79 - 88) up to F	0620
Citroën Xantia Petrol & Diesel (93 - 98) K to S	3082
Citroën XM Petrol & Diesel (89 - 98) G to R	3451
Citroën Xsara (97 - 00) R to W	3751
Citroën ZX Diesel (91 - 98) J to S	1922
Citroën ZX Petrol (91 - 98) H to S	1881
Citroën 1.7 & 1.9 litre Diesel Engine (84 - 96) A to N	1379
FIAT	
Fiat 500 (57 - 73) up to M	0090
Fiat Bravo & Brava (95 - 00) N to W	3572
Fiat Cinquecento (93 - 98) K to R	3501
Fiat Panda (81 - 95) up to M	0793
Fiat Punto Petrol & Diesel (94 - Oct 99) L to V	3251
Fiat Regata (84 - 88) A to F	1167
Fiat Tipo (88 - 91) E to J	1625
Fiat Uno (83 - 95) up to M	0923
Fiat X1/9 (74 - 89) up to G	0273

Title	Book No.
FORD	
Ford Capri II (& III) 1.6 & 2.0 (74 - 87) up to E	0283
Ford Capri II (& III) 2.8 & 3.0 (74 - 87) up to E	1309
Ford Escort (Sept 80 - Sept 90) up to H	0686
Ford Escort & Orion (Sept 90 - 97) H to P	1737
Ford Escort Mk II Mexico, RS 1600 & RS 2000 (75 - 80) up to W	0735
Ford Fiesta (76 - Aug 83) up to Y	0334
Ford Fiesta (Aug 83 - Feb 89) A to F	1030
Ford Fiesta (Feb 89 - Oct 95) F to N	1595
Ford Fiesta Petrol & Diesel (Oct 95 - 97) N to R	3397
Ford Granada (Sept 77 - Feb 85) up to B	0481
Ford Granada & Scorpio (Mar 85 - 94) B to M	1245
Ford Ka (96 - 99) P to T	3570
Ford Mondeo Petrol (93 - 99) K to T	1923
Ford Mondeo Diesel (93 - 96) L to N	3465
Ford Orion (83 - Sept 90) up to H	1009
Ford Sierra 4 cyl. (82 - 93) up to K	0903
Ford Sierra V6 (82 - 91) up to J	0904
Ford Transit Petrol (Mk 2) (78 - Jan 86) up to C	0719
Ford Transit Petrol (Mk 3) (Feb 86 - 89) C to G	1468
Ford Transit Diesel (Feb 86 - 99) C to T	3019
Ford 1.6 & 1.8 litre Diesel Engine (84 - 96) A to N	1172
Ford 2.1, 2.3 & 2.5 litre Diesel Engine (77 - 90) up to H	1606
FREIGHT ROVER	
Freight Rover Sherpa (74 - 87) up to E	0463
HILLMAN	
Hillman Avenger (70 - 82) up to Y	0037
HONDA	
Honda Accord (76 - Feb 84) up to A	0351
Honda Civic (Feb 84 - Oct 87) A to E	1226
Honda Civic (Nov 91 - 96) J to N	3199
HYUNDAI	
Hyundai Pony (85 - 94) C to M	3398
JAGUAR	
Jaguar E Type (61 - 72) up to L	0140
Jaguar MkI & II, 240 & 340 (55 - 69) up to H	0098
Jaguar XJ6, XJ & Sovereign; Daimler Sovereign (68 - Oct 86) up to D	0242
Jaguar XJ6 & Sovereign (Oct 86 - Sept 94) D to M	3261
Jaguar XJ12, XJS & Sovereign; Daimler Double Six (72 - 88) up to F	0478
JEEP	
Jeep Cherokee Petrol (93 - 96) K to N	1943
LADA	
Lada 1200, 1300, 1500 & 1600 (74 - 91) up to J	0413
Lada Samara (87 - 91) D to J	1610
LAND ROVER	
Land Rover 90, 110 & Defender Diesel (83 - 95) up to N	3017
Land Rover Discovery Petrol & Diesel (89 - 98) G to S	3016
Land Rover Series IIA & III Diesel (58 - 85) up to C	0529
Land Rover Series II, IIA & III Petrol (58 - 85) up to C	0314
MAZDA	
Mazda 323 (Mar 81 - Oct 89) up to G	1608

Title	Book No.
Mazda 323 (Oct 89 - 98) G to R	3455
Mazda 626 (May 83 - Sept 87) up to E	0929
Mazda B-1600, B-1800 & B-2000 Pick-up (72 - 88) up to F	0267
MERCEDES BENZ	
Mercedes-Benz 190, 190E & 190D Petrol & Diesel (83 - 93) A to L	3450
Mercedes-Benz 200, 240, 300 Diesel (Oct 76 - 85) up to C	1114
Mercedes-Benz 250 & 280 (68 - 72) up to L	0346
Mercedes-Benz 250 & 280 (123 Series) (Oct 76 - 84) up to B	0677
Mercedes-Benz 124 Series (85 - Aug 93) C to K	3253
Mercedes-Benz C-Class Petrol & Diesel (93 - Aug 00) L to W	3511
MG	
MGA (55 - 62)*	0475
MGB (62 - 80) up to W	0111
MG Midget & AH Sprite (58 - 80) up to W	0265
MITSUBISHI	
Mitsubishi Shogun & L200 Pick-Ups (83 - 94) up to M	1944
MORRIS	
Morris Ital 1.3 (80 - 84) up to B	0705
Morris Minor 1000 (56 - 71) up to K	0024
NISSAN	
Nissan Bluebird (May 84 - Mar 86) A to C	1223
Nissan Bluebird (Mar 86 - 90) C to H	1473
Nissan Cherry (Sept 82 - 86) up to D	1031
Nissan Micra (83 - Jan 93) up to K	0931
Nissan Micra (93 - 99) K to T	3254
Nissan Primera (90 - Aug 99) H to T	1851
Nissan Stanza (82 - 86) up to D	0824
Nissan Sunny (May 82 - Oct 86) up to D	0895
Nissan Sunny (Oct 86 - Mar 91) D to H	1378
Nissan Sunny (Apr 91 - 95) H to N	3219
OPEL	
Opel Ascona & Manta (B Series) (Sept 75 - 88) up to F	0316
Opel Ascona (81 - 88) (Not available in UK see Vauxhall Cavalier 0812)	3215
Opel Astra (Oct 91 - Feb 98) (Not available in UK see Vauxhall Astra 1832)	3156
Opel Calibra (90 - 98) (See Vauxhall/Opel Calibra Book No. 3502)	
Opel Corsa (83 - Mar 93) (Not available in UK see Vauxhall Nova 0909)	3160
Opel Corsa (Mar 93 - 97) (Not available in UK see Vauxhall Corsa 1985)	3159
Opel Frontera Petrol & Diesel (91 - 98) (See Vauxhall/Opel Frontera Book No. 3454)	
Opel Kadett (Nov 79 - Oct 84) up to B	0634
Opel Kadett (Oct 84 - Oct 91) (Not available in UK see Vauxhall Astra & Belmont 1136)	3196
Opel Omega & Senator (86 - 94) (Not available in UK see Vauxhall Carlton & Senator 1469)	3157
Opel Omega (94 - 99) (See Vauxhall/Opel Omega Book No. 3510)	
Opel Rekord (Feb 78 - Oct 86) up to D	0543
Opel Vectra (Oct 88 - Oct 95) (Not available in UK see Vauxhall Cavalier 1570)	3158
Opel Vectra Petrol & Diesel (95 - 98) (Not available in UK see Vauxhall Vectra 3396)	3523

* Classic reprint

Title	Book No.
PEUGEOT	
Peugeot 106 Petrol & Diesel (91 - 01) J to X	1882
Peugeot 205 Petrol (83 - 97) A to P	0932
Peugeot 206 Petrol and Diesel (98 - 01) S to X	3757
Peugeot 305 (78 - 89) up to G	0538
Peugeot 306 Petrol & Diesel (93 - 99) K to T	3073
Peugeot 309 (86 - 93) C to K	1266
Peugeot 405 Petrol (88 - 97) E to P	1559
Peugeot 405 Diesel (88 - 96) E to N	3198
Peugeot 406 Petrol & Diesel (96 - 97) N to R	3394
Peugeot 505 (79 - 89) up to G	0762
Peugeot 1.7/1.8 & 1.9 litre Diesel Engine (82 - 96) up to N	0950
Peugeot 2.0, 2.1, 2.3 & 2.5 litre Diesel Engines (74 - 90) up to H	1607
PORSCHE	
Porsche 911 (65 - 85) up to C	0264
Porsche 924 & 924 Turbo (76 - 85) up to C	0397
PROTON	
Proton (89 - 97) F to P	3255
RANGE ROVER	
Range Rover V8 (70 - Oct 92) up to K	0606
RELIANT	
Reliant Robin & Kitten (73 - 83) up to A	0436
RENAULT	
Renault 5 (Feb 85 - 96) B to N	1219
Renault 9 & 11 (82 - 89) up to F	0822
Renault 18 (79 - 86) up to D	0598
Renault 19 Petrol (89 - 94) F to M	1646
Renault 19 Diesel (89 - 95) F to N	1946
Renault 21 (86 - 94) C to M	1397
Renault 25 (84 - 92) B to K	1228
Renault Clio Petrol (91 - May 98) H to R	1853
Renault Clio Diesel (91 - June 96) H to N	3031
Renault Espace Petrol & Diesel (85 - 96) C to N	3197
Renault Fuego (80 - 86) up to C	0764
Renault Laguna Petrol & Diesel (94 - 00) L to W	3252
Renault Mégane & Scénic Petrol & Diesel (96 - 98) N to R	3395
ROVER	
Rover 213 & 216 (84 - 89) A to G	1116
Rover 214 & 414 (89 - 96) G to N	1689
Rover 216 & 416 (89 - 96) G to N	1830
Rover 211, 214, 216, 218 & 220 Petrol & Diesel (Dec 95 - 98) N to R	3399
Rover 414, 416 & 420 Petrol & Diesel (May 95 - 98) M to R	3453
Rover 618, 620 & 623 (93 - 97) K to P	3257
Rover 820, 825 & 827 (86 - 95) D to N	1380
Rover 3500 (76 - 87) up to E	0365
Rover Metro, 111 & 114 (May 90 - 98) G to S	1711
SAAB	
Saab 90, 99 & 900 (79 - Oct 93) up to L	0765
Saab 900 (Oct 93 - 98) L to R	3512
Saab 9000 (4-cyl) (85 - 95) C to N	1686
SEAT	
Seat Ibiza & Cordoba Petrol & Diesel (Oct 93 - Oct 99) L to V	3571
Seat Ibiza & Malaga (85 - 92) B to K	1609

Title	Book No.
SKODA	
Skoda Estelle (77 - 89) up to G	0604
Skoda Favorit (89 - 96) F to N	1801
Skoda Felicia Petrol & Diesel (95 - 99) M to T	3505
SUBARU	
Subaru 1600 & 1800 (Nov 79 - 90) up to H	0995
SUZUKI	
Suzuki SJ Series, Samurai & Vitara (4-cyl) (82 - 97) up to P	1942
Suzuki Supercarry (86 - Oct 94) C to M	3015
TALBOT	
Talbot Alpine, Solara, Minx & Rapier (75 - 86) up to D	0337
Talbot Horizon (78 - 86) up to D	0473
Talbot Samba (82 - 86) up to D	0823
TOYOTA	
Toyota Carina E (May 92 - 97) J to P	3256
Toyota Corolla (Sept 83 - Sept 87) A to E	1024
Toyota Corolla (80 - 85) up to C	0683
Toyota Corolla (Sept 87 - Aug 92) E to K	1683
Toyota Corolla (Aug 92 - 97) K to P	3259
Toyota Hi-Ace & Hi-Lux (69 - Oct 83) up to A	0304
TRIUMPH	
Triumph Herald (59 - 71) up to K*	0010
Triumph TR2, TR3, TR3A, TR4 & TR4A (52 - 67)*	0028
Triumph TR5 & 6 (67 - 75)*	0031
Triumph Spitfire (62 - 81) up to X	0113
Triumph Stag (70 - 78) up to T	0441
VAUXHALL	
Vauxhall Astra (80 - Oct 84) up to B	0635
Vauxhall Astra & Belmont (Oct 84 - Oct 91) B to J	1136
Vauxhall Astra (Oct 91 - Feb 98) J to R	1832
Vauxhall/Opel Calibra (90 - 98) G to S	3502
Vauxhall Carlton (Oct 78 - Oct 86) up to D	0480
Vauxhall Carlton & Senator (Nov 86 - 94) D to L	1469
Vauxhall Cavalier 1600, 1900 & 2000 (75 - July 81) up to W	0315
Vauxhall Cavalier (81 - Oct 88) up to F	0812
Vauxhall Cavalier (Oct 88 - 95) F to N	1570
Vauxhall Chevette (75 - 84) up to B	0285
Vauxhall Corsa (Mar 93 - 97) K to R	1985
Vauxhall/Opel Frontera Petrol & Diesel (91 - Sept 98) J to S	3454
Vauxhall Nova (83 - 93) up to K	0909
Vauxhall/Opel Omega (94 - 99) L to T	3510
Vauxhall Vectra Petrol & Diesel (95 - 98) N to R	3396
Vauxhall/Opel 1.5, 1.6 & 1.7 litre Diesel Engine (82 - 96) up to N	1222
VOLKSWAGEN	
Volkswagen Beetle 1200 (54 - 77) up to S	0036
Volkswagen Beetle 1300 & 1500 (65 - 75) up to P	0039
Volkswagen Beetle 1302 & 1302S (70 - 72) up to L	0110
Volkswagen Beetle 1303, 1303S & GT (72 - 75) up to P	0159

Title	Book No.
Volkswagen Golf & Bora Petrol & Diesel (April 98 - 00) R to X	3727
Volkswagen Golf & Jetta Mk 1 1.1 & 1.3 (74 - 84) up to A	0716
Volkswagen Golf, Jetta & Scirocco Mk 1 1.5, 1.6 & 1.8 (74 - 84) up to A	0726
Volkswagen Golf & Jetta Mk 1 Diesel (78 - 84) up to A	0451
Volkswagen Golf & Jetta Mk 2 (Mar 84 - Feb 92) A to J	1081
Volkswagen Golf & Vento Petrol & Diesel (Feb 92 - 96) J to N	3097
Volkswagen LT vans & light trucks (76 - 87) up to E	0637
Volkswagen Passat & Santana (Sept 81 - May 88) up to E	0814
Volkswagen Passat Petrol & Diesel (May 88 - 96) E to P	3498
Volkswagen Polo & Derby (76 - Jan 82) up to X	0335
Volkswagen Polo (82 - Oct 90) up to H	0813
Volkswagen Polo (Nov 90 - Aug 94) H to L	3245
Volkswagen Polo Hatchback Petrol & Diesel (94 - 99) M to S	3500
Volkswagen Scirocco (82 - 90) up to H	1224
Volkswagen Transporter 1600 (68 - 79) up to V	0082
Volkswagen Transporter 1700, 1800 & 2000 (72 - 79) up to V	0226
Volkswagen Transporter (air-cooled) (79 - 82) up to Y	0638
Volkswagen Transporter (water-cooled) (82 - 90) up to H	3452
VOLVO	
Volvo 142, 144 & 145 (66 - 74) up to N	0129
Volvo 240 Series (74 - 93) up to K	0270
Volvo 340, 343, 345 & 360 (76 - 91) up to J	0715
Volvo 440, 460 & 480 (87 - 97) D to P	1691
Volvo 740 & 760 (82 - 91) up to J	1258
Volvo 850 (92 - 96) J to P	3260
Volvo 940 (90 - 96) H to N	3249
Volvo S40 & V40 (96 - 99) N to V	3569
Volvo S70, V70 & C70 (96 - 99) P to V	3573
AUTOMOTIVE TECHBOOKS	
Automotive Air Conditioning Systems	3740
Automotive Brake Manual	3050
Automotive Carburettor Manual	3288
Automotive Diagnostic Fault Codes Manual	3472
Automotive Diesel Engine Service Guide	3286
Automotive Electrical and Electronic Systems Manual	3049
Automotive Engine Management and Fuel Injection Systems Manual	3344
Automotive Gearbox Overhaul Manual	3473
Automotive Service Summaries Manual	3475
Automotive Timing Belts Manual – Austin/Rover	3549
Automotive Timing Belts Manual – Ford	3474
Automotive Timing Belts Manual – Peugeot/Citroën	3568
Automotive Timing Belts Manual – Vauxhall/Opel	3577
Automotive Welding Manual	3053
In-Car Entertainment Manual (3rd Edition)	3363

* Classic reprint

CL11.3/01

Preserving Our Motoring Heritage

< *The Model J Duesenberg Derham Tourster. Only eight of these magnificent cars were ever built – this is the only example to be found outside the United States of America*

Almost every car you've ever loved, loathed or desired is gathered under one roof at the Haynes Motor Museum. Over 300 immaculately presented cars and motorbikes represent every aspect of our motoring heritage, from elegant reminders of bygone days, such as the superb Model J Duesenberg to curiosities like the bug-eyed BMW Isetta. There are also many old friends and flames. Perhaps you remember the 1959 Ford Popular that you did your courting in? The magnificent 'Red Collection' is a spectacle of classic sports cars including AC, Alfa Romeo, Austin Healey, Ferrari, Lamborghini, Maserati, MG, Riley, Porsche and Triumph.

A Perfect Day Out

Each and every vehicle at the Haynes Motor Museum has played its part in the history and culture of Motoring. Today, they make a wonderful spectacle and a great day out for all the family. Bring the kids, bring Mum and Dad, but above all bring your camera to capture those golden memories for ever. You will also find an impressive array of motoring memorabilia, a comfortable 70 seat video cinema and one of the most extensive transport book shops in Britain. The Pit Stop Cafe serves everything from a cup of tea to wholesome, home-made meals or, if you prefer, you can enjoy the large picnic area nestled in the beautiful rural surroundings of Somerset.

> *John Haynes O.B.E., Founder and Chairman of the museum at the wheel of a Haynes Light 12.*

< *Graham Hill's Lola Cosworth Formula 1 car next to a 1934 Riley Sports.*

The Museum is situated on the A359 Yeovil to Frome road at Sparkford, just off the A303 in Somerset. It is about 40 miles south of Bristol, and 25 minutes drive from the M5 intersection at Taunton.

Open 9.30am - 5.30pm (10.00am - 4.00pm Winter) 7 days a week, *except Christmas Day, Boxing Day and New Years Day*

Special rates available for schools, coach parties and outings Charitable Trust No. 292048